The EU Anti-Corruption Report

AF791301

This book analyses the development of anti-corruption as a policy field in the European Union with a particular focus on the EU Anti-Corruption Report. It reconstructs the origins of anti-corruption policy in the 1990s when the EU started to recognise corruption as a serious crime with a cross-border dimension. It also analyses the processes surrounding the downfall of the Santer Commission on charges of corruption in 1999 and the enlargement of the EU. This incorporation of transitional new member states was accompanied by a number of specific measures, instruments and monitoring mechanisms to combat corruption at the supranational level, finally leading to the introduction of the EU-wide Anti-Corruption Report in 2014. The book presents an in-depth analysis of its implementation, abandonment and the way forward under the European Semester as the new instrument for achieving EU anti-corruption reforms. It offers a new interpretation of the Report as a form of reflexive governance that operates at multiple levels and involves not only the European institutions and national governments, but also the role of civil society actors in the process of developing anti-corruption policy. It applies the theory of reflexive governance in analysing the impact of the Report in the UK, Romania and Albania, including the involvement of non-state actors in anti-corruption policymaking in these countries. The book concludes with a discussion on how future EU Anti-Corruption policy can make use of reflexive governance and offers recommendations to enhance anti-corruption policies of the EU, the member states and the candidate states.

Dr Andi Hoxhaj is a Teaching Fellow in Law at the University of Warwick, teaching EU law. He was awarded his doctorial title in 2017 at the University of Warwick. His work on corruption, good governance, EU enlargement policy and the migration of young people in the Western Balkans were referred to in three parliamentary inquiry reports published by the UK Parliament in 2018. In 2018, Dr Hoxhaj was awarded the 'British Academy Rising Star Engagement Award'. Dr Hoxhaj also holds an LLM in International Corporate Governance and Financial Regulation from the University of Warwick and an LLB (Hons) in Law from London Metropolitan University.

Law, Crime and Culture

Series editors:
Professor Susanne Karstedt, University of Leeds, UK;
Professor Ralf Rogowski, University of Warwick, Coventry, UK;
Professor Dirk Tänzler, University of Konstanz, Germany

The Law, Crime and Culture series explores an increasingly important and topical area of interdisciplinary research, covering a broad range of themes from understandings of social and legal order in individual cultures to intersections of criminological, legal and cultural inquiry. The series promotes cross-disciplinary and comparative research, and the series editors actively welcome submissions on the many and varied topics related to crime, social control and legal culture across the world.

Available titles in this series include:

The Social Construction of Corruption in Europe
Dirk Tänzler, Konstadinos Maras and Angelos Giannakopoulos

The EU Anti-Corruption Report
A reflexive governance approach
Andi Hoxhaj

The EU Anti-Corruption Report

A Reflexive Governance Approach

Andi Hoxhaj

Routledge
Taylor & Francis Group
LONDON AND NEW YORK

First published 2020
by Routledge
2 Park Square, Milton Park, Abingdon, Oxon OX14 4RN

and by Routledge
605 Third Avenue, New York, NY 10017

First issued in paperback 2021

Routledge is an imprint of the Taylor & Francis Group, an informa business

© 2020 Andi Hoxhaj

The right of Andi Hoxhaj to be identified as author of this work has been asserted by them in accordance with sections 77 and 78 of the Copyright, Designs and Patents Act 1988.

All rights reserved. No part of this book may be reprinted or reproduced or utilised in any form or by any electronic, mechanical, or other means, now known or hereafter invented, including photocopying and recording, or in any information storage or retrieval system, without permission in writing from the publishers.

Trademark notice: Product or corporate names may be trademarks or registered trademarks, and are used only for identification and explanation without intent to infringe.

Publisher's Note
The publisher has gone to great lengths to ensure the quality of this reprint but points out that some imperfections in the original copies may be apparent.

British Library Cataloguing-in-Publication Data
A catalogue record for this book is available from the British Library

Library of Congress Cataloging-in-Publication Data
A catalogue record has been requested for this book

Typeset in Galliard
by Integra Software Services Pvt. Ltd.

ISBN 13: 978-1-03-208762-7 (pbk)
ISBN 13: 978-1-138-55584-6 (hbk)

Contents

Acknowledgements

This book is based on research conducted on anti-corruption polices and laws in the European Union since the fall of the Iron Curtain to the present; parts of the book derive from research carried out for the PhD thesis that I wrote at the University of Warwick. I am grateful to a number of colleagues, family and friends in encouraging me to start the work, persevere with it and finally to publish it.

First and foremost, special gratitude goes to my former PhD supervisor Professor Ralf Rogowski for his unconditional support and guidance throughout my PhD and for having confidence in my ability to write this book and pursue an academic career. I would also like to thank colleagues at Warwick Law School, in particular to the EU law team, Professor Dora Kostakopoulou and Dr Jill Wakefiel—for their support, for the opportunity to teach parts of this book in the module 'Law and Policies of the European Union', and for supporting my early academic career in areas of EU law and policy. Without their patience and support, it would have not been possible. I will always be grateful to them for their unconditional support throughout my time at Warwick and in completing this project.

I am grateful to my fellow PhD candidates, Dr Catherine Arias and Dr Hassan Nizami, for their support during the PhD and while writing this book. I would also like to thank all other colleagues and administrative staff at the University of Warwick for their friendship and goodwill through the years, especially to Dr Stephen Connelly, Barbara Nastoll, Dr George Meszaros, Professor Mark Philp, Helen Riley, and to my former LLM lecturers, Dr Kathryn McMahon and Professor Dalvinder Singh. I would also like to thank Is Andrews for her great work in editing this book and looking through endless drafts of the manuscript. I am indebted for the opportunities you provided and for the conversations that gave me valuable insights into research questions and developing this book.

Gratitude is also due to Professor Susan Rose-Ackerman of Yale University, Dr Patrycja Szarek-Mason of Reading University, Professor Alina Mungiu-Pippidi of the Hertie School of Governance, Dr Blendi Kajsiu of the University of Antioquia, and colleagues at Transparency International in the EU and UK, Carl Dolan and Robert Barrington, whose research and advocacy for transparency and fighting corruption have inspired me to write this book. I greatly enjoyed hosting Dr Szarek-Mason, Carl Dolan, and members of TI-UK at a workshop at the University of Warwick in February 2014 and would like to thank them for their advice in developing my thoughts for the book. I was honoured to host Professor Susan Rose-Ackerman for her distinguished lecture, 'Are Corrupt Elites Necessary for Corrupt Countries?' at the University of Warwick in May 2015 and would like to thank Professor Ackerman for sharing her research with us and for taking the time to advise me in developing some ideas for this book.

Finally, I would like to acknowledge, with gratitude, the support and love of my family—my parents, Gëzim and Vjollca, my sister Anita, and my uncles Luli and Viktor for believing in me more than I could at times in myself and for their unconditional love and support on my academic journey. I would have not been able to carry out my education abroad in the first place without your unconditional support, love and help—I will always be there for you, as you sacrificed for me to get a better education than some of you had the chance to access. I would also like to thank my extended family, friends, and people that I have met throughout my life, as well as whilst writing my PhD and this book—for showing me kindness, supporting me in developing my research ideas, and offering me opportunities to develop further as a human, as well as an academic. You have all kept me going, and this book would have not been possible without all of you—I am grateful to have you in my life.

Abbreviations

AMTs	Autonomous Trade Measures
BAES	British Aerospace Systems
BEPG	Broad Economic Policy Guidelines
BoE	Bank of England
CAAT	Campaign Against the Arms Trade
CARDS	Community Assistance for Reconstruction, Development & Stabilisation
CPI	Corruption Perceptions Index
CSL	Civil Service Law
DNA	National Anticorruption Directorate (Romania)
EES	European Employment Strategy
EIB	European Investment Bank
EPPO	European Public Prosecutor's Office
EPRS	European Parliamentary Research Service
EU	European Union
FCA	Financial Conduct Authority
FPC	Financial Policy Committee
FSA	Financial Services Authority
FSMA	Financial Services and Markets Act 2000
GRECO	Group of States Against Corruption (Council of Europe)
IMF	International Monetary Fund
IPA	Instrument for Pre-Accession Assistance
JHA	Justice and Home Affairs
KNAB	Corruption Prevention and Combating Bureau (Lativa)
NBI	National Bureau of Investigation (Albania)
OECD	Organisation for Economic Co-operation and Development
OLAF	European Anti-Fraud Office
OMC	Open Method of Communication
OSCE	Organisation for Security and Cooperation in Europe
PAR	Public Administration Reform
PCBS	Parliamentary Commission on Banking Standards
PHARE	Poland and Hungary Assistance for the Restructuring of the Economy

PPERA	Political Parties, Elections and Referendums Act
PRA	Prudential Regulation Authority
SIPAR	Strategy for State Institution and Public Administration Reform
SPAK	Special Anti-Corruption and Organised Crime Structure (Albania)
SFO	Serious Fraud Office
SAA	Stabilisation and Association Agreement
SAP	Stabilisation and Association Process
SIPRI	Stockholm International Peace Research Institute
TI	Transparency International
TI-UK	Transparency International UK
The Commission	The European Commission
The Report	The EU Anti-Corruption Report
UCLAF	Unité de Coordination de La Lutte Anti-Fraude
UNCAC	United Nations Convention Against Corruption
UNTOC	United Nations Convention Against Transnational Organised Crime

Introduction

Since the fall of the Iron Curtain, corruption has gradually emerged as a major policy challenge in Europe. However, the European Union (EU) only started to take an interest in developing an anti-corruption policy in the late 1990s. This became more of a priority as plans developed for EU enlargement in the Central and Eastern Europe states (Czech Republic, Estonia, Cyprus, Latvia, Lithuania, Hungary, Malta, Poland, Slovakia and Slovenia) in 2004, (Bulgaria and Romania) in 2007, and Southeast Europe (Croatia) in 2013. Over this period, corruption emerged as a major political issue and has dominated the accession debate, posing a serious obstacle to economic and social development efforts in post-Communist countries.

The pre-accession process placed the EU in an influential position in the early 2000s, with the opportunity to direct the Central and Eastern European (CEE) and South Eastern Europe countries in their democratic, economic and social transitions. Fighting corruption in these countries gained unparalleled importance during this pre-accession process and became an explicit condition for their EU membership bids. During this period—and in particular in 2007, when Bulgaria and Romania joined the Union—the EU developed a more coherent anti-corruption policy by introducing the Cooperation and Verification Mechanism (CVM). Previously, the EU mainly adopted and supported international anti-corruption standards and measures as directed by the UN, the OECD and the Council of Europe. However, during the pre-accession process, the EU began to recognise that the anti-corruption policy field was a central element in promoting good governance reform and the rule of law and needed to be addressed more thoroughly by the EU's own mechanisms.

The CVM was developed by the EU specifically to monitor Bulgaria and Romania, reporting on an annual basis on their progress and efforts on judicial reform and the fight against corruption. However the mechanism also provided a lab experiment of sorts for the EU to develop further this form of anti-corruption monitoring for all member states—after the European debt crisis in 2010, corruption was considered to have been a major contributing factor. Thus, the EU announced the establishment of the EU Anti-Corruption Report in 2011, first published in 2014. The Report was to be published biannually, issuing key recommendations for all member states in improving their anti-corruption standards, laws and policies. The development and adoption of the EU Anti-Corruption Report (hereafter, the Report) was a bold initiative by the EU, demonstrating that it was taking the fighting against corruption more seriously. The Report approached corruption from a social and political dimension, as well as dealing with its economic impact on the development and progress of the member states, and ensured that civil society stakeholders were included in EU anti-corruption policymaking.

Despite the many benefits of the Report, and the welcome it found within the policy field, the European Commission decided to discontinue it in February 2017, after just the single 2014 publication. The Commission announced that corruption would henceforth be evaluated under the European Semester, arguing that the first and only Report had provided the basis for deeper work and consultation within the EU's anti-corruption framework, but was no longer required. However, the European Semester is limited in scope when evaluating corruption in member states, and its recommendations are mainly focused around economic policy, compared to the Report's broader remit and consideration of the negative impact of corruption on society, democracy and the rule of law.

This book offers an analysis of the EU's efforts to establish a separate policy field of anti-corruption, by looking at the development of the Report as the leading policy initiative that the Commission has developed to date. We evaluate how the Report tried to support member states' own efforts to establish a comprehensive anti-corruption policy field and how the involvement of non-state actors in anti-corruption policymaking was strengthened. The theory used in this analysis is the reflexive governance approach, and it will show how the EU, member states and candidate states can make better use of reflexive governance to develop comprehensive anti-corruption policy. The book will show how the EU has used its influence in anti-corruption policy development and give examples of how it has supported the member and candidate states to put in place adequate anti-corruption plans, laws and policies. We will also look at the inclusion of non-state actors in future EU anti-corruption policymaking, noting that there is currently still a deficit in this area.

We will consider five important questions:

- What is the EU policy against corruption within the member and candidate states, and what are the key findings of the Report?
- Was the Report an adequate initiative to address anti-corruption law and policy shortcomings in member states and EU institutions?
- Is the European Semester a suitable substitute for the Report in evaluating the member states' policy efforts in addressing corruption?
- Is the current EU anti-corruption policy under the European Semester sufficient to address the problem of corruption across member states?
- If not, how can the European Semester be strengthened, and how should the EU develop a more comprehensive policy in fighting corruption?

In discussing and answering these questions, we will review nine key findings:

1. The EU mostly plays a supportive role in developing anti-corruption policies and laws within the member states.[1]
2. The high level of corruption in the CEE and South Eastern Europe states and the 2018 EU enlargement strategy for the Western Balkans has pushed the EU to develop new anti-corruption strategies and instruments to make better use of its leverage over these countries during the pre-accession process, building an independent judiciary and anti-corruption agencies that can fight corruption without political interference.
3. The accession phase of Romania represented not only a challenge for the EU, but also an opportunity to develop further EU policy against corruption, such as the CVM—which provided the basis for developing the Report for all member states. The successes and shortcomings of the EU's approach in Romania have allowed for reflection and policy discussion on how the EU can be more effective in influencing anti-corruption in the current candidate countries in the Western Balkans.
4. The Report was the EU's anti-corruption flagship initiative and was—by far—its most inclusive mechanism for tackling the serious harm that corruption causes to all member states: economically, socially and politically. In the country report for all member states, the Report has tried to stimulate peer learning and the exchange of best practices against corruption, thus encouraging greater political will to enact anti-corruption policies. However, the Report's major shortcoming is that its recommendations are not legally binding and do not include European institutions.
5. The regulatory nature of the Report is different to previous EU anti-corruption approaches, which were based on a mixture of soft and hard law mechanisms in influencing the candidate and member states' anti-corruption laws and policies. The Report, on the other hand, displays clear signs of reflexivity and demonstrates a transformation of EU policy approach from the new governance to a reflexive governance approach. This is because it was consciously designed to support and strengthen member states' own anti-corruption efforts, playing a coordinative role.
6. The European Semester process is not an adequate substitution for the Report due to its narrow scope. Corruption is treated only as an element that contributes towards poor economic governance and the shadow economy; no social dimension is considered, and in the 2018 European Semester there were no recommendations issued which encompassed the political sphere of corruption. Additionally, in the 2018 European Semester's country-specific reports, only a quarter of the member states received recommendations addressing anti-corruption shortcomings, compared to

1 Although when the European Public Prosecutor's Office becomes operational in 2021–2022, the EU may change its approach to fighting large-scale financial crime across borders.

the Report's comprehensive reporting and recommendations for all member states.

7. Corruption continues to be an ongoing challenge in the member states and should continue to be a high priority for the EU's country engagement—whether with member states, candidates for membership or the rest of the world. The lack of a coherent anti-corruption framework within the EU, and the move to withdraw its broad approach, narrowing into the European Semester's purely economic focus is discouraging. Without the Report, the Commission lacks any mechanism or strategy to guide future EU anti-corruption policy—and therefore it should develop new policy along the lines of the Report, strengthening its reflexive approach.
8. Future EU anti-corruption policy should also include its own institutions, in particular the EU decision-making bodies. Furthermore, as part of the current consultation of the EU anti-corruption framework, since the cancelation of the Report in 2017, other important areas related to corruption should be made priorities in future anti-corruption policy. Particular attention for EU anti-corruption policy objectives should be paid to the fight against organised crime (including whistle-blower protection in member states and the EU, and the full implementation of the EU-wide whistle-blower directive proposed by the Commission in April 2018), and empowering specialised anti-corruption agencies at the member-state level.
9. The EU is hampered by limited and contested competence in the field of anti-corruption, with no legal powers in the area of anti-bribery legislation or political party financing. However, a concerted fight against corruption can rebuild trust in the EU project, and the EU has the potential to become an anti-corruption champion. In member states, there remains a significant implementation gap between anti-corruption law and practice, but the EU has not fully recognised the role that civil society and non-state actors can have in achieving better enforcement, as well as changing norms against corruption practices.

This book, by evaluating the EU Anti-Corruption Report 2014 and its impact, analyses the development of EU anti-corruption as a policy field. In order to identify key factors that shape anti-corruption policy in Europe, it applies the theory of reflexive governance to anti-corruption policymaking in the EU. The approach of reflexive governance focuses on the new form of interaction between the EU, member states and candidate states—in particular the dialogical nature of their relationships and how they influence each other in building ground and incentives for the sustainable development of anti-corruption as a policy field.

We begin with an examination of the five stages of the development of anti-corruption as a policy field in the EU so far, asking questions about the involvement of non-state actors in anti-corruption policymaking and the extent to which member and candidate states involve non-state actors in shaping anti-corruption policy in the national context. The middle section of the book is devoted to presenting and applying the theory of reflexive governance in analysing the Report and its impact and achievements in the UK, Romania and Albania. In the last part, we discuss insufficiencies of the Report and analyse whether the European Semester is an adequate substitute. Finally, we offer recommendations for future EU anti-corruption policy, in particular, by making proposals for how the legal framework can be improved in relation to the protection of whistle-blowers and how the EU can further strengthen the European Semester in addressing corruption and include non-state actors in shaping anti-corruption policy in the member states. We also make suggestions for how the EU, member and candidate states can make further use of reflexive governance in order to enhance their anti-corruption policies.

Section 1

We begin with an introduction to the history and evolution of anti-corruption policy in the EU and an examination of the origins of the EU Anti-corruption Report.

Chapter 1 *presents an overview analysis of the evolution of EU anti-corruption law and policy since 1997, leading to the production of the Report in 2014 and beyond. The chapter divides this development into five stages: firstly, we investigate motives behind the first communication on the issue of corruption by the EU Commission in 1997, in particular, in relation to enlargement of the EU in order to integrate former socialist countries in CEE. In the second stage, EU policy focusses on measures addressing corruption within EU institutions. The third stage is characterised by redefining the relationship of the EU and international anti-corruption policies—these latest efforts would seem to be attempts to develop anti-corruption as a separate policy field in the EU. The fourth stage of the chapter assesses the processes surrounding the introduction of the Report, and we discuss which forms of corruption the Report considers. The fifth stage of development is the Commission's decision in 2017 to discontinue the Report and the new ways the EU evaluates corruption under the European Semester Process.*

Chapter 2 *introduces the Report and its content in five stages. We first investigate the motives of the Commission to introduce the Report, the rationale behind its establishment, and its objectives and targets. Secondly, the chapter presents the perceptions and experience of corruption in the EU, as portrayed in the Report. The third part of chapter discusses the Report's thematic section, dedicated to public procurement. There then follows an analysis of the Report's recommendations for all 28 member states in 2014, and finally we examine the Report's shortcomings, comparing its theoretical design—as described by the Commission in 2011—to its reality, as published in 2014.*

Chapter 3 *examines the regulatory approach of the Report, in which we argue that it is best explained as a form of reflexive governance. This chapter is divided into four different parts: initially explaining the context of the regulatory approach of the Report, which relates to the emergence of new modes of governance in the EU. This involves a discussion of the key method of the new governance approach in the EU:*

the Open Method of Coordination, which has considerably changed the regulation and methods of governance at the supranational level. In the second part we introduce the concept of reflexive governance and explain the transformation of new governance into reflexive governance in EU policymaking. Here we also consider the growing use of reflexive forms of governance within the EU and how reflexive governance occurs. In the third part we introduce the theory of reflexive law, providing key insights into the regulatory nature of reflexive governance. Finally we apply the theory of reflexive governance to the Report and propose that the concept of regulation of self-regulation provides crucial insight into the Report's governance approach.

Section 2

This is the mid-section of the book, in which we present the first findings on the impact of the Report and the state of the anti-corruption policy field after the Report's cancellation. The insights are derived from three case studies on the United Kingdom, Romania and Albania (all states at different stages in their relationship to the EU), and the section accordingly comprises three chapters.

***Chapter 4** explains the recommendations that the Report issued for the UK and how the UK has applied the recommendations into concrete policy actions. It also evaluates to what extent the UK is characterised by reflexive governance in developing its own anti-corruption policy field and the interplay with the EU in improving its anti-corruption policy. Furthermore, it also looks at the implications Brexit might have for the UK's efforts to fight corruption and the risks the UK may now face in this regard.*

***Chapter 5** explains Romania's recommendations from the Report, and we observe the EU's approach to the country's anti-corruption policy reform, implemented prior to and post-accession, with a particular focus on the post-accession instrument known as the Cooperation and Verification Mechanism. Furthermore, we analyse the efforts Romania has made in applying the Report's recommendations and to what extent Romania engages in reflexive governance in establishing its own anti-corruption policy field. We also look at the latest political developments in Romania post-2016 and their impact on Romania's anti-corruption laws and Romania's National Anticorruption Directorate.*

***Chapter 6** analyses the case of Albania and the steps that it has taken in developing an anti-corruption policy field since 1990. We distinguish three different phases in the establishing of anti-corruption policy after the downfall of the Communist regime, up to the in-depth judicial reform begun in 2016. We evaluate the EU's support in encouraging Albania's efforts to establish an anti-corruption policy field and question whether these interactions reveal forms of reflexive governance.*

Section 3

This is the last-section of the book, in which we present the achievement and shortcomings of the Report in trying to develop a comprehensive anti-corruption policy, discussing the state of the anti-corruption policy field in the EU after the Report's cancellation in 2017. We also describe the current EU anti-corruption policy under the European Semester and analyse its country-specific reports issued in 2018. The section ends with recommendations on how the European Semester can be improved and considers the 'semester-isation' of EU anti-corruption policy and the associated damage done to the anti-corruption policy field as a consequence of the Report's cancellation.

***Chapter** 7 summarises the results of the foregoing analysis of the Report, and in it we address key areas of relevance for future EU anti-corruption policy. The chapter is divided into two main parts, the first assessing the Report's achievements in its efforts to establish a comprehensive anti-corruption policy field. We also analyse examples of reflexive governance occurring as a result of these achievements, and the Report's impact, and consider how reflexive governance can be helpful to member and candidate states in developing their own anti-corruption policies. In the second part of the chapter we discuss in depth the EU's decision to discontinue the Report and analyse the new approach of evaluating member states' efforts against corruption, under the European Semester process. We offer insights into the European Semester country-specific recommendations issued in 2018, examining each of these and asking why the corruption-related issues were only mentioned in recommendations for 7 out of 28 member states. In this part, we also analyse whether the European Semester process is an adequate or suitable substitute for the Report and whether its current format is lacking in as a truly comprehensive anti-corruption instrument. The chapter ends with offering some recommendations on how the EU can improve its future EU anti-corruption policy and an exhortation to the Commission not to abandon the policy areas and work that started under the Report.*

Conclusion

The book concludes by offering some remarks on the importance of Report in developing further the anti-corruption policy field in the EU and its impact in trying to improve the anti-corruption standards in the member states. Furthermore, we briefly summarise new policy initiatives based on reflexive governance which arose from the Report and the importance of how the report facilitated mutual learning between member states for sharing best anti-corruption practices and engaging instrumental non-state actors in policymaking. We finish with brief thoughts on how future EU anti-corruption policy could be improved and strengthened by using the reflexive governance approach and reflection on how the 'semester-isation' of the anti-corruption policy since the cancellation of the Report has harmed the progress of the policy field in the EU.

Section 1

1 An introduction

A short history of anti-corruption policy in the EU

Corruption is considered to be one of the biggest challenges currently facing the European Union (EU) and its society, after inequality and the rise of populism. It was only in the mid-1990s—in particular after the fall of the Iron Curtain—that corruption first emerged as a policy problem that could no longer be addressed just through domestic policy by individual member states and the EU. Corruption scandals continue to make headlines all around the world on a frequent basis, and the Special Eurobarometer[1] issued in December 2017 suggests that corruption is still very common in Europe—in public institutions, different branches of governments and a source for of party-political funding. The 2017 Eurobarometer suggests that over two-thirds (68 per cent) of Europeans think that corruption is widespread in their country, and a large majority (79 per cent) agree that there are clear links and interchange between business and political leaders in their country lead, based on favouritism and corruption practices. The 2017 Eurobarometer is an indication that corruption is still a systemic problem in Europe and, thus, collective effort is required to tackle the issue of corruption more effectively.

In a globalised and interconnected world, which is characterised by rising flows of capital, goods, people, exchange of information and knowledge, corrupt practices do take place not only within national contexts but also across borders.[2] Thus, the growing complication of corrupt practices presents a significant challenge for anti-corruption policy success and for anti-corruption institutions. The EU enlargement process has increased political and economic integration, and we should view corruption as a cross-border problem that concerns all the member states, even when corruption occurs at local or national level. As a result, the globalisation of corruption can have great implications for anti-corruption policy efforts, which have traditionally been within the

1 European Commission, 'Special Eurobarometer 470 "Corruption" Report' European Commission, Directorate-General for Migration and Home Affairs and co-ordinated by the Directorate-General for Communication (2017) <http://ec.europa.eu/commfrontoffice/publicopinion/index.cfm/Survey/getSurveyDetail/instruments/SPECIAL/surveyKy/2176> accessed 30 May 2019.

2 A Teixeira and others, *Corruption, Economic Growth and Globalization* (Routledge 2015) 41–51.

responsibility of national policy and law-making. Over the past two decades, there have been some efforts for collectively addressing the issue of corruption at international level, by introducing a number of international anti-corruption conventions, as well as at EU level, by attempting to develop anti-corruption as a separate policy field. Despite this, we can observe that the fight against corruption has not always been high on the EU agenda, and currently the EU focus is on the rise of populism, global warming, security threats and income inequality. However, in recent years, the EU has taken some more concrete policy steps in addressing the issue of corruption. In accordance with Ralf Rogowski, we can distinguish four different phases that characterise the development of EU anti-corruption policy as a policy field.[3] And from 2017, the EU anti-corruption policy has begun evolving into new, fifth phase, after the decision by the EU Commission (hereafter, the Commission) to address corruption concerns under the European Semester.

1.1 The first phase

The EU and other international organisations such as the UN, the World Bank and the IMF started to address the issue of corruption as a policy concern during the mid-1990s by promoting good governance, and during the process of preparing the EU for enlargement in Central and Eastern Europe (which took place in 2004, 2007 and 2011[4]). According to Patrycja Szarek-Mason, in 1995, Transparency International (hereafter, TI) identified in its memorandum to the EU institutions that 'the EU was not fully aware of its role in fighting corruption; rather, it leaves the issue of corruption to the EU member states or to other international organisations working on corruption.'[5] Therefore, one might observe that, at this stage, the EU did not engage in anti-corruption policy and left it to the member states to address corruption through their domestic means.

The Commission issued its first Communication on the EU policy against corruption in 1997—the first EU policy document to focus primarily on the issue of corruption.[6] This Communication can be characterised as the start of the first phase, in developing a separate anti-corruption policy at supranational level by the EU. The Communication highlighted that corruption was having a negative impact on fair competition in the EU and posed a direct threat to the

3 R Rogowski, 'ALACs and the Concept of Citizen Participation in the Light of European Law' *Warwick School of Law Research Paper No 2010/25* (25 October 2010).

4 D Schmidt-Pfister and H Moroff, *Fighting Corruption in Eastern Europe: A Multilevel Perspective* (Routledge 2013) 104–105.

5 P Szarek-Mason, *The European Union's Fight Against Corruption: The Evolving Policy Towards Member States and Candidate Countries* (CUP 2010) 78.

6 European Commission, 'Communication from the Commission to the Council and the European Parliament on a Union Policy Against Corruption' COM (97) 192 final. <https://eur-lex.europa.eu/LexUriServ/LexUriServ.do?uri=COM:1997:0192:FIN:EN:PDF> accessed 30 May 2019.

principles of open and free markets within the EU. In particular, corruption was viewed as affecting the proper functioning of the internal market, the financial interests of the EU and international trade. Furthermore, the Communication acknowledged that corruption had a negative impact on the functioning of good governance and the rule of law.[7] In the 1997 Communication, the Commission declared three main objectives for developing an anti-corruption policy: to protect the EU's financial interests, to protect officials of the EU and/or of the member states, and to protect the private sector. In all three areas, there were some superficial anti-corruption instruments in place. However, we will see in the following sections, the implementation of the anti-corruption instruments in the member states were inadequate, and their efforts were insufficient for addressing corruption as an issue, let alone tackling the issue of corruption more effectively.

The Commission's first Communication on EU policy on fighting corruption in 1997 also gave the first definition of corruption, as understood by the EU: 'any abuse of power or impropriety in the decision-making process brought about by some undue inducement or benefit'.[8] This definition was accepted in 1998 by the European Court of Auditors.[9] However, the EU's definition of corruption as the 'abuse of power for private gain' is a very broad one and, as such, hard to work with. There are questions over how to define the concepts such as 'abuse of power' or 'private gain', and it becomes difficult to clearly define or measure how great the 'private gain' must be in order to fall under the EU definition. In accordance with Patrycja Szarek-Mason, the EU definition starts from the assumption that formal and informal systems of law and norms exist and are accepted by all sides in the EU—which in fact, at this time, is not the case.[10] The Commission's definition of corruption is broad and embraces a socio-economic approach which looks to address corruption in the context of good governance.[11]

To date, defining corruption in the EU still remains a contested issue, stimulating debate over accepting a common definition. However, in this book, we will not engage in the discourse and literature of defining corruption, but rather accept the definition accepted broadly by Transparency International as 'misuse of public power for public gain'. When it comes to refining and developing an acceptable definition by all of the member states, the EU must take into account as many voices and perspectives as possible. Definitions and perceptions of corruption vary across many of the member states—which members comprise diverse political, cultural and social development. Therefore, coming to a collective definition of corruption in the EU is far from easy. We could argue that it is almost impossible to measure the level of

7 P Csonka, 'Corruption: The European Commission's Approach' in Barry AK Rider (ed), *Corruption: The Enemy Within* (Kluwer Law International 1997) 343–353.

8 European Commission (n 6).

9 Court of Auditors, 'Special Report No 8/98' *OJ C 230* 22 July 1998.

10 P Szarek-Mason, *The European Union's Fight Against Corruption: The Evolving Policy Towards Member States and Candidate Countries* (CUP 2010) 10.

11 ibid 11.

corruption across all of the member states, simply because the legal definitions, as well as the cultural understandings of a corrupt act, differ considerably from one member state to another. Therefore, the ongoing challenge for the EU is to adopt a definition that can incorporate numerous understandings of corruption across the member states.

At the same time as issuing the first Communication on EU policy on fighting corruption, the Commission also made a number of recommendations—in particular, the introduction of accounting and auditing standards, the blacklisting of corrupt companies and the banning of tax deductibility to EU member states.[12] The Commission's objective was to establish an EU strategy to respond to corruption issues within its member states,[13] because at this time a cross-border dimension started to be linked to serious corruption crimes, such as human trafficking, money laundering and the narcotic trade.[14] Furthermore, the accession process in Central and Eastern Europe (CEE) had begun to provoke the EU's interest in developing an anti-corruption policy, as many member states held deep reservations about the high level of corruption present in the CEE countries that would accede to the EU in 2004.

These concerns were taken on board by the Commission's overall report in 1998, on the progress towards accession by candidate countries. The report suggested that the fight against corruption needed to be strengthened further in the CEE states and that the efforts undertaken by the CEE candidate countries were not always adequate, commensurate to the severity of the problem. Although, as part of their accession process, a number of CEE states put in place programmes for the control and prevention of corruption (explained in detail later), these measures were deemed insufficient. We could view this lacklustre response as evidence of a lack of political will to tackle the issue of corruption in most of the CEE states—and that those efforts made were only to satisfy the EU accession conditions and meet the chapters of the Acquis Communautaire ('acquis').[15]

This view—of insufficient political will to address the high level of corruption in the CEE states—was reflected in the Commission's regular reports on each of the candidate country's progress report towards accession. Furthermore, the Commission's own conclusions of the individual country evaluations considered corruption a serious source of concern for Bulgaria, Czech Republic, Poland, Romania and Slovakia; an ongoing problem in Hungary, Latvia and Lithuania; and an issue of concern in Estonia and Slovenia. These and later assessments by the Commission in 2001 concluded that corruption remained a serious issue for

12 Council of the European Union, 'Action Plan to Combat Organized Crime' *OJ C 131* 15 August 1997.

13 European Commission (n 6).

14 The Council [1] adopted the Council Framework Decision 2003/568/JHA of 22 July 2003 on combating corruption in the private sector [2] pursuant to Title VI of the Treaty on European Union.

15 European Commission, 'Composite Paper: Reports on Progress Towards Accession by Each of the Candidate Countries' (4 November 1998) 6.

concern, and a potential barrier for EU accession for the CEE states.[16] The Commission did state, in many reports, its concern regarding the high levels of corruption in the CEE states and emphasised that making progress in the fight against corruption was a precondition for all the EU candidate states in order to fulfil the conditions for EU membership.

According to Stephan Leibfried, post-Communist countries are viewed in the EU as being more vulnerable to corruption, due to their inadequate institutional structures and lack of independent institutions.[17] Evaluating the levels of corruption in the CEE candidate states was, and still is, very challenging for the Commission—not because corruption in the CEE states is different to the corruption issues faced by the old member states, but because, at the time, the EU lacked a coherent anti-corruption policy and framework to address it.[18] The absence of such a framework in the late 1990s meant that the Commission did not establish any clear benchmarks for the EU candidate states in the area of corruption, nor in guidance to establish effective anti-corruption policy. This lack of clarity has since created many policy challenges for the EU.

Firstly, in the absence of a clear framework for evaluating the extent, nature and causes of corruption in CEE countries, the Commission evaluated those countries on the basis of how they prosecuted corruption acts under their criminal law. However, such an approach neglected the impact of some key aspects of corruption-related issues in the CEE countries, varying from societal tolerance of corruption to more or less deep-rooted traditions of allocating public resources on the basis of close networks, as was the common practice in the Communist era.

Secondly, the Copenhagen Criteria[19] under the EU chapters of the acquis—commonly known as the negotiation chapters—allowed the Commission to push for anti-corruption policies in the CEE candidate states, which the EU was unable to enforce on the existing member states. The Commission regularly pushed the EU candidate states' with additional conditions on meeting anti-corruption standards through its annual progress reports. In particular, the Commission required candidate states to sign and ratify the Council of Europe Criminal Law Convention on Corruption, by attaching it to the EU chapters of the acquis. By 2002, eight of the ten CEE candidate states had adopted the convention, compared to only three out of fifteen existing member states. Hence, we could argue that the CEE candidate states were being held to different standards from those already within the EU.

These elements and examples made the integration of any anti-corruption policy objective into the accession process challenging for the Commission.

16 WL Miller, AB Grodeland and YT Koshechkina, *A Culture of Corruption? Coping with Government in Post-Communist Europe* (Central European University Press 2001) 279.

17 S Leibfried, *The Oxford Handbook of Transformations of the State* (OUP 2015) 607.

18 Szarek-Mason (n 10).

19 J Sargentini and A Dimitrovs, 'The European Parliament's Role: Towards New Copenhagen Criteria for Existing Member States?' *Journal of Common Market Studies 54* (5) (2016) 1085–1092.

Furthermore, the main focus of accession negotiations on harmonisation and implementation of the acquis limited the scope for inclusion of anti-corruption policy in the CEE states. Therefore, the anti-corruption acquis was rather limited and the effectiveness of anti-corruption policy was beyond the scope of EU.

As a result of an inadequate EU policy towards corruption, a number of CEE candidate states—where corruption had been persistent as a serious problem, even by the standards of the Commission's progress reports—were admitted into the EU later than others. However, the inadequacy of a clear anti-corruption policy at the EU, particularly in terms of the candidate states, was a cause for concern for two main reasons. Firstly, the EU paid insufficient attention to the issue of corruption, focusing only on CEE countries demonstrating that they meet the acquis conditions, rather than showing a track record of implementation—despite the fact that there were credible signs that corruption in some CEE countries was a major threat to the functioning of democracy and the common market. Secondly, the high level of corruption and inadequate anti-corruption policies in a number of candidate states in the CEE undermined the quality of governance in the EU. The corruption observable in the CEE undermined some of the fundamental values to which the EU subscribes and presented the Commission with additional challenges to establishing effective instruments and mechanisms that would promote more effective anti-corruption policy in all the member states and ensure that the Copenhagen Criteria was honoured.

The EU institutions were involved in corruption scandals themselves in late 1990s, which caused a halt in anti-corruption policy development at European level until 2003. The 1999 scandals faced by EU institutions—in particular the Commission—mark the start of the second phase of the development of the EU anti-corruption as a policy field within its institutions.

1.2 The second phase

The second phase can be mainly characterised by the internal problems facing the EU institutions in 1999 and, in particular, the scandals involving the Santer Commission—all members of which had to resign over serious allegations of corruption. The collapse of the Santer Commission exposed the need to implement effective measures for the protection of the EU institutions against corruption. In response, the EU established the Commission's integrity[20] and its intention to increase ethics and good governance standards. Additionally, the EU reformed the anti-fraud unit UCLAF (*Unité de Coordination de La Lutte*

20 European Commission, 'Communication from the Commission to the Council, the European Parliament and the European Economic and Social Committee on a Comprehensive EU Policy Against Corruption' COM (2003) 317 final <https://eur-lex.europa.eu/legal-content/EN/TXT/PDF/?uri=CELEX:52003DC0317&from=EN> accessed 30 May 2019.

Anti-Fraude), creating instead the European Anti-Fraud Office (OLAF), whose main responsibility is to investigate corruption in EU institutions.[21]

OLAF is an independent administrative body entrusted with powers to investigate cases related to corruption and fraud, as well as other illegal activity affecting the EU budget. OLAF was set up to protect the financial interests of the EU in fighting corruption and any other illegal activities, as well as to protect the reputation of the European Institutions. Furthermore, OLAF was entrusted with power to investigate any misconduct of the EU institutions' personnel that might result in disciplinary or criminal proceedings. OLAF also supported the Commission in developing and implementing anti-corruption policy. The overall objective for establishing OLAF was to create an institution that was more effective and had more independence than its predecessor UCLAF when investing corruption practices.

In addition to the re-organisational structure of OLAF, the Commission also took other policy measures, starting the process of developing a broad good governance framework—in particular the White Paper on European Governance, published in 2001.[22] The White Paper established a framework to reform the Commission, based on principles of accountability, independence and transparency.[23] It included a strategy for establishing an internal audit service, improving public access to documents of the European Parliament, the Council and the Commission, and strengthening its fraud prevention legislation.[24] The White Paper also laid the foundation for developing a tougher code of conduct for members of the European Parliament and EU Commission officials.

The collapse of the Santer Commission made the EU Commission more aware of the need to promote and ensure better accountability and transparency within EU institutions. The Commission implemented a series of measures aimed at improving the integrity and ethics among its staff[25] and rules on how to report serious wrongdoings related to corruption.[26] The European Transparency Initiative was launched shortly after the collapse of the Santer Commission and was designed to foster dialogue about areas where transparency at the EU level appeared to need further improvement.[27] The EU Commission acknowledged at this time that transparency is an important element in preventing

21 European Commission, 'Decision of 28 April 1999 Establishing the European Anti-Fraud Office' *(OLAF) OJ L 13620* 31 May 1999.

22 European Commission, 'White Paper on European Governance' COM (2001) 428 final 7–11.

23 ibid.

24 Jill Wakefield, 'Good Governance and the European Anti-Fraud Office' *12 European Public Law* (4) (2006) 549–575.

25 Szarek-Mason (n 10) 72.

26 European Commission (n 6).

27 European Commission (2006), Green Paper on European Transparency Initiative, COM (2006) 194 final.

corruption[28] and, thus, began to publish data about EU funds beneficiaries, lobbying regulation, strengthening the ethics in the EU institutions and adjusting the regulation of access to documents at the EU level.[29]

Further efforts were also taken by the Council of Europe to promote transparency and integrity, developing 20 'guiding principles'[30] to support national dialogue in improving anti-corruption policy. These guiding principles were mainly aimed at improving key sectors of public administration that were perceived as exposed to corruption practices. They supported the development of precautionary measures, including raising public awareness, ethical behaviour, independence of the judiciary and prosecution, restrictions of immunity for public officials, supporting more stronger codes of conduct for public officials, and adequate auditing procedures for public administration, supervision of financing of political parties and freedom of media.[31] The 20 guiding principles are a form of soft law measures, and not legally binding. Therefore, national governments were only encouraged to implement these principles when drafting their national anti-corruption policy.

The Council of Europe developed an anti-corruption monitoring body known as the Group of States Against Corruption (GRECO) to monitor the performance of the 20 guiding principles. GRECO ensured that the non-binding nature of the guiding principles did not diminish their achievement in encouraging adequate anti-corruption policies. Furthermore, GRECO has become an important monitoring instrument in evaluating its members' compliance with the anti-corruption standards through a process of mutual evaluation and peer pressure.[32] GRECO is also an important institution in supporting its members' capacity to fight corruption and has developed important anti-corruption conventions, such as the Criminal Law Convention on Corruption (*Criminal Law Convention*)[33] and the Civil Law Convention on Corruption (*Civil Law Convention*).[34] The Criminal Law Convention focuses on the criminalisation of active and passive bribery of public officials, therefore including national and foreign officials, officials of international organisations and members of national and foreign public legislatures.[35] Similar to the OECD convention, these convention goals ensure the legal protection for informants cooperating with investigating

28 Szarek-Mason (n 10) 84.

29 European Commission, 'Protection of the Communities' Financial Interests—Fight Against Fraud—Annual Report 2005' COM (2006) 378 final.

30 Council of Europe, 'Resolution (97) 24 on the Twenty Guiding Principles for the Fight Against Corruption' (1997)

31 C Eckes and T Konstadinides, *Crime Within the Area of Freedom, Security and Justice: A European Public Order* (CUP 2011) 48.

32 Szarek-Mason (n 10) 37.

33 Neil Boister and Robert J Curry, *Routledge Handbook of Transnational Criminal Law* (Routledge 2015) 79–80.

34 Szarek-Mason (n 10) 254.

35 Ilias Bantekas and Susan Nash, *International Criminal Law* (Routledge 2007) 282.

and prosecuting authorities.[36] However, none of these conventions were ratified by the member states until late 2014. Therefore, the EU anti-corruption framework remained mainly non-binding and inadequate. There are two possible reasons for this.

Firstly, the nature and level of corruption appeared to differ widely across the member states—reflecting different national traditions and historical backgrounds. There is a clear difference between the bureaucratic traditions of integrity and probity characteristic of the Northern EU member states, on the one hand, and the more informal style of public service characteristics of South and Eastern European member states, on the other hand. These differences can be observed in numerous examples, witnessed throughout the following chapters of this book. One such is the departure of Eva Joly, the judge in charge of the investigation into the Elf Aquitaine affair in France.[37] The scandals that surrounded the former French President Jacques Chirac,[38] the former Italian Prime Minister Silvio Berlusconi[39] and the former Romanian Prime Minister Victor Ponta all highlight that corruption is a serious issue of concern throughout the EU. Secondly, the EU Commission's internal problems, with the collapse of the Santer Commission, made it hard to push member states to address the issue of corruption in policy terms during the second phase of reforms.

Hence, there was a contradictory situation in the EU. On the one hand, it had embarked on a number of important steps to implement good governance practices at the EU administration level; and on the other hand, efforts to support common anti-corruption standards and policies across member states were challenging because of the EU's own internal issues with corruption. This was despite the fact the EU, through the Copenhagen Mandate, had sufficient legal power to push for anti-corruption measures, but had lost some credibility from the collapse of the Santer Commission.

1.3 The third phase

Anti-corruption policy gained further momentum at international level at the start of the new millennium in 2000, as many important international anti-corruption instruments were established.[40] This marked the third phase of development of an EU anti-corruption policy, in which the EU mainly adopted international anti-corruption standards. In particular, the EU

36 Boister and Curry (n 33).

37 Transparency International, 'Global Corruption Report 2007: Corruption in Judicial Systems' *TI* (2007) 84–88.

38 J Henley, 'Gigantic Sleaze Scandal Winds Up as Former Elf Oil Chiefs Are Jailed' *The Guardian*, 13 November 2003 <www.theguardian.com/business/2003/nov/13/france.oilandpetrol> accessed 30 May 2019

39 D Tänzle, A Giannakopoulos and K Maras, *The Social Construction of Corruption in Europe* (Ashgate 2012) 134.

40 Rogowski (n 3).

promoted to its member states the adoption of the OECD Convention on Combating Bribery of Foreign Public Officials in International Business Transactions[41] and the UN Convention against Corruption.[42] According to Ralf Rogowski, the shift of attitudes in the EU to support international initiatives indicated that the EU at this point gave up in pursuing their own anti-corruption policy, but rather adopted international measures.[43] The EU saw its role during the third phase to support international efforts against corruption and become a global player in policymaking.

The EU's objective to fight corruption was further intensified in 2003, when the Commission issued the second 'Communication on a Comprehensive EU Policy against Corruption'.[44] The Commission's understanding of a 'comprehensive policy against corruption' meant reducing the level of corruption within the EU institutions and tackling the EU member states more forcefully.[45] Transparency International considered the second Communication as a game changer,[46] as it included clearer policy recommendations for the EU member states in comparison to the first 1997 Communication.[47] For example, one policy recommendation was to establish specialised anti-corruption agencies and guarantee the independence of specialised anti-corruption authorities in order to fight corruption more effectively. Another policy recommendation was to introduce rules and codes of conduct for public officials, in order to prevent conflicts of interest, ensuring freedom of the media, and freedom of information.[48] Furthermore, the second Communication developed the concept of corruption at EU level, defining it as 'an abuse of power for private gain'.[49] Therefore, the Commission went further in 2003, embracing both public and private sectors within this definition.

In defining corruption for the purposes of EU policy, the Commission included a narrow criminal law definition and a broader notion of corruption used for the purposes of preventive policy.[50] The distinction—between the criminal law definition, and the broader concept of corruption adopted for the

41 C Pacini, AJ Swingen and R Hudson, 'The Role of the OECD and EU Conventions in Combating Bribery of Foreign Public Officials' *Journal of Business Ethics 37* (4) (2002) 385–405.
42 D Schmidt-Pfister and H Moroff, *Fighting Corruption in Eastern Europe: A Multilevel Perspective* (Routledge 2013) 104–105.
43 Rogowski (n 3).
44 European Commission (n 6).
45 M Beblavý and EB Sičáková, 'The Changing Faces of Europeanisation: How Did the European Union Influence Corruption in Slovakia Before and After Accession?' *Europe-Asia Studies 66* (4) (2014) 536–556.
46 Szarek-Mason (n 10) 7.
47 European Commission (n 6).
48 European Commission, 'Report on the Stabilisation and Association Process for South East Europe: First Annual Report' COM (2002) 163 final.
49 European Commission (n 6).
50 J Carver, 'Combating Corruption: The Emergence of New International Law' *International Law Forum 5* (2) (2003) 119–123.

purposes of preventing it—is important. Criminal law definitions constitute a basis for prosecuting offenders and must be unambiguous and specific. The clarity of definition is preserved against the discretionary power of public authorities. As a result, EU criminal law recognises only discrete corrupt practices, such as taking or offering bribes, and fails to cover the full range of corrupt activities which might be involved.[51] Bribery is simply one type of corruption. There are many others, such as buying votes, favouritism, nepotism, trading in influence, and illegal political party financing; at this point the EU policy neither focussed on nor developed policy or law to address these.[52]

The Commission's anti-corruption policy changed during the pre-accession stage, because of the perception of high-level of corruption in the CEE states, which were about to join the EU in 2004. The candidate states were under extreme political pressure to comply with the Commission's recommendations set out in the regular country reports. As a result, the Commission made fighting against corruption one of the key objectives of the European Neighbourhood Policy.[53] Furthermore, the Commission moved its anti-corruption instrument from Chapter 24 to the new Chapter 23 of the European Neighbourhood acquis, which placed the judiciary, and fighting against corruption and organised crime higher on the agenda. This change was aimed to reinforce the structure of the EU anti-corruption policy approach in candidate and potential candidate states.[54]

The Commission tried to reinforce anti-corruption instruments, support member states in joining GRECO, and the ratification of the United Nations Convention Against Transnational Organized Crime (UNTOC) and the United Nations Convention Against Corruption (UNCAC). For the candidate states, the Commission made the ratification of these anti-corruption instruments a compulsory part of the negotiating chapters. However, the weakness of EU policy was the fact that it ended on the day of accession of the CEE countries to the EU, in May 2004.[55]

As a policy field, EU anti-corruption up to this point was characterised largely by fragmentation and the lack of a strategic vision on how to fight corruption, with a focus mainly on candidate states. Through regular reports on the CEE states, the Commission supported an adequate set of anti-corruption standards, but the CEE countries failed to apply them consistently. The acknowledgment of such shortcomings forced the Commission to change strategy during the accession for Bulgaria and Romania.[56] As a result, on 13 December 2006, the Commission adopted a decision, on the basis of Articles 37 and 38 of the

51 ibid.

52 Agata Stachowicz-Stanusch, *Organizational Immunity to Corruption: Building Theoretical and Research Foundations* (Information Age Publishing 2010) 135.

53 Sara Poli, *The European Neighbourhood Policy—Values and Principles* (Routledge 2016) 90.

54 ibid.

55 Szarek-Mason (n 10) 21.

56 G Noutcheva, *European Foreign Policy and the Challenges of Balkan Accession, Conditionality, Legitimacy and Compliance* (Routledge 2012) 84.

Treaty of Accession, to establish the 'Co-operation and Verification Mechanism' (CVM) for Bulgaria[57] and Romania.[58] This was the first time that such a monitoring mechanism and post-conditionality was used post-accession in the history of EU policies. The establishment of the CVM opened up a second generation of conditionality and marked the beginning of the fourth phase of the EU anti-corruption policy as a policy field.[59]

1.4 The fourth phase

The EU enlargement expansion in 2004 made the Commission go beyond its single market objectives, and focus also on promoting liberal democracy and strengthening the rule of law in Europe, due to the high level of corruption in CEE. The fight against corruption became at this time a key objective to the EU enlargement policy—but anti-corruption policy was still less significant than the economic and administrative reforms that supported the proper functioning of the single market. After the accession of the CEE states in 2004, the Commission acknowledged corruption as a serious problem and tried to avoid a similar mistake with Bulgaria and Romania, which were scheduled to join the EU in 2007.[60]

The Treaty of Accession with CEE states implemented three exclusive safeguard clauses in relation to the economy, the internal market and the area of Justice and Home Affairs (JHA), which can be enforced for three years after accession. Therefore, any new or old EU member state had leverage to invoke these clauses in the case of any serious economic crisis, or risk causing a serious violation of the functioning of the internal market until 2007.[61] The JHA safeguarding clauses allowed the existing member states to have the power to reject any application of judgments and arrest warrants from the CEE states in case of forthcoming risks in the implementation and application of the acquis, concerning mutual recognition in civil and criminal cases.[62] These safeguarding clauses

57 European Commission, 'Decision on Establishing a Mechanism for Cooperation and Verification of Progress in Bulgaria to Address Specific Benchmarks in the Areas of Judicial Reform and the Fight Against Corruption and Organised Crime' (2006/929/EC) *OJ L 354/58* 14 December 2006.

58 European Commission, 'Decision on Establishing a Mechanism for Cooperation and Verification of Progress in Romania to Address Specific Benchmarks in the Areas of Judicial Reform and the Fight Against Corruption and Organised Crime' (2006/928/EC) *OJ L 354/56* 14 December 2006.

59 Ramona Coman, 'The Normative Power of the EU and Contentious Europeanization: The Case of Judicial Politics' *Journal of European Integration 36* (6) (2014) 533–548.

60 Soeren Keil and Zeynep Arkan, *The EU and Member State Building: European Foreign Policy in the Western Balkans* (Routledge 2015) 41–49.

61 Christine Chiva and David Phinnemore, *The European Union's 2007 Enlargement* (Routledge 2012) 12–14.

62 ibid.

were put in place as an 'emergency brake' instrument for the existing member states, but they were never used.

In the case of Bulgaria and Romania's accession, the Commission policy changed when the Treaty of Accession with Bulgaria and Romania was signed in 2005. There was an observable shift in the Commission's approach, which was now making combating corruption the main issue for both countries. The-Commission began to monitor Bulgaria and Romania more strongly than the previous CEE countries which had entered the EU in 2004. In addition to the increasing emphasis on seriously tackling corruption, this marked change may be linked to a couple of factors. In practical terms, it was easier to monitor just two countries rather than eight; also the issue of corruption was perceived to be more widespread in the public administration in Bulgaria and Romania, in comparison to the previously acceding CEE countries.[63]

Yet, there were other reasons behind the Commission's new approach. The changing political climate within the member states and their relationship with the EU was a major factor in policy change: the refusal of the Constitutional Treaty in the Dutch and French referendums showed public disapproval for various aspects of EU policy, including the enlargement policy. As a result, and under pressure, the Commission had to adapt and develop a more rigorous monitoring mechanism in addressing the outstanding legal and policy concerns related to anti-corruption instruments in Bulgaria and Romania. Furthermore, the EU also learned from the previous round of enlargement in the CEE states that corruption was a widespread concern and better tools needed to be developed to ensure that the implementation of anti-corruption legislation was operational and intact.[64] As a consequence, the EU policy towards Bulgaria and Romania was reinforced in two ways: firstly, by introducing a sanction option of possibly postponing accession by another three years. Secondly, by introducing the CVM to monitor progress in the area of anti-corruption *after* Bulgaria and Romania joined the European Union.[65]

As a result, in December 2006, the Commission made a decision, based on Articles 37 and 38 of the Treaty of Accession, to establish the CVM as a transitional measure to assist the two countries to remedy these shortcomings in the fields of judicial reform, corruption and organised crime. Bulgaria and Romania were allowed to join the EU on 1 January 2007, under the condition that they met certain anti-corruption benchmarks which were to be monitored under the CVM.

63 Florian Trauner, 'Post-Accession Compliance with EU Law in Bulgaria And Romania: A Comparative Perspective' *European Integration Online Papers (EIoP) 2* (13) Art 21 (2009) <http://eiop.or.at/eiop/texte/2009-021a.htm> accessed 30 May 2019.

64 Mason-Szarek (n 10) 227.

65 Radu Carp, 'The Struggle for the Rule of Law in Romania as an EU Member State: The Role of the Cooperation and Verification Mechanism' *Utrecht Law Review 10* (1) (2014) 1–16.

The benchmarks for Romania related to the effectiveness and transparency of the judicial system, reforming institutional integrity, building institutional capacity to fight against corruption at all levels more effectively and to develop effective anti-corruption prevention tools. The benchmarks for Bulgaria were related to issues concerning the independence, professionalism and efficiency of the judicial system, and its institutional capacity to fight against corruption more effectively and crack down on organised crime networks.

The benchmarks for the CVM can be understood as a structured approach for organisational procedures to develop new and higher standards in terms of legalisations and anti-corruption preventive instruments.[66] The EU mainly used this practice during the pre-accession process, and it was linked into the EU enlargement policy. However, the anti-corruption benchmarks were broad, i.e. subscribing to a set of good governance principals, and not systematically implemented throughout the EU candidate states before 2007. The new monitoring mechanism gave the Commission some leverage to maintain pressure on Bulgaria and Romania in establishing effective anti-corruption reforms—at least in theory. The EU seemed to act on the notion that it might be better to work with Bulgaria and Romania once they were inside the European Union, rather than to try to push for reforms from outside of the EU and lose the EU enlargement momentum in these countries and within the Union.[67]

This new approach did not only extend to the application of pre-accession monitoring instruments but also improved the EU enlargement policy and anti-corruption policy. As we have seen, the greatest shortcomings of the EU policy towards the CEE states was that it lacked coherent and tailored anti-corruption benchmarks for each country. In the case of Bulgaria and Romania, if these two states failed to implement these benchmarks, the Commission now had the power to apply safeguarding measures and sanctions.[68]

The benchmarks designed in the CVM for Bulgaria and Romania—which will be elaborated on further in Chapter 5—supported fundamental reforms. They required that both Bulgaria and Romania fulfilled the principal membership condition of having an independent and effective judicial system, central to being an EU member and fulfilling the Copenhagen Criteria.[69]

At its core design, the monitoring instrument under the CVM (as a post-accession monitoring system) is very different from the pre-accession strategy. It involves meeting specific policy goals and targets for Bulgaria and Romania on the basis of setting up specific anti-corruption benchmarks, periodical monitoring of compliance with those benchmarks using independent sources of

66 Ana Ramalho, *The Competence of the European Union in Copyright Lawmaking: A Normative Perspective of EU Powers for Copyright Harmonization* (Springer 2016) 216–217.

67 Chiva and Phinnemore (n 61) 1–3.

68 Eli Gateva, *European Union Enlargement Conditionality* (Palgrave Macmillan 2015) 102.

69 Jan-Werner Müller, 'Should the EU Protect Democracy and the Rule of Law Inside Member States?' *European Law Journal 21* (2) (2015) 141–160.

information and providing financial and technical assistance to support anti-corruption reforms. This procedure of benchmarking is modelled after the Council of Europe's GRECO evaluations of the 20 guiding principles against corruption. However, the CVM reports, issued annually by the Commission since 2007, cover more detailed evaluations than any other pre-accession instruments. This new approach shows that the EU understood that the anti-corruption policy established for the purpose of the 2004 enlargement policy was inadequate and insufficient—thus a policy change was necessary.[70]

The Commission issues an annual formal report under the CVM, based on careful analysis and monitoring, and drawing on a continuous dialogue between the Bulgarian and Romanian authorities and the Commission services. The Commission issued its first report on 27 June 2007; the reports contain assessment and recommendations to the Bulgarian and Romanian authorities and are complemented by a staff-working document which sets out the Commission's detailed analysis against each of the benchmarks under the CVM. Each CVM report, including methodology and conclusions, is discussed and endorsed by the Council of Ministers before publication.

By establishing the CVM, the EU responded to the corruption problems in Bulgaria and Romania, and in addressing them, took them more seriously than in the previous round of enlargement. The EU policy against corruption also became more systematic, not only because new member states were asked to achieve better results in fighting corruption but also because the EU developed clearer and more coherent anti-corruption guidelines and objectives.[71] Furthermore, the CVM reports also intensified contacts with the other EU countries, civil society, international organisations, independent experts and a variety of other sources working on anti-corruption policy. The former Romanian justice minister, Monica Macovei, endorsed the CVM as a post-accession monitoring instrument, because she believed that the reforms of the judiciary and the fight against corruption must continue even after Romania joined the EU.[72] However, the imposition of CVM in Bulgaria and Romania as a monitoring system can be viewed as an admission of previous failure by the EU: the accession process had not ensured that these countries met the EU standards, and still were not ready, even though they joined the EU in 2007.

In theory, the CVM as a post-accession monitoring instrument is more comprehensive in terms of guidelines for pushing for quality anti-corruption instruments. However, its effectiveness largely depends on the application of

70 Heather Grabbe, 'European Union Conditionality and the Acquis Communautaire' *International Political Science Review 23* (3) (2002) 249–68.

71 Teresa Cierco, *The European Union Neighbourhood: Challenges and Opportunities* (Routledge 2013) 25–26.

72 Anitta M Hipper, *Beyond the Rhetorics of Compliance: Judicial Reform in Romania* (Springer VS 2015) 221–222.

sanctions by the EU Commission, i.e. freezing EU funding assistance to Bulgaria and Romania, rather than on its soft approach.

In summary, the CVM offers only a provisional ground to push Bulgaria and Romania towards anti-corruption reform, but does not solve the problem in the long term. Corruption is still widespread in Bulgaria and Romania, even though the CVM has been in place for the past ten years. The EU enlargements policy challenges and experience in addressing anti-corruption shortcomings presented by Bulgaria and Romania have provided a number of lessons, which are now being reflected in the pre-accession strategy towards the current candidate states, which will be elaborated in the case study for Albania in Chapter 4.

As a policy field, the EU anti-corruption policy developed further in 2010, with the establishment of the Stockholm Programme, which sets out key priorities for the EU in the areas of justice, freedom and security for the period 2010–2014. It aimed at addressing key challenges in the areas of justice, freedom and security, and it also included fighting against corruption.[73] With the adoption of the Stockholm Programme, the Commission had a political mandate to evaluate efforts in the fight against corruption and further develop its anti-corruption policy, in close co-operation with the Council of Europe Group of states against Corruption.[74]

Subsequent to the Lisbon Treaty, the legal grounds for developing more efficient instruments to fight corruption were consolidated further, and efforts were taken to support better anti-corruption policy. By abolishing the pillar structure, the Treaty permitted for an effective decision-making procedure and better implementation by the member states of the actions in areas of freedom, security and justice, while making them subject to better parliamentary and judicial control, in order to greater enhance the balance between judicial and security safeguarding of citizens.[75]

Article 83 TFEU defined corruption among the serious crimes with a cross-border dimension for which minimum rules on the definition of criminal offences and sanctions might be established. Furthermore, after adopting the 'Stockholm Program',[76] the European Council supported the Commission to develop further indicators for assessing efforts in the fight against corruption more effectively (for example, in areas related to public procurement, financial control and the establishment of a coherent anti-corruption policy). Since then, the European Parliament has, on numerous occasions, requested a comprehensive anti-corruption policy and

73 Richard Ball, *The Legitimacy of the European Union Through Legal Rationality: Free Movement of Third Country Nationals* (Routledge 2014) 217–218.

74 Rogowski (n 3).

75 Mark Dawson, *New Governance and the Transformation of European Law: Coordinating EU Social Law and Policy* (CUP 2011) 99.

76 Council of European Union, 'The Stockholm Programme—An Open and Secure Europe Serving and Protecting the Citizens' Adopted by the European Council on 10–11 December 2009, 17024/09.

the establishment of clear mechanisms monitoring corruption in the EU member states on a more regular basis.

As a result, the Commission decided to set up an EU Anti-Corruption Report (hereafter known as the Report, or the 2014 Report) to evaluate and monitor all member states' efforts against corruption. In June 2011, the Commission announced its plans to establish the Report, and in the words of the Commission 'to address more robustly the serious damage that corruption causes to EU—economically, socially and politically'.[77] The new Report announced that it would also evaluate the capacity of EU institutions to fight corruption. The Commission issued a Communication on the fight against corruption in the EU, known as a 'Commission Decision Establishing an EU Anti-Corruption Report',[78] for building and implementing more effective policies against corruption at the EU and national levels.[79] The publication of objective fact-based reports that the Report would present would be applicable to all of the EU member states every two years. It was designed to offer a more complete overview of the existence and efficiency of the anti-corruption efforts in the EU and its tools in addressing corruption. A group of experts[80] and a network of researchers were set up to assist the Commission in its preparation.[81]

Furthermore, this new Report was building on existing tools, in terms of evaluating anti-corruption policies, aiming to add innovative measures in addressing anti-corruption policy shortcomings. The evaluation and recommendations that the Report would produce would serve as a useful tool to see the level of corruption and policy shortcomings throughout the EU, available to everyone including politicians, the public, the media and practitioners. The Report was also designed to monitor and evaluate the member states in addressing corruption and to stimulate political commitment in pushing for anti-corruption reform. Supported by a specialist group and a network of research correspondents, the Report was to be managed by the EU Commission Home Affairs. The Report was designed to present a rational reflection of the achievements, commitments and vulnerabilities of all the member states efforts in preventing and fighting corruption; its main objective was to identify trends and weaknesses that needed addressing, as well as to facilitate more peer-learning and exchange of best practices in areas of anti-corruption policy throughout the EU.[82]

77 European Commission, 'Communication on Fighting Corruption in the EU' COM (2011) 308 final.

78 ibid.

79 Emilija Taseva, 'New European Commission Anti-Corruption Package: Towards a More Efficient Fight Against Corruption?' *The New Journal of European Criminal Law 3* (3–4) (2012) 344–362.

80 European Commission, 'Decision on setting up the Group of Experts on Corruption' 28 September 2011 (2011/C 286/03).

81 European Commission, 'Communication on Fighting Corruption in the EU' COM (6 June 2011) 308 final.

82 ibid.

The Commission was careful in its wording, stating that the Report would try to avoid any duplication with existing mechanisms and instruments and to fill their gaps with other available means. To this end, the Commission collaborated with the existing monitoring and evaluation mechanisms and involved other participants such as independent experts, researchers, EU Commission services and the European Anti-Fraud Office, Europol and Eurojust, the European Anti-Corruption Network, surveys and civil society. The Report was created on the basis of existing international instruments from the Council of Europe, UN and OECD, while concentrating on the cross-cutting problems of particular concern at the EU level, as well as certain issues specific to each of the member states.

The EU Anti-Corruption Report was published in February 2014 for the first time. It drew on existing data sets to monitor trends and to identify policy weaknesses in all the member states, which consisted of 28 country-specific reports and a summary report that offered thematic analyses in all of the member states. We will analyse this first Report in more depth in Chapter 2.

The Report mainly served to make each individual member state aware of its own shortcomings in its laws and institutional capacity to combat corruption effectively. It also provided important information on corruption cases, in particular offering a description of the level of corruption throughout the EU. The Report also identified cross-cutting corruption risks with cross-border dimensions for the EU and offered recommendations to each individual member state in areas which they identified as most vulnerable to corruption practices.

The preparation of the second iteration of the Report was scheduled for publication in 2016 and was in progress, until the Commission Vice President Frans Timmermans announced in January 2017 that the Commission had decided to drop the Report altogether. Timmermans suggested that the Report published in 2014 served well as the basis for dialogues with the member states, which was a useful instrument for background information. He also stated that the Report opened a wider debate on the issue concerning corruption, both at EU level and in individual member states.

However, the Commission's view, since 2017, is that fighting corruption should be addressed through economic policy—and Timmermans indicated in his announcement that combating corruption is becoming part of the 'European Semester' process of economic governance, where a number of the country reports now also include specific analysis of corruption risks and related challenges that were associated with corruption practices.

What we can observe is the Commission shifting its approach by integrating anti-corruption policy into the EU economic policy coordination, marking the start of a new phase of the EU anti-corruption policy post-2017. Subsequently, the Commission made the decision to drop the Report after only one publication—the final chapter of this book evaluates in more depth the reasons behind this decision, and how successful the Commission has been so far in integrating anti-corruption monitoring instruments into the 'European Semester'. We will consider whether the Report was an effective tool in driving anti-corruption policy reform and analyse whether the 'European Semester' process is fit for purpose in addressing anti-corruption shortcomings in member states, in addition to coordinating economic policy.

In the next chapter, we will examine the 2014 EU Anti-Corruption Report's objectives and offer some key insights into the overall design of the Report and its approach to addressing key public sectors exposed to corruption practices within member states. We will consider in detail how the Report worked in practice, and give an overview of its key findings for the 28 member states, examining the main recommendations for each, in anti-corruption terms.

1.5 Conclusion

It is unlikely that all of EU member states will accept the same definition of corruption and treat the issue similarly from a policy and legal perspective. At the EU level, corruption is understood as an abuse of power for private gain, and almost all member states have adopted a similar definition. However, corruption takes many forms, such as bribery, trading in influence, abuse of political and economic functions. Furthermore, corruption can also hide behind nepotism, conflicts of interest or revolving doors between the public and the private sectors, in public procurement contracts in particular. As we have seen in this chapter—and many more examples will illustrate this throughout the book—corruption effects are serious and widespread in the EU and its member states and constitute a significant security threat as an enabler for crime and terrorism. Furthermore, corruption acts as a drag on economic growth in the EU by creating uncertain business environment, hampering the fair operation of the internal market and reducing investment, which the EU is trying to address through the European Semester process under its current policy approach against corruption.

Throughout the five phases that we have distinguished in this chapter, the EU anti-corruption policy has developed in response to initiatives by international organisations, most notably the OECD, the UN and the Council of Europe, in particular in the 1990s. Thus, international standards against corruption set out by these organisations have impacted the way the EU anti-corruption policy has developed—but the EU and its member states have seemed to fall behind in their progress on adopting these standards, at least until late 2014.

However, the scandals of Jacques Santer (the former prime minister of Luxembourg), the president of the Commission between 1995 and 1999—which became the first Commission to resign *en masse* due to allegations of corruption—had a major impact on the EU institutions' reputation and triggered an internal process on how senior EU officials and employees should conduct themselves. Romano Prodi (the former prime minister of Italy), who took over as EC president following the scandal, introduced a series of codes of conduct for European institution employees and created the new anti-fraud body known as OLAF, with powers that also included conducting investigations within EU institutions. These events forced the EU to focus its efforts against corruption and unethical behaviour within its institutions—clean its own house first—before engaging with member states in addressing developing an anti-corruption policy.

At the turn of the millennium, the EU planned for enlargement in CEE states, and in this chapter, we have observed that the EU focus was on promoting democracy and the rule of law; in both domains, the fight against corruption plays a crucial role for the new member states. However, the EU did not effectively use this opportunity to emphasise the problem of corruption in the accession process with the CEE, and the conditions of accession were ill-equipped in evaluating the progress in the fight against corruption therein. Furthermore, there was a lack of the political will from the member states to make corruption an issue and support the EU to develop more preventive anti-corruption measures. In 2007, the EU acknowledged the superficial and inadequate efforts made in 2004 and was pushed by founding member states to change accession policy in addressing corruption and for Romania and Bulgaria to introduce the CVM, a mechanism evaluating both countries annually on the progress on judicial reform, corruption and organised crime.

The CVM served as a laboratory for the Commission to further develop the EU anti-corruption policy towards member states—which led, in 2011, to the EU introducing plans for the 2014 Report. The Commission's grand plan for the Report was to evaluate the state of corruption within the member states, the EU institutions and candidate states and to include an array of areas affected by corruption—for the first time, the EU was developing a comprehensive anti-corruption policy. However, when the Report was published in 2014, it only included a snapshot of corruption issues in the 28 member states and EU institutions, and candidate states were dropped from the Report's findings. Nonetheless, the 2014 Report was by far the most inclusive EU anti-corruption monitoring mechanism and anti-corruption policy encouragement.

However, the Commission dropped the Report in 2017, for reasons unknown. It is widely believed that this was a political decision by the Commission—pressured by founding members to avoid calling out member states on corruption-related issues and scandals in a biennial report. Subsequently, the Commission transferred the work of the Report to the European Semester process, with a view to strengthening the economic governance policy. This decision, viewed from a policy and legal perspective, would indicate that the EU is focusing its efforts on safeguarding the EU's internal market, engaging with member states only as far as corruption affects the function of the single market.

Thus far, we have sketched a useful background of EU policy against corruption, and how its strategy has developed between 1996 and 2018. In the next chapter, we will discuss the EU Anti-Corruption Report in detail—the EU flagship initiative of the past two decades, addressing corruption and issuing specific recommendations for each of the 28 member states. We will also open a broader discussion about EU anti-corruption policy, analysing to what extent the Commission's legal mandate allows it to address the problem of corruption within the EU.

2 The EU anti-corruption report

On 6 June 2011, the Commission proposed an anti-corruption reporting mechanism for periodic assessment, which would be known as the EU Anti-Corruption Report.[1] The Report defines corruption as 'abuse of power for private gain',[2] a definition which received international acceptance. This covers specific acts of corruption, and thus, supports member states in taking steps to prevent or punish corrupt acts as defined by law. This new anti-corruption mechanism's objective was to address the effects of corruption on politics, society, the economy and the judiciary in the EU—an aim which falls well within the scope of the Commission's main objective of encouraging more political engagement and dialogue with member states through the Report, with a view to enhancing better anti-corruption policy and supporting member states in enforcing legislation and complying fully with their anti-corruption commitments.

The development and design of the Report was the Commission's direct response to the member states' request, in the Stockholm Programme recommendation, to develop additional anti-corruption indicators on the basis of existing systems and common benchmarks that would ensure measuring anti-corruption efforts within the EU on more regular basis.[3]

The Report was published for the first time by the Commission on 3rd February 2014,[4] which presented an overview of corruption-related issues within each of the EU's member states, suggesting some steps for states to prevent and combat corruption more effectively. The Report also provided a platform for discussion across different levels of government and civil society to improve anti-corruption tools.

The Report was designed to support the ongoing anti-corruption work in the EU member states and improve the political commitment in addressing corruption across the EU and to identify how the EU dimension could support

1 European Commission, 'Communication on Fighting Corruption in the EU' COM (2011) 308 final. <https://ec.europa.eu/home-affairs/sites/homeaffairs/files/e-library/docs/pdf/com_decision_c%282011%29_3673_final_en_en.pdf> accessed 30 May 2019.

2 European Commission, 'EU Anti-Corruption Report' COM (2014) 38 final.

3 C Closa and D Kochenov, *Reinforcing Rule of Law Oversight in the European Union* (CUP 2016) 286.

4 European Commission (n 2).

member states efforts in fighting corruption more successfully;[5] it was an instrument for promoting higher standards of integrity in the member states, thus contributing positively to this broad Commission aim of robust regional growth.

The Report was based on the principle that through periodical evaluation and the publication of fact-based reports, additional impetus would be created for member states to implement internationally recognised anti-corruption standards throughout the Union. With this in mind, the Report was applicable to all member states, which encouraged them to develop a domestic framework for improving anti-corruption measures based on best practice standards. Another of the Report's objectives was to support member states in identifying causes of corruption at domestic level, which would lead to paving the way for future, wider EU policy actions against corruption. The Report was also designed to be a catalyst in identifying potential risks deriving from corruption at member state level, which could later develop into a more serious economic and political crisis.[6]

The Report[7] covers all of the member states and has the following structure:

a) Introduction, presenting the policy background and key objectives.
b) Results of 2013 Eurobarometer surveys on perceptions of corruption and experience of corruption in the EU member states.
c) Thematic chapter, focused on assessing public procurement, and corruption and anti-corruption measures. Public procurement is crucial for the internal market and can be a source of corruption.
d) Annex on methodology, describing how the Report was prepared, as well as methodological choices and limitations encountered.
e) Country chapters—these cover all of the member states' policy shortcomings, mainly highlighting selected key shortcomings identified through the individual assessment of each country and offering general recommendations for each of the countries. These chapters do not provide a comprehensive description of corruption-related concerns and anti-corruption legislation.

2.1 Overview of general objectives and findings of the EU anti-corruption report

According to Jeremy Horder and Peter Alldridge, the goal of the Report was to provide an overview of corruption within the member states and the steps that they can take to prevent and fight corruption collectively.[8] Furthermore, the Report's main objective was to launch a wider discussion at different government

5 European Commission (n 1).
6 European Commission (n 1).
7 European Commission (n 2).
8 J Horder and P Alldridge, *Modern Bribery Law: Comparative Perspectives* (CUP 2014) 185.

levels—including the Commission, member states, the European Parliament and civil society—to assist the anti-corruption work at national level and to identify new methods in which the European dimension can support the member states to fight corruption more successfully.[9]

At the time of publication of the Report, member states had in place adequate legal instruments and institutions to prevent and fight corruption. However, the results they were delivering were not satisfactory across the EU.[10] Anti-corruption laws were not always properly enforced, systemic problems of corruption were not addressed effectively and the relevant anti-corruption institutions did not always have adequate capacity to enforce anti-corruption rules. Promising intentions from member states' governments were still too vague in making commitments and turning these into concrete action. The political will to address corruption appeared to be largely missing in many of member states.

The Report focuses on key selected issues of particular concern to each member state, described in more detail in section 2.4. It also highlights good practices and weaknesses and identifies steps by which member states might possibly be able to address corruption more effectively. The Commission recognised that some of these issues are unique to the national competencies and structures of individual member states and, therefore, attempted to convey a broadly supportive and positive message through the Report, while identifying state-specific challenges and weaknesses. However, it is in the common interest across the EU to ensure that all member states have sufficient anti-corruption policies in place and that the EU as a whole supports each member state in developing a sufficient anti-corruption policy.

The Report views corruption as a complex phenomenon that is entrenched in economic, social, political and cultural dimensions, and which cannot be easily eliminated just by the work of the Report or Commission support.[11] In other words, an effective policy response to the Report by the member states as a whole is insufficient—there is no 'one size fits all' solution. Hence, the Report examines the main corruption-related issues within the national context of each member state individually and offers individually tailored recommendations according to the most pressing needs of each member state.

However, there was also a broader policy objective from the EU when it established the Report. The global financial crisis in 2007–2008 put more pressure on member states' governments and EU economic performance, which required the EU to respond by promoting higher levels of integrity and transparency in public expenditure, according to Kemal Dervis and Jacques Mistral.[12] The Eurobarometer used for the Report found that citizens expected the EU to

9 ibid 186.

10 European Commission (n 2).

11 ibid.

12 K Dervis and J Mistral, *Europe's Crisis, Europe's Future* (The Brookings Institution 2016) 87–88.

play an important role in supporting member states to protect their economy against organised crime, financial and tax fraud, money laundering and corruption, particularly in times of budgetary austerity and economic crises, such as the EU has faced in the past decade.[13]

As a result, the Report supports the Europe 2020 objectives to foster a smart, sustainable and inclusive economy, but it highlights that the Europe 2020 strategy will also depend on institutional factors, such as the proper application of good governance, rule of law, and in particular, the control of corruption.[14] Therefore, fighting corruption can contribute to the EU's competitiveness in the global economy and the Report tries to embody this notion, recommending that anti-corruption measures are put in place by member states as part of the European Semester, an annual cycle of economic policy coordination involving a detailed analysis of member states' programmes for economic and structural reform.

Broadly speaking, the Commission (communicating through the Report) contends that improving the efficiency of public administration, especially if combined with greater transparency, would help in mitigating corruption-related risks and improve the general economic and investment climate.[15] As a result, the Commission Communication for European Industrial Renaissance in January 2014 paid particular attention to the quality of public administration as a driving aspect of the EU's growth strategy.[16]

2.2 Perceptions of corruption and experience of corruption in the EU

2.2.1 Private citizen responses

In preparing the background to the Report, the Commission conducted two Eurobarometer surveys in early 2013. The first was the Special Eurobarometer,[17] which surveyed citizens in general; the second was a business-focused 'Flash Survey'.[18] The Commission also used the rankings of the Corruption Perceptions Index (CPI) used by Transparency International to evaluate the answers given by the Eurobarometer respondents for balancing the Report, as a way of fact-checking the responses.[19]

13 European Commission, 'Special Eurobarometer 397 on Corruption' (2013) <http://ec.europa.eu/public_opinion/archives/ebs/ebs_397_en.pdf> accessed 30 May 2019.

14 European Commission (n 2).

15 ibid.

16 European Parliament 'How Can European Industry Contribute to Growth and Foster European Competitiveness?' *Study for the ITRE Committee* (August 2014).

17 European Commission (n 13).

18 European Commission 'Flash Eurobarometer 374 on Business' Attitudes Towards Corruption in the EU' (2014) <http://ec.europa.eu/public_opinion/flash/fl_374_en.pdf> accessed 30 May 2019.

19 European Commission (n 13).

The general responses from the citizens participating in the Eurobarometer found that there was a low perception and experience of paying bribery in the Nordic countries, like Denmark, Finland and Sweden.[20] Barely any respondents in the surveys in these member states suggested that citizens had been asked to pay a bribe or had engaged in a corrupt act (less than one per cent), and the number of citizens who thought that corruption is widespread was 20 per cent in Denmark, 29 per cent in Finland and 44 per cent in Sweden.[21] These numbers are considerably below the EU average and among the best performers against corruption practices. In the case of the UK, the Eurobarometer found that only five citizens out of 1,115 had paid a bribe or engaged in a corrupt act (less than one per cent), showing the best result in the EU. Nevertheless, the public perception data in the Eurobarometer found that around 64 per cent of UK respondents that took part in the surveys thought that corruption was widespread in the country.[22]

In member states like Germany, the Netherlands, Belgium, Estonia and France, more than half of the respondents taking part in the Eurobarometer surveys consider corruption to be a widespread phenomenon, although the actual number of citizens who had paid a bribe was lower than two per cent.[23] These member states are also among the best performers in the TI Index. Austria also shares similar characteristics with these member states, with the exception of a somewhat high number of respondents—around five per cent—who, according to the Eurobarometer survey, have been expected to pay a bribe or engaged in a corrupt act.[24]

In other member states, Hungary (13 per cent), Slovakia (14 per cent) and Poland (15 per cent) have a relatively high number of citizens who had personal experience of bribery or engaged in corrupt act in a number of sectors.[25] In these member states, the public healthcare system provided the bulk of instances of bribery, and there is evidence that the structural problems in the public healthcare system provide incentives to engage in bribery or corruption with medical staff to have access to better healthcare.[26] Citizens were frequently asked to pay a bribe in the public healthcare system,[27] while in other sectors such as police, customs, politicians and public prosecutors' services, less than one per cent of respondents engaged in some form of corruption, according to the Eurobarometer survey. Corruption, in a broader sense, is perceived as widespread in these member states, and participants' responses indicated that they thought that corruption occurs around 82 per cent of the time in Poland, 89 per cent in Hungary and 90 per cent in Slovakia.[28]

20 ibid.
21 ibid.
22 ibid.
23 European Commission (n 2).
24 European Commission (n 13).
25 European Commission (n 2).
26 ibid.
27 European Commission (n 13).
28 European Commission (n 2).

In member states like Portugal, Slovenia, Spain and Italy, paying a bribe was perceived as rare, but corruption in a broader sense was a serious concern. In the Eurobarometer surveys, a relatively low number of respondents claimed that they were asked or expected to engage in a corrupt act in the past 12 months,[29] and personal experience of bribery was rare, at around one to three per cent. One explanation for public perception of corruption levels compared to personal experience is the strong influence of political scandals and the economic performance in these member states, which is reflected in the respondents' negative impression about corruption as an issue overall.[30] The Eurobarometer surveys found that the general perception was that of corruption being widespread, at 90 per cent in Portugal, 91 per cent in Slovenia, 95 per cent in Spain and 97 per cent in Italy.[31]

Member states including Croatia, the Czech Republic, Lithuania, Bulgaria, Romania and Greece lagged behind in the scores concerning both perceptions and actual experience of citizens engaged with corruption.[32] In these member states, between 6 and 29 per cent of respondents indicated that they were asked or expected to engage in some form of corruption in the past 12 months,[33] and between 84 and 99 per cent of citizens thought that corruption was widespread in their country.[34] In member states like Croatia and the Czech Republic, it appears that there is a somewhat more positive impression, with slightly better scores than the rest of the countries from the same group.[35] Member states like Latvia, Malta, Ireland and Cyprus do not show results that diverge as much from the EU average on any of these aspects shown above.

At European level, over three-quarters of respondents (nearly 76 per cent) think that corruption is widespread in their own country according to the Eurobarometer survey.[36] The member states where respondents are most likely to think that corruption is extensively widespread are Greece (99 per cent), Italy (97 per cent), and Lithuania, Spain and the Czech Republic (all at 95 per cent). A quarter of Europeans (about 26 per cent) considered that they are directly affected by corruption in their daily lives[37]; this compared to 29 per cent found by the 2011 Eurobarometer survey. Citizens are most likely to say that they are directly affected by corruption in Spain and Greece (63 per cent), Cyprus and

29 European Commission (n 13).
30 A Mungiu-Pippidi, *The Quest for Good Governance: How Societies Develop Control of Corruption* (CUP 2015) 161–185.
31 European Commission (n 13).
32 Tanja A Börzel, 'Coming Together or Drifting Apart? Political Change in New Member States, Accession Candidates, and Eastern Neighbourhood Countries' *MAXCAP Working Paper Series, No 3 May 2014 'Maximizing the Integration Capacity of the European Union: Lessons of and Prospects for Enlargement and Beyond'* (2014) (MAXCAP ISSN 2198–7653).
33 European Commission (n 2).
34 European Commission (n 13).
35 European Commission (n 2).
36 European Commission (n 13).
37 European Commission (n 2).

Romania (57 per cent) and Croatia (55 per cent).[38] The least likely citizens to think that they are directly affected by corruption are those in Denmark (three per cent) and France and Germany (both at six per cent). Around one in twelve EU citizens (or eight per cent) say that they have experienced or witnessed a case of corruption in the past 12 months.[39] Respondents were most likely to say that they personally have experienced or witnessed corruption in Lithuania (25 per cent), Slovakia (21 per cent) and Poland (16 per cent).[40] The very least likely citizens to say that they personally have experienced or witnessed corruption are those in Finland and Denmark (three per cent in each) and Malta and the UK (with four per cent in each).[41]

Around three-quarters of Europeans (around 73 per cent) considered that corruption and use of personal connections are often the easiest paths to get access to certain public services in their country.[42] Member states like Slovakia and Croatia (89 per cent in each), Cyprus (92 per cent) and Greece (93 per cent) have a high number of respondents who share this belief.[43]

Similar to the 2011 Eurobarometer survey, around two of three Europeans (67 per cent) think that the financing of political parties is not sufficiently transparent nor is it properly supervised[44]; member states such as Spain (87 per cent), Greece (86 per cent) and the Czech Republic (81 per cent) take this view.[45] In member states like Denmark (47 per cent), the UK (54 per cent), Sweden (55 per cent) and Finland (56 per cent), citizens share similar views with respect to the supervising and transparency of financing of political parties.[46] Around a quarter (23 per cent) of EU citizens agree that their governments' efforts are sufficient in tackling and addressing the issue of corruption, and a similar number (26 per cent) think that there are adequately successful prosecutions in their country to deter people from bribery and corrupt practices.[47]

2.2.2 Commercial responses

The business-focused survey conducted for the Report showed some striking variations amongst the member states in the levels of perceived corruption in conducting business by the investment and business community. Greece was the member state that was perceived as the most corrupt member state in business (at an astonishing 99 per cent) and the lowest is Denmark (at 10 per cent).

38 European Commission (n 13).
39 ibid.
40 European Commission (n 2).
41 European Commission (n 13).
42 European Commission (n 2).
43 European Commission (n 13).
44 European Commission (n 2).
45 European Commission (n 13).
46 European Commission (n 2).
47 ibid.

This corresponds to a similar result reflected in the 'Special Eurobarometer' presented above from citizens, which varies between 20 per cent for Denmark and 99 per cent for Greece.[48]

At European level, more than four out of ten companies consider corruption as an obstacle to doing business, and this is also the case for patronage and nepotism.[49] When asked directly whether corruption is a concern for doing business in the survey, 50 per cent of the construction sector and 33 per cent of the telecoms and IT companies thought that it was a problem to a serious degree.[50] The business-focused survey found that the smaller the company, the more often corruption and nepotism were seen as a problem in doing business. According to the business-focused survey, corruption in member states such as Greece and Slovakia (both at 66 per cent), Portugal (68 per cent) and the Czech Republic (71 per cent) were most likely to consider corruption as a major problem when doing business with other companies.[51]

2.3 Public procurement

Nearly one-fifth of the EU's GDP is spent every year by public authorities in public-procuring works, goods and services; thus, public procurement constitutes an important element of the national economies in the EU.[52] The Commission estimates that the total value of calls for tenders above those EU thresholds is approximately EUR 425 billion.[53] These figures indicate that public procurement is an area where corruption can prevail, and as a result, the Commission chose public procurement as a thematic chapter for the Report to make member states aware of the serious threat that corruption poses to this area.

The Report identified that in eight member states (France, Italy, Hungary, Lithuania, the Netherlands, Poland, Romania and Spain), the direct costs of corruption in public procurement for key sectors (including rail, road, water, waste, urban, utility construction, training and research and development) were between EUR 1.4 and 2.2 billion.[54] These findings suggest a significant need for greater awareness and more preventive instruments in place regarding corruption in public procurement.

The Report used responses to the flash Eurobarometer 2013, and the survey found that more than three out of ten (or around 32 per cent) companies in the member states participating in public-procurement tenders reported that corruption had prevented them from winning a public contract.[55] This response

48 European Commission (n 18).
49 ibid.
50 European Commission (n 2).
51 European Commission (n 18).
52 European Commission, 'Flash Eurobarometer 398 on Internal Market Report' (2013) <http://ec.europa.eu/public_opinion/archives/ebs/ebs_398_en.pdf> accessed 30 May 2019.
53 European Commission (n 18).
54 European Commission (n 2).
55 European Commission (n 18).

and related concerns were widely shared amongst companies in the sectors such as construction (at around 35 per cent) and engineering (around 33 per cent) in all member states.[56] In member states like the Czech Republic (51 per cent), Cyprus (55 per cent), Slovakia (57 per cent) and Bulgaria (58 per cent), company representatives suggested that this is also the case in engineering and construction.[57]

The flash Eurobarometer 2013 survey also found that the main reason companies have not taken part in a public-procurement tendering process in the last three years is because of 'red tape'.[58] Approximately four out of ten companies say that a variety of illegal practices in public-procurement procedures are common, in particular:

- Specifications tailor-made for certain corporations (≈ 57%)
- Conflict of interest in bid assessment (≈ 54%)
- Collusive bidding (≈ 52%)
- Unclear selection (≈ 51%)
- Involvement of bidders in setting up the specifications for tendering (≈ 48%)
- Violation of negotiated procedures (≈ 47%)
- Modifications to the procurement terms after conclusion of the public contract (≈ 44%).[59]

Furthermore, the flash Eurobarometer 2013 survey found that engineering and construction companies are the most likely to claim that all of these practices are widespread in business.[60]

Based on these findings, the Report indicated that more than half of all companies say that corruption in public procurement managed by national governments amounts to 56 per cent; corruption in public procurement managed by regional and local governments amounts to 60 per cent.[61]

The Special Eurobarometer 2013 survey on corruption found that nearly 45 per cent of the Europeans citizens interviewed believe that bribery and the abuse of positions of power for personal gain are prevalent among officials who award public contracts.[62] The member states where respondents were most likely to believe that there is widespread corruption practiced by officials awarding public contracts were Italy and Greece (both about 55 per cent), Croatia (58 per cent), Slovenia (60 per cent), the Netherlands (64 per cent) and the Czech Republic (69 per cent). The member states with the most positive perceptions of officials awarding public contracts were the UK (33 per cent), Luxembourg and Ireland (both at 32 per cent), Finland (31 per cent) and Denmark (22 per cent).[63]

56 European Commission (n 52).
57 ibid.
58 ibid.
59 ibid.
60 ibid.
61 ibid.
62 European Commission (n 2).
63 ibid.

When analysing the figures from the two surveys, it becomes clear why the Report finds that public procurement is one of the areas most vulnerable to corruption practices, and therefore, merits a thematic chapter of its own.[64] The significance of public procurement in the European economy cannot be underestimated. As a result, the Report suggested a number of possible actions for member states to take in addressing the policy shortcomings in respect of public procurement.[65]

Firstly, the Report suggested that member states consider adjusting their risk assessment in order to identify corruption within public procurement.[66] Member states should consider the following:

a) Developing risk assessments at the level of public-procurement oversight, with the support of law enforcement or anti-corruption and integrity agencies, regardless of their institutional setting.
b) Ensuring data centralisation for detecting corrupt practices and patterns—including those of conflicts of interests and revolving door practices.
c) Developing based-on risk assessments—developing tailor-made instruments to measure vulnerable sectors more regularly.
d) Implementing targeted anti-corruption policies for regional and local government—to effectively detect corruption practices at the local level.
e) Developing common guidelines for developing red-flagging indicator systems and supporting independent authorities to detect corruption—in particular favouritism and conflicts of interest.

Secondly, the Report recommended that member states should consider implementing higher standards for transparency in respect to awarding procurement contracts,[67] with the following general recommendations:

a) Considering ensuring common standards for transparency at local and regional level for public-procurement procedures.
b) Ensuring free access to public contracts, including the provisions on rights, obligations and penalty clauses.
c) Considering further improving their transparency in public-procurement procedures, pre- and post-award, through online publication in all of the administrative structures—including at central, regional and local level. Furthermore, member states should consider ensuring more transparency of procurement, especially to state-owned companies.

64 G Piga and T Tatrai, *Public Procurement Policy* (Routledge 2015) 5.
65 European Commission (n 2).
66 ibid.
67 ibid.

Thirdly, the Report recommended that member states should consider strengthening internal and external control instruments for the entire procurement cycle and also during contract implementation.[68] The following are general recommendations for member states to consider:

a) Ensuring that there is in place adequate capacity of public-procurement review bodies, consultative and oversight bodies, as well as courts of audit to carry out their verification in case of violation.
b) Strengthening the internal control mechanisms for purposes of prevention and detection of corrupt practices and conflicts of interests. Furthermore, member states should consider developing common methodologies for anti-corruption and conflict of interest detection tools during the public-procurement cycle.
c) Ensuring the recommendations of the courts of audit identifying irregularities in public-procurement tendering.
d) Carrying out more effective checks on ownership of bidders and subcontractors.
e) Ensuring that there are satisfactory control mechanisms for procurement in place for state-owned companies.

Fourthly, the Report suggested that member states should raise more awareness about the need for preventing and detecting corrupt practices at all levels of public procurement.[69] The Report suggested the following general recommendations for member states to consider:

a) Improving coordination between different public authorities overseeing public procurement.
b) Raising more awareness and developing coherent guidelines on prevention of corrupt practices and conflict of interests in public procurement, especially regional and local governments.
c) Providing adequate training on technical and legal aspects of the public-procurement process to prosecutors and the judiciary staff who investigate public-procurement violation.

Finally with regard to public procurement, the Report suggested that member states should strengthen the sanctioning regimes for those that breach public-procurement contracts,[70] with the following recommendations:

a) Ensuring proper application of dissuasive sanctions in relation to corrupt practices, favouritism or conflicts of interests in public-procurement contracts.
b) Developing effective mechanisms for repealing decisions or annulling public-procurement contracts.

68 ibid.
69 ibid.
70 ibid.

These are general recommendations for all member states, through which the Report aims to raise the profile of addressing corruption in public procurement. They are not legally binding, making member states aware of what they should have in place. Furthermore, these recommendations were used to prepare the ground in 2014 for the implementation of EU directives on public procurement in 2016 (the Directive 2014/24/EU on public procurement,[71] the Directive 2014/25/EU on procurement by entities operating in the water, energy, transport and postal services sectors[72] and the Directive 2014/23/EU on the award of concession contracts into national law[73]).

Having considered general recommendations, let us now consider in more detail the Report's recommendations for each individual member state.

2.4 The EU anti-corruption report recommendations for each of the member states

2.4.1 Austria

The Report identified that in Austria's case, there were obstacles to investigators having access to banking information, which it deemed necessary for effective prosecution in cases relating to corruption and bribery.[74] Additionally, Austria was recommended to make the investigation and prosecution of foreign bribery a priority, and to improve the capacities of the specialised prosecutors working on domestic and foreign corruption cases. Austria should also introduce a monitoring mechanism to check the declarations of assets and interest for elected and appointed senior officials and use sanctions for non-compliance with rules on declaring interests, incomes and assets.

2.4.2 Belgium

The Report identified that Belgium has not consistently addressed corruption and should therefore prioritise anti-corruption-related policy at regional and

71 'Council Directive 2014/24/EU on Public Procurement and Repealing Directive 2004/18/EC' [2014] *OJ L 94/65* <https://eur-lex.europa.eu/legal-content/EN/TXT/PDF/?uri=CELEX:32014L0024&from=EN> accessed 30 May 2019.

72 'Directive 2014/25/EU on Procurement by Entities Operating in the Water, Energy, Transport and Postal Services Sectors' [2014] *OJ L 307* <https://eur-lex.europa.eu/legal-content/EN/TXT/PDF/?uri=CELEX:02014L0025-20160101&from=EN> accessed 30 May 2019.

73 'Directive 2014/23/EU on the Award of Concession Contracts' [2014] OJ L 094 <https://eur-lex.europa.eu/legal-content/EN/TXT/PDF/?uri=OJ:L:2014:094:FULL&from=FR> accessed 30 May 2019.

74 European Commission, 'Annex 20: Austria to the EU Anti-Corruption Report' COM (2014) 38 final, <http://ec.europa.eu/dgs/home-affairs/what-we-do/policies/organized-crime-and-human-trafficking/corruption/anti-corruption-report/docs/2014_acr_austria_chapter_en.pdf> accessed 30 May 2019.

federal levels.[75] In particular, Belgium should introduce an integrity policy in the administration and supporting integrity schemes at regional and federal level, in order to prevent conflict of interest for all appointed and elected officials at federal, regional and local levels. The Report also recommended that Belgium increase its justice system capacity, to avoid lengthy criminal proceedings related to corruption cases that in the past have not been prosecuted in time, due to the expiry of the statute of limitations. A more comprehensively successful prosecution rate could be secured by providing sufficient capacity—for both the police to detect and investigate corruption-related offences and the judiciary to deliver. Lastly, Belgium should enhance legislation on political party funding and develop an effective supervisory mechanism to audit political parties at federal and local levels, under a unified supervision and audit structure.

2.4.3 Bulgaria

The Report identified that, for Bulgaria, fighting corruption should still be a high priority, because corruption continues to remain a serious challenge at every level. Furthermore, petty corruption continues to be reported in healthcare, police, customs, local authorities and beyond.[76] Bulgaria needs to improve the independence and effectiveness of anti-corruption institutions, and in particular the judicial system, shielding its anti-corruption institutions and the judiciary from any political influence. In addition, Bulgaria must increase the integrity and accountability of elected officials and put safeguarding measures in place to prevent electoral irregularities. Finally, the Report found that Bulgaria should adopt a code of ethics for members of the National Assembly and establish an effective supervisory mechanism in order to ensure dissuasive sanctions for electoral fraud.

2.4.4 Croatia

In Croatia, politicisation and favouritism of the public administration and the integrity standards in the political system is a cause for concern.[77] The country should establish an effective mechanism to prevent corruption in state-owned

75 European Commission, 'Annex 1: Belgium to the EU Anti-Corruption Report' COM (2014) 38 final <http://ec.europa.eu/dgs/home-affairs/what-we-do/policies/organized-crime-and-human-trafficking/corruption/anti-corruption-report/docs/2014_acr_belgium_chapter_en.pdf> accessed 30 May 2019.

76 European Commission, 'Annex 2: Bulgaria to the EU Anti-Corruption Report' COM (2014) 38 final <http://ec.europa.eu/dgs/home-affairs/what-we-do/policies/organized-crime-and-human-trafficking/corruption/anti-corruption-report/docs/2014_acr_bulgaria_chapter_en.pdf> accessed 30 May 2019.

77 European Commission, 'Annex 11: Croatia to the EU Anti-Corruption Report' COM (2014) 38 final <http://ec.europa.eu/dgs/home-affairs/what-we-do/policies/organized-crime-and-human-trafficking/corruption/anti-corruption-report/docs/2014_acr_croatia_chapter_en.pdf> accessed 30 May 2019.

companies and implement an effective anti-corruption action plan therein to promote high accountability standards. Furthermore, Croatia should develop effective protective mechanisms in both the public and private sectors for whistle-blowers to report corruption-related misconduct. Croatia was identified as having inadequate rules concerning the conflict of interests of public officials at central and local levels, and it should comply with the Constitutional Court decision of 2012 in ensuring that there is full compliance in this area. The Report also suggested that Croatia needs to improve its practises of verification, swift access to relevant information and cooperation with other authorities in investigating corruption cases. Finally, Croatia should implement a merit-based recruitment and promotion for public officials at mid-management and lower levels, by developing an adequate code of conduct for elected officials at central and local levels.

2.4.5 *Cyprus*

The Report identified that, in Cyprus, there should be more focus on political party financing,[78] and a code of conduct should be introduced for elected and appointed officials, to declare any assets and disclose any potential conflicts of interest. Cyprus should lower its thresholds for donations to political parties, limit the possibilities of state-owned companies to sponsor political events and regulate donations for election candidates and campaigns. There should be regulations for political party finance, whereby parties publish their financial statements and accounts online, including the identity of donors, as well establishing external supervision for election candidates' income and expenditure. Finally, the Report recommended that Cyprus reinforce its disciplinary body for public servants and endow the necessary powers to anti-corruption institutions for a more effective implementation of anti-corruption policies.

2.4.6 *Czech Republic*

In the Czech Republic, corruption represents a major obstacle in doing business and creates significant potential for the misuse of public funds.[79] The Czech Republic should introduce civil service legislation addressing the conflicts of interest of public officials, enhancing civil service stability by safeguarding it against political interference. Additionally, the Report recommended that the country should introduce an ex-ante verification mechanism to prevent the

78 European Commission, 'Annex 13: Cyprus to the EU Anti-Corruption Report' COM (2014) 38 final <http://ec.europa.eu/dgs/home-affairs/what-we-do/policies/organized-crime-and-human-trafficking/corruption/anti-corruption-report/docs/2014_acr_cyprus_chapter_en.pdf> accessed 30 May 2019.

79 European Commission, 'Annex 3: Czech Republic to the EU Anti-Corruption Report' COM (2014) 38 final <http://ec.europa.eu/dgs/home-affairs/what-we-do/policies/organized-crime-and-human-trafficking/corruption/anti-corruption-report/docs/2014_acr_czech_republic_chapter_en.pdf> accessed 30 May 2019.

conflicts of interest and corrupt practices in relation to the European Structural and Investment Funds programmes and to make further efforts to strengthen the independence of all bodies responsible for the implementation of EU funds. The country should regulate electoral campaign expenditure and establish an impartial supervision of political party financing, thus ensuring that the financial reports of political parties are easily accessible to the public, and disclose party and electoral campaign expenditure in detail, through annual financial reports. Finally, the Report recommended that the Czech Republic strengthen its capacity for prosecutors handling corruption-related cases in an independent way, by re-examining the criteria for nomination of prosecutors and pursuing reforms to strengthen the independence of anti-corruption bodies.

2.4.7 Denmark

The Report emphasised that Denmark is among the EU's leading countries in terms of transparency and integrity, and has very few corruption practices.[80] However, there is still some room for improvement, and further attention is needed in addressing the political party financing, considering the GRECO recommendations to improve the transparency and supervisory instruments for the financing of political parties and individual candidates. Denmark can improve its framework for prosecuting and sentencing Danish corporations on grounds of foreign bribery, and it should review the provision of dual criminality in respect of foreign bribery offences, ensuring that the small facilitation payment defence is clearly defined, and the foreign bribery legal framework is in line with OECD Anti-Bribery Convention.

2.4.8 Estonia

In the case of Estonia, corruption is low in comparison to other post-Communist states, and petty corruption hardly affects citizens' everyday lives.[81] However, the country should further improve transparency in the political party financing, develop an effective monitoring instrument for political parties and apply dissuasive sanctions in case of any violation. The Report also recommended that Estonia develop guidelines on monitoring compliance with anti-corruption requirements at local government level and provide sufficient training to local governments. Estonia should also implement a parliamentary code of

80 European Commission, 'Annex 4: Denmark to the EU Anti-Corruption Report' COM (2014) 38 final <http://ec.europa.eu/dgs/home-affairs/what-we-do/policies/organized-crime-and-human-trafficking/corruption/anti-corruption-report/docs/2014_acr_denmark_chapter_en.pdf> accessed 30 May 2019.

81 European Commission, 'Annex 6: Estonia to the EU Anti-Corruption Report' COM (2014) 38 final <http://ec.europa.eu/dgs/home-affairs/what-we-do/policies/organized-crime-and-human-trafficking/corruption/anti-corruption-report/docs/2014_acr_estonia_chapter_en.pdf> accessed 30 May 2019.

conduct, together with a supervision body to ensure scrutiny of economic interest declarations of public officials. Finally, Estonia should conduct an independent in-depth analysis into the risk of politicisation of local official appointments in public administration, state-owned companies.

2.4.9 Finland

Finland is a leading country in Europe and the champion of anti-corruption.[82] However, corruption cases in Finland do appear in terms of favouritism—there are instances of exchanges on the basis of informal relationships and lobbying by business people providing campaign financing to politicians. Therefore, the Report recommended that Finland works with local authorities to ensure an adequate level of transparency in public contracts with private entrepreneurs, and additionally, to support the country's anti-corruption unit (the National Bureau of Investigations) to investigate corruption-related cases and coordinate anti-corruption procedures between government agencies more effectively.

2.4.10 France

Corruption in France is related to politics[83]; French politics has been subject to allegations of corruption and nepotism, spreading to high-ranking politicians and public officials. Therefore, France should take into account the GRECO recommendations on party findings, thereby increasing the transparency of financial information in election campaigns and strengthening the supervisory capacity of the National Commission for Campaign Accounts and Political Funding. The Report recommended that France continue to pursue its on-going reforms on the asset disclosure and conflicts of interest concerning appointed and elected public officials. France should also improve its legislation on foreign bribery and include rules on dual criminality and jurisdiction in line with the recommendations by the OECD, GRECO and the UNCAC review mechanism. Finally, France should allocate more resources to investigators and prosecutors dealing with corruption cases and protect the operational independence of prosecutors of related corruption cases.

82 European Commission, 'Annex 26: Finland to the EU Anti-Corruption Report' COM (2014) 38 final <http://ec.europa.eu/dgs/home-affairs/what-we-do/policies/organized-crime-and-human-trafficking/corruption/anti-corruption-report/docs/2014_acr_finland_chapter_en.pdf> accessed 30 May 2019.

83 European Commission, 'Annex 10: France to the EU Anti-Corruption Report' COM (2014) 38 final <http://ec.europa.eu/dgs/home-affairs/what-we-do/policies/organized-crime-and-human-trafficking/corruption/anti-corruption-report/docs/2014_acr_france_chapter_en.pdf> accessed 30 May 2019.

2.4.11 Germany

The Report identified that Germany is among the top-ranking member states in the EU and one of the best performers of transparency and integrity.[84] However, Germany should improve sanctions for elected officials who have been found to misuse public office. The absence of a revolving door policy, particularly in the public sector, was also noted. Germany should further strengthen its preventive measures regarding political party funding, and preventive measures should be in line with the GRECO recommendations on electoral campaign accounts and donations. The country should also expand the legislation transposing the Framework Decision 2003/568/JHA on fighting corruption in the private sector with respect to some elements of bribery. Finally, the Report recommended that Germany raises greater awareness in SMEs regarding foreign bribery offences.

2.4.12 Greece

For Greece, the Report noted that the institutions fighting and preventing corruption are facing the same resource pressure as the whole public administration.[85] The first recommendation from the Report is for the country to support the national anti-corruption coordinator in effective anti-corruption policy implementation and to strengthen an independent functional review of the anti-corruption framework in line with the national anti-corruption action plan. These measures should ensure that the national anti-corruption action plan is effectively implemented across corruption-vulnerable sectors such as healthcare and tax administration. The second recommendation is that Greece should address political party financing and strengthen the party funding supervision body, ensuring the independence, efficiency and transparency of the Control Committee. Greece should reinforce the mechanisms for tracing donations and loans to political parties and ensure sufficient resources for the Supreme Court of Audit to carry out effective verification of party funding. The third recommendation is that Greece should establish an in-depth ethical code of conduct for elected officials at national and local levels, and effective accountability tools for potential violations of these codes, in particular including corrupt practices and conflicts of interests. Greece should seek to reduce any potential barrier to the investigation of corruption offences by releasing any high-ranking officials'

84 European Commission, 'Annex 5: Germany to the EU Anti-Corruption Report' COM (2014) 38 final <http://ec.europa.eu/dgs/home-affairs/what-we-do/policies/organized-crime-and-human-trafficking/corruption/anti-corruption-report/docs/2014_acr_germany_chapter_en.pdf> accessed 30 May 2019.

85 European Commission, 'Annex 8: Greece to the EU Anti-Corruption Report' COM (2014) 38 final <http://ec.europa.eu/dgs/home-affairs/what-we-do/policies/organized-crime-and-human-trafficking/corruption/anti-corruption-report/docs/2014_acr_greece_chapter_en.pdf> accessed 30 May 2019.

immunity protection from investigations. In particular, the country should simplify the procedure for lifting immunities and ultimately reform the statute of limitations rules concerning current and former members of the government.

2.4.13 Hungary

The Report identified that clientelism, favouritism and nepotism in public administration remain matters of concern in Hungary, and there is a strong informal relationship between businesses and political actors at local level, making local governments more vulnerable to corrupt practices.[86] Firstly, the Report recommended that Hungary ensures independency in the verification mechanism process for asset declarations and conflicts of interest of elected and appointed officials, both at national and local levels. Furthermore, Hungary should develop codes of conduct for elected officials at central, regional and local levels, covering conflicts of interest and ensuring sufficient accountability instruments for detecting any potential violations of such codes. The Report also recommended that Hungary take a tougher stand in addressing the corruption risks connected with clientelism and favouritism within public administration. Secondly, Hungary should establish clearer rules on political party financing and strengthen the transparency and the independence of auditing of political parties checking party finance. Thirdly, the Report recommended that Hungary fight corruption in the healthcare system by eliminating the practice of gratitude payments, rewards or other forms of informal payments to public employees in the healthcare sector.

2.4.14 Ireland

The Report found that, even though in recent years the Irish Government has undertaken reforms at legislative and policy levels to address many of the issues concerning corruption and improving transparency, accountability and integrity, still more consideration could be given to ensure that corrupt behaviour is sanctioned.[87] Firstly, Ireland should improve its record of prosecutions in corruption cases by the Standards in Public Office Commission, the Director of Corporate Enforcement and the police, offer more resources to the relevant investigatory authorities and extend their responsibilities to prosecute conflicts of interest at both regional and local levels. Secondly, Ireland should put in

86 European Commission, 'Annex 17: Hungary to the EU Anti-Corruption Report' COM (2014) 38 final <http://ec.europa.eu/dgs/home-affairs/what-we-do/policies/organized-crime-and-human-trafficking/corruption/anti-corruption-report/docs/2014_acr_hungary_chapter_en.pdf> accessed 30 May 2019.

87 European Commission, 'Annex 7: Ireland to the EU Anti-Corruption Report' COM (2014) 38 final <http://ec.europa.eu/dgs/home-affairs/what-we-do/policies/organized-crime-and-human-trafficking/corruption/anti-corruption-report/docs/2014_acr_ireland_chapter_en.pdf> accessed 30 May 2019.

place a threshold on the overall amount an individual may give to a political party, electoral candidates or elected representatives who are members of that party, in line with the recommendations made by the Mahon Tribunal. The country should regulate referendum campaign financing and impose a sensible time limit for political parties to release their financial disclosure obligations. Thirdly, the Report recommended that Ireland offer more power and capacity to the independent urban planning regulator to investigate local authority fraud and corruption. Finally, Ireland should implement a plan for local authority corruption prevention, ensuring effective detection mechanisms for conflicts of interest at local level.

2.4.15 Italy

The Report found that corruption remains a serious challenge in Italy.[88] Firstly, Italy must strengthen the integrity regime for elected and appointed officials at national, regional and local levels and revise and implement thorough ethical codes of conduct together with adequate accountability instruments and tough sanctions for violations. The Report also recommended that Italy consider promoting codes of ethics within political parties and strengthen the legal framework on party funding. Secondly, Italy should address the deficiencies of the statute of limitations, as recommended in July 2013 in the context of the European Semester, and introduce more flexible rules on suspension and interruption. Thirdly, Italy should evaluate the risks of pending corruption cases becoming time-barred and ensure the prioritisation of cases running such risks. The country should strengthen the capacities of the national anti-corruption agency, and supervisory functions at regional and local levels, implementing a uniform framework for internal controls and using external independent audits at regional and local levels with regard to public spending, in particular for public contracts. Finally, Italy must improve the independency of institutions that deal with the verification of conflicts of interest and asset declarations of elected and appointed public officials.

2.4.16 Latvia

In the case of Latvia, the Report found that even though anti-corruption laws are gradually being developed and refined, the implementation in practice remains unsatisfactory.[89] Firstly, the Report recommended that Latvia continue strengthening the capacities and independence of the Corruption

88 European Commission, 'Annex 12: Italy to the EU Anti-Corruption Report' COM (2014) 38 final <http://ec.europa.eu/dgs/home-affairs/what-we-do/policies/organized-crime-and-human-trafficking/corruption/anti-corruption-report/docs/2014_acr_italy_chapter_en.pdf> accessed 30 May 2019.

89 European Commission, 'Annex 14: Latvia to the EU Anti-Corruption Report' COM (2014) 38 final <http://ec.europa.eu/dgs/home-affairs/what-we-do/policies/organized-crime-and-human-trafficking/corruption/anti-corruption-report/docs/2014_acr_latvia_chapter_en.pdf> accessed 30 May 2019.

Prevention and Combating Bureau (KNAB) from potential political interference, particularly in supervisory and budgetary procedures. Latvia should promote better use of centralised e-procurement for public contracts and further enhance KNAB's efforts to detect corruption in public contracts. Secondly, Latvia should pay more attention to improving the transparency of state-owned companies and redefine the professional selection criteria for supervisory and management posts. Thirdly, Latvia must strengthen the judiciary's capabilities and resources in handling corruption-related cases in an independent way, by reinforcing the role of self-governing judicial bodies in relation to appointments and career progression. Restricting Parliament's powers regarding the confirmation of judicial appointments and implementing further measures to uphold due process in disciplinary proceedings are important regulations necessary to achieve this. The country should modify and apply more strictly Parliament's Code of Ethics, develop guidelines on conflicts of interest of public officials and lift administrative immunities for MPs.

2.4.17 Lithuania

Lithuania lacks independency in its anti-corruption body and must address corruption-related issues in public contracts, political party financing and healthcare.[90] Firstly, the Report recommended that Lithuania prioritise fighting corruption in public contracts and develop additional preventive instruments within contracting authorities to assist detecting corruption at various stages of tendering, with a particular focus on local level and the healthcare sector. Secondly, Lithuania should enhance the resources of its Special Investigation Service, by focusing more on the number of indictments and seriousness of cases, and better coordinate its institutions to more proactively investigate high-level corruption cases. Thirdly, the country should reinforce its capacities and the power of the Chief Official Ethics Commission, in order to improve procedures for checking the declarations of conflicts of interest of elected and appointed officials and for monitoring violations more effectively. The Report's final recommendation was that Lithuania should improve political party financing by providing adequate information on sources of funding and enhancing the Central Electoral Commission's capacity to monitor the expenditure and income of political parties more effectively.

90 European Commission, 'Annex 15: Lithuania to the EU Anti-Corruption Report' COM (2014) 38 final <http://ec.europa.eu/dgs/home-affairs/what-we-do/policies/organized-crime-and-human-trafficking/corruption/anti-corruption-report/docs/2014_acr_lithuania_chapter_en.pdf> accessed 30 May 2019.

2.4.18 Luxembourg

The Report identified that in Luxembourg there is an absence of rules on access to information, lobbying and there is no revolving-door policy in place, all of which raises the risk of conflicts of interest and other undetected instances of corruption-related acts.[91] Firstly, the Report recommended that Luxembourg should increase the resources to fight financial and economic crime, including within the judiciary and police. Secondly, Luxembourg should introduce a supervisory mechanism applicable to the financing of individual candidates and campaign accounts and make sure that the rules on donations from legal persons to individual candidates comply with the rules applicable to parties. Luxembourg should ensure an independent mechanism for properly verifying the conflicts of interest of elected officials and civil servants at national and local levels. Finally, the country must implement legislation on access to public information—this should establish the responsibility of the public authorities to provide access to information and documents of public interest and clearly define the conditions under which requests may be denied.

2.4.19 Malta

Even though addressing corruption has been a priority in Malta, the financing of political parties remains largely unregulated and is a matter of concern.[92] Firstly, the Report recommended that Malta introduce a disclosure rule and cap on political donations. There should be a ban on anonymous donations beyond a reasonable threshold and independent audits of political parties' accounts. Secondly, Malta should improve the coordination among anti-corruption units to optimise the collection of evidence and prioritise investigation and prosecution in corruption-related cases. Additionally, the country should further empower the Permanent Commission Against Corruption and allocate more resources to appoint specialists on anti-corruption. Thirdly, the Report recommended that Malta strengthen the capacity of the judiciary in dealing with corruption-related cases, improving the appointment and dismissal procedures for judges, enhancing more transparent and merit-based selection and removal of judges, and enforce the decisions of the Commission for the Administration of Justice when finding ethical breaches in the judiciary. Finally, the Report recommended that Malta continue its reforms in the Malta Environmental Planning Authority to build further public confidence in its integrity and impartiality.

91 European Commission, 'Annex 16: Luxembourg to the EU Anti-Corruption Report' COM (2014) 38 final <http://ec.europa.eu/dgs/home-affairs/what-we-do/policies/organized-crime-and-human-trafficking/corruption/anti-corruption-report/docs/2014_acr_luxembourg_chapter_en.pdf> accessed 30 May 2019.

92 European Commission, 'Annex 18: Malta to the EU Anti-Corruption Report' COM (2014) 38 final <http://ec.europa.eu/dgs/home-affairs/what-we-do/policies/organized-crime-and-human-trafficking/corruption/anti-corruption-report/docs/2014_acr_malta_chapter_en.pdf> accessed 30 May 2019.

2.4.20 The Netherlands

The Report found that, in the Netherlands, integrity is traditionally highly valued and there continues to be a strong public demand for transparency and accountability, both in the public and in the private domains.[93] However, the Netherlands should extend its rules on the assets and interests to elected officials and members of government, supporting a transparent verification system and developing a framework for post-employment conflicts of interest of former elected officials. Secondly, the Report recommended that the Netherlands focus more of its efforts on the prosecution of both natural and legal persons for corruption in international business transactions, increase the resources and capabilities to the investigative office dealing with the prosecution of foreign bribery and increase the level of fines applicable to the legal persons of Dutch firms engaging in foreign bribery acts.

2.4.21 Poland

The Report found that fighting corruption has been a priority in Poland prior to joining the EU, and the authorities have implemented adequate policies that have contributed to progress in fighting corruption, especially against petty corruption.[94] However, Poland's existing reforms to safeguard the independence and effectiveness of anti-corruption institutions should be taken further. Firstly, Poland must develop a long-term strategy against corruption, with a realistic timeframe for implementing the strategy across different sectors that are vulnerable to corruption. The anti-corruption strategy should also aim at reforming and increasing the capacities of the anti-corruption bodies. Secondly, the Report recommended that Poland ensure that there are measures in place to safeguard against potential politicisation of the Central Anti-Corruption Bureau, by introducing an impartial and transparent procedure for the appointment of its director. Poland should also improve the cooperation and coordination with police, other special anti-corruption services and prosecution to deal with corruption-related cases more efficiently. Thirdly, the Report recommended that Poland should implement more effective measures in order to supervise state-owned companies and increase transparency, professionalism and integrity standards in the public and the healthcare sectors.

93 European Commission, 'Annex 19: The Netherlands to the EU Anti-Corruption Report' COM (2014) 38 final <http://ec.europa.eu/dgs/home-affairs/what-we-do/policies/organized-crime-and-human-trafficking/corruption/anti-corruption-report/docs/2014_acr_netherlands_chapter_en.pdf> accessed 30 May 2019.

94 European Commission, 'Annex 21: Poland to the EU Anti-Corruption Report' COM (2014) 38 final <http://ec.europa.eu/dgs/home-affairs/what-we-do/policies/organized-crime-and-human-trafficking/corruption/anti-corruption-report/docs/2014_acr_poland_chapter_en.pdf> accessed 30 May 2019.

2.4.22 Portugal

The Report found that, over the past decade, Portugal has demonstrated a political commitment to fight corruption.[95] However, key institutions that fight corruption in Portugal are facing the same pressures on resources as the whole of the public administration. Therefore, in the context of the state reform currently being introduced in Poland after the economic crisis, the country should pay more attention to anti-corruption initiatives. However, there is no national anti-corruption strategy in place in Portugal. Thus, the Report recommended Portugal to keep a track record of successful prosecution of corruption cases and to allocate resources and financial support to assist further the law enforcement agencies, the prosecution service and the judiciary. Portugal should strengthen its preventive anti-corruption tools on party funding, taking into account GRECO recommendations on political party financing, and develop codes of conduct for elected officials at central and local levels, accompanied with sufficient accountability instruments to address any possible violations of these codes. Portugal should develop ethical codes of conduct within political parties, and finally, the Report recommended improvement to the transparency of decision-making at local level, in particular in planning permission and addressing corruption-related cases in local government.

2.4.23 Romania

The Report found that both petty and political corruption remain a systemic problem in Romania;[96] the political will to address corruption and promote high standards of integrity has been inconsistent in Romania. The January 2014 CVM Report highlighted that even though progress was made in many areas of judiciary and anti-corruption policies, the political will remains low to pursue the objectives set by the CVM. Thus, firstly, the Report first recommended that Romania safeguard the independence of anti-corruption institutions and the judiciary regarding non-partisan investigations. Furthermore, Romania should ensure that there is no political intervention in court proceedings concerning high-level corruption cases related to elected and appointed officials. Integrity standards should be reinforced in the judiciary, and corruption within the judiciary system should be addressed more efficiently. Secondly, the Report recommended that Romania implement codes of conduct for elected and appointed officials and ensure that accountability instruments are in place for more

95 European Commission, 'Annex 22: Portugal to the EU Anti-Corruption Report' COM (2014) 38 final <http://ec.europa.eu/dgs/home-affairs/what-we-do/policies/organized-crime-and-human-trafficking/corruption/anti-corruption-report/docs/2014_acr_portugal_chapter_en.pdf> accessed 30 May 2019.

96 European Commission, 'Annex 23: Romania to the EU Anti-Corruption Report' COM (2014) 38 final <http://ec.europa.eu/dgs/home-affairs/what-we-do/policies/organized-crime-and-human-trafficking/corruption/anti-corruption-report/docs/2014_acr_romania_chapter_en.pdf> accessed 30 May 2019 2018.

efficiently detecting corrupt practices and conflicts of interest. Romania must develop ethical codes for political parties and establish ethics pacts between parties to promote higher integrity standards in the political system. Romania should ensure that there is no obstruction of justice for politicians and that immunities are lifted for elected officials. Romania should also implement an anti-corruption national strategy to develop tools that prevent/reduce the level of informal payments, particularly reducing the level of informal payments in public contracts at central and local governments and in the public healthcare system. Romania should improve the working conditions for medical staff and raise the level of professionalism within the Ministry of Health. Finally, the Report recommended the implementation of rules on revolving-door practices in public contracts and raising awareness of the risks such practices entail, including EU-funded projects.

2.4.24 Slovakia

The Report found that Slovakia faces serious problems with the independence of the judiciary and identified that the close ties between the political and business elite undermines the functioning of anti-corruption efforts.[97] Thus, Slovakia should be prioritising structural reforms and measures to address conflicts of interest between the political and business elites and good coordination in investigations. Firstly, the Report recommended that Slovakia increase the independence of the judiciary, in particular implementing rules to clearly define the criteria for the removal of presidents and vice presidents from office of court; the country should strengthen the procedural guarantees in disciplinary proceedings against judges found to have misused their position and ensure the independence of disciplinary panels. Secondly, Slovakia should support a merit-based approach to appointments to management positions within police departments and develop a strategy to detect and prosecute more effectively corruption-related crimes. Thirdly, the country should increase the transparency of political party financing at local and regional levels, establishing an independent body to investigate and supervise party financing, ensuring that the sanctions are applied accordingly in case of any violations of political funding rules. Fourthly, the Report recommended that Slovakia develop an effective policy to fight corruption cases affecting EU funds, public contracts and corruption in the healthcare system, and reinforce its efforts of law enforcement, prosecution and the judiciary to pursue corruption cases affecting EU funds and public tenders at central and local levels.

97 European Commission, 'Annex 25: Slovakia to the EU Anti-Corruption Report' COM (2014) 38 final <http://ec.europa.eu/dgs/home-affairs/what-we-do/policies/organized-crime-and-human-trafficking/corruption/anti-corruption-report/docs/2014_acr_slovakia_chapter_en.pdf> accessed 30 May 2019.

2.4.25 Slovenia

The Report found that Slovenia, in recent years, has seen a decline in the political will to fight corruption, and that there is also a decline in the integrity levels of high-level officials, both elected and appointed, and other officials within the public administration and state-owned companies.[98] Therefore, the first recommendation of the Report is for Slovenia to apply tougher penalties to elected and appointed officials at central and local levels for conflicts of interest and unjustified wealth. Slovenia should develop codes of conduct and adequate accountability and preventive tools for violations of such codes for elected officials and appointed officials. Secondly, Slovakia must develop ethical codes within political parties, and establish a supervision body to check party funding and electoral campaigns more effectively. Thirdly, the Report recommended that the country should support and ensure that the independence of the Commission for Prevention of Corruption is preserved, and its powers and capacity are further reinforced. Slovenia must maintain the operational independence of prosecution services specialising in fighting financial and economic crime and encourage more effective collaboration of all relevant public institutions that combat corruption in Slovenia.

2.4.26 Spain

The Report found that Spain has pushed forward in investigating corrupt practices at central and local levels.[99] However, recent large-scale corruption cases have revealed a number of alleged corrupt practices affecting public funds and financing of political parties. Public spending at regional and local levels has been particularly challenging, and public tenders and urban development appear to be among the most vulnerable areas in Spain. Therefore, firstly, the Report recommended that Spain develop a tailor-made strategy for regional and local administrations to prevent corruption practices, and establish monitoring mechanisms to increase transparency of decision-making at local and regional governance. Secondly, the Report recommended that Spain develop codes of conduct for elected officials at central, regional and local levels, and develop ethical codes within political parties as recommended by the resolution of the Spanish Parliament in February 2013, implementing clear rules on asset disclosure and conflicts of interests for elected and appointed officials at central, regional and local

98 European Commission, 'Annex 24: Slovenia to the EU Anti-Corruption Report' COM (2014) 38 final <http://ec.europa.eu/dgs/home-affairs/what-we-do/policies/organized-crime-and-human-trafficking/corruption/anti-corruption-report/docs/2014_acr_slovenia_chapter_en.pdf> accessed 30 May 2019.

99 European Commission, 'Annex 9: Spain to the EU Anti-Corruption Report' COM (2014) 38 final <http://ec.europa.eu/dgs/home-affairs/what-we-do/policies/organized-crime-and-human-trafficking/corruption/anti-corruption-report/docs/2014_acr_spain_chapter_en.pdf> accessed 30 May 2019.

levels. Spain should reinforce the resources of the Office of Conflicts of Interests to carry out verifications in an independent and effective way. Finally, the Report recommended that Spain implement new laws on transparency and access to public information and increase good governance, supported by an independent supervisory mechanism matched with a strict sanctioning system.

2.4.27 Sweden

Sweden is among the least corrupt countries in the EU and has taken an ambitious approach to fighting corruption, implementing several effective anti-corruption initiatives.[100] However, the Report found a few areas of concern remain: corruption practice at local levels and loopholes in the Swedish legal framework for prosecuting and sentencing Swedish corporations on grounds of foreign bribery. Thus, the Report first recommended Sweden that it ensures the liability of legal persons for foreign bribery is activated in cases where the offence is committed through lower-level employees, intermediaries, subsidiaries or third-party agents including non-Swedish nationals. Sweden should raise the level of penalties for corporations and other legal entities. Finally, the Report recommended that Sweden improve the transparency of political party funding and of individual candidates, in line with recommendations suggested by GRECO, and extend future legislation on party financing at regional and local levels.

2.4.28 United Kingdom

In the UK, foreign bribery continues to be an issue, and detailed guidelines to the Bribery Act 2010 should be issued in order for companies to make use of the legislation.[101] Firstly, the Report recommended that the UK continue its efforts in tackling foreign bribery and provide sector-specific guidelines to companies in areas which may be at increased risk, in particular in the defence industry. Secondly, the UK should also strengthen accountability in the governance of banks, thus including stricter law enforcement and ensure that the beneficial owners of UK-registered companies are declared fully and in a transparent manner. Thirdly, the Report recommended that the country should impose limits on electoral campaign spending and capping donations to political parties, ensure more proactive monitoring misuse of political party donations and prosecution of potential violations and consider

100 European Commission, 'Annex 27: Sweden to the EU Anti-Corruption Report' COM (2014) 38 final <http://ec.europa.eu/dgs/home-affairs/what-we-do/policies/organized-crime-and-human-trafficking/corruption/anti-corruption-report/docs/2014_acr_sweden_chapter_en.pdf> accessed 30 May 2019.

101 European Commission, 'Annex 28: United Kingdom to the EU Anti-Corruption Report' COM (2014) 38 final <http://ec.europa.eu/dgs/home-affairs/what-we-do/policies/organized-crime-and-human-trafficking/corruption/anti-corruption-report/docs/2014_acr_united_kingdom_chapter_en.pdf> accessed 30 May 2019.

lowering the thresholds for the reporting of financial holdings and for the registration of received gifts to elected officials, thus providing clear guidance on acceptable gifts for Members of Parliament. Finally, the UK should address the issues identified by the Leveson Inquiry, in particular regarding the legitimate interaction between the press and the police, and such time limits on the employment of former police officers by the media should be clearly regulated.

2.5 General limitations of the EU anti-corruption report

The Report included little new data, drawing heavily on work conducted by UN, GRECO, OECD, TI and other regional organisations that are specialists in anti-corruption issues. The Report included some original data collection—in particular from the survey—but it still faced a challenge in demonstrating its added value and usefulness to the public and policymakers. This is because the Report risks duplication of the information and data by other international organisations that have a longer history in anti-corruption work. The biggest contribution that the Report has made is to raise awareness of the sectors that are more affected by corruption, and the policy and strategy shortcomings in dealing with corruption in the member states—in particular, putting anti-corruption policy high on the agenda and creating opportunities for exchanging ideas and policy integration in different areas to address corruption also as law and policy issues. Even were the Commission to be criticised for collecting existing evidence (rather than conducting new analysis about corruption), the Report acts as an important reference for understanding the lack of policy and supporting member states in developing key tools and policies to prevent corruption. This is as well as engaging the Commission, member states and civil society in ongoing dialogue to enhance further their anti-corruption efforts.[102]

There is no formal assessment procedure in the current Report, for instance, similar to the GRECO's evaluation[103] (though some follow-up on country-specific recommendations was envisaged in the second Report). However, no formal assessment procedures were established within the framework of the Report up to this point. Other limitations are the areas covered by the recommendations in the Report. TI evaluations of the Report point out the lack of its specific recommendations: in particular, on the protection of whistle-blowers, access to information and lobbying. In fact, communication from the Commission in 2011 on the Report mentioned that these areas would be evaluated in depth when the Report was issued (in February 2014). Furthermore, in its Report evaluation, TI observed a lack of attention to

102 Wouter van Ballegooij and Thomas Zandstra, 'Organised Crime and Corruption: Cost of Non-Europe Report' Annex II—Corruption European Parliament, EPRS PE 579.319 (March 2016) 72–88.

103 Diana Schmidt-Pfister and Holger Moroff, *Fighting Corruption in Eastern Europe: A Multilevel Perspective* (Routledge 2013) 78–85.

the cross-border element—a factor most in need of scrutiny within the EU dimension.[104]

There were other areas and sectors that corruption has a negative impact upon, which were initially promised to be assessed in the first Commission communication in 2011; for example, an evaluation of law enforcement, judicial and police cooperation within the EU. The Report was also supposed to cover asset recovery, accounting standards, statutory audit for EU companies and enhancement of integrity in sport and match-fixing, as well as an evaluation of the EU's external policies in regard to the EU candidate states, potential candidates and neighbouring countries to make recommendations on policy reforms in addressing their anti-corruption policy shortcomings.[105] The 2014 Report did not, in fact, pay attention to any of these areas.

Furthermore, the Commission also initially suggested that the Report would evaluate the level of corruption within EU institutions and offer some suggestions for these policy reforms.[106] Research found that the DG Home Affairs dropped such an idea because the Commission perceived it to be biased in its approach in evaluating its own institutions. The Commission may commission someone outside of the EU institutions to make an evaluation and analysis of the level of corruption within these institutions in the future.

As a result, the evaluation of corruption within the EU institutions did not fall within the scope of the Report. From the perspective of the EU and its Report, monitoring and evaluation procedures with regards to corruption at the EU level and within its institutions are weaker than their counterparts relating to the state of corruption in the member states. In order to offer some kind of evaluation and to remedy this gap, TI made a study of corruption and integrity risks within EU institutions and pertaining to the EU's budget, in its 2014 EU Integrity System Report.[107] This report is an evaluation of ten EU institutions and agencies: the European Parliament, European Council, Council of the EU, the Commission, Court of Justice of the European Union, European Court of Auditors, European Anti-Fraud Office, Europol and Eurojust, and the Ombudsman.[108] As such, TI's report represents a comprehensive and independent study on the state of corruption at the EU level.[109] EU institutions are subject to external review through their membership in UNCAC, but such a review has not been conducted at this point, and it is difficult to make a concrete

104 Carl Dolan, 'We Have an Anti-Corruption Report: So Now What?' *Politico* (2 May 2014) <www.politico.eu/article/we-have-an-eu-anti-corruption-report-now-what/> accessed 30 May 2019.

105 European Commission (n 1).

106 ibid.

107 Transparency International, 'Report on the EU Integrity System' (2014) <https://transparency.eu/wp-content/uploads/2016/10/EU_Integrity_System_Report.pdf> accessed 30 May 2019.

108 ibid.

109 Van Ballegooij and Zandstra (n 102) 104–110.

evaluation. Should the EU and its institutions accede to GRECO, it would face similar scrutiny and can be evaluated more clearly. In the next section, we will evaluate some key areas that a theoretical future EU Anti-Corruption Report might have considered, in order to cover and raise more awareness of the policy shortcomings in future Reports.

2.6 Conclusion

The EU Anti-Corruption Report was an outcome of the EU decision in June 2011, wherein the Commission proposed a set of measures to address more actively the serious harm corruption causes to the European Union—economically, socially and politically, in its member states, candidate states and its institutions. The Commission began developing the Report, and this new mechanism was viewed positively, in its design to encourage more political anti-corruption engagement throughout the EU. Therefore, once published in 2014, the Report's main target was to support member states in better enforcing their legislation and fully implementing their international commitments against corruption, as well as improving the coherence of their anti-corruption legal tools and policy actions in the EU. In other words, the Report's overarching goal was to develop higher anti-corruption standards.

However, as we have seen in this chapter's discussion, the 2014 Report did not include an assessment of the corruption posed by the European institutions and the candidate states as was originally promised; dropping these elements and features was a disappointing development, reducing as it did the fullness of the corruption-threat picture faced in the EU. Nevertheless, the Report provided interesting findings about the serious economic harm caused by corruption to the EU, estimated at approximately €120 billion per year. Furthermore, the Report identified some of the main corruption trends through its two surveys and offered a good snapshot of the policy and legal weaknesses which need to be addressed in all of the member states. Thus, the Report had good potential for influencing the policies of member states in taking corruption more seriously.

The EU initiatives in the field of anti-corruption up to 2011 were closely linked to supporting the proper function of the internal market, and they had achieved this objective well. However, with the introduction of the Report in 2014, the EU extended its objectives to focus the anti-corruption policy in areas where corruption had a social and political impact on member states. Through a detailed country report for all 28 member states, the Report tried to stimulate peer learning and exchange of best practices against corruption, thus creating a synergy throughout the EU to address the issue of corruption more effectively. An important question to consider is whether the Report influenced member states to embed higher anti-corruption standards and encouraged more political will to enact anti-corruption policies. This will be discussed in detail throughout parts two and three—but first, we will consider the theory behind the Report and analyse it as a form of reflexive governance that supports member states to enhance their anti-corruption policy shortcomings.

3 The EU anti-corruption report and reflexive governance

3.1 Introduction

In this chapter, we argue that the regulatory approach of the EU Anti-Corruption Report is best described as reflexive governance. We'll consider this in four sections. The first section considers the context of the Report and the emergence of new modes of governance in the EU. It includes a discussion of key methods of the new governance approach in the EU—the open method of coordination—which has significantly changed the regulation and methods of governance at the supranational level. The second section introduces the concept of reflexive governance and explains the transformation of new governance into reflexive governance in EU policymaking. Here also we'll explain the growing use of reflexive forms of governance within the EU and see examples of how reflexive governance occurs. The third section introduces the theory of reflexive law that provides core insights into the regulatory nature of reflexive governance. The final section discusses the application of the theory of reflexive governance to the Report and demonstrates that the concept of 'regulation of self-regulation' provides the key insight into the governance approach of the Report.

3.2 New governance in the European Union

The emergence of new modes of governance in the EU dates back to the Maastricht Treaty in 1992 and the introduction of the European Economic and Monetary Union (EMU). Ten years of successful experimentation with economic policy coordination enabled the launch of the EMU in 2002 and triggered a reorientation of European policymaking and a change of methods of governance at the supranational level. The economic and fiscal policies coordination model was adopted for the coordination of employment policies, in the form of the European Employment Strategy (EES), as well as other coordination policies in several new policy areas. The underlying concept of governance based on policy coordination was outlined in the Commission's White Paper on European Governance in July 2001.[1]

1 European Commission, 'White Paper on European Governance' COM (2001) 428 final 7–11.

In the white paper, the Commission identified its four strategic objectives at the beginning of the new millennium, which included the reform of European governance alongside democracy, transparency and subsidiarity.[2] The white paper made use of the global debate on good governance to discuss opportunities for internal reform aimed at bringing the EU closer to its citizens, rendering it more effective, and consolidating the democratic legitimacy of its institutions.[3] The Commission's white paper on governance established five basic principles that could strengthen the good governance approach: openness, participation, accountability, effectiveness and coherence.[4]

Openness is largely related to the importance of communication between the European institutions and the member states, as far as the decisions that the EU makes are concerned; this includes the use of a practical language in the public documents. Participation means the broad involvement of institutional bodies, agencies, social partners and civil society at all stages; from designing a policy concept to implementation of a policy, participation constitutes a key condition for the quality and the effectiveness of the EU's policies. Accountability relates to trust and the explicit roles of the participants in the process of decision-making. Effectiveness concerns the degree of achievement of targets that have been put in place on the basis of assessment processes of applied policy areas. Lastly, coherence relates to the synchronisation between the policies and the actions, as well as their easy understanding. The applications of these five principles are intended to strengthen the principles of proportionality and subsidiarity in the Commission.[5]

Each principle is important by itself. However, they cannot be achieved through discrete actions or approaches. Policies can no longer be effective unless they are prepared, implemented and enforced in an inclusive way. The white paper calls for renewing the Commission's method, by following a less top-down approach and enlarging its policy tools through an increased use of non-legislative instruments.

The white paper acknowledges the vital role that civil society plays in giving 'voice to the concerns of citizens and offering services to people's needs', and involving civil society organisations at all levels of the policy process.[6] One of the white paper's concluding proposals aims to institutionalise the EU's relationship with civil society, by introducing a code of conduct that identifies responsibilities and improves accountability of all partners.[7] In involving EU-level civil society, organisations can be part of the EU policymaking process through more

2 Tanja A Börzel and Vera Van Hüllen, *Governance Transfer by Regional Organizations: Patching Together a Global Script* (Palgrave Macmillan 2015) 33

3 Tanja A Börzel, Yasemin Pamuk and Andreas Stahn, 'Good Governance in the European Union' *Berlin Working Paper on European Integration No 18* (2008) 5–22.

4 European Commission (n 1).

5 European Commission (n 1) 11–28.

6 ibid.

7 ibid.

structured processes of consultation.[8] This approach leads to a 'transnationalisation' of policy process, meaning it is reinforced by provisions of the Lisbon Treaty on participatory democracy.[9]

We'll now analyse the key guiding instrument for improving European governance proposed in the white paper: the open method of coordination (OMC). OMC was a new form of integrative policymaking, enabling it to meet both external and internal pressures.[10] It promotes a soft policy approach, which is now applied to a growing number of policy areas, including social exclusion, pensions, education, health care, and research and development.[11]

3.3 The open method of coordination

The introduction of new forms of governance in the EU, and in particular the OMC, has significantly changed the regulation and methods of governance at supranational level.[12] The OMC was presented at the European Council in Lisbon as the central tool for fulfilling the Lisbon agenda. However, elements of this method have a longer history within international governance; for instance, benchmarking and evaluations have been the main tools for the IMF and the OECD for decades.[13] In the context of the EU, the OMC is rooted in treaty-based EU policy coordination processes introduced during the 1990s, such as Broad Economic Policy Guidelines (BEPG), and the EES, developed in order to coordinate the economic policies of the member states after ratification of the Maastricht Treaty.[14] At the Lisbon Socio-Economic Summit in 2000, the OMC was defined as a broadly applicable governance instrument for EU policymaking:[15] a specific ensemble of procedural elements involving iterative benchmarking of national progress towards common European objectives and organised mutual learning. A four-step governance architecture (modelled on

8 Börzel and Hüllen (n 2).

9 European Council, 'Presidency Conclusions' (21–22 June 2007) 11177/1/07.

10 Tanja A Börzel and Rachel A Cichowski, *The State of the European Union: Law, Politics, and Society* (OUP 2003) 2–29.

11 Charles F Sabel and Jonathan Zeitlin, 'Learning from Difference: The New Architecture of Experimentalist Governance in the EU' *European Law Journal 14* (3) (2008) 271–327.

12 Jonathan Zeitlin, 'The Open Method of Coordination in Action: Theoretical Promise, Empirical Realities, Reform Strategy' in Jonathan Zeitlin and Philippe Pochet with Lars Magnusson (eds), *The Open Method of Co-ordination in Action: The European Employment and Social Inclusion Strategies* (Peter Lang 2005) 447–503.

13 ibid.

14 The BEPG procedure, which is based on Article 99 of the Treaty, is as follows: on the basis of a Commission recommendation, the Council, by a qualified majority vote, produces draft BEPGs that are submitted to the European Council, which adopts a conclusion. On this basis, the Council, again acting by QMV, adopts the relevant recommendation. The EP is informed of the recommendations.

15 Zeitlin (n 12).

the EES and its four steps) can be distinguished in relation to the OMC, summarised here by Ralf Rogowski in his white paper analysis:[16]

1 Setting up guidelines supplemented by timetables for achieving the goals in the short, medium and long terms (the Commission makes proposals on the guidelines).
2 Introducing quantitative and qualitative indicators and benchmarks as a means of comparing best practices (the Commission organises the exchange of best practices and makes proposals on indicators).
3 Translating the European guidelines into national action plans by setting specific targets and adopting measures, thereby taking into account national and regional characteristics.
4 A follow-up system: monitoring and evaluation combined with peer review (this provides support to the processes of implementation and peer review). In their review of the national action plans, the Commission and the Council regularly provide comments and recommendations that are often based on comparisons with the best performers and create additional benchmarks for each member state.

The non-binding nature of the OMC, in comparison to traditional hard supranational legislation, is designed to facilitate the achievement of the EU's main goals by enhancing transparency, mutual learning and peer review, while leaving decision-making to the member states.[17]

The OMC is an iterative method: the policy cycle is repeated, depending on the policy area, every one to three years. An OMC is created by the European Council in areas encountering problem of interdependence requiring policy coordination, but in which member states are not willing to delegate authority to the EU. After discussions with relevant committees, public and private stakeholders, and outside experts, the Commission makes a proposal for a common strategy for dealing with identified problems[18] (examples where this practice has taken place are employment and pensions). The Commission then suggests a series of guidelines and objectives to the Council of Ministers, who might adjust the guidelines and objectives before approving them. Generally, the guidelines are presented under a few overarching strategic pillars; for example, the guidelines for the employment OMC were initially presented under the four pillars of Employability, Entrepreneurship, Adaptability and Equal Opportunities. In addition to

16 R Rogowski, *Reflexive Labour Law in the World Society* (Edward Elgar 2013) 189–206.

17 Joanne Scott and David M Trubek, 'Mind the Gap: Law and New Approaches to Governance in the European Union' *European Law Journal 8* (1) (2002) 1–18.

18 Jonathan Zeitlin, Egidijus Barceviius and J Timo Weishaupt, *Assessing the Open Method of Coordination: Institutional Design and National Influence of EU Social Policy Coordination* (Palgrave Macmillan 2014) 24.

the policy guidelines, the Commission proposes quantifiable targets or objectives with either short or medium timetables for completion.[19]

Firstly, in contrast to objectives pursued by using the traditional 'Community method', objectives in OMC guidelines must be reaffirmed at the beginning of each cycle and can be amended or removed in the light of experience. Jonathan Zeitlin and his colleagues view this as a strong indication of Lisbon's institutionalisation, particularly if one considers the separate benchmarking devices and norms adopted by the European Council.[20]

Secondly, OMC facilitates several new mechanisms and instruments designed to enhance monitoring of policy and performance, such as indicators, benchmarks and quantitative targets. The member states are expected to produce National Action Plans or National Reports that outline the state of affairs in the related policy domains and actions taken or planned in response to Commission objectives. Throughout the course of the process, the Commission and the experts assigned thereby monitor the progress in each of the states, and in the European Community as a whole. At the end of the annual, biennial or triennial cycle, the Commission—after consultations with the relevant experts, social partners, Parliament and other Commission entities—presents a draft report of the progress made. For example, the EES and the BEPG could make explicit recommendations from the EU member states. The designated council body or joint council must approve the Joint Report and submit it to the European Council.[21]

Thirdly, institutional devices have been introduced to assist cross-national learning. One significant institutional innovation is the creation of hybrid expert groups that involve supranational and intergovernmental experts in a consultative body for the Council and the Commission. These expert groups hold non-public meetings approximately every few months, aiming to facilitate mutual learning processes by incorporating expertise into the OMC.[22] Though they have no official power, the informal settings where discussions take place encourage a free exchange of ideas and help to build trust between the Commission and member state experts. In addition to the technical evaluation and monitoring, these groups or committees are responsible for the establishing policy and performance indicators, critical for assisting the monitoring process

19 E Szyszczak, 'Experimental Governance: The Open Method of Coordination' *European Law Journal 12* (4) (2006) 486–502.

20 Zeitlin, Barcevičius and Weishaupt (n 18) 25.

21 KA Armstrong, 'The Lisbon Strategy and Europe 2020: From the Governance of Co-ordination to the Co-ordination of Governance' in Paul Copeland and Dimitris Papadimitriou (eds) *The EU's Lisbon Strategy: Evaluating Success, Understanding Failure* (Palgrave Macmillan 2012) 208–28.

22 DM Trubek and LG Trubek, 'The Open Method of Co-ordination and the Debate over "Hard" and "Soft" Law' in Jonathan Zeitlin and Philippe Pochet with Lars Magnusson (eds), *The Open Method of Co-ordination in Action: The European Employment and Social Inclusion Strategies* (Peter Lang 2005) 83–103.

and exchanging comparable information.[23] Also, in some OMCs, the Commission arranges voluntary peer reviews, in which member state, stakeholders, the Commission and national independent experts engage in a qualitative review of members' best practice, which may include site visits and exchange of expert reports, and in-depth discussions on the policy area at stake.[24]

The Lisbon European Council described the OMC as a fully decentralised approach, incorporating regional and local governments, and the Commission develops benchmarking exercises for managing change by networking with different providers and users, namely the interest groups, companies and NGOs. OMC is a particularly flexible EU governance tool, which has been designed to fit the policy logic of different domains, such as employment, pensions, education, healthcare, the level of problem interdependence and the national sensitivity around relevant areas.[25]

After the relaunch of the Lisbon Strategy in 2005, on the bases of the recommendations of the two Kok reports,[26] the OMC for economics and employment policies was integrated under the Lisbon agenda. This redesign of the OMC was effective, insofar as it addressed the problems of effectiveness, legitimacy and visibility by calling for a broader set of actors to be involved at member state level.[27] However, other issues (like the specificity of policy targets and democratic participation, for example) remain problematic.[28] When the Lisbon Strategy expired in 2010, it was replaced by the Europe 2020 Strategy, which broadened the commitment to EU social cohesion objectives by introducing new headline targets and integrated guidelines aimed—inter alia—at reducing poverty and social exclusion.[29]

From a legal perspective, the OMC is non-binding and, ultimately, voluntary in nature. It is designed to be flexible; its voluntary nature allows member states to amend reforms in accordance with the structures of their regimes, institutional networks and their specific circumstances.[30] It allows for a wide-ranging participation of social partners. Nevertheless, if a member state decides not to

23 ibid.

24 Helga Pülzl and Marius Lazdinis,'May the Open Method of Coordination be a New Instrument for Forest Policy Deliberations in the European Union?' *Forest Policy and Economics 13* (6) (2011) 411–418.

25 Poul F Kjaer, *Between Governing and Governance: On the Emergence, Function and Form of Europe's Post-National Condition* (Hart 2010) 110–112.

26 European Commission, 'Communication to the Spring European Council 'Working Together for Growth and Jobs: A New Start for the Lisbon Strategy' (2005) <https://eur-lex.europa.eu/LexUriServ/LexUriServ.do?uri=COM:2005:0024:FIN:en:PDF> accessed 30 May 2019.

27 R Rogowski, 'The European Social Model and Law and Policy of Transitional Labour Markets in the European Union' in R Rogowski (ed), *The European Social Model and Transitional Labour Markets—Law and Policy* (Ashgate 2008) 9–27.

28 Kjaer (n 25).

29 Barcevičius, Zeitlin and Weishaupt (n 18) 2–3.

30 ibid 25.

cooperate, or chooses à la carte which policies it wishes to follow while resisting others, there are no hard sanctions that can be imposed.

Therefore, the effectiveness of the OMC mainly depends on the participants' willingness to cooperate—or to use the language of reflexive law, to engage in self-regulation.[31] However, from a policy-oriented view, it is a widely shared belief that in areas such as employment and social policy, the OMC is the suitable method, because member states are largely unwilling to transfer sovereignty beyond coordination. The soft law approach of the OMC appears to have advantages for national governments, as through this mechanism, they can receive guidance on reforming their systems without losing their sovereignty.[32]

In theory, the OMC prompts a learning process, in which member states are subjected to benchmarking, peer review and evaluations of their progress.[33] However, the outcomes of the 'OMC in action' show few examples of successful learning,[34] although there seems to be some evidence of learning from negative experience. The results of evaluations and benchmarking can lead to open criticism of member states governments. The so-called soft sanctions of 'naming and shaming' can harm the reputation of member states that score less favourably and put their governments under pressure to conform.[35]

The OMC has been criticised in a number of ways. Doubts have been voiced, for example, about the implementation process, alleging that the production of the National Action Plan is often an affair solely involving technocrats and government officials.[36] Furthermore, sociological accounts of the monitoring process see it riddled with cultural misunderstandings and linguistic ambiguities. It has also been suggested that a proper theoretical account of the use of OMC in economic, employment and social policies is lacking.[37]

3.4 Reflexive governance

Since the emergence of OMC, we have witnessed a gradual transformation of *new governance* into *reflexive governance* in EU policymaking. There is a growing use of reflexive forms of governance within the EU that transforms the technocratic limits of the OMC in order to develop more effective policies, regulations and laws.

31 Rogowski (n 16) 191.

32 S Deakin and R Rogowski, 'Reflexive Labour Law, Capabilities and the Future of Social Europe' in R Rogowski, R Salais and N Whiteside (eds), *Transforming European Employment Policy—Labour Market Transitions and the Promotion of Capability* (Edward Elgar 2011). 229–54.

33 Kjaer (n 25).

34 M Van der Meer, J Visser and T Wilthagen, 'Adaptive and Reflexive Governance: The Limits of Organized Decentralization' *European Journal of Industrial Relations 11* (3) (2005) 347–365.

35 DM Trubek and LG Trubek, 'The World Turned Upside Down: Reflections on New Governance and the Transformation of Law' *Wisconsin Law Review* (2) (2010) 719–26.

36 Zeitlin (n 12).

37 Rogowski (n 16) 189–206.

Reflexive approaches view the diversity of policies, laws and practices across the EU member states as the basis for experimentation and mutual learning within the overall process of European governance. There are three main aspects that distinguish OMC and new governance from reflexive governance.

Firstly, the Commission uses new governance and OMC as a top-down approach. It operates on the model that ideas developed at the EU level gradually influence developments at national or sub-national level—change occurs as a result of shaming by the Commission. Reflexive governance suggests instead a holistic approach and argues that policy change may result as much from bottom-up as top-down pressures. Key to change are processes of diffusion through mimesis or discourse, deliberation, learning and networks.

Secondly, reflexive governance emphasises the multilevel nature of governance. The multilevel approach transcends a new governance approach, insofar as decision-making authority is distributed across more than one level of relatively autonomous public sector institutions; reflexive governance promotes a shift of responsibilities to a lower level of governance and views governance as supportive of self-regulation.

Thirdly, reflexive governance is based on this shift of responsibilities being reflected in the use of new legal instruments. The OMC approach resorts to moral or political pressure as a second-best solution. The flexibilisation of exiting legal instruments constitutes a core concern of reflexive governance.

Reflexive governance has been introduced as a new concept that responds to a shift in understanding processes of decision-making, policymaking and policy implementation. This can broadly be described as a shift from a primary focus on the top-down activities of government (whether operating through regulatory, financial or educational instruments) to governance, which recognises a much broader mix of participants involved in policymaking and implementation processes.[38] These participants are active at various governance levels, ranging from global to local, with often overlapping and conflicting jurisdictions. It is through networks around government ministries responsible for a policy sector at regional, national and local levels that policy gets formulated and implemented.

Reflexive forms of governance enable stakeholders to frame and tackle problems in collaboration. A key component to the success of reflexive governance is to include individuals, organisations and agencies in collective learning and collaboration. This means breaking away from routines that are no longer appropriate to the problem, and experimenting, adapting and reviewing new measures in a search for more flexible relations.[39] This includes viewing the policy process as

38 Olivier De Schutter and Jacques Lenoble, *Reflexive Governance: Redefining the Public Interest in a Pluralistic World* (Hart 2010) 60–62.

39 Colin Scott, 'Reflexive Governance, Meta-Regulation and Corporate Social Responsibility: The "Heineken Effect"' in N Boeger, R Murray and C Villiers (eds), *Perspectives on Corporate Social Responsibility* (Edward Elgar 2008) 170–85.

a shared problem, and searching for collective solutions. Since various groups of people conceive of the world in different ways, different actors will frame the object of governance and its boundaries differently. How these different framings are interactively and mutually negotiated has an important bearing on reflexive governance. According to Schutter and Lenoble, there are four key characteristics of reflexive governance: collective learning, active participation, global interaction and innovative problemsolving.[40]

Collective learning: it is a key element of reflexive governance approaches. The aim is to provide a platform for dialogue and mutual learning between different levels of governance and actors engaged in different practices. The line of communication here is not vertical, and not a feedback mechanism. Reflexive governance transcends a top-down approach by shifting decision-making responsibilities into an organised discussion, where there is the possibility for a broader spectrum of perspectives that can be shared, and in which compromise must be reached between the participants on the basis of rational argument and experiences. However, the reflexive approach to governance transcends collaborative-deliberative approaches, represented by the work of Charles Sabel and his colleagues,[41] which promotes local experimentalism and uses Habermas's discourse theory of communicative action.[42] Reflexive governance does not privilege consensus and allows room for as much dissensus as necessary. The basis of success for reflexive governance depends on the participants actively engaging and participating in dialogue and experimentation, and thereby engaging in the process of mutual learning. Learning is conceived as a continuous process of reflexive learning, in which knowledge is developed through a feedback circle between different actors. This is characterised by double-loop learning[43] that focuses on rethinking existing policies and strategies. This approach suggests a new set of dynamics that enables learning between a mixture of governmental and non-governmental participants.[44] The work on reflexive learning contributes to the previous literature on reflexive approaches to governance, by integrating theories of collective and mutual learning with organisational theory, and links the process of collective learning to the three other core aspects of reflexive governance, leading to implementation of knowledge.

40 De Schutter and Lenoble (n 37).

41 Sabel and Zeitlin (n 11) 278–80.

42 Jürgen Habermas, *Between Facts and Norms: Contributions to a Discourse Theory of Law and Democracy* (Polity 1996).

43 Alice Y Kolb and David A Kolb (2011) 'Experiential Learning Theory: A Dynamic, Holistic Approach to Management Learning, Education and Development' in SJ Armstrong and C Fukami, (eds) *The SAGE Handbook of Management Learning, Education and Development* (Sage 2011) 42–68; and C Argyris and D Schön, *Organizational Learning II: Theory, Method and Practice* (Addison Wesley 1996) 39–43.

44 BI Crona and JN Parker, 'Learning in Support of Governance: Theories, Methods, and a Framework to Assess How Bridging Organizations Contribute to Adaptive Resource Governance' *Ecology and Society* 17 (1) (2012) 32.

Active participation: reflexive governance emphasises that active participation of a wider set of actors at domestic, regional and local levels is key to successful policymaking. It allows for interest groups and expert individuals to become active participants and engage in exchange of knowledge between different levels of actors involved in the process of policymaking. This is unlike the 'new governance' approach, where the Commission and governments of member states are the main actors participating in the process of policymaking. Reflexive governance means inclusion of civil society and citizen groups in consultation processes, and in supporting governance in shaping policy and regulation.[45] It also means shifting responsibility to lower levels and engaging citizens in policymaking.[46] In new governance, the representation of different interests of stakeholder groups is possible, although the representation of larger sections of citizens cannot be guaranteed by this procedure, and complex collective choice must be part of a concept of active participation.[47] Nevertheless, from a reflexive governance perspective, it is important to collaborate and involve local movements, NGOs and individual experts at local level in policymaking and in the process of preparing policies and regulations.[48]

Global interaction: the theory of reflexive governance emphasises that governance at national and local levels has to be understood as part of global responses to global problems. Thus, globalisation is an opportunity for reflexive governance to gain useful knowledge and to benchmark national policy and regulations against international standards. Furthermore, reflexive governance takes into account that national and local initiatives must be evaluated and enriched in the light of fast-changing global conditions.[49] The reflexive approach recognises the need for global knowledge transfer and the willingness and ability to exchange useful knowledge—global knowledge transfer involves a number of steps that include idea creation, sharing, evaluation, dissemination and adoption.[50] These five steps are key for reflexive governance, because decision-making processes in reflexive governance usually are not based on a single event, but rather on a series of interactions and discoveries that make use of knowledge in different local, national and global settings.[51]

45 PJ Vergragt and HS Brown, 'Sustainable Mobility: from Technological Innovation to Societal Learning' *Journal of Cleaner Production 15* (11–12) (2007) 1104–1115.

46 R Rogowski, 'ALACs and the Concept of Citizen Participation in the Light of European Law' *Warwick School of Law Research Paper No 2010/25* (2010).

47 De Schutter and Lenoble (n 37) 97–102

48 MJ Magone, *Routledge Handbook of European Politics* (Routledge 2015) 31–32.

49 De Schutter and Lenoble (n 37) 97–102.

50 SS Levine and M Prietula, 'How Knowledge Transfer Impacts Performance: A Multi-Level Model of Benefits and Liabilities' *Organization Science 23* (6) (2012) 1748–1766.

51 Beatrice I Crona and John N Parker, 'Learning in Support of Governance: Theories, Methods, and a Framework to Assess How Bridging Organizations Contribute to Adaptive Resource Governance' *Ecology and Society 17* (1) (2012) 32.

Innovative problem solving: the theory of reflexive governance pays particular attention to innovation and experimentation in solving policy shortcomings. This includes capacities to create new solutions to policy shortcomings, as well as improving regulations, trainings, structures, technology and knowledge transfers. However, new instruments and policy do not automatically emerge from old instruments and policy. This requires innovative experimentalism. For example, exchanges between different regions can foster innovation, as each region will have to redefine its policies and strategies, and improve on them in light of the successes and failures of others using a particular instrument.[52] An important condition in order to successfully produce new ideas is innovative training, which then can lead to the discovery of new effective instruments. In order to learn from experience innovatively, it is crucial to design mechanisms that can monitor failure and success of past experience. In other words, knowledge has to be converted from tacit to explicit knowledge.[53] This process requires tools such as databases, or apps that can allow access to best practice examples.

Technology has been fundamental to innovation, and it has enhanced wider participation throughout the world.[54] For instance, surveys can be carried out through online platforms, and the use of technology has helped us evaluate knowledge through such surveillance, which then leads to further innovation and experimentation of policies. Finally, online platforms have been key to lowering dramatically the barriers for the dissemination of knowledge and obtaining knowledge for innovation. It is easier than ever before to target and inform people in both desirable and rather less desirable ways. For instance, groups can discuss new ideas through online tools and spread valuable information on an independent basis. Such global participants can make citizens a valuable information source and can help to create acceptance and transparency tools, which potentially leads to innovative and better policies.[55]

The four elements of reflexive governance above, when applied to EU policies and initiatives, can explain why new governance is gradually transforming into reflexive governance. Furthermore, the theory of reflexive governance can be enhanced by using the social system theory as demonstrated by Ralf Rogowski. In doing so, it quickly becomes clear that the notion of reflexive governance is based on the concept of reflexive law. Reflexive law is a means to develop and find new ways to support reflexive policymaking in the EU. Next, we will consider the theory of reflexive law and its role in reflexive governance.

52 De Schutter and Lenoble (n 37) 97–102.

53 Stephen P Turner, *Understanding the Tacit* (Routledge 2014) 3–17.

54 Manuel Castells and Gustavo Cardoso, *The Network Society from Knowledge to Policy* (Johns Hopkins Center for Transatlantic Relations 2005) 3–23.

55 Derk Loorbach, 'Transition Management for Sustainable Development: A Prescriptive, Complexity-Based Governance Framework' *Governance 23* (1) (2010) 161–183.

3.5 Reflexive law

Reflexive law theory adds important elements to the theory of reflexive governance, in accordance with social systems theory. Reflexive law views and understands the legal system as an autonomous function system within society, on the same level as the economy and the political system. According to Niklas Luhmann, the legal system is guided by the necessity to safeguard its self-reference and self-reproduction; in other words, its autopoiesis.[56] Reflexive law provides not only the basis for an evaluation of the limits but also the potentials of law as a mechanism for social change.[57]

According to Luhmann's theory of society,[58] subsystems such as law and politics are *operationally closed* and *cognitively open* systems of communication. Operational closure means that these subsystems can reproduce themselves through self-regulations of communication.[59] This leads, in the case of law, to a normatively closed system of counterfactually stabilised expectations. Only law transmits normative validity to its elements, and this process allows for legislation and adjudication to take place, which enables law to create law.

In Luhmann's theory of societal development, possibilities for reflexive processes increase when society has adopted functional differentiation as its mode of integration.[60] Luhmann demonstrated this in relation to what he calls 'positivisation of law'; the argument is as follows: reflexivity takes place when the legal system becomes an autonomously functioning system of society, arising as a by-product of norm application in decision-making. It defines the process of presenting new types of norms for the regulation of norm application, and, by evolving second-order norms, the legal system becomes able to carry out decision-making founded on the application of the binary code 'legal/illegal'. Therefore, reflexivity contributes to the closure of the system and to its autonomy.[61]

Reflexivity in the sense of 'norming of norms' is not unfamiliar to legal theory and is discussed in numerous ways. An example is Hans Kelsen's idea of a pyramid of norms as a self-validating mechanism of law, in which higher norms provide legitimacy to lower-ranking norms.[62] Another example is HLA Hart's concept of secondary legal laws as norms of ordering primary legal norms.[63] Reflexivity as an instrument of self-control of law and as

56 R Rogowski, 'Luhmann, Niklas (1927–98)' *Wiley Blackwell Encyclopaedia of Sociology* (2nd edn, Wiley Blackwell 2015) 1–6.

57 Rogowski (n 16) 33.

58 Niklas Luhmann, *Theory of Society Vol 1* (Stanford UP 2012) 18–99.

59 Niklas Luhmann, 'Some Problems with Reflexive Law' in G Teubner and A Febbrajo (eds), *European Yearbook in the Sociology of Law—State, Law and Economy as Autopoietic Systems: Regulation and Autonomy in a New Perspective* (Giuffrè 1992) 389–415.

60 Niklas Luhmann, 'The Self-Reproduction of Law and Its Limits' in Niklas Luhmann, *Essays on Self-Reference* (Columbia UP 1990).

61 Niklas Luhmann, *A Sociological Theory of Law* (2nd edn, Routledge 2014) 164.

62 H Kelsen, *Pure Theory of Law* (2nd edn, University of California Press 1967).

63 HLA Hart and others, *The Concept of Law* (2nd edn, Clarendon Press 1997).

a stabiliser of positivisation of law can be distinguished from the founding reflexivity connected to the stabilisation of expectations. According to Luhmann, fundamental for the development of law as a system is the development of reflexive expectations. The processing of normative expectations lies at the heart of the evolution of law as an autonomous legal system in society.[64]

Ralf Rogowski distinguishes between internal and external reflexivities in system theoretical accounts of the legal system.[65] Niklas Luhmann's main interest was in reflexive processes inside systems. Within the concept of reflexive law, Gunther Teubner[66] focuses on external reflexivity in inter-systemic links; in his new theory of regulations, reflexivity refers to the law's capability to reflect on its regulatory abilities. The theory of reflexive law is not merely an abstract interpretation of modern law, but it has solid implications for regulatory design. It argues that, in seeking to influence other autopoietic systems which are operationally closed to their environment, the legal system resorts to indirect means of regulation.

The main reasons for this are that legal intervention is dependent on self-regulation within the systems, which are themselves the target of legal intervention. For regulation to be successful, it has to facilitate self-reflection and self-regulation. The forms of law have to shift from substantive to procedural law.[67] This law becomes reflexive when it understands that regulation depends on processes of self-regulation within other social systems. The regulation of other social systems needs a sophisticated reinterpretation of societal prerequisites into legal facilitation. Regulation of other social systems differs because there are no essential internal guidelines for the legal system to constrain any potentially destructive use of regulations. Thus, the legal system has to rely on external sources to assess its impact.[68]

Teubner's well-known regulatory trilemma is a good example of an analysis of the limits of regulation. Hugh Collins describes this trilemma as,

> either the legal rules may fail to have an impact on social practice, or they may subvert the desirable social practices by making impractical demands, or the law may lose the coherence of its own analytical framework by seeking to incorporate sociological and economic perspective in its reasoning.[69]

64 Luhmann (n 60).

65 Rogowski (n 16) 35.

66 Gunther Teubner, *European University Institute Press Series: Law as an Autopoietic System* (Wiley Blackwell 1993) 1–13.

67 Gunther Teubner, 'Substantive and Reflexive Elements in Modern Law' *Law and Society Review 17* (2) (1983) 239–85.

68 Rogowski (n 16) 44.

69 Hugh Collins, *Regulating Contracts* (OUP 1999) 68–69.

Teubner called his account of the trilemma a 'strategy for post-regulatory law', but it is, in fact, a complex account of modern limits and potentials of legal regulation.

Teubner proposes, as a solution for the trilemma, that regulation has to become regulation of self-regulation. Rogowski, in his account of successful legal regulation, adds that self-regulation requires law's own self-regulation as a precondition. Reflexive law means that law transforms itself, so that it becomes capable of facilitating self-regulation in other systems. This means, in practical terms, the development of new forms of law—in particular soft law—and a shift to procedural tools that allow law to influence self-regulation indirectly.[70]

The idea of proceduralism is inspired by a number of debates, among them is the legal philosophy of Jürgen Habermas. In Habermas's opus magnum on law, *Between Facts and Norms*, he suggests that proceduralism is not just an important form of law in modern societies but also part of a paradigm shift towards deliberation as a form of regulation.[71] For Jacques Lenoble, the paradigm shift to procedure in governance results from the failure of the dominant formal and material programmes of modern law.[72] Others argue that proceduralisation is linked to formalisation, and, according to Rudolf Wietholter, a particular form of juridification.[73]

However, the reflexive law transience proceduralism (based on Habermas's theory of modern law as deliberation) is ill suited to an analysis of supranational forms of law-making. OMC leaves the idea of polity behind.[74] Indeed, the OMC is an example of reflexive governance and reflexive new forms of law that facilitate self-regulation in member states.[75]

The Commission uses methods such as recommendations, monitoring and peer review to create new forms of soft law that facilitate self-regulation. These new modes of governance are not legally binding. From the beginning, European Community and EU practice has relied on a range of not-legally-binding instruments, and the European institutions themselves envisaged soft law and self-regulation as regulatory alternatives.

The European instruments and mechanisms that are discussed under the heading of 'soft law' are numerous. They can be categorised in different ways, according to Linda Senden.[76] For example, action programmes created by the

70 Rogowski (n 16) 37.

71 Mark Dawson, *New Governance and the Transformation of European Law: Coordinating EU Social Law and Policy* (CUP 2011) 105–118.

72 Jacques Lenoble and Marc Maesschalck 'Renewing the Theory of Public Interest: The Quest for a Reflexive and Learning-based Approach to Governance' in *Reflexive Governance: Redefining the Public Interest in a Pluralistic World* (Hart 2010) 3–21.

73 Jen Hendry, 'Governance, Proceduralisation and Justice: Some Challenges to the Legal Paradigm' *Law and Critique: Special Issue on Governance, Civil Society & Social Movements 19* (3) (2008) 345–361.

74 Armstrong (n 21).

75 Rogowski (n 16) 190–192.

76 Linda Senden, *Soft Law in European Community Law* (Bloomsbury 2004) 124–132.

Commission and adopted by the Council are preparatory and informative instruments.[77] Some researchers also include green and white papers issued by the Commission among the informative instruments and qualify them also as soft law.[78] In particular, 'communications' published by the Commission are *informative instruments* that are addressed to the wider public, including other institutions, private stakeholders and civil society.

In addition, *interpretative* and *decisional* instruments, whose role is to interpret primary or secondary EU law, are also called 'communications'.[79] Generally, interpretative communications are issued by the Commission and other EU institutions.[80] Decisional instruments are decisional guidelines, codes and frameworks that are also issued by the Commission. Their objective is to support rulemaking in areas where the Commission assists member states.

Soft law also comes in the form of steering instruments, such as Council declarations, joint declarations, inter-institutional agreements and Council resolutions,[81] as are Council and Commission ethical codes of conduct or practice. The Code of Good Administrative Behaviour, adopted by the Commission on 13 September 2000, and which applies to Commission staff in their dealings with the public, is an example of regulation of self-regulation after the scandals of the Santer Commission in 1999.[82] In this case, soft law is used by the Commission to regulate itself and constitutes a European form of self-regulation and reflexive governance of EU law and policy.

3.6 An analysis of the EU anti-corruption report as reflexive governance

In the final section of this chapter, we will apply seven components of the theories of reflexive governance and reflexive law, in order to analyse the Report as a form of reflexive governance. These components are collective learning, active participation, global interaction, innovative problemsolving, proceduralism, soft law and regulation of self-regulation.

The first component of reflexive governance, 'collective learning', is a key characteristic of the Report. One of its main aims is to support different actors to engage in learning best practice from each other. Curial information for collective learning is provided in the section classified as 'the main findings of the

77 B Van Vooren, *EU External Relations Law and the European Neighbourhood Policy: A Paradigm for Coherence* (Routledge 2012) 181–182.

78 Linda Senden, 'Self-Regulation and Co-Regulation in European Law: Where Do They Meet?' *Electronic Journal of Comparative Law 9* (1) (2005) 1–26.

79 Birgitte E Olsen and Karsten E Sørensen, *Regulation in the EU* (Thomson 2006) 179–184.

80 Senden (n 77).

81 Udo Diedrichs, Wulf Reiners and Wolfgang Wessels, *The Dynamics of Change in EU Governance* (Edward Elgar 2011) 26.

82 Angelina Topan, 'The Resignation of the Santer-Commission: The Impact of "Trust" and "Reputation"' *European Integration online Papers (EIoP) Vol 6* (2002) 1–14.

EU Anti-Corruption Report'. This section of the Report analyses the state of corruption in all EU member states and identifies sectors vulnerable to corruption. For example, urban development and construction are sectors identified in the Report as being vulnerable to corruption in some member states; in response to this, the Report suggests that member states establish a specialised prosecution service. Additionally, the Report finds that environmental planning is an area vulnerable to corruption in some member states, in the granting of planning permits, particularly for large-scale projects. Another vulnerable sector is healthcare, especially regarding procurement and the pharmaceutical industry; tax administration is another highlighted area.

Finally, in its thematic chapter, the Report highlights the corruption risks for public procurement in all of the member states, suggesting a far-reaching anti-corruption agenda to tackle corruption in public procurement that covers politics, banking, police, local government and other corruption-related sub-sectors.

By identifying vulnerable areas, the Report suggests learning from negative experience. Furthermore, collective learning is supported by the Report in offering indicators of corruption where it poses a direct risk in vulnerable sectors. Good practices are presented as sources of inspiration for collective learning. An example of best practices is in 'Financing of Political Parties', where Finland is noted to have a 'well-regulated and transparent funding system'. This can serve as best practice in the EU, and other member states can learn from it in improving their own regulation of political party financing.

An area of successful collective learning from best practice is preventative policies according to the Report. The Commission singles out the Netherlands and its 'public sector integrity' initiative as the best model to promote integrity in the public sector, with the aim of preventing corruption in public administration. The Commission suggests that other member states can collectively learn from the Netherlands model to reform their own polices and regulations to promote higher integrity in the public sector.

The Commission also mentions a number of anti-corruption agencies that the EU has assisted in establishing. They include the Slovenian Commission for Prevention of Corruption, the Romanian National Anti-Corruption Directorate, the Latvian Bureau for Prevention and Combating of Corruption, the Spanish Specialised Anti-Corruption Prosecution Office and the Croatian Bureau for Combating Corruption and Organised Crime. These agencies are examples of sharing best practice suggested by the Report for other member states to reflect on when designing their own anti-corruption policy. Those member states that received a recommendation to establish or enhance their anti-corruption agencies are also encouraged to assess the experience and models of agencies mentioned above as best practice for establishing an effective anti-corruption organisation.

The best practices strategy of the Commission can be interpreted as a form of reflexive governance, by which the Report provides a platform for learning between different levels of governance, and in which participants are able to actively engage and participate in dialogue and experimentation, and thereby engage in a process of learning.

The second component of reflexive governance, 'active participation', is a key element of the reflexive governance approach. For collective learning to occur, active participation must take place at domestic, regional and local levels. This component of reflexive governance focuses in particular on civil society to get involved in policymaking and is viewed as key for active participation from a different range of actors. Reflexive governance differs in this respect from the new governance approach, where the Commission and member states are the main actors participating in the process as active participants in developing a certain policy. In other words, the active participation concept requires that the Commission is shifting responsibilities to develop anti-corruption policy and measures to lower levels.

The central concern with 'active participation' is widely evident in the Report, as its overall goal is to involve a wide range of participants from the governmental and non-governmental sectors in shaping policies, laws and regulations at EU, member state, regional and local levels; this foundational element of the Report demonstrates concern for reflexive governance. It does not impose standards, but encourages actors to revisit and redefine their interests and actions through ongoing deliberative processes.

A good example of support for active participation—in particular, shifting responsibilities to local level—can be identified in the Report's thematic chapter. The risk of public procurement at regional and local levels is addressed here, and the Report finds that public procurement at these levels raises particular issues where local authorities have wide discretionary powers that are not matched with sufficient checks and balances mechanisms. Furthermore, the Report finds that, in some regions and municipalities, a strong network of clientele was developed around small interest groups. In some member states, local administrations have developed their own anti-corruption action plans. The Report also shows that, in a few cases, civil society initiatives have had a beneficial effect on the accountability of local administrations with regard to transparency of public spending. Thus, from a reflexive governance theory perspective, the active participation occurs—in particular, shifting responsibilities to local level and local experimentation.

The Report recommends two best practices from member states' local governments' own initiatives. The first example is the 'Slovakia Open Local Government Initiative'. The Report suggests that this initiative is an external monitoring of public spending mechanisms in Slovakia, run by TI, ranking 100 Slovak towns according to a set of criteria based on transparency in public procurement, access to information, availability of data of public interest, public participation, professional ethics and conflicts of interests. The second example is the German model, which has developed 'guidelines for prevention of corruption in public procurement at local level'. The Report singles out the 'Brochure on the Prevention of Corruption in Public Tendering', jointly approved by the German Association of Towns and Municipalities and the Federal Association of Small and Medium-Sized Building Contractors. The Brochure provides an overview of preventive measures against corruption in public procurement at the level of towns and municipalities. The objectives of this German initiative are to enhance codes of conduct to regulate sponsorship and acceptance of gifts, establish centralised authorities for public tenders, increase use of e-procurement, exclude enterprises found guilty of corruption offences and establish blacklists/corruption registers.

From a reflexive governance perspective, these two examples can be understood as attempts by the Report to support local experimentation and active participation at local and regional levels, in order to develop instruments that can prevent and fight corruption effectively. The Report presents two examples of successful local initiatives that other member states can learn from and adapt to their own local initiatives in fighting corruption.

Reflexive governance, in the form of supporting active participation, also characterises the processes that led to the introduction of the Report itself. A wide range of actors participated in the establishing of the Report: these included the Commission, member states, government officials, non-governmental organisations, civil society and academia. The most prominent examples of active participation came in the form of two regional workshops held during the process of preparing the Report. The first regional workshop took place in Sofia, Bulgaria, on 10–11 December 2012, and the second regional workshop took place in Gothenburg, Sweden, on 5 March 2013. In both workshops, there were representatives from the DG Home Affairs, representatives from each of the member states' national authorities, civil society, independent experts and groups of experts selected by the Commission, academia, NGOs, journalists and business representatives. The participants came from a wide variety of backgrounds and actively engaged in supporting and consulting the Commission in preparing the Report. Thus, the process of creating the Report was a result of reflexive governance in the form of active participation.

The third crucial component, 'global interaction', is another key element of reflexive governance. This emphasises the importance of global challenges for local, national and supranational efforts. Both corruption and anti-corruption must be understood as a result of the increasingly global, highly integrated world society and its economy. The global interaction component of the theory of reflexive governance is evident in the Report in viewing its response to fight corruption as part of global efforts.

As illustrated in Chapter 2, this Report is part of a global response to improve legal regulation and policies of anticorruption, acknowledging the influences of international bodies such as GRECO, UN and the OCED on its design and content. The Report itself is a response to pressures on the EU and its member state governments to pay closer attention to informal and corrupt practices after the 2008 global financial crisis. For example, the Report is a means to implement the UN convention against corruption (known as UNCAC). In the light of economic challenges, both in Europe and elsewhere, stronger guarantees of integrity and transparency of public expenditure were seen as necessary after the global financial crisis of 2008. In surveys and opinion polls conducted in research preparing for the Report, citizens responded that they expected the EU to play an important role in assisting member states after the global financial crisis and the Euro crises to protect their economy against organised crime, financial and tax fraud, money laundering and corruption. The Report indicates that the responses by citizens to implement international anti-corruption initiatives were positive, especially in times of economic crisis and budgetary austerity.

Another example of global interaction in the Report is the use of international indicators, corruption indices and, in particular, the TI Corruption Perceptions Index (CPI). The Report makes use of the CPI, firstly to understand the ranking of each of the member states and, secondly, the sectors that are perceived to be mostly affected by corrupt practices. From reflexive governance perspectives, the Report uses global instruments such as the CPI to prepare some of its policy objectives and to double-check its own research, in particular the Special Eurobarometer and the business-focused flash survey. The involvement of international indicators such as this is another example of the Report engaging in global interaction, a key component of reflexive governance.

The Report openly acknowledges that it is an anti-corruption instrument in response to global efforts fighting corruption—and this is itself an indication of reflexive governance, thereby making a valuable contribution to strengthening global efforts in fighting corruption. Furthermore, it engages in reflexive governance, insofar as it makes member states aware of opportunities and obligations in the global fight against corruption.

The fourth element of the theory of reflexive governance, 'innovative problem-solving', also characterises the governance approach of the Report. This is true in relation to evaluation of existing capacities in order to create new solutions to policy shortcomings and enhancing instruments to improve regulations, policy, training, technology and knowledge transfer between member states. The Report suggests that member states find innovative solutions in two additional ways: by learning from best practices from other member states and by creatively implementing international standards in fighting corruption. In fact, the Report itself can be seen as a mutual experience-sharing programme to develop innovative tools to prevent corruption practices.

The Report encourages, in particular, finding innovative solutions in fighting corruption in public procurement—this is a very important area for the EU economy, as approximately one-fifth of the EU's GDP is spent every year by public entities. The Report calls for stronger integrity standards in the area of public procurement and suggests improvements in control mechanisms in a number of member states. The detailed information and specific points suggested for further improvement are given in country chapters, as detailed in Chapter 2. The main section suggests that the Report should raise awareness of the rules among all public-procurement actors and promote a culture of integrity in public service. Thus, from the viewpoint of a theory of reflexive governance, the Report supports member states in reflecting on their shortcomings and introducing innovative new tools and instruments to promote integrity in public service. Research shows[83] that member states are testing new ways and using technology to better collect and analyse data in order to improve public-procurement governance—thus ensuring a better collection of data on procurement—and also to establish contract registries for public-procurement contracts, to establish public-procurement irregularities databases based on remedies and audits, to develop anomalies detection tools and to ensure interconnectedness between public-procurement data and public and business registries and EU funds databases. A good example of innovative use of technology in the member states is the introduction of an e-procurement system. The Commission aimed for all member states to have an e-procurement system in place by 2018; such an achievement, when fulfilled, will help to meet the Report objectives of promoting a culture of integrity in public service, as well as reducing corruption in public procurement. This means that any communication within public-procurement processes must be fully electronic and this is entrenched in the Directive 2014/24/EU of the European Parliament and of the Council of 26 February 2014 on public procurement.[84]

In addition to the four key components of reflexive governance identified above, the Report is innovative in terms of reflexive law. Its approach is characterised by proceduralism, use of soft law and regulation of self-regulation. These features are used in order to support member states to enhance their anti-corruption policies, laws, programmes and agendas to fight corruption.

There are signs that the Report takes seriously the paradigm shift towards deliberation as a form of regulation. It uses insights of the theory of reflexive law on 'proceduralism' that expresses a new understanding of law in modern society. Proceduralism supports the idea that a broader range of actors is involved in the process of policymaking, with a key feature relating to the function of procedure and procedural requirements in structuring participation.

The importance of participatory procedure can also be detected in the creation of the Report. In its preparation, a procedure was followed that involved a group of experts from a wide variety of backgrounds being assembled to advise the Commission. In addition, a network of research correspondents collected and processed information from each of the member states. Furthermore, the Commission held expert meetings with the participation of national authorities, researchers, NGOs, journalists and business representatives. Proceduralism guaranteed the involvement of civil society, and that civil society actors became part of the process in preparing the Report. Furthermore, proceduralism characterises the structure and the process of dialogue between the Commission,

83 European Parliament 'eGovernment: Using Technology to Improve Public Services and Democratic Participation EPRS Author—PE 565.890 (2015).

84 'Directive 2014/25/EU of the European Parliament and of the Council of 26 February 2014 on Procurement by Entities Operating in the Water, Energy, Transport and Postal Services Sectors and Repealing Directive' 2004/17/EC <https://eur-lex.europa.eu/legal-content/EN/TXT/HTML/?uri=CELEX:32014L0025&qid=1552850266102&from=EN> accessed 2 April 2019.

member states and civil society, as well as the involvement of different actors that went beyond the Commission and national authorities, including the findings of civil society in the Report.

Proceduralism also typifies the organisation of the Report itself. The Report's biannual cycle and the request made to the member states to respond to the Report's recommendations and outstanding issues are both procedural devices. The member state response is expected to take the form of a national action plan. A number of member states, including the UK and Romania, have already adopted an anti-corruption national action plan, with a clear timetable and procedures as to what each sector should do in enhancing measures and regulations to address corruption and irregular practices more effectively.

Overall, the nature of the Report is characterised by proceduralism; the procedure for regulation by dialogue used in the Report is not dissimilar to the procedure and the technique of the OMC and new governance in general. The Report is, in fact, a monitoring instrument that observes and reports on the level of corruption and on the measures to fight it in each of the member states.

Another sign of the reflexivity of the governance approach of the Report is the choice of 'soft law' as its main legal instrument. It does not operate with legally binding 'hard law', but instead favours soft law instruments, well known in international and European law, such as 'codes of conduct', 'guidelines', communications' and other non-treaty obligations. Reference to these forms of soft law can be found throughout the Report, including the national chapters, the thematic chapter on public procurement and in particular the recommendations issued for each member state.

The choice of 'Recommendation' as the main legal instrument in conducting a dialogue with the member states is one of the clearest indications of the reflexive governance nature of the Report. Recommendations are suggestions for the member states to take action but are not automatically binding. However, they are instruments of governance because they aim at closer cooperation and coordination among the member states within the EU. In addition to promotion and coordination of national policies, they also aim at contributing to the establishment of anti-corruption as a policy field at supranational level. The Report itself is a major stepping stone in the construction of this policy field.

The final component, 'regulation of self-regulation', is probably the key concept offered by the theories of reflexive governance and reflexive law. It captures the overarching approach to governance taken in the Report. Ralf Rogowski, in his account of reflexive law, suggests that reflexive legal regulation means that legal regulation has to transform itself so that it becomes capable of facilitating self-regulation in other systems. This means, in practical terms, the development of new forms of law that allow law to assist self-regulation.

The way regulation of self-regulation operates in practice can be demonstrated in relation to how the recommendations of the Report were generated. In the first instance, member states were asked to identify their anti-corruption policy shortcomings and engage with the Commission in writing up their own recommendations in the Report. The recommendations that were finally issued for each of the national chapters were officially written by the Commission, but followed closely the reports of each of the member states. In practice, the Commission was inviting member states to reflect on their own policy shortcomings in addressing the issue of corruption and write their own recommendations in the Report. Thus, the recommendations of the Report are truly reflexive, as they simply mirrored self-identified problems and thereby became part of the member states' self-regulations.

3.7 Conclusion

The EU policy against corruption over the past 15 years can be characterised as a mixture of soft and hard law mechanisms in influencing the candidate and member states ant-corruption laws and policies. However, the EU policy against corruption has undergone major transformations, and with the introduction of the EU Anti-Corruption Report, it now displays clear signs of reflexivity. Since 2000, the main instrument in the new governance architecture, OMC, has been used successfully in different policy fields, having a positive impact during the enlargement process, as it helped candidate states in CEE to catch up in their reforms, arriving at a similar level to current member states. However, since the Europe 2020 project was presented in 2010, the EU policy approach is driven through policy coordination in member states. Therefore, one can predict that there will be an increased approach for reflexive coordination of policies at the European level, and thus a more comprehensive transformation from the new governance into reflexive governance approach.

When we applied the theory of reflexive governance to the EU Anti-Corruption Report, the seven components of the theory of reflexive governance were found to be in evidence, characterising its governance approach. Furthermore, the theory of reflexive governance offered key insights into the regulatory nature of the Report's main objective, which was regulation of self-regulation, thereby actively supporting member states to design and conduct their own anti-corruption policies. The theory of reflexive governance showed that the governance approach of the Report is not just new governance, as the pre-2104 policy approach was applied, but reflexive in its nature. This is because it consciously aims at creating a European anti-corruption policy, through supporting and strengthening member state anti-corruption policies, and thus the EU plays a coordinating role. The next part of this book discusses the EU anti-corruption policy, its approach to member states and its strategy in the policy towards member states and candidate states.

Section 2
Country Case Studies

Introduction: country case studies on the UK, Romania and Albania

This section of the book takes a particular lens in considering the findings of the EU Anti-Corruption Report in the member states, and analyses the impact and achievements of the EU in pursuing its anti-corruption policy. The insights are derived from three country case studies on the United Kingdom, Romania and Albania, and this part of the book is accordingly divided into three chapters. The aim of these case studies is to study a long established (soon to be former) member state such as UK, a recent member state such as Romania—in this case one of the latest to join the EU—and a candidate state for the EU such as Albania. In this way we can explore the EU's interactions in supporting and developing anti-corruption policy across different states.

The first part of this section is dedicated to the UK. It explains the recommendations that the Report issued for the UK and how the UK has implemented those recommendations into concrete anti-corruption policy actions. It also evaluates to what extent the UK engages in reflexive governance in developing its anti-corruption policy field and the interplay with the EU in enhancing its anti-corruption policy. Furthermore, it also discusses the impact that Brexit might have in the UK anti-corruption laws and policies and its resources to maintain its anti-corruption international role.

The second part is a chapter on Romania, explaining the Report's recommendations. The chapter offers analysis on the EU approach towards Romania and the anti-corruption policy reforms it has implemented before and after accession to the EU. There is a particular focus on the post-accession instrument Cooperation and Verification Mechanism (CVM), established in 2007. We analyse the efforts Romania has made in implementing the recommendations of the Report and to what extent the country makes use of reflexive governance in establishing its anti-corruption policy field.

The final chapter focuses on Albania, analysing the steps an EU candidate state has taken in developing an anti-corruption policy field. The Albanian chapter distinguishes three phases through which the country has tried to develop an anti-corruption policy after the downfall of the Communist regime in 1991. The focus of this chapter is to evaluate the assistance of the EU to support Albania in its efforts in establishing an anti-corruption policy field and asks whether the interaction between the EU and Albania reveals forms of reflexive governance.

4 The United Kingdom

4.1 The EU anti-corruption report for the UK

The Report country chapter for the UK suggests several steps for the country to take into consideration when addressing the issue of corruption more effectively. The Report highlights that the UK does not have any issues concerning petty corruption; the UK has made positive steps in encouraging companies to resist involvement in corruption acts and in preventing bribing officials overseas through good practice guidelines and rigorous legislation, most nobly under the Bribery Act 2010.

Historically, the UK has a long-lasting tradition in promoting and advocating for high ethical standards in public service and addressing corruption. However, the Report suggested that more rigorous efforts are necessary in addressing the risks of corruption in some sectors—the UK needs to establish more effective measures to prevent and address the potential risks of foreign bribery in particular. The Report encourages the UK to establish sector-specific guidelines to companies in areas that might be at higher risk of being exposed to corrupt acts, particularly in the defence sector, and, in addition, further steps must be taken to ensure more transparent and dissuasive sanctions in out-of-court settlements.

In the light of the banking and large-cooperative scandals in the UK prior to 2014, the Report suggested that the UK needs to further strengthen accountability bank governance. Strengthened features include better enforcement of the sanctions when wrongdoing occurs, and government should ensure that the beneficial owners of UK-registered companies are fully declared. These steps are important in order to tackle bribery and corruption within the UK's financial sector, which came under intense scrutiny after criticism of the Financial Services Authority and its subsequent abolition in April 2013.

The Report finds that the UK needs to pay more attention to encouraging higher standards of integrity for elected officials and address political corruption. Furthermore, the country should make additional efforts to cap donations to political parties, impose limits on electoral campaign spending, and ensure practical monitoring instruments in overseeing campaign spending and prosecuting potential violations. The Report also suggested that the UK should consider lowering the thresholds for the reporting of financial holdings and for the registration of received gifts for public office holders, and provide clear guidelines on what is and what is not acceptable in terms of gifts for Members of Parliament.

Finally, the UK should carefully address the issues classified by the Leveson Inquiry, concerning the legitimate collaboration between the press and the police. There must be a clear time limit set by the UK for the employment of former police officers by the media industry.

4.1.1 The UK attitude to ethics

Ethics are generally defined as a set of principles that provide a structure for appropriate action in accordance with that set of principles. Ethical issues in the UK are perceived to be those issues that are distinct from law, politics or society, that are concerned with right and wrong activities, and that are outcomes for the organisations or individuals.[1] Recent UK history has displayed various examples of unethical behaviour, from the scandals implicating property development and local authority contracting in the 1960s, and the so-called 'Poulson Affair' in 1972, to more modern events, such as the 'cash for questions' furore that saw the end of the Conservative government in 1997 and led to the establishment of the Committee on Standards in Public Life and the drafting of the Principles of Public Life, the 'Nolan Principles'.[2]

It is important to define the UK approach to ethics, as it helps us understand the discussion about corruption in politics. Political behaviours are culturally and socially defined in different ways in different local, national or international settings. Some national cultures see certain forms of political behaviour—such as patronage and clientelism—as corrupt acts, while others see these as acceptable instruments of political association. Even so, there can be value clashes within societies that might constitute different acts as unethical, or even corrupt. This is because values change over time, and the public accordingly change their estimation of what is and what is not acceptable. This has occurred in the case of the UK. In the last 15 years, the public have responded to a series of questionable acts by parliamentarians. The increasingly high levels of concern from the public and the media have led the UK to reform standards of public behaviour. However, such a process has not been as straightforward or fully effective as the Report suggests.

Huberts, Pijl and Steen classify as unethical behaviour those acts that violate the integrity of a public office holder if their behaviour contained acts that can fall under the categories of fraud, corruption, theft, conflicts of interest, improper use of authority, misuse of information or discrimination. Harassment

1 G Little and D Stopforth, 'The Legislative Origins of the MPs' Expenses Scandal' *The Modern Law Review 76* (1) (2013) 83–108.

2 P Bew, 'The Committee on Standards in Public Life: Twenty Years of the Nolan Principles 1995–2015' *Political Quarterly Journal 86* (3) (2015) 411–8.

and bullying are also seen as unethical in the UK. That being said, it is not always clear as to what might constitute unethical behaviour, as it sometimes also falls under the classification of being illegal or inappropriate behaviour. Thus, there is frequent overlap, as ethical issues are regulated by legislation, and there still exist grey areas between what constitutes a gift or a bribe, despite numerous legislative attempts to define borderlines. As is shown for the UK in the Report, a clear list is required, defining what constitutes a gift and whether Members of Parliament may accept certain items or monies.

Considering when a gift becomes a bribe raises complex issues of cultural relativity, especially in the context of the EU—with its 27 member states representing a wide variety of national and cultural diversity. However, there are also common problems that hold particular meanings locally. In other words, inequality and injustice are common problems that occur in different forms at the local level. This is manifested when developing codes of conduct for government ministers, MPs, civil servants and judges. Most codes of conduct include a register of interests, either as an important part of the code or as a separate document. Such a register of interests exists to ensure transparency, mainly where there might be possible conflicts of interest.[3] This issue was also included in the Report for the UK. Therefore, gifts that must be registered include those given to family members—but there again, classifying family can be difficult and complex. For instance, family members might not benefit from the post or position of the registree. From a Western perspective, family members mean the partner and children of the registree, and those who live in the same home. In other cultures, the notion of the family is not only extensive, but it is probable that the head of the family will seek to favour those extended members. Therefore, it would be unrealistic to expect one homogeneous culture or set of principles to be applied across all administrations in the UK, a country fast becoming multicultural.[4]

4.2 Foreign bribery in the UK

The Report for the UK suggested further preventive measurements to effectively address risks of foreign bribery. Furthermore, the UK should consider developing sector-specific guidelines to companies in areas that could be at increased risk. The UK has already implemented the Organisation for Economic Co-operation and Development (OECD) convention on combating bribery of foreign public officials and enacted the UK Bribery Act 2010, which addresses the risk of foreign bribery. This Act is a broad amendment of all UK bribery statutes, and it applies to foreign as well as domestic bribery.

3 R Rhodes, 'Recovering the Craft of Public Administration' *Public Administration Review 76* (4) (2016) 638–47.
4 Rhodes (n 3).

The UK Bribery Act has broad territorial jurisdiction, and it is built upon the most extensive foreign act to date, which was the US Foreign Corrupt Practices Act of 1977 (FCPA). The UK Bribery Act applies to bribery and corruption in both the public and private sectors, and penalties apply for those that facilitate payments or fail to prevent bribery by someone, i.e. a mediator paying a bribe on a business or cooperation. Under the UK Bribery Act, these are strict liability offences. Its implementation created a responsibility to implement, preserve and enforce effective anti-bribery policies and procedures. Moreover, groups will be liable for a bribe paid on their behalf, unless they can prove that they had applied sufficient procedures designed to prevent bribery. The bribery of foreign public officials is also a punishable offence, and the Act contains specific offences for senior company officials agreeing to or overlooking bribery. Under European legislation, companies sentenced due to an offence of fraud, bribery or money laundering are excluded from tendering for public contracts.

The UK Bribery Act 2010 received Royal assent in April 2010 and entered into force in July 2011.[5] The legislation implements the UN Convention against Corruption 2003 and replaces a number of out-of-date statutes in England and Wales, Northern Ireland and Scotland, which also include the Public Bodies Corrupt Practices Act 1889 and the Prevention of Corruption Acts 1906 and 1916. In addition, it also repeals the provisions contained in part 12 of the Anti-Terrorism, Crime and Security Act 2001[6] relating to bribery of foreign public officials and abolishes the common law offence of bribery.

The Act was established to improve the UK anti-corruption regulations and laws in order to prevent the risk of bribery by UK businesses around the world,[7] but its extraterritorial jurisdiction has more far-reaching implications for UK businesses, companies, their subsidiaries and supply chains. In addition to criminalising bribery, the legislation has made a new offence of failing to prevent bribery, although a business can escape possible prosecution if they can prove that it carried out sufficient procedures to prevent the possibility of bribery. All the same, the UK does not have a satisfactory record of prosecuting cases of bribery in international business. This raises some questions; if this legislation does not put enough pressure on UK businesses in the international sphere, this leaves the responsibility of fighting bribery and corruption to less resourced business associates and supply chains in emerging countries.[8]

The Act designed two general offences of bribery: an offence of bribery of a foreign public official and an offence of failure by a business to prevent bribery

5 J Maton, 'UK Bribery Act 2010' *Employee Relations Law Journal 36* (3) (2010) 37–45.

6 Anti-Terrorism Crime and Security Act 2001, 108–110 <www.legislation.gov.uk/ukpga/2001/24/pdfs/ukpga_20010024_en.pdf> accessed 30 May 2019.

7 LM Yanga, 'UK Bribery Act 2010: Implications for Business in Africa' *International Journal of Law and Management 56* (1) (2014) 3–28.

8 The International Bar Association, 'Report of the Task Force on Extraterritorial Jurisdiction' IBA Legal Practice Division (London 2009) <http://tinyurl.com/taskforce-etj-pdf> accessed 30 May 2019.

being conducted on their behalf. Section 1 of the Act[9] creates the offence of bribing another and Section 2 of the Act[10] creates the offence of being bribed; Section 6 of the Act[11] creates the offence of bribing a foreign public official and Section 7 of the Act[12] creates a new offence of failing to prevent bribery. The Act doesn't give an explicit definition of bribery, but it does explain the actions believed to constitute an act of bribery. This means that there are essentially two definitions of bribery set out in Sections 1, 2 and 6. The first requires the intention to induce or reward inappropriate conduct, and the second does not. Thus, there are ramifications for profitable organisations in preparing appropriate procedures and policies, since one definition has clear criminal implications and the other does not. Nonetheless, there is no clarification in the Act as to why the same offence of bribery may be committed under such different conditions. Gift-giving, hospitality and facilitation payments made by organisations or their agents and other liaisons acting on their behalf are prohibited.[13]

The Act enforces penalties on individuals and business organisations found guilty of bribery offences. Under Sections 1, 2 and 6, if convicted, an individual can face imprisonment for a maximum term of 12 months, or a monetary fine, and in some cases, both. Under Section 7 of the Act, organisations can be liable to unlimited fines by the authorities, and civil remedies are not acceptable.[14] What is interesting about this part of the legislation is that it provides a legal defence for a commercial organisation if it can show that it had proper procedures in place to prevent bribery being made on its behalf. In addition, the Act provides a legal defence for bribery committed in relation to the intelligence services or armed forces, where it may be shown that there are arrangements in place to ensure that such action is necessary for the purpose of persons carrying out these tasks.[15]

4.2.1 Risk-based principles for preventing bribery

Under Section 9 of the Act, the Secretary of State for Justice is mandated to publish guidelines about procedures that commercial organisations can put in place to prevent bribery.[16] The guidelines do not suggest any specific procedure and there is no regulatory framework to monitor compliance; they simply set

9 Bribery Act 2010, s 1 (c23).
10 Bribery Act 2010, s 2 (c23).
11 Bribery Act 2010, s 6 (c23).
12 Bribery Act 2010, s 7 (c23).
13 Yanga (n 7).
14 ibid.
15 K Harrison and N Ryder, *The Law Relating to Financial Crime in the United Kingdom* (Routledge 2016) 142.
16 Neil Mcinnes, 'Never judge a book by its cover: Why the first 'Bribery Act' case isn't' (thebriberyact.com, 22 November 2011) <http://thebriberyact.com/2011/11/22/never-judge-a-book-by-its-cover-why-the-first-bribery-act-case-isnt/> accessed 30 May 2019.

out six general risk-based principles, designed to be flexible in order to let the organisations make their own appropriate guidelines and procedures. These guidelines do not impose any direct obligation on organisations. The principles are as follows (Table 1):

Table 1 Guidance About Commercial Organisations Preventing Bribery (Section 9 of the Bribery Act 2010)

Principle 1	Proportionate procedures
Principle 2	Top level commitment
Principle 3	Risk assessment
Principle 4	Due diligence
Principle 5	Communication (including training)
Principle 6	Monitoring and review

Source: Ministry of Justice[17]

The above principles seem to represent an approach to the design of anti-bribery procedures and for policies of compliance purposes. However, from a legal perspective, there are some concerns with both the guidelines and the substance of the law. In discussion about the guidance, the respondents of the International Bar Association note that the principles do not contain the rule of law—a fundamental legal principle which is essential for effective enforcement and legislative control.[18] Its presence would enable commercial cooperation to be more effective in fighting corruption. Furthermore, the Act appears to lack suitable substance. In particular, in Section 6 of the Act, the penalty of criminality is too low. As there is no need for any element of unforeseen intent in order for an offence to be committed under Section 6 of the Act, any expenditure intended to promote a business' goods or services, whether small or large, might be criminalised.[19] Although the Serious Fraud Office has suggested that prosecutors will use their own discretion to ensure that only those abusing

17 Ministry of Justice, 'Guidance About Commercial Organisations Preventing Bribery (Section 9 of the Bribery Act 2010), Response to Consultation CP11/10 (CP(R) 7/11) (2011) <http://data.parliament.uk/DepositedPapers/Files/DEP2010-1705/DEP2010-1705.pdf> accessed 30 May 2019.

18 'Risks and Threats of Corruption and the Legal Profession' *International Bar Association* Joint Report by IBA, OECD and UNODC (2010).

19 'Response of the Working Group of the International Bar Association (IBA) Anti-Corruption Committee to the Ministry of Justice Consultation on Guidance About Commercial Organisations Preventing Bribery' *International Bar Association* (2010).

corporate hospitality and marketing will be pursued, such flexible measures do not stipulate the necessary legal conviction.[20] Thirdly, business organisations will face problems in drafting clear procedures and policies that will be compliant with the Act, as its wording prohibits such expenditure. Regardless of prosecutorial discretion, any promotional expenditure relating to a foreign public official would, in any case, breach Section 328 of the Proceeds of Crime Act 2002, except when a business gets consent from the Serious Organised Crime Agency—which is very unlikely and impractical.[21]

4.2.2 Bribery of foreign public officials

Section 6 of the Act cites that a person who bribes a foreign public official indirectly or directly with intent to obtain or maintain business, or take an advantage in the conduct of business, is to be found guilty of an offence of bribery. The bribe might be given in the form of an agreement of a financial exchange or other advantage to encourage the official to omit the performance of his or her public functions or influence the performance of a role. The Bribe Payers Index (BPI) 2011[22] ranked the UK 8th out of the 28 leading economies whose businesses are least anticipated to pay bribes overseas. The BPI score is on a scale from 0 to 10. A high score suggests that the likelihood of companies from that country engaging in overseas bribery is low. The UK's BPI was 7.9, 8.6 and 8.3 during 2006, 2008 and 2011, respectively.[23] However, there is a suggestion that UK businesses often use bribes to circumvent national laws and regulations, by bribing foreign public officials to win contracts, or speed up the processes of the services that they are demanding. Furthermore, UK businesses allegedly pay bribes to officials in customs and tax revenue authorities, the police, the judiciary, and registry and permit offices.[24] The TI-UK Report suggested that nearly 30 per cent of directors in the UK reported in the TI-UK survey that their businesses used liaisons to avoid anti-corruption laws abroad.[25] These claims are supported by various high-profile cases involving UK businesses, including the famous British Aerospace Systems (BAES) defence contracts

20 'Financial Services Authority (FSA) Anti-Bribery and Corruption Systems and Controls in Investment Banks' *FSA*, FSA/PN/035/2012 (2012) <www.fsa.gov.uk/static/pubs/other/anti-bribery-investment-banks.pdf> accessed 30 May 2019.

21 'Guidance on Proceeds of Crime Act 2002 (POCA) Money Laundering Provisions' *Gov.uk* 7–8, <www.gov.uk/government/uploads/system/uploads/attachment_data/file/257962/30-poca.pdf> accessed 30 May 2019.

22 'The Bribe Payers Index' *Transparency International* (2011) <http://issuu.com/transparencyinternational/docs/bribe_payers_index_2011/31?e=0> accessed 30 May 2019.

23 'Business Principles for Countering Bribery' *Transparency International* (2013) <www.transparency.org/whatwedo/publication/business_principles_for_countering_bribery> accessed 30 May 2019.

24 Jeremy Horder and Peter Alldridge, *Modern Bribery Law: Comparative Perspectives* (CUP 2013) 128–59.

25 Transparency International (n 23).

around the world, including Saudi Arabia, Tanzania and South Africa; the Lesotho Highlands Water Project in Southern Africa; and the TSKJ Consortium in Nigeria.[26] The main argument is that there is a poor record of the UK prosecuting bribery cases in international business.

The cases investigated and prosecuted by the Serious Fraud Office (SFO) are foreign bribery-related cases—except for defence-related contracts, as they are dealt with by the Ministry of Defence. This division has developed a conflict of interest, as observed by the BAES case.[27] The company was investigated for false accounting and alleged bribery. The Saudi Arabia case was eventually dropped on the grounds of national security interest. This was despite the fact that the OECD Convention on bribery mentioned that the prosecution must not be dropped due to national security reasons.[28] One justification was that a shortcoming in the law made it problematic to determine corporate criminal liability, as there needed to be a direct connection with the business involved in the corrupt act—but there were theories that investigations were withdrawing due to lack of political will and blackmail.[29] In the Tanzanian case, it was argued that that restitution could not be made since there were no victims of crime. Leaving aside these allegations, BAES continues to attract contracts from foreign governments.[30] The Director of the SFO put forward an insightful question that reflects a deeper underlying socio-economic motivation in the way that governments prosecute and settle cases of corruption: what is the right approach for a prosecutor dealing with a prosecution of a corporation while recognising that, behind the corporation lie employees, pensioners, customers, families and others whose livelihood depends upon that corporation?[31]

Therefore, the UK's foreign policy on international corporations has been largely impractical and insufficient for fighting corruption. The lack of implementation of anti-corruption measures in the UK is also reflective of the strong corporate lobby in pursuit of international trade and the government's plea for less regulation. Although the UK is a signatory to a number of regional anti-corruption and international conventions, the UK has not strengthened its reputation by establishing its own strategies to support these measures, and this is reflected in the Report.

A report by the Foreign and Commonwealth Office cited that one of the country's international priorities is to help UK businesses win contracts in foreign markets and lobby against regulatory and political barriers.[32] Corporations

26 Yanga (n 7).
27 N Lord, *Regulating Corporate Bribery in International Business: Anti-Corruption in the UK and Germany* (Routledge 2014) 182.
28 ibid.
29 C Fletcher and Daniela Herrmann, *The Internationalisation of Corruption: Scale, Impact and Countermeasures* (Routledge 2012) 144.
30 ibid.
31 Yanga (n 7).
32 R McCourquodale and P Simons 'Responsibility beyond Borders: Responsibility for Extraterritorial Violations by Corporations of International Human Rights Law' *Modern Law Review 70* (4) (2007) 598–625.

are encouraged to self-regulate, using voluntary measures and guidelines—such as the UN Global Compact's tenth principle against corruption, the International Chamber of Commerce rules against extortion and bribery, and the Extractive Industry Transparency Initiative. The UK considered these to be examples of best practice.[33] The government makes a case that these voluntary measures and guidelines play a significant role in trying to discover innovative solutions to problems preventing corruption and other issues encountered by international businesses working in diverse business environments.[34]

The OECD has been critical about the UK's reluctance to prosecute bribery offences, referring to outdated laws, vague fragmentation of investigative and genuine efforts, and overlapping powers.[35] Besides which, the SFO, the City of London Overseas Crime Unit and the Serious Organised Crime Agency all deal with overseas corruption and money laundering cases. In addition, the OECD also showed concerns about the UK's lack of experts and their transparency in dealing with bribery cases. From 1997 to 2008, the UK had not investigated a single case of bribery of foreign public officials[36]; the first conviction was made in 2009. Under enormous pressure, the government issued the Foreign Bribery Strategy in 2010, which set out how the government planned to address and administer the growing challenges of enforcement, and establish a clear legal, regulatory and policy framework for action against foreign bribery.[37] The Bribery Act is part of the legislative reforms towards meeting these challenges. The White Economic Crimes Agency was set up to improve implementation and enforcement efforts. Even so, its mandate is to pay attention mainly to economic issues.[38]

However, since the UK Bribery Act 2010 came into force, there have been suggestions that the Act is insufficiently enforced. As a result, in May 2018, the UK House of Lords appointed a Select Committee, chaired by Lord Saville of Newdigate, to scrutinise the implementation and enforcement of the UK Bribery Act 2010.[39] The Committee took evidence throughout 2018 and will be reporting in 2019.

The purpose of the review, according to the House of Lords, is an opportunity for post-legislative scrutiny, given that nearly all corrupt conduct is now

33 Yanga (n 7).

34 M Berinde and A Andreescu, 'Business Ethics Implementation in the Organizational Culture of Companies' *Annals of the University of Oradea Economic Science Series 22* (1) (2013) 44–53.

35 Fletcher and Herrmann (n 29) 129–30.

36 ibid.

37 Berinde and Andreescu (n 35).

38 J Van Erp, W Huisman and G Vande Walle, *The Routledge Handbook of White-Collar and Corporate Crime in Europe* (Routledge 2015) 94.

39 'Lords Select Committee Appointed to Examine Bribery Act 2010' *House of Lords* (2018) <www.parliament.uk/business/lords/media-centre/house-of-lords-media-notices/house-of-lords-media-notices—2018/may-2018/lords-select-committee-appointed-to-examine-bribery-act-2010/> accessed 30 May 2019.

prosecuted under the UK Bribery Act 2010. On 4th June 2018, the Ministry of Justice published a memorandum of post-legislative scrutiny on the Bribery Act 2010, and the memorandum presents, overall, a positive assessment of the Act.[40] However, it indicates that the Act has been insufficiently used, inconsistently applied, and—so far—failed to meet expectations.

Since the commencement of the Bribery Act, prosecutors have proceeded against 22 individuals under Section 1 (bribing another person) and 13 individuals under Section 2 (being bribed by another person). Of these 35 prosecutions, a total of 27 have led to convictions, of which 17 resulted in custodial sentences. These are unimpressive figures, given the broad scope of the Bribery Act.

Of greater concern are the figures relating to Section 6 of the Bribery Act (bribery of a foreign public official) and Section 7 (corporate failure to prevent bribery).[41]

So far there have been no prosecutions under Section 6 and according to the memorandum issued by the Ministry of Justice in June 2018:

> the reason for the lack of prosecutions under Section 6 of the Bribery Act is not clear, but it may be in part because any individuals perpetrating bribery overseas on behalf of businesses seeking publicly funded business opportunities will typically not be UK nationals or non-nationals ordinarily resident in the UK.[42]

This explanation ignores the fact that the offence under Section 6 may be committed directly or through a third party, and such a justification risks indicating to businesses that such behaviour conveyed outside the UK by overseas agents will not be prosecuted or investigated. This criticism would be less valid if such behaviour had been prosecuted under Section 7 of the Bribery Act.

4.2.3 Improving the accountability in the governance of banks

The Report suggests briefly that the UK should further strengthen the accountability of governance in banks, including stricter enforcement and implementation. The financial crisis of 2008 exposed significant shortcomings in governance within banks and the culture and behaviour which underpinned the banking system in the UK. As a result, in June 2012, the Parliamentary Commission on Banking Standards (PCBS) was appointed to conduct an inquiry into the professional standards and culture

40 'Bribery Act 2010: Post Legislative Scrutiny Memorandum' *Ministry of Justice* (2018) <https://assets.publishing.service.gov.uk/government/uploads/system/uploads/attachment_data/file/713452/bribery-act-2010-post-legislative-scrutiny-memorandum.pdf> accessed 30 May 2019.

41 ibid.

42 ibid.

within the UK banking sector. The Commission was appointed as a result of the London Interbank Offered Rate rigging scandal, which was followed by the financial crisis and a series of high-profile conduct failures within the UK banking industry.

The PCBS published its findings and recommendations on 19th June 2013. The report highlighted many shortcomings and, in its conclusion, stressed that a lack of accountability contributed heavily to the mismanagement of key risks and led to public distrust in the industry. The PCBS made a number of recommendations in relation to improving individual accountability in the banking sector, which were incorporated into the Financial Services (Banking Reform) Act 2013. At the same time, the Financial Conduct Authority (FCA) and the Prudential Regulation Authority (PRA) also released a joint consultation on the implementation of new remuneration rules (FCA/PRA CP15/14), which sought to introduce changes to structure. The regulators saw the two consultations as a package that would reinforce the trend of greater responsibility and accountability across the financial and banking industry.

The collapse of financial institutions—followed subsequently by the spread of the financial crisis—triggered policymakers to re-examine the supervision of banks and to develop more accountability for the restoration of financial stability.[43] Since 2008 there has been a heavy emphasis and much work put into addressing the causes of the financial crisis and the supervisory shortcomings at an international level.

In the UK, the financial crisis began in 2007, with the unexpected failure of Northern Rock, and subsequently spread throughout the UK banking system. This resulted in the collapse of a number of other financial institutions, the bail-out of the Royal Bank of Scotland, and the acquisition of HBOS bank by Lloyds, amongst other failures.[44] The turmoil of the banking and financial sector led to an understanding that there was a loophole in the overall structure of financial regulation.[45] Thus, regulatory reform for banking and finance was placed at the top of the political agenda in the UK. In 2010, the newly elected Coalition Government revealed its strategies for a broad overhaul of the regulatory structure and put forward an ambitious programme for reforms, hoping to prevent potential crises for the future and restore public confidence.

The adoption of Financial Services Act 2012 was the UK's official response to the crises, which came into force on the 1st April 2013.[46] The new legislation saw the split of the Financial Services Authority (FSA) into two separate authorities: the PRA and the FCA. In addition, a new committee, the Financial Policy

43 Nichola Ryder, Umut Turksen and Sabine Hassler, *Fighting Financial Crime in the Global Economic Crisis* (Routledge 2015) 16–18.

44 ibid.

45 Financial Services Act 2012, Explanatory Notes, para 3.

46 Andreas Kokkinis, 'The Financial Services Act 2012: The Recent Overhaul of the United Kingdom's Financial Regulatory Structure' *International Company and Commercial Law Review 24* (9) (2013) 325–8.

Committee (FPC), was established within the Bank of England (BoE) in order to perform macro-prudential oversight functions.[47]

4.2.4 A review of the failures of the financial system

The Labour Government that came into power after the 1997 elections announced its objective to engage in a radical reform of the financial services regulatory structure that would strip the BoE of its supervisory responsibilities.[48] Subsequently, this led to the introduction of the FSA, which became the UK's single regulator. Thus, the Treasury, the BoE and the FSA mutually shared responsibility for financial stability in the UK.[49] The Bank of England Act 1998 and the Financial Services and Markets Act 2000 (FSMA) gave the legal bases on which this multilateral regulatory structure was certified. The joint roles of the three institutions were embedded in a Memorandum of Understanding that created the background structure for co-operation between the three institutions, in order to achieve the common objective of financial stability.[50] The BoE was responsible for maintaining stability of the monetary and financial system. The Treasury was responsible for supervising the multilateral organisation of the three institutions' regulatory framework and for authorising support operations in case of a potential crisis with responsibility for sagacious supervision, in addition to conducting business aspects in assigned to the FSA.[51]

It was observed at the time that the consolidated model of supervision and regulation would be a model for improving the dynamics within the financial services sector. The arrangement and overlap of practicality and conduct of business regulatory goals—rather than a distinction between them—made strong claims that the joint regulatory structure was the most appropriate model in effectively and efficiently resolving situations of ambiguous objectives.[52] Thus, coordinated institutions were considered to be more efficient in evaluating the big picture of the financial industry and increase effectiveness by preventing duplicated support functions.[53] However, post-1997, the climate of financial

47 Javier Bilbao-Ubillos, *The Economic Crisis and Governance in the European Union: A Critical Assessment* (Routledge 2014) 39–42.

48 ibid.

49 Financial Services and Markets Act 2000 'Memorandum of Understanding between the Financial Conduct Authority and the Bank of England, including the Prudential Regulation Authority' (2015) <www.bankofengland.co.uk/-/media/boe/files/memoranda-of-understanding/bank-fca-psr-and-pra-supervision-of-payment-systems.pdf> accessed 30 May 2019.

50 George G Kaufman and Robert R Bliss, *Financial Institutions and Markets: The Financial Crisis: An Early Retrospective* (Palgrave Macmillan 2012) 94–111.

51 ibid.

52 John Armour and others, *Principles of Financial Regulation* (OUP 2016) 513–4.

53 ibid.

stability was steady, and the UK's approach to regulation was considered important in making the UK's financial markets prosperous at the time.

A decade later, during the 2008 crisis, the whole financial system was put to test and found to be inadequate. The extensive mandate of the FSA, which included both prudential regulation and conduct of business, was evidenced to be too ambitious to be efficient.[54] The financial crisis showed that placing financial regulation for the entire financial system into the hands of one institution led to failings of numerous objectives. Conduct of business supervision became the top priority of the FSA, and this was done at the expense of prudential supervision.[55]

In addition, there were serious problems with macro-prudential analysis. A lack of macro-prudential strategy and the failure to utilise macro-prudential instruments to detect systemic risks that occurred were, according to Turner, 'far more important to the origins of the crisis than any specific failure in supervisory process relating to individual firms.'[56] Also, the FSA's approach to macro-prudential supervision was rather unclear. It was mainly dependent on tick box compliance with regulations, while an adequate in-depth and strategic analysis—key in terms of the effectiveness of prudential regulation—was put on the sidelines, consequently leading to significant loopholes.[57]

The crisis highlighted the significant weakness of the coordinated system as a whole, rather than the FSA individually.[58] The multilateral agreement was upheld to have numerous inherent failings in dealing with the financial crisis.[59] The system's successful stability was mainly dependent upon a robust cooperation between the FSA, the BoE and the Treasury. During the financial crisis, it became clear that the association between these three organisations was not working sufficiently. The triple authorities did not have a defined management structure, and there were difficulties with respect to communication between the three institutions. Furthermore, among the most significant shortcomings of the triple structure was that the BoE could exercise a veto authority over the Treasury's recommended programmes, thus making coordinated action between the BoE and the Treasury difficult.[60]

54 Ian P Dewing and Peter O Russell, 'Whistleblowing, Governance and Regulation Before the Financial Crisis: The Case of HBOS' *Journal of Business Ethics 134* (1) (2016) 155–69.

55 ibid.

56 Joanna Gray and Orkun Akseli, *Financial Regulation in Crisis? The Role of Law and the Failure of Northern Rock* (Edward Elgar 2011) 80–82.

57 Samuel McPhilemy, 'Formal Rules versus Informal Relationships: Prudential Banking Supervision at the FSA Before the Crash' *New Political Economy 18* (5) (2013) 748–67.

58 Nigel Clayton, 'An Overview on the Inconsistencies of Approach in Regulating the Capital Position of Banks: Will the United Kingdom Step out of Line with Europe?' *Journal of Banking Regulation 14* (2) (2013) 107–33.

59 ibid.

60 'A New Approach to Financial Regulation: Building a Stronger System' *HM Treasury* (2011) <www.gov.uk/government/uploads/system/uploads/attachment_data/file/81411/consult_newfinancial_regulation170211.pdf> accessed 30 May 2019.

Furthermore, the actual structure of the multilateral arrangements between the bodies was flawed; the structure of the FSA (the authority to supervise individual banks) was different from that of the BoE (the institution with the necessary funds and means to act as the lender of last option upon a possible failure of a particular bank). Thus, even as the BoE had legislative responsibility for financial stability, it had inadequate instruments to deliver on them.[61]

Alastair Darling, the Chancellor of the Exchequer at the time, noted that the problem was that the system had been operating for over a decade in good fashion, and it was not anticipated that there would be a crisis[62]: the financial system had been thought to be operating effectively during that prior ten-year period. The BoE had focused mainly on its monetary policy duties, and even though it was in charge of supervising the financial stability, it never seemed necessary for the BoE to understand the dangerous relationships in operation within the banking system. At the same time, the FSA had mainly focused on its concern with consumer issues, instead of observing systemic risks, while the Treasury had not considered financial regulation as a main priority.[63]

It would be inadequate to say that the failing of the tripartite system was the *main* reason the banking crisis occurred. Most experts argue that the roots of the crisis have a global origin—particularly due to global economic imbalances, a failure to understand and assess risk, the continuing debt figures across the financial system, as well as a failure to guarantee capital liquidity.[64] Certainly, there were major shortcomings in the way the tripartite system treated the causes of the crisis, and these failures have significantly contributed to its magnitude. If a different regulatory model had been in place, it is questionable whether it might have coped better with such enormous forces.[65]

4.3 Political corruption in the UK

There are several aspects open to exploitation in the UK's current political system, and the Report makes the following recommendations in addressing these:

- Capping donations to political parties
- Encouraging higher integrity for elected officials
- Furthering efforts to limit electoral campaign spending
- Developing a practical monitoring instrument to supervise campaign-spending violations

61 Alastair Darling, *Back from the Brink: 1000 Days at Number 11* (Atlantic Books 2012) 20.
62 ibid.
63 ibid.
64 Armour and others (n 53).
65 Armour and others (n 53).

- Setting a clearer time limit for when former public officials can be employed by the media industry

The Report highlights the issue of party finance—a complex problem for reform, debated at great length in the UK political discourse. Sir Hayden Phillips, in his comprehensive review of party finance, found that, in the last 20 years, there has been an intermittent but persistent debate about how to reform the funding of political parties.[66] Furthermore, this debate must be reflected in a wider perspective, based on the ongoing changes in the environment of the political parties according to Johnston and Pattie.[67] Johal, Moran and Williams's study of the post-2008 financial crisis discovered that the continuous crisis of party funding in the UK has opened a window to allow financial interests to have a strong influence in the parties.[68] On the other hand, the Committee on Standards in Public Life found that all parties require their leaders to spend time soliciting those individuals or organisations for the funds they need in order to survive.[69] Reflecting upon the context of the financial crisis and more general paradigms raised by the Committee on Standards in Public Life findings, it would seem obvious that this dependency cannot be beneficial for democracy.[70] As a result, political finance in the UK is tainted by institutional corruption.

The Report also suggests donor-dependency as an issue, but it is important to ascertain the degree to which dependency causes harm. In Fisher's account, this is not always clear, but rather ambiguous regarding party election spending, because even though there is evidence that levels of campaigning are noticeably linked with turnout,[71] the paradigm suggesting that political party spending has an encouraging effect on electoral prosperities is difficult to prove.[72] On the basis that the electoral result of spending appears somewhat ambiguous, we might reason that fundraising is not such a significant activity for parties after all. However, the opposite argument is supported by the fact that an annual donation of £50,000 to the Conservative Party confers membership of the so-called 'Leader's Group', conferring a right to meet the Party leader—at the

66 Jennifer Van Heerde-Hudson and Justin Fisher, 'Parties Heed (With Caution): Public Knowledge of and Attitudes towards Party Finance in Britain' *Sage Journals Party Politics 19* (1) (2013) 41–60.

67 Ron Johnston and Charles Pattie, 'Funding Local Political Parties in England and Wales: Donations and Constituency Campaigns' *British Journal of Politics and International Relations 9* (3) (2007) 365–95.

68 Johal Sukhdev, Michael Moran and Karel Williams 'Power, Politics and the City of London after the Great Financial Crisis' *Journal of Government and Opposition 49* (3) (2015) 400–25.

69 Committee on Standards in Public Life, 'Political Party Finance: Ending the Big Donor Culture. Thirteenth Report' Cm 8208 (London, Nov 2011) 105.

70 ibid.

71 Justin Fisher, David Denver, and John Benyon *Central Debates in British Politics* (Routledge 2015) 405.

72 ibid.

time David Cameron—and other senior figures from the Conservative Party at dinners, post-Prime Minister's Questions lunches, drinks receptions and important election events.[73] It is clear that there exists a disparity in members' access to top-level leadership, arising from the party's methods of securing funding. This raises serious questions about possible favouritism that might involve in return to the most generous donors.

However, the actual harm caused by donor-dependency might not be the most problematic issue. As Lawrence Lessig notes, once a dependence is established, even perfectly benign behaviour can become corruption in the form of trading of influence.[74] Despite a significant legislative overhaul in 2000 by the Political Parties, Elections and Referendums Act, the public in the UK remains concerned about the dependence of the parties on donors.[75] In Johnston and Pattie's account, this concern relates to the possibility of influence—if not actual influence—that donors may have on party policies and programmes.[76] In other words, just the *potential* for an unhealthy donor-dependency is sufficient grounds to distrust the political system. In this sense, institutional corruption occurs within the UK political system and, as a consequence, has an influence on key economic processes. This weakens the effectiveness of the institution and also weakens the public's trust of the institution.[77]

In 2000, the Political Parties, Elections and Referendums Act (PPERA) was adopted to regulate party finance in the UK. The 2000 Act established, for the first time, an electoral commission, regulation of donations and limited election spending.[78] Since it was adopted, various amendments have been made to PPERA, particularly in response to a scandal in 2006, where it appeared that political parties had been receiving loans at lower than commercial rates as a way of avoiding requirements to declare donations, in exchange for which some of the loan donors were put forward as nominations for peerages. According to Fisher, the House of Lords Appointments Committee rejected all nominations. The loans-for-peerages scandal resulted in a lengthy and expensive police investigation, but ultimately no charges were made.[79] Subsequently, regulations were amended to include loans within the classification of regulated donations.

These examples show that campaign spending limits have been a long-standing and dominant feature of British political finance, long before the Report was

73 Holly Watt, 'The Tory Leader's Group Donor Club: "A Chance for Like-Minded People to Talk"' *The Guardian* (2015) <www.theguardian.com/politics/2015/may/04/tories-leaders-group-donor-club-david-cameron-conservatives-dinners> accessed 30 May 2019.

74 Lawrence Lessig, 'Institutional Corruptions' *Edmond J Safra Working Papers No 1* (2013) 15.

75 Fisher, Denver and Benyon (n 72).

76 Johnston and Pattie (n 68).

77 Lessig (n 74).

78 Fisher, Denver and Benyon (n 72) 405–07.

79 ibid.

introduced. According to Ewing's observations, such limits play a dual role: firstly, as a policy for dealing with electoral corruption and secondly as a method of encouraging equality of electoral opportunity.[80] If the first of these two functions is based on old governance regulations against individual corruption, it appears that the second requires additional attention. Fisher outlines the potential significance of spending limits, by suggesting that uncontrolled funds are superior to any other form of resources that go into political life.[81]

Alongside spending caps, transparency is also another key issue of the British political establishment, indirectly mentioned in the Report. According to guidelines from the Electoral Commission, the Political Parties and Elections Act 2009 asks that political parties declare all donations or loans of more than £7,500.[82] According to Fisher, only three donations of over £1 million were made, with a further five over £100,000. Fisher found that the top three Conservative donors accounted for almost £8.5 million.[83] Research by the Edmond J Safra Centre for the Ethics on the Electoral Commission's database found that there were 46 donations, excluding those from public funds, of over £100,000 made to the three main political parties.[84] It is not really clear if these two research findings are comparable, in order to suggest an increase in large gifts over time, but it is a clear indication that the dependence of the Conservative Party on large individual donors went from three in 2001 to eight in 2011, compared with only one individual donating to the Labour Party and none to the Liberal Democrats.[85]

4.3.1 Implementing a donation cap in the UK

The discussion of campaign-spending ceilings, voluntarism in party income and a general lack of regulation on party finance has been dominant in UK politics for over a century, and the Report's suggestion of a donations cap is a reiteration of the general debate in the UK.[86] However, after the introduction of PPERA in 2000, the discussion of increased regulation has been more central to the UK agenda in addressing the issue. For example, Fisher found that more comprehensive proposals, such as far-reaching state funding, would have been more likely to obtain support now than in 2000 when the PPERA was adopted.[87] The (latest)

80 Keith Ewing, Jacob Rowbottom and Joo-Cheong Tham, *The Funding of Political Parties: Where Now?* (Routledge 2012) 256–57.

81 Fisher, Denver and Benyon (n 72).

82 The Electoral Commission, 'Donations and Loans: Guidance for Regulated Donees in Great Britain' (2010) <www.electoralcommission.org.uk/__data/assets/electoral_commission_pdf_file/0019/13708/026-regulated-donees-guidance-final.pdf> accessed 30 May 2019.

83 Fisher, Denver and Benyon (n 72).

84 Lessig (n 74).

85 Fisher, Denver and Benyon (n 72).

86 Paul Heywood, *Routledge Handbook of Political Corruption* (Routledge 2015) 3–9.

87 Fisher, Denver and Benyon (n 72).

Thirteenth Report of the Committee on Standards in Public Life notes that the only safe way to eliminate big money from party funding is to put a cap on donations, set at £10,000.[88] Some agreement around a £50,000 cap had been reached, but later collapsed in October 2007—at £50,000; such a cap would have been significantly higher than in most other systems operating donation limits.[89]

The Report rightly makes the case for a cap in party donations. However, for the UK to agree on this raises some important issues. One of the key challenges for reaching agreement on a donation cap on is how to replace the lost funds, in order that the parties maintain their capacity to achieve their roles within the political system. As a general suggestion for the possibility of eliminating large donations, parties would increase their democratic base by increasing their efforts to involve more political supporters. However, whilst this might provide some compensation, a cap could mean that parties could operate with far greater probity under regulated income, and a fixed cap could be monitored under state funding—private donations tend to put pressure on political parties to provide something in return to the donors.[90] The Committee on Standards in Public Life supports such a shift and has estimated the cost of replacing the lost funding at around £23 million per annum, equivalent to approximately £50 million per elector per year.[91] This figure seems to be fairly modest if it decreases the dependence of political parties on third-party donors and subsequently improves public trust in the institution of government. Such changes would certainly reduce and ultimately eliminate institutional corruption.

4.3.2 Integrity in elected officials

The Report suggested that the UK should further increase the integrity of elected officials. Traditionally, the UK has been considered to be a country maintaining a high standard of ethics and integrity within public life. Almond and Verba stated that the UK enjoys a model of a civic culture for fairness and impartiality, commensurate with active and educated citizens contributing in public life.[92] In fact, integrity and ethical standards in public life in the UK were considered to be of a model standard because many scandals have in fact been hidden from the public. They were dealt with quietly and have been isolated by the public, such as in the historical cases of Stanley in 1948, Profumo in 1963 and Poulson in 1972.[93] The UK

88 Committee on Standards in Public Life (n 69).
89 ibid.
90 Fisher, Denver and Benyon (n 71) 405–07.
91 Committee on Standards in Public Life (n 70).
92 Paul M Heywood, 'Integrity Management and the Public Service Ethos in the UK: Patchwork Quilt or Threadbare Blanket?' *International Review of Administrative Sciences 78* (3) (2012) 474–93.
93 Paul M Heywood and Jonathan Rose (2015), 'Curbing Corruption or Promoting Integrity? Probing the Hidden Conceptual Challenge' in Peter Hardi, Paul M Heywood and Davide Torsello (eds), *Debates on Corruption and Integrity: Perspectives from Europe and the US* (Palgrave Macmillan 2015) 102–19.

made a strong commitment to establishing high ethical standards and integrity amongst its public office holders, and in particular, civil servants are generally noted for their commitment to core values of integrity, objectivity, honesty and independence; these are found in the Civil Service Code (2010). These standards have a long history and can be traced back in the hallmarks of a professional system following the 1854 Northcote-Trevelyan report.[94] The 'Haldane model', based on the eponymous 1918 report, supported the development of close relationships between civil servants and ministers' departments. The constitutional convention mainly held ministers to account for their ministry's actions, but after 1945, the development of expert parliamentary select committees began to also hold other public officials to account over policy matters.[95]

Lord Adonis described the UK as widely seen to be the model of a non-corrupt industrial democracy.[96] This observation has come under increasing scrutiny, as a series of political scandals have unfolded in recent years. That said, most of these scandals have been coterminous with the development of what Hood and Lodge have characterised the 'civil service reform syndrome',[97] a development that originated under the Conservative administration of 1979–1997 and continued with the Labour administration of 1997–2010. However, since the MPs' expenses scandal, the UK is perceived to be more corrupt in its political system. The report by TI-UK reveals that the UK crashed dramatically, from 11th to 20th in the league table of countries perceived to be the cleanest in the world after the scandal was revealed.[98] Numerous recent scandals in the UK have indicated serious faults in the political system, growing particular concerns about the regime for parliamentary expenses, lobbying of politicians by those who could buy access that can influence legislation, policy decisions and spending priorities. A recent report on UK corruption by TI-UK revealed that the British public now view political parties to be the most corrupt sector in the UK and parliament to be the third most corrupt sector.

The expenses scandal was considered to be one of the most controversial Parliamentary events of modern times—these events had a profound impact on public perceptions of MPs and led to the Parliamentary Standards Act 2009,[99] lowering public confidence—not just in those individual politicians involved, but also in political institutions as a whole. The danger is that the public will cease respecting the decisions made by parliament and the government, and no longer perceive them to be legitimate and fair. This poses a serious threat to UK democracy.[100]

94 Kenneth O Morgan, *The Oxford History of Britain* (OUP 2010) 546.

95 P Jones and P Tickner, *Fraud and Corruption in Public Services* (Routledge 2016) 250–2.

96 Jean-Bernard Auby, Emmanuel Breen and Thomas Perroud, *Corruption and Conflicts of Interest: A Comparative Law Approach* (Edward Elgar 2014) 88.

97 Rhodes (n 3).

98 'National Integrity Systems TI Country Study Report United Kingdom' *Transparency International* (2009).

99 House of Commons Committee on Members' Expenses, The Operation of the Parliamentary Standards Act 2009: First Report of Session 2010–2012 vol 2 (2012).

100 Heywood (n 94).

Thus, the Commission recommends in the Report that the UK should address the issue of increasing the integrity of public officials. The debate in British public life has many elements, concerning conflicts of interest, trading of influence, party finance and post-employment of office-holders. Most of the time, this internal debate and the accompanying literature evaluate the issues of ethics and integrity in the UK. The Report takes up these issues and reflects them back to the UK, thereby supporting ongoing efforts of reforming and strengthening public standards.

4.3.3 Corruption concerns in the defence sector

The defence and security sectors have, for decades, been two of the more closed sectors of society in the UK, and there are few accounts of anti-corruption reform of militaries and ministries of defence. A culture of secrecy, close relations with politics, and the sector's size and complexity all help to create an environment where corruption can thrive. In 2016 alone, the total sales of global arms and military services amounted to more than US $374.8 billion.[101] Furthermore, with global defence spending rising, competition for arms contracts is intense, as well as the potential financial reward, making it a prime target for corrupt practices. The UK is the largest arms producer in Europe, and third biggest in the world, after the United States and Russia. According to a new report on global arms sales, issued in December 2018 by the Stockholm International Peace Research Institute (SIPRI), in 2017 the US topped the list, with 57 per cent of total arms sales, Russia ranked second with 9.5 per cent, just ahead of the UK with 9.0 per cent.[102] The UK total arms sales in the last year was about US $35.7 billion (£28.3 billion), rising by 3.3 per cent from 2016 to US $22.9 billion (£18.4 billion). Furthermore, the combined arms sales of British companies were 2.3 per cent higher since 2016, largely due to increases in the sales of UK companies such as the BAES, Rolls-Royce and aerospace components company GKN. According to SIPRI report, seven UK companies were listed in the top 100 in the world, and these companies play an important part in the UK economy with their arm productions and sales.[103]

Significant efforts have been made to reduce corruption within the industry in the UK in the last two decades, yet corruption remains a regular feature in international arms deals. In 2017 alone, four investigations into Airbus were opened,[104] while lengthy investigations were concluded and judicial decisions

101 'Global Arms Industry: First Rise in Arms Sales Since 2010, Says SIPRI' (*SIPRI* 2017) <www.sipri.org/media/press-release/2017/global-arms-industry-first-rise-arms-sales-2010-says-sipri> accessed on 30 May 2019.

102 ibid.

103 ibid.

104 'Airbus Group Serious Fraud Office' *SFO* (7 September 2016) <www.sfo.gov.uk/cases/airbus-group/> accessed 30 May 2019; 'Airbus to Cooperate with France's Parquet National Financier in Preliminary Investigation' (*Airbus*, 15 March 2017) <www.airbus.com/newsroom/press-releases/en/2017/03/Airbus-cooperate-France-Parquet-National-

were reached against Rolls Royce, both UK companies. Furthermore, in recent years, many of the UK and world's largest defence companies have faced significant allegations of corruption. For example, in 2010, BAES was ordered to pay £500,000, plus £250,000 in costs, to settle a Serious Fraud Office investigation into unexplained payments as part of a £28 million sale of a radar and air traffic control system to the Tanzanian government. BAES was found guilty of failing to adhere to accounting standards and was ordered to make nearly £30 million in ex-gratia payments to Tanzania.[105] Furthermore, BAES entered into another settlement, but this time with the US Department of Justice in 2010, relating to similar allegations of bribery in its dealings with the Czech, Hungarian and Saudi governments.[106] Under the settlement, BAES pled guilty to a count of conspiring to defraud the US government and was ordered to paid a fine worth US $400 million. After the settlement with the US Department of Justice, BAES suggested that it will commit to strengthening its compliance programme in the future. In 2014, the arms company, a UK subsidiary of AgustaWestland SpA (now under Leonardo), was fined €300,000—while its parent company Agusta-Westland was fined €80,000—to settle an investigation in Italy into allegations of bribery relating to the sale of 12 helicopters to the Indian military[107]; the Italian court ordered the confiscation of €7.5 million in company profits. In January 2017, Rolls Royce entered into record-breaking settlements in the US, UK and Brazil to settle numerous bribery and corruption allegations, involving its cover-up and use of traders over two decades.[108] The UK and US settlements involved deferred prosecution

Financier.html> accessed on 30 May 2019; David Pegg and Rob Evans, 'Airbus Braces For a Difficult Landing After Corruption Allegations' *The Guardian* (5 November 2017) <www.theguardian.com/business/2017/nov/04/airbus-year-corporate-confessions-difficult-landing> accessed 30 May 2019.

105 'Sentencing Remarks' Regina v BAE Systems PLC, Southwark Crown Court (21 December 2010) <www.bailii.org/ew/cases/Misc/2010/16.pdf> accessed 30 May 2019; Jonathan Russell, 'BAE Pays Fine to Settle Tanzania Corruption Probe' *The Telegraph* (21 December 2010) <www.telegraph.co.uk/finance/newsbysector/industry/defence/8216551/BAE-pays-fine-tosettle-Tanzania-corruption-probe.html> accessed 30 May 2019.

106 Plea Agreement United States v BAE Systems PLC (4 February 2010) <http://fcpa.stanford.edu/fcpac/documents/4000/002716.pdf> accessed 30 May 2019; 'Press Release: BAE Systems PLC Pleads Guilty and Ordered to Pay US $400 Million Criminal Fine' *Department of Justice* (1 March 2010) <http://fcpa.stanford.edu/fcpac/documents/3000/002249.pdf> accessed 30 May 2019.

107 'Finmeccanica: The Italian judge accepts the requests made by Augusta Westland to bring to an end the Indian case' (*Leonardo* 28 August 2014) <www.leonardocompany.com/en/-/finmeccanica-accolte-gip-richieste-agustawestland> accessed 30 May 2019.

108 'Rolls-Royce Settles Bribery Probes in UK, US and Brazil' (*Reuters*, 16 January 2017) <www.reuters.com/article/us-rolls-royce-hldg-fraud-settlement-idUSKBN15025C> 'Rolls Royce PLC' (*SFO*, 17 January 2017) <www.sfo.gov.uk/cases/rolls-royce-plc/> accessed 30 May 2019.

agreements worth about £497 million and US $170 million, respectively, while an agreement with Brazilian prosecutors amounted to almost £21 million.[109]

These cases and examples show that defence sector is especially vulnerable to corruption, and the Report noted that there is a need for the UK to explore developing stronger anti-corruption measures. Since 2000, TI-UK has been a strong advocate for the UK to reform procurements of arm deals and transparency with defence companies. In a recent study, entitled 'Out of the Shadows: Promoting Openness and Accountability in the Global Defence Industry', published by in TI-UK September 2018, it suggested that there are four key components that make the defence sector vulnerable to corruption: secrecy, high-value contracts, complexity of defence contracts and political connections.

Secrecy is a major facilitator of defence corruption because national security considerations may require some confidential spending on defence not be disclosed to the public. Furthermore, the extent of independent oversight on classified budgets also varies widely, as well as the restrictions to accessing information about the budget for classified spending. Without transparent oversight, spending cannot be properly audited, thus enabling corrupt actors to operate with impunity.

Secondly, contracts involving large-scale arms are often extremely lucrative—for example, in 2015, the UK licensed around £5 billion in arms to Saudi Arabia; these types of contracts are accompanied by a plethora of associated contracts in services and support. The rewards for winning such contracts are substantial and have a great impact in the economy and employment; therefore, the competition is intense, and corruption may play a role in facilitating the winning bids.

The element of the complexity of defence contracts is a third important factor because even straightforward defence contracts can take years to negotiate, usually including joint venture partnerships, extensive supply chains and local contractors. Furthermore, the technical nature of defence equipment can also require corporations to switch contractors or adjust to local political developments throughout the cycle of the contract.

Finally, corruption in the defence industry is deeply political, and arms trades are made based on political connections. Government decisions are mostly motivated by the projection of power, foreign policy objectives, the desire to maintain a domestic industry, and retain control in the arms trade market. Decision-making on defence purchases and sales frequently involves senior political figures. Furthermore, the lobbying is significant in the arms trade, exacerbated by the close and opaque relationship between defence companies and government. Thus, it is no

109 'Deferred Prosecution Agreement' SFO v Rolls Royce PLC (17 January 2017) <www.judiciary.uk/wp-content/uploads/2017/01/sfo-v-rolls-royce.pdf> 'Deferred Prosecution Agreement' United States v Rolls Royce PLC (17 January 2017) <www.justice.gov/criminal-fraud/fcpa/cases/rolls-royce-plc> 'MPF firma acordo de leniência com Rolls-Royce' *Ministério Público Federal* (17 January 2017) <www.mpf.mp.br/pr/sala-de-imprensa/noticias-pr/mpf-firma-acordo-de-lenienciacom-rolls-royce> accessed 30 May 2019.

surprise that the top nine European arms manufacturers declared nearly €3.6 billion in defence-lobbying expenditure in 2014. To make matters worse, defence spending is rising in the markets at most risk of corruption within their defence institutions.

The above components illustrate how the defence sector and arms trade are prone to corruption. In the case of the UK, it shows how difficult is to address corruption, and the biggest issue concerns UK arms exports abroad. The UK government prides itself that it operates 'one of the most robust arms export control regimes in the world',[110] and there have been encouraging steps made by UK arms companies to put in place higher anti-corruption and compliance standards. However, there are also many ethical questions around the export of goods to rogue countries and nations that oppress their own people, violate international humanitarian law, and countries with poor human rights records. The Middle East is a major market for the UK, accounting for just under half the UK's total defence exports in 2017. The £5 billion arms deal with Saudi Arabia in 2015 has proven particularly controversial in recent years, and a range of voices have called on the government to suspend the arms exports out of concern that these weapons have been used to commit violations of international humanitarian law in Yemen. Although the UK government's current policy on arms sales to Saudi Arabia does not break any UK law, it raises major questions about the UK's policy towards arms trade, and the vulnerability of the defence and security sectors to corruption.

Overall, the UK has adequate legislation in place to control the arms trade, and the UK Bribery Act 2010 has been another useful tool for dealing with corruption in relation to the arms trade. However, Brexit implications will pose new challenges to legislation in this area. The government has said relatively little on arms export controls post-Brexit, but as the UK forges a new relationship with the EU, it is likely the country will have to amend or introduce national legislation on issues relating to exports. The UK-based not-for-profit organisation Campaign Against the Arms Trade (CAAT) has been raising concern about the potential increase in arms exports post-Brexit[111]; the exporting of military equipment to the world's most troubling governments and military forces looks likely to be exacerbated in the search for post-Brexit trade deals.

110 House of Commons Foreign Affairs Committee, 'The Use of UK-Manufactured Arms in Yemen' House of Commons Fourth Report of Session 2016–2017 (2018) 33. <https://publications.parliament.uk/pa/cm201617/cmselect/cmfaff/688/688.pdf> accessed 30 May 2019.

111 House of Commons Foreign Affairs Committee, 'UK arms exports during 2016' House of Commons Committees on Arms Export Controls, First Joint Report of Session 2017–2019 (2018) 45–50 <https://publications.parliament.uk/pa/cm201719/cmselect/cmquad/666/666.pdf> accessed 15 March 2019.

4.4 UK responses to the EU anti-corruption report

Just as the EU has a different relationship with Romania and Albania than with the UK, so we can also notice a different level of effort made by the EU in supporting an anti-corruption policy in the UK, compared to its approach to Romania and Albania.

The interplay between the EU and the UK in developing anti-corruption policy is different to other EU member states, insofar as the EU mostly supports the UK's efforts in developing their own anti-corruption policy without demanding different standards. This assessment is also reflected in the Commission's recommendation to the UK in the Report.

As a brief reminder, let's recap the topics that the Commission has recommended for the UK, all of which concern ongoing efforts to develop a coherent anti-corruption strategy within the country. These include:

- the risks of foreign bribery and providing sector-specific guidelines to companies in areas that might be at increased risk,
- strengthening accountability in the governance of banks,
- capping donations to political parties,
- providing guidance on acceptable gifts for Members of Parliament, and
- implementing the Leveson Inquiry recommendation on the limits on the employment of former police officers by the media.[112]

In December 2014, the UK responded to most of the recommendations made in the Report by introducing the UK's first ever 'UK Anti-Corruption Plan'. For the first time, the Anti-Corruption Plan introduces the UK's anti-corruption efforts under one cross-departmental national action plan for the next two years.[113] However, it is important to mention that the UK enhanced its efforts fighting corruption not only by responding to the recommendations made in the Report, but also by responding to global and civil society demands—in particular, demands made by TI-UK in 2011 to develop an Anti-Corruption National Action Plan.[114] From a reflexive governance perspective, the Report had an amplifying effect in the UK, which made commitments to address corruption in many policy fields that go beyond those mentioned in the Report's recommendations.

112 European Commission Annex 28, 'United Kingdom to the EU Anti-Corruption Report' COM (2014) 38 final.

113 HM Government, 'The UK Anti-Corruption Plan' (2014) 10–56. <www.gov.uk/government/uploads/system/uploads/attachment_data/file/388894/UKantiCorruptionPlan.pdf> accessed 15 March 2019.

114 'Corruption in the UK' *Transparency International UK* (2011) 16–26 <www.transparency.org.uk/publications/corruption-in-the-uk-overview-policy-recommendations/> accessed 15 March 2019.

The Anti-Corruption Plan (hereafter, the Plan) represents an important step forward in the UK's efforts to fight corruption, notably in that it reveals political will to acknowledge corruption as a serious threat. The Plan was well-received, and civil society organisation TI-UK has given a qualified welcome to its launch, which comprises a 60-page document containing 66 actions.[115] The Plan recognised in its content the threat corruption poses to the UK's economy as well as to society, thus shifting the long-standing narrative that corruption happens only overseas and rarely in the UK. The content of the Plan managed to establish a coordinated strategy to tackle corruption, by drawing widely on findings from several government departments, law enforcement agencies, the business community and civil society research—especially from TI-UK.

Thus, we can say that the UK has responded positively to the recommendations of the Report by taking concrete action; steps taken by the UK reflect successful reflexive governance in the form of regulation of self-regulation. In a report issued by the UK government in May 2016 on the progress of the Plan, concrete steps were shown in implementing the 66 actions that the Plan set out, of which 62 actions having been delivered thus far.[116] The UK's Report recommendations are fully integrated throughout the different priorities in the Plan.

The Home Office has established a new offence of 'police corruption', which came into force on 13th April 2015. This offence, carrying a maximum penalty of 14 years imprisonment, is exclusively an offence for a police officer.[117] The UK has taken some steps here in the recommendations made by the Leveson inquiry to regulate police corruption in some form (recommendations also supported in the Report). However, time limits on the employment of former police officers by the media are yet to be clearly outlined. The other recommendation concerns the conduct of MPs on the registration of received gifts and clear guidance on acceptable gifts; the Plan's May 2016 progress report suggests that the House of Commons approved the revised Guide to the Rules relating to the conduct of Members on 17th March 2015.[118] Furthermore, the UK has taken steps in ensuring that the beneficial owners of UK-registered companies are declared, which was also a brief recommendation in the Report. The

115 R Barrington, 'Reflections on a Decade in the Fight against Corruption and the Coming'. *Transparency International UK* (2019) <www.transparency.org.uk/reflections-on-the-fight-against-corruption/> accessed on 15 March 2019.

116 'Progress Update on the UK Anti-Corruption Plan' HM Government (2016) 2–7 <www.gov.uk/government/uploads/system/uploads/attachment_data/file/522802/6.1689_Progress_Update_on_the_UK_Anti-Corruption_Plan_v11_WEB.PDF> accessed 15 March 2019.

117 Home Office, 'Annual Report and Accounts 2014–2015' (2015) 9 <www.gov.uk/government/uploads/system/uploads/attachment_data/file/441284/HO_AR_14-15_print.pdf> accessed 15 March 2019.

118 House of Commons, 'The Code of Conduct and The Guide to the Rules relating to the Conduct of Members' Chapter 1 and 2 (2015) <www.publications.parliament.uk/pa/cm201516/cmcode/1076/107601.htm>

May 2016 progress report suggests that the UK will implement a central register of UK company beneficial ownership information after the necessary primary and secondary legislation are in place.[119]

The Plan is a clear success story of reflexive governance through the Report. The government's May 2016 progress report responds positively to TI-UK recommendations and strengthens communication and involvement of society in policymaking.[120] The Plan takes into account the sound research produced by TI-UK in the Defence Companies Anti-Corruption Index 2015, in which TI-UK provided an analysis of what the biggest defence companies—and fail to do—to prevent corruption.

Overall, the UK has responded positively to the recommendations of the Commission's Report and has exhibited promising efforts in making use of the reflexive governance theory. This is in striking contrast to the widespread negative attitude in the UK towards EU policies.

4.5 Post-Brexit: the UK anti-corruption initiatives

Since the UK voted to leave the European Union on June 2016, Brexit has dominated the political scene and will continue to do so in the coming years. The ever-complicated divorce from EU in combination with economic uncertainty and the ongoing domestic political instability that has shaken the UK since Brexit are not the best of conditions for fighting corruption. So far, it appears that the UK government priorities and resources will be allocated to other policy areas and searching for new international partners and trade agreements with states that do not have the same anti-corruption standards. Therefore, it is possible that the UK's anti-corruption standards may decline until the UK finds its new place in the world.[121]

So far, the UK has maintained an exemplary standing in its anti-corruption laws and policies: for example, the Bribery Act 2010, the UK Anti-Corruption Strategy 2017–2021,[122] and the Global Anti-Corruption Summit hosted by the UK Government in 2016, which have all been acclaimed by the EU, the OECD and TI.[123] However, there are serious reasons for concerns about the

119 HM Government (n 118).

120 ibid.

121 Lorenzo Pasculli, 'Corruptio Legis: Law as a Cause of Systemic Corruption: Comparative Perspectives and Remedies also for the Post-Brexit Commonwealth' in *Proceedings of 6th Annual International Conference on Law Regulations and Public Policy (LRPP 2017) 5–6 June 2017 Singapore (2017)* 189–97.

122 HM Government, 'UK Anti-Corruption Strategy 2017-2022' (2017) <www.gov.uk/government/publications/uk-anti-corruption-strategy-2017-to-2022> accessed 27 February 2019.

123 'Fighting Corruption: A Manifesto for a More Secure, Prosperous and Resilient UK' *Transparency International* (2017) <www.transparency.org.uk/publications/ge-2017-manifesto/> accessed 27 February 2019.

negative impact that Brexit may have on the UK's commitments to address corruption and its international influence in upholding anti-corruption standards.[124]

Firstly, in order for the UK to retain its competitiveness, it must find new trade opportunities in its post-Brexit phase. The conditions may arise that banks and businesses put pressure on the government to adopt policies of deregulation in various areas, including those against foreign officials covered in the Bribery Act.[125] So far, the UK government has promised to keep intact the high regulatory standards and anti-corruption measures—the risk of backsliding on these standards has been closely monitored during the immediate post-Brexit period by media watchdogs and NGOs such as Global Witness and TI-UK. Secondly, to date, Brexit negotiations have diverted the government's attention and resources away from the anti-corruption agenda to some extent, and, during the transition period, resources will be focused on restructuring the trade agreement.[126] For example, the seemingly endless delay on long overdue promised UK Anti-Corruption Strategy can be interpreted to mean that fighting corruption is not a current priority. Another example of the descaling of importance of the anti-corruption agenda is the closing of the case on Rolls-Royce by the Serious Fraud Office in February 2019 after the company entered into a Deferred Prosecution Agreement deal. As part of the agreement, no individual prosecutions were brought, and a £671 million deal was agreed jointly with the Serious Fraud Office and the authorities in Brazil and the U.S.A., following allegations of conspiracy to corrupt and failure to prevent bribery by Rolls-Royce in ten countries, including China, India, Indonesia and Thailand.[127] In the post-Brexit phase, there may be more similar cases, and a failure to prosecute gives the impression that fighting corruption is no longer a high priority for the UK.

Since Brexit, the main issue for concern for the government is the allocation and prioritising of resources, and thus, anti-corruption policies may slip down the list of UK government priorities. However, the country has so far maintained its anti-corruption commitments, in particular with the adoption of the 'Anti-Corruption Strategy 2017–2022' issued in 2017, and the launch of the

124 D Hough, 'Will Brexit Britain Lose Its Lead in the Fight Against Corruption?' *The Conversation* (2018) <https://theconversation.com/will-brexit-britain-lose-its-lead-in-the-fight-against-corruption-72128> accessed 27 February 2019.

125 'Brexit: What Next for the Anti-Corruption Movement in the UK?' *Corruption Watch* (2016) <www.cw-uk.org/single-post/2016/07/05/Brexit-What-Next-for-the-Anti-Corruption-Movement-in-the-UK> accessed 27 February 2019.

126 R Barrington, 'What Does Brexit Mean For the UK's Fight Against Corruption?' (2016) <www.transparency.org.uk/what-does-brexit-mean-for-the-uks-fight-against-corruption/> accessed 27 February 2019.

127 'UK's Serious Fraud Office drops investigations of Rolls Royce individuals, GSK' *Reuters* (2019) <www.reuters.com/article/britain-sfo/uks-serious-fraud-office-drops-investigations-of-rolls-royce-individuals-gsk-idUSL5N20H3D1> accessed 27 February 2019.

International Anti-Corruption Coordination Centre in July 2017.[128] Furthermore, two new important pieces of legislation have been recently enacted: the Criminal Finances Act 2017, and the Money Laundering, Terrorist Financing and Transfer of Funds Regulations 2017.[129] These pieces of legislation were introduced to fight money laundering, corruption and terrorist financing more effectively, and they are also aimed at addressing illegal campaign financing. In this legislation, two new corporate offences have been created regarding failure to prevent facilitation of tax evasion, which has been a serious concern for the UK.

Furthermore, in January 2018, the FCA established the Office for Professional Body Anti-Money Laundering Supervision to oversee the effectiveness of the anti-money laundering supervisory arrangements of more than 20 professional bodies. The UK has also announced the establishment of a new national economic crime centre to deal with high-profile fraud and corruption. Furthermore, in May 2018, the UK Parliament voted in favour of requiring any British overseas territory that has not already done so to introduce public registers that reveal the individuals behind companies based there by the end of 2020.[130] TI-UK and Global Witness have strongly advocated for years for the UK government to require British overseas territories to introduce such public registers of beneficial ownership; research finds the UK's overseas territories and Crown Dependencies' financial systems are widely used in money laundering and grand corruption cases. Moreover, almost 70 per cent of corruption cases surveyed by the World Bank relied on anonymously owned companies' help to obscure what they were doing, and the UK's overseas territories were the most popular destination for the corrupt to hide their wealth.[131] Furthermore, 75 per cent of UK properties under investigation for corruption in the last ten years were registered with offshore shell companies.[132] It must be noted that the 5th EU Anti-Money Laundering Directive has already made a public register a requirement for EU

128 HM Government, 'Home Secretary Announces New National Economic Crime Centre to Tackle High Level Fraud and Money Laundering' (2017) <www.gov.uk/government/news/home-secretary-announces-new-national-economic-crime-centre-to-tackle-high-level-fraud-and-money-laundering> accessed 27 February 2019.

129 J Harvey, 'The Limitation of the Law in Relation to Financial Crime: Back to Basics' *Journal of Criminal Law 82* (3) (2018) 193.

130 'UK overseas territories to open up ownership registers' *Financial Times* (2018) <www.ft.com/content/5a924560-4d45-11e8-8a8e-22951a2d8493> accessed 1 March 2019.

131 'Unexplained wealth orders: How to catch the corrupt and corrupt money in the UK' *Transparency International* (2017) <www.transparency.org/news/feature/unexplained_wealth_orders_how_to_catch_the_corrupt_and_corrupt_money_in_the> accessed 1 March 2019.

132 'The Companies We Keep: What the UK's Open Data Register Actually Tells Us About Company Ownership' *Global Witness* (2018) <www.globalwitness.org/en/campaigns/corruption-and-money-laundering/anonymous-company-owners/companies-we-keep/#chapter-0/section-1> accessed 10 March 2019.

countries, and the UK decided to introduce one in 2015, but this is new positive development for the UK overseas territories.[133]

The following chapter will assess the next case study on Romania and explains the recommendations of the EU Anti-Corruption Report issued to Romania in 2014. Furthermore, the next chapter offers an analysis of the EU approach towards Romania in support anti-corruption reforms and to what extent Romania makes use of reflexive governance in establishing its anti-corruption policy field. In the case of UK as an old (former) Member State, it was evident that the UK made use of reflexive governance approach, and it involved the main anti-corruption civil society actors such as TI-UK and Global Witness in its anti-corruption policymaking. In the case of the Romania as of the latest Members that joined the EU 2007, however, corruption was prior to its accession and still is now that the country it's over ten years a Member States of the Union as the main topic of the discussion between the EU and the Romania governments—the following chapter will show the interaction between the two in developing and anti-corruption policy field and whether the EU Anti-Corruption Report had a positive impact in the country.

133 N Mugarura, 'The Implications of Brexit for UK Anti-Money Laundering Regulations' *Journal of Money Laundering Control 21* (1) (2018) 5.

5 Romania

5.1 The EU anti-corruption report for Romania

The Report country chapter for Romania finds that petty and political corruption remain a systemic problem. Whilst some anti-corruption reforms have been pursued over the years, their results proved to be ineffective and easily reversible. The Report finds that when it comes to prosecution of high-level corruption cases in Romania, the political will to address corruption and promote high standards of integrity has been inconsistent.[1] Nevertheless, there have been some positive steps made in the efforts to fight the systemic problem of corruption. The Commission suggested that Romania should build on the progress that it has made so far under the Cooperation and Verification Mechanism (CVM).

The Report identified four key areas for further improvement in Romania, mainly concerned with the dysfunctional impact that corruption has on the judiciary, politics, the healthcare system and public procurement (this last, an area of particular interest for the Commission in all of the EU member states[2]).

5.1.1 The judicial system

According to Marian Enache, the judicial system in Romania is vulnerable to corrupt practices.[3] Despite the structural development that the judiciary went through as part of the EU integration process, Romania still cannot fully meet the standards of efficiency, independence and impartiality required of a member of the EU. Romania's justice system, together with the political system, according to Martin Mendelski,[4] remains the most visible sectors prone to corrupt practices. Further reforms and restructuring of the judiciary to prevent corruption and

1 Alan T Belasen and Roxana Toma, *Confronting Corruption in Business: Trusted Leadership, Civic Engagement* (Routledge 2016) 127–66.

2 Gustavo Piga and Tunde Tatrai, *Public Procurement Policy* (Routledge 2016) 1–9.

3 Marian Enache, 'The Evolution of the Justice Reform in Romania' *US-China Law Review 9* (3) (2012) 175–83.

4 Martin Mendelski, 'EU-Driven Judicial Reforms in Romania: A Success Story?' *East European Politics 28* (1) (2012) 23–42.

prosecute high corruption cases are stipulated in the Report, as well as in the January 2016 CVM report. The need to develop and implement a set of adequate corruption-combating policies and strategies in the justice system has become increasingly imperative, and reforming the justice system has been a large part of the EU and Romanian relationship in preparing the country for EU membership.[5] According to Sebastian Văduva—despite the many studies and strategies supported by the Commission in Romania—according to the public and NGOs, the judiciary is still far from ensuring its integrity and independence.[6]

As a result, the Report country chapter for Romania suggested that the country must ensure all necessary guarantees remain in place to protect the stability, independence and maintenance of the track record of anti-corruption institutions and the judiciary, with regard to non-partisan investigations and effective court proceedings concerning high-level corruption cases[7]—in particular, those of elected and appointed officials. Furthermore, the Report suggested implementing preventive measures, accompanied by an effective sanctioning regime to strengthen the integrity standards in the judiciary. This would include all the relevant stakeholders in the judicial system, such as the Superior Council of Magistracy, the Judicial Inspection, magistrates' associations, courts and prosecutors' offices.[8]

Michael Hein observes that Romania has been going through two essential phases in reforming the judicial system: firstly, the enactment of the new Constitution of Romania in 1991, and secondly, the accession of Romania to the EU.[9] The EU has been an external driver for judicial reforms in Romania, especially since the introduction of the CVM in December 2006. The judicial reform actions were subjected to benchmark-based monitoring since the CVM was introduced, focussing on several projects of judicial strengthening. These projects included the judicial capacity building of specific judicial bodies, the unification of the jurisprudence of courts and prosecutor offices, strengthening the public ministry's institutional capacity, improving the judicial statistics system, strengthening the probation system, and improving management and media training for magistrates.[10] However, the Commission has mixed views in its evaluation of judicial improvement in the post-accession phase, noted by the CVM, the Report and researchers in the anti-corruption field.[11] Meanwhile, strengthening the

5 Anitta M Hipper, *Beyond the Rhetorics of Compliance: Judicial Reform in Romania* (Springer 2015) 17–33.

6 Sebastian A Văduva, *From Corruption to Modernity: The Evolution of Romania's Entrepreneurship* (Springer 2016) 4–24.

7 Radu Carp, 'The Struggle for the Rule of Law in Romania as an EU Member State: The Role of the Cooperation and Verification Mechanism' *Utrecht Law Review 10* (1) (2016) 1–16.

8 Lin A Hammergren, *Justice Reform and Development: Rethinking Donor Assistance to Developing* (Routledge 2014) 118–28.

9 Michael Hein, 'The Fight against Government Corruption in Romania: Irreversible Results or Sisyphean Challenge?' *Europe-Asia Studies 67* (5) (2015) 747–76.

10 Hammergren (n 8) 118–28.

11 Mendelski (n 4).

judiciary continues to be an area in which the EU asks for more support, in regard to human resources and integrity shortcomings in the Romanian judicial system. The third section of this chapter will analyse in more depth the issue of corruption in Romania's judicial system and draw on analysis of the historical factors in greater depth.

5.1.2 The political system

According to Iuliana Precupetu, the political system has similar corruption problems to the judicial system and has dominated Romanian political discourse for many years, becoming a structural feature of post-socialist transformation in Romania.[12] The large majority of the political elite has continuously opposed the prosecution and conviction of corrupt offenders in Romania. After a long constitutional conflict that seriously inhibited the fight against political corruption between 2006 and 2009, law enforcement agencies started to experience some success in prosecuting high government officials who misused their public power for personal gain. Nevertheless, the extent of political corruption remains consistently high, and punishing public office holders against corruption remains relatively low.[13]

Thus, the Report country chapter suggested that Romania should implement a comprehensive code of conduct for elected officials and ensure consistent accountability tools and sanctions for corrupt practices, conflicts of interest and incompatibilities.[14] Furthermore, Romania should consider developing an ethical code for political parties and take into consideration establishing an ethical pact between political parties to encourage higher standards of integrity. Romania should also ensure that all the decisions concerning lifting of immunities are rational and taken promptly.[15] Finally, the political elite should avoid obstructing justice and fully cooperate with law enforcement.

Alina Mungiu-Pippidi identifies three sets of factors with regard to high-level corruption in the political system.[16] Firstly, political culture is regarded as one of the main factors that cause corruption in Romania, to the extent in which it predetermines the ways that political elites socialise.[17] Secondly, researchers find

12 Dirk Tänzler, Konstadinos Maras and Angelos Giannakopoulos, *The Social Construction of Corruption in Europe* (Ashgate 2012) 6–8.

13 Antoaneta Dimitrova, 'The Effectiveness and Limitations of Political Integration in Central and Eastern European Member States: Lessons from Bulgaria and Romania', 'Maximizing the Integration Capacity of the European Union: Lessons of and Prospects for Enlargement and Beyond' MAXCAP Working Paper Series No 10 (June 2015).

14 Ulrich Sedelmeier, 'Anchoring Democracy from Above? The European Union and Democratic Backsliding in Hungary and Romania after Accession' *Journal of Common Market Studies 52* (1) (2014) 105–21.

15 ibid.

16 A Mungiu-Pippidi, 'How Media and Politics Shape Each Other in the New Europe' *Romanian Journal of Political Science Romanian Academic Society 8* (1) (2008) 69–78.

17 Åse B Grødeland, 'Public and Elite Perceptions of Supranational Courts: The European Perspective' *Review of Central and East European Law 39* (1) (2014) 41–94.

that the influence of Communist legacies explains the degree of corruption: the governance nature that was more autocratic, undemocratic, unaccountable and lacking in transparency.[18] Thirdly, poor economic development in Romania is also observed as a central explanatory factor for corruption. Poor wages for civil servants, difficulties in political party funding and the lack of sufficient resources for anti-corruption policies lead to a higher degree of political corruption in Romania.[19] These three factors continue to contribute to the high level of corruption in the political system in Romania, and the Report acknowledges that Romanian political culture is characterised by an antagonistic relationship between the state and the society, in which the political elites are perceived as misusing public office. As a result, the Commission suggested further action is required. In the next section of this chapter, we will consider corruption in the political system and analyse the challenges that have occurred in the fight against corruption in the Romanian political system since the introduction of the CVM in 2006.[20]

5.1.3 Healthcare

The healthcare system is characterised as a sensitive issue in Romania because of bad management and underfunding. Since the collapse of Communism, there has been increasing use of informal payments and corruption to get access to healthcare treatment in the country.[21] Healthcare is one of the sectors where informal payments are often used, and this has been noticed by the Commission and the literature to be problematic because of the social impact on Romanian society. Patients give doctors, nurses and hospital staff money or gifts for services in exchange for health services.[22] The country has severe problems with informal payments in the public healthcare system, and the Report suggested further action to tackle this, implementing more effective strategies such as improving the wages and working conditions for medical staff.[23]

Furthermore, Romania should ensure operational independence of the Integrity Agency within the Ministry of Health, allowing this internal agency to supervise budget and procurement and ensure that the agency's findings are

18 Richard Connolly, *The Economic Sources of Social Order Development in Post-Socialist Eastern Europe* (Routledge 2013) 141–75.

19 Tatiana Kostadinova, *Political Corruption in Eastern Europe: Politics After Communism* (Lynne Rienner 2012) 33–34.

20 Michael Baun and Dan Marek, *The New Member States and the European Union: Foreign Policy and Europeanization* (Routledge 2013) 175–89.

21 Andrada Moldovan and Steven Van de Walle, 'Gifts or Bribes? Attitudes on Informal Payments in Romanian Health Care' *Public Integrity 15* (4) (2013) 383–99.

22 ibid.

23 Tetiana Stepurko, Milena Pavlova, Irena Gryga and Wim Groot, 'Informal Payments for Health Care Services—Corruption or Gratitude? A Study on Public Attitudes, Perceptions and Opinions in Six Central and Eastern European Countries' *Communist Post-Communist Studies 46* (4) (2013) 419–31.

followed up.[24] In other words, the Ministry should engage in regulation of self-regulation more effectively. This is a clear example of the Report supporting Romania to engage in a reflexive governance exercise.

The Romanian health system suffers from a range of difficulties, including extensive management deficiencies, absent or inadequate medical equipment, and limited or no access to medical care in rural areas. Empirical evidence suggests that the use of informal payments is widespread in the country, and interactions between health professionals are filled with informal payments, constituting corruption by patients.[25] Employees in medical centres and hospitals in Romania also act as gatekeepers to health facilities, treatments, and non-medical care such as food or clean sheets. In Romania, offering gifts and even paying bribes is, therefore, quite common practice within the healthcare system. Thus, the distinction between a gift and a bribe is often quite narrow,[26] and the same behaviours that are observed as corruption by some researchers may be interpreted as acts of gratitude by others, unconnected with expectations of preferential treatment. The healthcare sector-related research often uses the concept of 'informal payments' to label the exchange of money, gifts or services between patients or their families and healthcare personnel.[27] Later in this chapter, we will investigate the exchange of informal payments in Romania, and the factors behind common practices such as these, as well as the Report's approach to addressing them.

5.1.4 Public procurement

As demonstrated in Chapter 2, the Commission has given prominence to public procurement in the Report in assessing costs of corruption for the EU economy.[28] These costs vary considerably between each member state, and in Romania, public procurement accounted for 11 per cent of GDP.[29] The Report, together with the Europe 2020 strategy, considers tackling corruption in public procurement as an important factor to improve the business environment and to enhance the performance of businesses in the EU.[30] In line with this focus on public procurement, the Report country chapter for Romania suggests public procurement as a main area of concern.

24 European Commission, 'Annex 23: Romania to the EU Anti-Corruption Report' COM (2014) 38 final <http://ec.europa.eu/dgs/home-affairs/what-we-do/policies/organized-crime-and-human-trafficking/corruption/anti-corruption-report/docs/2014_acr_romania_chapter_en.pdf> accessed 30 May 2019.

25 Stepurko, Pavlova, Gryga and Groot (n 23).

26 N Cohen, 'Informal Payments for Health Care—The Phenomenon and its Context' *Health Economics, Policy and Law* 7(3) (2012) 285–308.

27 Stepurko, Pavlova, Gryga and Groot (n 23).

28 Antionette Calleja, *Unleashing Social Justice through EU Public Procurement* (Routledge 2016) 107–25.

29 Piga Tatrai (n 2).

30 ibid.

The Report suggested that Romania should consider developing uniform and effective prevention tools within contracting authorities and public-procurement supervisory bodies, with a particular focus on conflicts of interest. Furthermore, Romania should ensure that there is a systematic monitoring and transparency of the implementation of large-scale public contracts, especially those projects that are EU-funded. There should be a constancy of the legal framework on conflicts of interests and the incompatibility rules related to elected representative officials, and Romania should develop a more efficient system to detect and sanction conflicts of interest in public procurement. Romania should also establish an effective control mechanism targeting the allocation of government funds to local administrations and state-owned companies by implementing safeguards against discretionary allocation to the detriment of the public interest—i.e. strengthening anti-corruption tools for public-procurement processes within state-owned companies.

The Report and related research find that public procurement is a sector vulnerable to corruption in Romania, as well as EU funds in particular. Mihály Fazekas argues that external funds (such as EU funds) may deteriorate the quality of government and as a result increase the risk of corruption in member states.[31] Fazekas suggest that there are three reasons for this: firstly, EU funds are often spent on public projects, such as road construction, where public discretion is fairly high and spending is more likely linked to corruption than non-discretionary spending. Secondly, EU funds offer a large pool of public resources for rent extraction of public agencies. Thirdly, EU funds weaken the link between domestic civil society, taxation and policy performance. Some of these vulnerabilities have been demonstrated in Romania, and we will evaluate and analyse these issues in greater depth later in this chapter.[32]

To sum up, the Report's recommendations for Romania's next steps are mainly focused on the four key areas we have outlined above:

- Pursuing the investigations and effective court proceedings of high-level corruption cases and strengthening `the integrity standards in the judiciary;
- Implementing a comprehensive code of conduct for elected officials, developing an ethical code for political parties, and ensuring that lifting of immunities are taken promptly to avoid obstruction to justice;
- Addressing corruption in the healthcare system and implementing effective strategies to reduce the level of informal payments; and
- Establishing an effective control mechanism and procurement supervisory bodies concerning the allocation of government funds to local administrations, and making state-owned companies public.

31 Mihály Fazekas and others, *Are EU Funds a Corruption Risk? The Impact of EU Funds on Grand Corruption in Central and Eastern Europe* (Corruption Research Centre 2014) 1–23.
32 ibid.

In the following section, we will analyse the recommendations for Romania made in the Report in the light of the long-term efforts and interactions of the Commission and the various Romanian governments that have focused on fighting corruption. It will become apparent that the four key areas addressed in the Report are linked to ongoing discussions as part of special monitoring of Romanian policy developments; of particular relevance in this context is the CVM.

5.2 The EU anti-corruption strategy towards Romania—the CVM

During the pre-accession stage, Romania was regularly ranked as one of the most corrupt countries in Central and Eastern Europe (CEE) and one of the most corrupt EU candidate countries at the time according to TI-UK. As a result, Romania was considered to be a challenging case for accession to the EU and regularly lagged behind all other EU candidate states. Despite this, Romania received full EU membership in January 2007.

The accession of Romania and Bulgaria in 2007 completed the enlargement in the CEE that began in 2004, but it also marked the start of a policy change in evaluating anti-corruption reform post-accession, as both countries possessed significantly high levels of corruption. As illustrated in Chapter 1, the EU did not apply any instrument to monitor progress in fighting corruption within the CEE countries after their accession in May 2004.[33]

Since 2005, when the Treaty of Accession with Romania and Bulgaria was signed, one could observe a change in the Commission's strategy in pushing for rigorous anti-corruption policies and preventive measures before a country joined the EU.[34] At this stage, corruption emerged as one of the most serious issues and was regarded as an obstacle for EU accession. The Commission also started to monitor Romania more thoroughly than the other CEE states that joined the EU in 2004. We can distinguish two reasons for the Commission's different approach to Romania: it is easier to monitor two countries compared to eight countries, and the issue of corruption was much more serious in the case of Romania.[35]

Another factor that contributed to the Commission taking a more complex and demanding approach with Romania was the change of political climate within the EU. The rejection of the Constitutional Treaty in the Dutch and French referendums indicated a public disapproval of various aspects of EU policy, including that of the enlargement policy.[36] In a more difficult political environment, the

33 Gergana Noutcheva, 'Bulgaria and Romania's Accession to the EU: Postponement, Safeguards and the Rule of Law' *CEPS Policy Briefs No 102 15 May 2006* <http://shop.ceps.eu/downfree.php?item_id=1329> accessed 30 May 2019.

34 Venelin I Ganev, 'Post-Accession Hooliganism: Democratic Governance in Bulgaria and Romania after 2007' *East European Politics and Societies 27* (1) (2013) 26–44.

35 Eli Gateva, 'Post-Accession Conditionality—Translating Benchmarks into Political Pressure?' *East European Politics 29* (4) (2013) 420–42.

36 Gergana Noutcheva and Dimitar Bechev 'The Successful Laggards: Bulgaria and Romania's Accession to the EU' *East European Politics and Societies 22* (1) (2008) 114–44.

Commission was under pressure to require more tangible evidence of a strong commitment from Romania to fight corruption. In addition, the Commission had experience from the previous enlargement in applying pressure on new member states to tackle corruption and recognising their anti-corruption policy shortcomings at an earlier stage. The Commission also had more experience in monitoring new member states, guaranteeing effective and appropriate implementation of anti-corruption measures and the adoption of good governance tools. Thus, the strategy towards Romania was reinforced in two ways. Firstly, the Commission introduced a tool for possible accession postponement, and secondly, the introduction of the CVM to monitor progress in the area of anti-corruption reform after the accession process was completed.[37]

The postponement clause, as Lazowski argues, served as a tool to discipline Romania in their very last phase of the pre-accession.[38] The postponement clause was also part of the special list of anti-corruption commitments, which were to be followed even after the accession negotiations were closed for Romania.[39] Only Poland had been presented with one special recommendation in the previous round of enlargement in introducing liability of legal persons for corruption.[40] In contrast, the list presented to Romania clearly suggested that the Commission was taking a much tougher stand in developing policy to fight corruption in the 2007 enlargement round. Thus, emerged the first signs of a separate EU anti-corruption policy field.

Despite continuous problems with corruption and the lack of progress observed in the Commission's reports about Romanian's effort to tackle corruption, to delay the Romania's accession until 2008 would have carried significant political risks. Thus, the EU acknowledged all these risks and decided not to delay the accession of Romania, even though corruption was high and Romania did not fulfil the EU membership criteria, as Noutcheva noted.[41] The Commission found itself in a position where, on the one hand, it could not delay the accession of Romania without losing its political credibility. On the other hand, Romania's accession in its current state—with high levels of corruption and inadequate structures against organised crime—could undermine the functioning of the EU.

Hence, the Commission found itself under pressure and ultimately opted for a third scenario: establishing a regime of post-accession monitoring mechanisms

37 Antoaneta Dimitrova and Aron Buzogany, 'Post-Accession Policy-Making in Bulgaria and Romania: Can Non-state Actors Use EU Rules to Promote Better Governance?' *Journal of Common Market Studies 52* (1) (2014) 139–56.

38 Adam Lazowski, 'And Then They Were Twenty-Seven … A Legal Appraisal of the Sixth Accession Treaty' *Common Market Law Review 44* (2) (2007) 401–30.

39 Philip Levitz and Grigore Pop-Eleches, 'Monitoring, Money and Migrants: Countering Post-accession Backsliding in Bulgaria and Romania' *Europe-Asia Studies 62* (3) (2010) 461–79.

40 Patrycja Szarek-Mason, *The European Union's Fight against Corruption: The Evolving Policy towards Member States and Candidate Countries* (CUP 2010) 225.

41 Noutcheva (n 33).

called the Cooperation and Verification Mechanism (CVM), which no new member state had faced before. As illustrated in Chapter 1, this new development also marked the very first post-accession conditionality to which new member states were obliged to respond. Thus, Romania was accepted to join the EU under the condition that they would meet certain key anti-corruption standards and benchmarks after its accession to the EU.[42] We will now analyse the CVM, a key aspect of the EU support in developing a coherent anti-corruption policy field in Romania.

5.2.1 The Cooperation and Verification Mechanism for Romania

The CVM is an anti-corruption mechanism designed to maintain the reform momentum in Romania and avoid reversal of the rule of law reforms and to implement key anti-corruption measures. The monitoring mechanism allows the EU to retain some leverage in the area of anti-corruption policies after Romania accessed to the EU. It has been noted that the EU acted on a hypothesis that, on balance, it may be preferable to work with the country when they are inside the Union, rather than to try to push for anti-corruption reforms from the outside.[43] Every six months, the Commission issues a report on Romania that evaluates the progress on the bases of the established benchmarks and stresses important issues necessary to be addressed before the next report.[44] These monitoring reports have been acknowledged as very detailed designed for following the progress of administrative reforms, judicial improvements and political developments. The reports have played a vital role in gathering information about the government reforms in Romania.[45]

The main CVM report is published in the summer of each year and contains a detailed evaluation of progress and recommendations for further anti-corruption reforms in Romania. Each winter, the Commission publishes an interim report providing a technical update on important developments having occurred in the last six months. However, the interim report does not include an evaluation of progress accomplished. The progress report issued in the summer remains the main point of reference for the assessment of progress in Bulgaria and Romania.[46] The CVM was supposed to come to an end after five years in 2012—however, the Commission decided to leave the CVM in place, even after the introduction of the EU Anti-Corruption Report, in order to keep

42 Mihaiela R Gugiu, 'EU Enlargement and Anticorruption: Lessons Learned from Romania' *Journal of European Integration 34* (5) (2012) 429–46.

43 Szarek-Mason (n 40).

44 R Rogowski, 'ALACs and the Concept of Citizen Participation in the Light of European Law' *Discussion Paper Series 1 Konstanz* (2010) <www.soziologie.uni-konstanz.de/alacs/project/papers1/> accessed 30 May 2019.

45 Levitz and Pop-Eleches (n 39).

46 European Commission, 'Commission Decision of 13/XII/2006', C (2006) 6570 final.

the pressure on Romania to enhance the rule of law and establish a comprehensive anti-corruption policy field.

The CVM for Romania contains some objectives (known as 'the four benchmarks', shown below) against which Romania is evaluated. The Commission issues its CVM reports every year to Romania against these benchmarks and tracks their degree of fulfilment. If they are not achieved, the Commission offers technical assistance to do so. The **four benchmarks** against which Romania is evaluated mainly focus on the function of the rule of law:[47]

(1) Ensure a more transparent and efficient judicial process, notably by enhancing the capacity and accountability of the Superior Council of Magistracy. Report and monitor the impact of the new civil and penal procedural codes.
(2) Establish, as foreseen, an integrity agency with responsibilities for verifying assets, incompatibilities and potential conflicts of interest, and for issuing mandatory decisions on the basis of which dissuasive sanctions can be taken.
(3) Building on progress already made, continue to conduct professional, non-partisan investigations into allegations of high-level corruption.
(4) Take further measures to prevent and fight against corruption, in particular within local government.

Typically, a benchmark is a standard of best practice against something that can be measured.[48] However, we would argue that these so-called benchmarks more resemble *targets* that Romania should meet, rather than a standard against which objectives can be measured. Furthermore, the CVM does not give any tools for assessing or measuring progress, which would normally be an important part of any benchmarking instrument.[49]

In fact, the CVM has provided a set of targets, most of which are expressed in a rather abstract manner: for instance, 'continue the reform of the judiciary' or 'take further measures to prevent and fight corruption'. Patrycja Mason's analysis shows that drawing up such general targets clearly indicates that the CVM is more of a political instrument than a technical mechanism.[50] This analysis examines whether or not Romania has adequately addressed the benchmarks. Their wide definition leaves the door open for the Commission to put certain targets throughout its regular reports under the CVM, even continuing beyond the seven years it was initially designed to serve as an instrument.

Belgian prosecutor Willem de Pauw, an expert reviewer of the Commission, stated in a CVM report mentioned by *The Economist* that 'the Romanian judiciary system appears to be unable to function properly when it comes to applying the rule of law against high-level corruption', and the situation would soon revert to

47 ibid.
48 Szarek-Mason (n 40).
49 ibid.
50 ibid.

the pre-accession level of 2003.[51] De Pauw's report also suggested the apparent paradox that the judges cannot be blamed for this situation, as it would be illogical to impute to the judiciary a lack of 'corruption awareness'. The fight against corruption is generally defined as a policy imperative with which judicial function has nothing to do—judges apply the law independently and impartially to individual cases.[52]

The benchmarks set out for Romania refer to certain shortcomings in the areas of judicial reform and the fight against corruption; failure to sufficiently address these issues would have resulted in the activation of the Justice and Home Affairs (JHA) safeguarding clause.[53] However, the Commission did not activate any such clause, and their decision not to trigger any of the safeguarding measures is related to the scope of the explicit threats and more accurately to the penalising power of the remedial and preventive sanctions established by the safeguarding clauses. The remedial and preventive sanctions are considered to be limited and inadequate—there was even some discussion at the European Council meetings to activate the clause, but it was deemed to be an inadequate solution in the long term. However, the Dutch Minister of EU affairs sent a letter to the former Justice Commissioner Barrot, asking the Commission to consider activating the JHA safeguarding clause if the CVM reports to Romania failed to make any tangible progress,[54] even though the applicability of their sanctions expired at the end of 2009.

In Romania, the political will to tackle domestic institutional reform has been uneven since before it joined the EU, and the 2014 Report suggests that it remains so. There was a surge in activity in the run-up to accession, but much of the political elite responded by closing ranks and working to dilute or remove the curbs on corruption that were implemented at that time. Unlike in CEE states, where new parties exploited the failure of the government to fight corruption, in Romania, some of the old parties worked to push the issue under the rug. Nevertheless, when the EU has put strong pressure on Romania, the government has responded under the CVM, mainly by passing legislation in the parliament.[55] Mihaiela Gugui supports such an analysis, as in Romania there has been progress in the fight against corruption when EU leverage and electoral pressures have created political incentives for some domestic elites to spearhead reforms—although in the main, these are not due to the CVM.[56] This is a clear

51 'In Denial—The European Union Conceals Romania's Backsliding on Corruption' *The Economist* (3 July 2008) <www.economist.com/node/11670671> accessed 30 May 2019.

52 Bogdan Iancu, 'Post-Accession Constitutionalism with a Human Face: Judicial Reform and Lustration in Romania' *European Constitutional Law Review 6* (1) (2011) 28–58.

53 European Commission (n 46).

54 Eli Gateva, *European Union Enlargement Conditionality* (Palgrave Macmillan 2015) 102.

55 Mihaiela R Gugiu, 'The Politics of Corruption: Political Will and the Rule of Law in Post-Communist Romania' *Journal of Communist Studies and Transition Politics 26* (3) (2010) 341–62.

56 ibid.

example that there is not much of the theory of reflexive governance approach in evidence. The former Romanian justice minister, Monica Macovei, recommended that the reforms of the judiciary and the fight against corruption should continue after accession to the EU and that the post-accession monitoring process was needed to keep up the pressure.[57]

Overall, the CVM has helped the Commission to monitor progress in important cases and put pressure on the judiciary and the parliament to act appropriately. However, progress with respect to fighting corruption still remains very slow. Many corruption cases never go to trial. The Commission has called for urgent action to fast-track trials that risk dragging on past the statute of limitations, and so avoid successful prosecution simply through inertia.[58] The work of government representatives in various areas still remains poor, since accountability is mostly absent, and political allegiance is the leading determinant of success.[59] The CVM, however, has shown important factors that have helped to draw a general picture of the issue of corruption in Romania and provided the basic model for establishing the EU Anti-Corruption Report.

However, as an incitement over the years, the CVM has only offered temporary results and has not solved the problem in the long term. The fact that the CVM was extended beyond the initially designated five-year objective and continues to be used by the Commission—even with the Report in place—shows that it is not as effective a solution as planned. The decision on the continuance of the CVM is based on the mechanism being applied until all the benchmarks set under the mechanism are satisfactorily fulfilled. However, even after ten years of Romania's inclusion in the EU, these benchmarks are still not fully met. It is not realistic to expect that the problems of corruption will be cured anytime soon in Romania, even with some policy success. Even if sanctions were applied to Romania, they would affect innocent citizens and companies, as the court judgments affecting their legal position will not be recognised elsewhere in Europe.

In summing up the EU anti-corruption policy towards Romania, we can argue that much of the Romania-EU relationship has been based on establishing key anti-corruption measures to fight corruption more effectively in many sectors. Thus, much of this relationship is characterised by Romania implementing key measures and reforms that the EU requested in the CVM and the pressures that the Commission has placed on the Romanian Government to implement those reforms. In many cases, the Commission also supports Romania in developing an anti-corruption policy field, but this support has not been based on the theory of reflexive governance, at least up to this point. The theory of

57 Gateva (n 54).

58 European Commission 'Interim Report from the Commission to the European Parliament and the Council on Progress in Romania/Bulgaria under the Cooperation and Verification Mechanism' COM (2012) 56/57 final.

59 Romanian Academic Society, 'Beyond Perception: Has Romania's Governance Improved After 2004?' (2011) <www.sar.org.ro/polsci/?p=573> accessed 30 May 2019.

reflexive governance would require the Commission and Romania to engage in a dialogue for establishing an anti-corruption policy, more engagement of civil society, and a multi-level approach to establish an anti-corruption policy field. So far, much of the discussion has been dominated by the Commission requiring and pushing Romania to implement key reforms. These would ultimately contribute to establish an anti-corruption policy field and meet policy aims, but they are not being created or implemented in a reflexive arena. Now we will evaluate the Report's recommendations for Romania and what progress has made since the Report was issued; we will also analyse whether the Report's recommendations embody elements of the theory of reflexive governance.

5.2.2 Recommendations for Romania's judicial system

The Report suggested that Romania must still work on safeguarding the stability and independence of the judiciary. It also emphasised the importance of continuing to maintain a record of anti-corruption institutions and ensure that there are non-partisan investigations regarding high-level corruption cases. The Report also highlighted that there should be evidence in tackling corruption and prosecutions of elected and appointed officials in particular. Romania needs to implement coherent preventive measures, supplemented by an effective sanctioning regime, in order to strengthen integrity in the judiciary. This is specifically aimed at all the relevant stakeholders in the judiciary, such as the Superior Council of Magistracy, the Judicial Inspection, magistrates' associations, courts and prosecutors' offices.

Corruption is viewed as a serious threat to judicial performance in CEE states overall and a particular challenge for post-Communist transition. Many countries found judicial corruption to be an obstacle for European membership and had to go through immense restructuring, adopting preventive tools to combat corruption in the justice system.[60] This included implementing anti-corruption policies and strategies in conjunction with the EU to address the issue of corruption in the judiciary more coherently. However, not all efforts have been very effective, and Romania is an example of a country that, even after joining the EU, still has high levels of corruption in the judiciary. In particular, this applies proportionally to the rule of law.[61] Corruption and applying the rule of law are also a topic for intense political debate at times between the EU and Romania, as the political elite has put consistent pressure on the justice system and attempts to control the judiciary in Romania. It should be noted that the recommendation in the Report is a reiteration of the same issue concerning

60 Tom Gallagher, *Romania and the European Union: How the Weak Vanquished the Strong* (Manchester University Press 2010) 240–242.

61 Radu Carp, 'The Struggle for the Rule of Law in Romania as an EU Member State: The Role of the Cooperation and Verification Mechanism' *Utrecht Law Review 10* (1) (2016) 1–16.

the judicial system that has been raised in the CVM, since its first publication in 2007.

Defining corruption is a difficult task, and research has been unable to find a common working definition, as illustrated in Chapter 1; a common definition for judicial corruption may be more challenging still. However, according to Buscaglia, judicial corruption can be specifically defined as the use of public authority for the private benefit of court personnel when this use undermines the rules and procedures to be applied in the provision of court services.[62] In analysing the complicated relationship between judicial institutions and corruption, researchers distinguish between different types of judicial corruption, such as administrative corruption, operational corruption,[63] functional, and dysfunctional corruption.[64] Romania has a particular issue with administrative and operational judicial corruption, which the Report observed as highly problematic.

In Romania, and in most CEE countries, there is a distinct requirement for the political networks to increase their pressure and control the judicial system. The external pressure used on judicial personnel, which takes the form of judicial corruption, is applied in order to either lower the legal penalties or change the court decision.[65] Therefore, having control of the judiciary can provide great advantages to political networks, such as political influence on key decisions and protection. According to Buscaglia, such corrupt acts—which encompass politically motivated court decisions—are returned as favours for career development within the judicial system.[66] Such acts are fairly complex, yet despite the hidden character of operational corruption, academics have identified several indicators, such as follows: conflicting and overlapping authority, political power struggles over access to resources, manipulation and denial of truthful information, and personal relationships of necessity and loyalty. In other words, there is a weak separation between the civil service and party politics, a weak professionalisation of the public institutions, and a lack of administrative accountability and transparency. These acts are also a testament to the deficient political control in most post-Communist states.[67]

Further indicators also recognised include the delay of judicial decisions, extended undue procedures and, occasionally, judges rejecting laws on the basis of unconstitutionality. In Tom Gallagher's account regarding judicial corruption, he observed that judges picked indirect strategies as a way to review legislation, rather than declare the whole statute to be unconstitutional (although judges

62 Daniela Piana, *Judicial Accountabilities in New Europe: From Rule of Law to Quality of Justice* (Routledge 2016) 132–34.

63 ibid.

64 ibid.

65 Szarek-Mason (n 40) 232.

66 Edgardo Buscaglia, 'An Analysis of Judicial Corruption and Its Causes: An Objective Governing-Based Approach' *International Review of Law and Economics 21* (2) (2001) 233–49.

67 Susan Rose Ackerman, *International Handbook on the Economics of Corruption* (Edward Elgar 2011) 278–82.

have on occasion struck down portions of the law as unconstitutional and unlawful[68]). Thus, judicial dependence on outside pressure is diminished in the Romanian justice system.

So, we could say that the judiciary in Romania is both a perpetrator as well as a victim of corruption. Political networks may find the financial and power gain from corruption irresistible, and it has been demonstrated that this has been the case over the years with different governments. Once corrupted, political networks reduce the effectiveness of the legal and judicial systems through manipulation of resource allocation and appointments to key positions. For example, just four months after Romania joined the EU, the minister of justice, Macovei, was dismissed from office—despite the fact that the EU regarded Macovei as having done a good job in pushing for anti-corruption reform in the judiciary.[69] Another example was President Traian Bilsescu, who was impeached twice. Although he survived both referendums, the impeachment procedures (particularly the last, on 10 July 2012) resulted in significant political and economic costs for Romania.[70] Therefore, reducing resources will make it difficult for the legal system to fight corruption and allow more room for corruption to increase. As a result, a weak judicial system becomes open to corrupt practices, as the Report reflects.

Nonetheless, it must be noted that, as explained in Chapter 1, reinforcing the performance of the judicial system will depend a lot on the will and application of the rule of law proportionally. Independent and professional behaviour by the judiciary will translate into respect for the rule of law and institutional suitability.[71] However, this would require political will to build both structural and institutional mechanisms to protect the independence of the justice system. Without strengthening the institutional side of the judiciary and the independence from political networks, it would be hard to implement the integrity that the Report calls for in the Romanian justice system. Next, we will evaluate the issues concerning corruption in the Romanian political system, linked to the other sectors that politics tries to control—identified by Prado as an obstacle to strengthening the rule of law itself.[72]

5.2.3 Recommendations for the political system

The Report suggested that Romania must implement a far-reaching code of conduct for elected officials and establish accountability tools and sanctions for corrupt practices and conflicts of interest. The Report also suggested that Romania

68 Gallagher (n 60) 115–17.

69 Anitta M Hipper, *Beyond the Rhetorics of Compliance: Judicial Reform in Romania* (Springer VS 2015) 25–40.

70 Wojciech Sadurski, *Rights before Courts: A Study of Constitutional Courts in Post-Communist States of Central and Eastern European* (2nd edn, Springer 2014) 329–77.

71 Hipper (n 69).

72 Mariana M Prado, 'The Paradox of Rule of Law Reforms: How Early Reforms Can Create Obstacles to Future Ones' *University of Toronto Law Journal 60* (2) (2010) 555–78.

should ensure that all the decisions concerning lifting of immunities are correctly reasoned and taken promptly, with no obstruction of justice by the political elite. The Report also identified that the country should consider developing an ethical code for political parties and encouraging high-integrity standards within the political system.

Corruption within the Romanian political system and elites has been under the EU's scrutiny for a long period, and the country has suffered many political scandals related to bribery and corruption. Governments are either voted out of office or resign due to corruption-related issues, as in November 2015, when the government of Victor Ponta fell, and a team of technocrats came in led by Dacian Ciolos, a former European Commissioner.[73]

The CVM report of 27 January 2016 was positive for the Ciolos-led government when the Commission's First Vice President Frans Timmermans noted that:

> *Romania and Romanians have shown their willingness to fight corruption and to protect the independence of the judiciary. The mass demonstrations against corruption have shown how these issues matter to Romanian citizens. Over the last year we have seen the professionalism, commitment and good track record of the judiciary and the anti-corruption prosecution and reforms being internalised.*[74]

The resignation of former Prime Minister Ponta, in November 2015, had a positive impact in improving the CVM issued in early 2016. However, the Commission stated that the reform of the judiciary does not enjoy the full consensus necessary to assure sustainable progress and required full participation by the political parties to get consensus.[75] This highlights that, even in 2016—after ten years of the CVM—the judicial independence and respect for court decisions continue to be challenging in Romania. This indicates that since the Report was issued, there has not been substantive reform in ensuring the independency of the judicial system due to a lack of political will.

The first high-profile case of fighting corruption in the political ranks was when the High Court of Cassation and Justice sentenced the former Romanian Prime Minister Adrian Nastase to two years in prison[76] and banned him from running

73 Marian Chiriac, 'Romania Names Ex-Commissioner as New PM' *Balkan Insight* (11 November 2015) <www.balkaninsight.com/en/article/ex-commissioner-is-romania-s-new-prime-minister-11-10-2015> accessed 30 May 2019.

74 European Commission, 'On Progress in Romania under the Cooperation and Verification Mechanism' Report from the Commission to the European Parliament and the Council, COM (2016) 41 final.

75 Adelina Marini, 'Problems in Bulgaria are Systemic, in Romania—Political' *EU Inside* (2016) <www.euinside.eu/en/news/problems-in-bulgaria-are-systemic-in-romania-political> accessed 30 May 2019.

76 N Buckley, 'Former Romanian Prime Minister Jailed for Taking Bribes' *The Financial Times* 6 January 2014 <www.ft.com/cms/s/0/a43e56b8-7707-11e3-a253-00144feabdc0.html #axzz41gLEJh9z> accessed 30 May 2019.

for public office. Nastase was then found guilty of having illegally funded his presidential election campaign in 2004, using his position as the head of the government to illegally collect about €1.6 million from various companies (by officially announcing their payments as attendance fees for a governmental symposium).[77]

In the last few years, the Romanian political system has experienced a period of some success in fighting corruption: in particular, from April 2011 until October 2013, the Court handed down no fewer than eleven verdicts in corruption cases against former members of government.[78] Since 2011, there is evidence that elected public high office holders were successfully put on trial for the first time since the collapse of Communism. These positive developments were promising evidence of Romania having the will to tackle corruption in the political system and restoring some degree of public trust to the judiciary in holding their elected officials accountable.[79]

Some of these investigated political cases give an indication of the seriousness of the corruption embedded in politics. In Romania, in the last ten years, there were no fewer than two prime ministers, 21 ministers and 19 secretaries of state subject to investigation by the prosecution offices for acts committed in the exercise of their public office.[80] The EU, civil society actors and the media began to dominate the political discourse in Romania at the beginning of the year 2000[81]—as a result, numerous laws and regulations have been implemented and amended, as well as new state institutions being established to fight political corruption more efficiently.[82]

The EU has given technical assistance and support to the Romanian anti-corruption institutions over the years, and these bodies have developed their own dynamics since 2005. Research indicates an institutional independency of Romanian law-enforcement bodies, supported by the fact that these anti-corruption institutions have investigated corruption-related cases committed by members of all political parties.[83] These developments are viewed as positive—but we might suspect they were only superficial, as a means to get into the EU.

Since Romania joined the EU there have been some attempts to develop an effective anti-corruption policy, but the general political environment in the country has been characterised by instability, which has had a negative impact in

77 Leslie A Schwindt-Bayer and Margrit Tavits, *Clarity of Responsibility, Accountability and Corruption* (CUP 2016) 7.

78 Jenny Andersson and Eglė Rindzevičiūtė, *The Struggle for the Long-term in Transnational Science and Politics* (Routledge 2015) 165–95.

79 Tanja A Börzel, 'Coming Together or Drifting Apart? Political Change in New Member States, Accession Candidates, and Eastern Neighbourhood Countries' *MAXCAP Working Paper Series No 03 May 2014* Freie Universität Berlin (2014) 16–25.

80 Gallagher (n 60) 205.

81 ibid.

82 Hipper (n 69).

83 Sabina Schnell, 'Mimicry, Persuasion, or Learning? The Case of Two Transparency and Anti-corruption Policies in Romania' *Public Administration and Development 35* (4) (2015) 277–87.

building on the progress. In particular, the years 2008–2012 were dominated by a deep economic and financial crisis, prompting two successive Romanian governments to take radical steps to obtain the International Monetary Fund (IMF) bailout loans. This led to a serious loss of popular confidence and culminated in massive street protests which saw a change of two governments in 2009 and 2012.[84] As a result, after four years of political instability in Romania, the fight against corruption was undermined.

However, after the Ponta's government came into power, the fight against political corruption was relatively steady, even though there were many institutional changes due to changes of administration which contributed to general instability and a specific failure to prioritise the fight against corruption. Insufficient anti-corruption measures remain, as the court proceedings frequently go on for many years—the result of numerous procedural delays.[85] However, this procrastination is also due to the lack of capacity in the justice system and courts frequently hesitating to sentence high-level/high-profile corruption cases to long prison sentences. The judgments in such high-level corruption cases frequently remain below the legal minimum, and about 60 per cent of the sentences are suspended, according to the CVM.[86] Such practices on the part of the courts significantly diminish their deterrent effect, making prosecution rather superficial. That said, this problem is also due to the fact the judiciary itself is highly affected by corruption, as we have seen.

As a result of Romanian compliance with EU recommendations on anti-corruption, three important improvements in the legal framework were designed to prevent corruption in politics. Firstly, an amendment to the Constitutional Court Law in September 2010, eliminating the rule which specified that, during the review proceeding before the Constitutional Court, cases which were pending on corruption cases before the ordinary court had to be suspended.[87] Secondly, in July 2011, the High Court of Cassation and Justice in Romania (ICCJ) decided by an interpretative ruling that, for the length of a tangible review before the Constitutional Court, the statute-barred period of the related case must be extended.[88] Thirdly, in October 2010, the Romanian parliament approved a law known as the 'Small Reform Law' according to Hein, which amended the codes of procedure in order to accelerate judicial proceedings.[89]

84 Petia Kostadinova and Magda Giurcanu, 'Political Blackmail, Institutional Infighting, and Electoral Politics: The Fate of Governing Parties during the Great Recession (2008–2012) in Romania and Bulgaria' *Politics and Policy 43* (6) (2015) 789–821.

85 David Clark, 'Fighting Corruption with Con Tricks: Romania's Assault on the Rule of Law' The Henry Jackson Society new edition (4 January 2017) <http://henryjacksonsociety.org/wp-content/uploads/2017/01/Romania-paper.pdf> accessed 30 May 2019.

86 European Commission, 'On Progress in Romania under the Cooperation and Verification Mechanism' COM (2012) 410 final.

87 Adrian D Matei, 'Could the Present Economic-Financial Crisis Give a New Impetus to the Fight against Corruption and the Underground Economy?' *Internal Auditing and Risk Management 8* (2) (2013) 35–46.

88 Hein (n 9).

89 ibid.

In 2012, the government approved a new 'National Anti-Corruption Strategy 2012–2015' drafted by the parliament, which mainly answered the demands and recommendations put forward by the Commission, and declared that they would no longer misuse the immunity rights from prosecution that they enjoyed. The Strategy was designed to strengthen the integrity of parliamentary members. In particular, this was done by amending the regulations of the Chamber of Deputies and the Senate and other legislation in this field, in order to put on the agenda of the first plenary session requests for lifting immunity of Parliamentarians and resolve these requests within a maximum of 72 hours.[90] In fact, the Report calls for an application of such a rule, and that is why it is mentioned as a key issue to be addressed by Romania.

Nevertheless, the government has tried to influence some decisions of the prosecutors—for example in 2012, by delaying the nomination of the new Prosecutor General attached to the ICCJ and the DNA Chief Prosecutor. Since the regular term of the incumbent Prosecutor General was to end in October 2012, and DNA Chief Prosecutor Daniel's term had already expired in February 2012, the Ponta government delayed the appointment procedures during the summer of 2012 whilst trying to impeach President Basescu.[91] In doing so, the government attempted to clear the way to appoint prosecutors close to the Ponta Government, who were much less committed to building on previous anti-corruption gains.

After the failure of the presidential dismissal of Basescu, it was not until May 2013 that the then Prime Minister Ponta and President Basescu reached an agreement on the appointment of Romania's two leading prosecutors. Those appointed were portrayed respectively as the 'president's candidate', who became the DNA Chief Prosecutor, and the 'government's candidate', who became the ICCJ Prosecutor General.[92]

The academic discourse in Romania finds that such acts are motivated by the political elite in further politicising the judicial system. However, it's clear that politicians from all parties use allegations of corruption for other political purposes besides a sincere motive to eliminate corruption, and these patterns have been highly visible in post-Communist transition states.

5.2.4 Recommendations for public procurement

The Report suggested that Romania has to take into account the development of effective tools within contracting authorities and public-procurement supervisory bodies, and in particular, focus on conflicts of interest at local and regional level,

90 Ministry of Justice, 'National Anticorruption Strategy for the Period 2012–2015' op 11 <www.anticorruption-romania.org/docman/doc_download/83-nationalanticorruption-strategy-2012-2015-annex-1> accessed 30 May 2019.

91 Kostadinova and Giurcanu (n 84).

92 Hein (n 9).

as corruption in public procurement in Romania is an area of particular concern for the EU.

According to the 2015 flash Eurobarometer survey on corruption relevant to businesses,[93] more than 34 per cent of EU companies and 51 per cent of Romanian domestic companies that participated in public procurement say corruption prevented them from winning a contract. A 2005 survey done by the World Economic Forum, in a sample of 125 countries, placed Romania among the last 25 countries concerning the frequency of bribery and additional payments in public procurement. Compared to ten years ago, Romania has not made enough progress in transparency on this issue, considering all the financial assistance it has received from the EU. At that time, Romania was the only EU candidate country to be placed with such a poor ranking, while most of the EU member states were placed among the best 25 performers.[94] The 2015 flash Eurobarometer survey showed that nearly 74 per cent of the population believed that contracts are not awarded in a fair and transparent way.[95]

However, the CVM reports are the best source to offer a perspective on corruption in public procurement for Romania: analysing reports from 2010 to 2014 (the 2016 report is mainly based on judicial independence and judicial reform), we see several common ideas. Firstly, all the CVM reports find that progress seems very inadequate in the prevention and sanctioning of corruption related to public procurement in Romania; progress made against high-level corruption in general has not been matched in public procurement. Secondly, nearly all of the CVM reports and the Report address similar shortcomings, including frequent changes of the legal framework, and an institutional set-up that lacks sufficient capacity, as well as an absence of key tools for effective controls, such as an inclusive register of public tenders and weak protection of public procurement against conflicts of interest; few cases of conflicts of interest are pursued in public procurement. Thirdly, almost all of the CVM reports and the Report put emphasis on creating ex-ante verifications in order to detect conflicts of interest in the early stages of the award procedure.[96]

Public-procurement procedures in Romania are highly dysfunctional and corrupt because of the absorption of structural funds. Recent studies show that the spending of EU funds across many new and old member states is a contributing factor in public-procurement corruption.[97] Even if only a fraction of EU funding

93 Flash Eurobarometer 406, 'The Cooperation and Verification Mechanism for Bulgaria and Romania—Second Wave' European Commission (2015) <http://ec.europa.eu/commfrontoffice/publicopinion/flash/fl_406_en.pdf> accessed 30 May 2019.

94 OECD 'Integrity in Public Procurement—Good Practice from A to Z' *OECD* (2013).

95 Gabriella M Racca and Christopher R Yukins, *Integrity and Efficiency in Sustainable Public Contracts: Balancing Corruption Concerns in Public Procurement Internationally* (Bruylant 2014) 69–101.

96 Beate Sjåfjell and Anja Wiesbrock, *Sustainable Public Procurement Under EU Law: New Perspectives on the State as Stakeholder* (CUP 2016) 133.

97 Fazekas and others (n 31).

is impacted by corruption, still this is in a context in which the EU funds between 1.9 per cent and 4.4 per cent of GDP and well above 50 per cent of public investment. The Commission criticised this weakness in the country and pushed for an enforcement of instruments to protect EU funds contributing to public-procurement contracts. In June 2013, the Romanian government replied to the requests and critiques coming from the Commission and adopted a joint ministerial order regarding the support of the guide encompassing the central risks identified in the field of public procurement.[98]

An example of these risks is the unjustified shortening of deadlines as a result of the publication of notice of an intention to purchase. Use of an accelerated award procedure can be done only if the emergency situation is clearly justified by the contracting authority, and it is not connected to its own fault.[99] This involves putting in place an award criterion, i.e. the most economically advantageous tender, with the inclusion of irrelevant or unquantifiable evaluation factors. Automatic exclusion of the lowest tender occurs, as this is often done based on the justification that such a low price will most likely generate problems during the execution of the contract.[100]

The Report suggested that Romania builds upon these guidelines and makes a proper application. However, as there are conflicts of interest in awarding public-procurement contracts in Romania, appropriate measures should be taken to prevent this. Conflicts of interest represent one of the most widespread forms of corruption in public procurement in the country. In March 2013, Horia Georgescu, the president of the National Agency for Integrity for Romania, attended the conference 'Combating Criminality in the Field of Public Procurement, an Operational Approach'. While referring to an internal study conducted by the Agency, Georgescu declared that at local and county authority level, conflicts of interest are no longer controlled by the state authorities, due to a legal framework that is outdated and does not meet the challenges in practice.[101] More than 78 elected officials at the local level were found to have received and earned public money through corrupt practices in public procurement.

In the field of conflicts of interest, the legal and institutional framework has changed constantly over the last ten years. Currently, the Romanian national

98 A Mungiu-Pippidi, *A Quest for Good Governance: How Societies Develop Control of Corruption* (CUP 2015) 61–185.

99 Bogdana Neamtu and Dacian C Dragos, 'Fighting Corruption in Public Procurement: The Case of Romania in Gabriella' in Gabriella M Racca and Christopher R Yukins (eds) *Integrity and Efficiency in Sustainable Public Contracts: Balancing Corruption Concerns in Public Procurement Internationally* (Bruylant 2015) 1–22.

100 Francesco Decarolis, 'Awarding Price, Contract Performance, and Bids Screening: Evidence from Procurement Auctions' *American Economic Journal: Applied Economics* 6 (1) (2014) 108–32.

101 'Public Procurement: An Operational Approach' *Freedom House* (20 March 2013) <http://freedomhouse.ro/en/index.php/stiri/events/item/134-press-release-conference-public-procurement-an-operational-approach> accessed on 30 May 2019.

public-procurement legislation does not include a clear definition of conflicts of interest; instead, the law mentions several situations that can lead to a case of conflicts of interest.[102] In regard to the persons involved in verifying and evaluating the candidates for tenders, the conflict might be created by an interest that can influence the impartiality and objectivity of those persons throughout the evaluation process.[103] The most recent piece of legislation addressing the issue of conflicts of interest cited that the conflicts of interest should be understood broadly as a conflict between the professional duties and the private interest of a public servant, in which it could be observed as having the potential to obstruct the independent and objective execution of duties.[104] In the light of this wide definition, even non-patrimonial interests have the potential to influence the behaviour of a person. However, very often the NGOs and press monitoring the field of conflict of interest have identified situations presenting conflicts of interest in public procurement.

Researchers find the current legal framework in Romania needs a complete makeover[105]; these requirements are also observed in the CVM report of 2014, as well as in the Report. The legal and institutional frameworks in place, as found in the research, can no longer provide results in the fight against corruption. The 2014 CVM report suggests that Romania should pay more attention to the prevention side, in order to reduce the continuous vulnerability of public-procurement procedures towards corruption, and it should establish early detection tools of conflicts of interest through an ex-ante verification procedure of conflicts of interest.[106] This means a combined framework and cooperation between National Agency for Integrity (the national entity involved in monitoring and sanctioning conflicts of interest in Romania) and the government agency responsible for monitoring procurement procedures.

What is clear from the research, the CVM report and the Report is that potential conflicts of interest should be identified and avoided in advance before contracts are awarded. Thus, a legal obligation on public-procurement authorities to respond to problems identified in both reports will be key to making the system work more efficiently. However, as the previous section on political corruption in Romania has shown, during the past five years, governments have been very unstable, and thus the priority has been more on the judiciary and reforming politics, rather than implementing new laws to prevent conflicts of interest and fight corruption more effectively within public procurement.

102 European Commission, 'Country Report Romania on Including an In-Depth Review on the Prevention and Correction of Macroeconomic Imbalances' SWD 91 final (2016).
103 Neamtu and Dragos (n 99).
104 ibid.
105 Freedom House (n 101).
106 European Commission (n 86).

5.2.5 The threat of corruption in healthcare

The Report suggested that Romania should implement effective strategies to cut the level of informal payments in the public healthcare system by considering improving wages and working conditions for medical staff in order to prevent some forms of corruption. Also, Romania could ensure operational independence of departments within the Ministry of Health, allowing them to control their budget and procurement.

Informal payments in the healthcare system are becoming an increasingly debated topic, especially in developing and transitional countries in CEE—and Romania is no exception. Lewis defines informal payments as:

> *payments to individual and institutional providers, in kind or in cash, that are made outside official payment channels or are purchases meant to be covered by the health care system. This encompasses envelope payments to physicians and contributions to hospitals, as well as the value of medical supplies purchased by patients and drugs obtained from private pharmacies, but intended to be part of government-financed healthcare services. Such informal payments are a form of corruption.*[107]

The healthcare systems are still underdeveloped across the CEE region; healthcare is a complex issue in Romania, as in most CEE states. The deficiencies encompass issues related to other areas, such as governance, laws, the economic and socio-political situation, including levels of corruption, as well as cultures of moral and financial incentives in obtaining services at state facilities. In Romania, out-of-pocket payments have become a common feature for healthcare delivery, which is in major contrast to the free-of-charge service provision during the Communist era.[108] Patients are now paying, either formally or informally, to have access to or satisfactory quality for healthcare. Although some governments in Romania have ignored the existence of informal practices in the healthcare sector, there is now a recognition by the EU (included in the Report) to drive Romania to adopt strategies to eliminate informal payments in the healthcare system, which the EU perceives will reduce the level of corruption.

Surveys conducted in Romania find that around almost 56 per cent of the population have paid a bribe to have access to healthcare.[109] The research and reporting on the issue of corruption in healthcare is still not as advanced as in other areas such as politics or the judiciary, as corruption in healthcare has not

107 M Lewis, 'Informal Payments and the Financing of Health Care in Developing and Transition Countries' *Health Affairs 26* (4) (2007) 984–97.

108 W Bartlett, J Božikov and B Rechel, *Health Reforms in South East Europe* (Palgrave Macmillan 2012) 130–47.

109 Tetiana Stepurko, Milena Pavlova, Irena Gryga and Wim Groot, 'To Pay or Not to Pay? A Multi-country Study on Informal Payments for Health-care Services and Consumers' Perceptions' *Health Expectations 18* (6) (2014) 2978–93.

been a concern of the government, nor on the EU's preventive mechanisms agenda. Even so, the issue is complex, and recent reporting finds that corruption in healthcare has become systemic.

Firstly, doctors in much of CEE argue that abysmal wages in official healthcare systems leave them no choice but to demand payments on the side. In Romania, resident doctors at public hospitals earn about €200 per month, while specialists can earn up to €500.[110] It is unsurprising, then, that about 7,000 Romanian doctors (about 30 per cent) have emigrated according to the head of the country's college of physicians.[111] Britain's National Health Service alone is estimated to employ over 2,000 Romanian doctors.[112]

This institutional impoverishment is a leading factor contributing to informal payments in the Romanian healthcare system, and the situation has become even worse in Romania compared to other EU countries because the country's healthcare system is underfunded and its drug regulation is inadequate. Romanian doctor Maria Barbu reported in *The Independent* in 2014 that during her search for work, a hospital manager wanted €5,000 to hire her in a small town of 8,000 inhabitants.[113] She shared her experience further, contending that at every step of their careers, Romania's doctors and nurses must negotiate a system accused of rewarding bribery and nepotism instead of being based on merit. Research finds that not many health professionals hold out against this corruption. Doctors sometimes pay money 'under the table' in order to secure employment and promotion in the healthcare system,[114] and this also contributes to doctors supplementing their income by receiving bribes in order to advance or keep their jobs.

At the same time, according to Teodora Menea, patients are willing participants in this bribe-ridden economy, pressing money upon doctors out of gratitude or fear in order to get access to healthcare.[115] Menea argues that there has been a culture of social acceptance of informal payments in healthcare, which poses a policy challenge for Romania.[116]

110 'Patients Bearing Gifts: In Central and Eastern Europe, Patients Offer Bribes and Low-Paid Doctors Accept Them' *The Economist* (24 March 2015) <www.economist.com/news/europe/21647087-central-and-eastern-europe-low-paid-doctors-accept-bribes-and-patients-offer-them-patients-bearing> accessed 30 May 2019.

111 ibid.

112 Denis Campbell, Haroon Siddique, Ashley Kirk and James Meikle, 'NHS Hires up to 3,000 Foreign-trained Doctors in a Year to Plug Staff Shortage' *The Guardian* (28 January 2015) <www.theguardian.com/society/2015/jan/28/-sp-nhs-hires-3000-foreign-doctors-staff-shortage> accessed 30 May 2019.

113 *The Economist* (n 110).

114 Rasma Karklins, *The System Made Me Do It: Corruption in Post-communist Societies* (Routledge 2005) 219.

115 T Manea, 'Medical Bribery and the Ethics of Trust: The Romanian Case' *Journal of Medicine and Philosophy 40* (1) (2015) 26–43.

116 ibid.

Despite the difference in overall perceptions regarding cash and in-kind informal payments discussed above, some research find positive or indifferent attitudes towards both types of payments in Romania, though the largest cluster groups are based on negative attitudes.[117] The research analysis finds that, despite the overall public support for the eradication of informal patient payments, these payments are inevitable due to the low funding of the public healthcare sector. This was also the case with the cancer drug crisis in Romania, where cancer patients struggle every day to find the drugs their lives depend on—the government, after facing strong public pressure, lent €800,000 to Unifarm, the Romanian state company in charge of acquiring and distributing drugs to medical institutions around the country to reduce the crisis.[118] Thus, informal patient payments fill the gaps in the public healthcare system.

Aside from the impact at an individual level, informal payments also have affected the performance of the healthcare system in Romania. This effect is observed in the distribution of services, such as in the example of the supply of cancer drugs, and resource allocation. Furthermore, informal payments are contributing to the obstruction of healthcare reform, since they create a strong incentive for individuals in high hierarchical positions to block reform attempts. This discussion has been summed up by Gaal and McKee, who proposed two alternative hypotheses: donation and fee-for-service.[119] The donation hypothesis rests on socio-cultural and ethical explanations and involves a voluntary action on the patient's part, whereas the fee-for-service hypothesis stresses shortage and always involves a certain degree of pressure. Coercion is not always, or even mainly external, but often internal. Although the two hypotheses seem conflicting and mutually exclusive, they could co-exist in Romania as alternatives.[120] Thus, policy efforts to address informal payments and corruption may benefit from considering these alternative hypotheses.

There is currently no strategy to overcome corruption in the healthcare system in Romania, nor is there enough literature addressing the issue. Filiasi suggests that the Health Ministry does not have a human resources strategy, nor a clear strategy for the healthcare system.[121] Furthermore, Filiasi suggests that the Ministry of Health does not collect statistics to show how medicine has

117 Tetiana Stepurko, Milena Pavlova, Irena Gryga and Wim Groot, 'The Formal-Informal Patient Payment Mix in European Countries: Governance, Economics, Culture or All of These?' *Health Policy 113* (3) (2013) 284–95.

118 Ajay Aggarwal, Ophira Ginsburg and Tito Fojo, 'Cancer Economics, Policy and Politics: What Informs the Debate? Perspectives from the EU, Canada and US' *Journal of Cancer Policy 2* (1) (2014) 1–11.

119 Manea (n 115).

120 ibid.

121 Elena Stancu, 'Mass Exodus: Why Corruption in Romania's Healthcare System Is Forcing Its Doctors to Work Abroad' *The Independent* (2014) <www.independent.co.uk/news/world/europe/mass-exodus-why-corruption-in-romanias-healthcare-system-is-forcing-its-doctors-to-work-abroad-9035108.html> accessed 30 May 2019.

changed, and the head of the medical watchdog indicates that the government rejects the criticisms of underperformance and corruption in the healthcare system.[122] Therefore, despite the fact that informal payments have been reported in Romania, there is still a lack of institutional initiative to address the issue of informal payments. The Commission's reports criticise Romania for not making enough judicial changes and effort to fight corruption. Since 2007, when Romania joined the EU, more than €12 million from the EU budget has been invested in supporting the fight against corruption and judicial reform in Romania.[123] The healthcare system, on the other hand, seems especially affected by everyday bribery or informal payments. Thus, the situation is quite paradoxical because Romanians show concern about this kind of small bribery, but at the same time regularly practice it—and this contradiction makes conditions difficult for successful policy change. Thus, these informal payments and forms of corruption have an impact on patients, healthcare providers and the system as a whole—but at the same time there is no coherent strategy to address the issue of informal payments in Romania's healthcare sector.

5.3 Post-EU anti-corruption report

Corruption continues to be a serious concern and challenge for Romania, despite the anti-corruption prosecutors cracking down on high-level public officials, with a success record of jailing a prime minister, 18 ministers, and thousands of mid-level public officials and politicians on charges of corruption and abuse of public office.[124] The Romania's National Anticorruption Directorate (DNA) has been very effective in this respect, having an outstanding conviction rate of 90 per cent for all cases brought forward on corruption and abuse of power for private gain.[125] The Report has acknowledged that the Romanian DNA is one of five examples of good practices in anti-corruption agencies across the EU. The Report stated that:

> *DNA has built a notable track record of non-partisan investigations and prosecutions into allegations of corruption at the highest levels of politics, the judiciary and other sectors such as tax administration, customs, energy, transport, construction, healthcare, etc. In the past seven years, DNA has indicted over 4700 defendants. 90.25 per cent of its indictments were confirmed through final court decisions. Nearly 1500 defendants were convicted through final*

122 ibid.

123 Manea (n 115).

124 A Mungiu-Pippidi, 'Romania's Italian-Style Anticorruption Populism' *Journal of Democracy Issue 29* (3) (2018) 104–16.

125 European Commission, 'Report from the Commission to the European Parliament and the Council on Progress in Romania under the "Co-operation and Verification Mechanism"' (2016) 10 <https://ec.europa.eu/transparency/regdoc/rep/1/2016/EN/1-2016-41-EN-F1-1.PDF> accessed 15 February 2019.

> *court decisions, almost half of them holding very high-level positions. Key to these results has been DNA's structure which incorporates, apart from prosecutors who lead and supervise investigations, judicial police and economic, financial and IT.*[126]

The DNA's impressive track record also continued in 2015, with the following numbers of filed corruption cases against high-level politicians and company CEOs: about 1,250 civilians were prosecuted (including then Prime Minister Victor Ponta), 5 ministers and 21 members of the Romanian parliament.[127] Also in 2015, €194.37 million in illegal assets were recovered from those convicted on corruption charges. 2016 was another successful year for the DNA, as more than 1,270 people were brought to trial, including 3 ministers, 17 members of the Romanian parliament, 47 mayors, 16 judges and 21 company CEOs.[128] In addition to the convictions, €226 million in illegal assets were recovered. In 2017, about 1000 people were prosecuted and found guilty, including the former Speaker of the Lower House, 6 members of the Romanian parliament, 3 ministers, 49 mayors, 6 judges and 11 company CEOs.[129] Further to the convictions, €159.5 million in illegal assets were also recovered. These high prosecution rates show that the DNA is a very effective anti-corruption agency. Between 2010 and 2017, there were 4,720 final corruption sentences thanks to DNA investigation—an impressive average of nearly 600 convictions per year.[130]

However, since the Social Democratic Party won the general election in 2016, the new government has pushed to relax the fight against corruption and to remove the head of DNA, Laura Kovesi. The first step was to modify the Penal and Procedure Codes under a pretext of fixing the problem of overcrowding of prisons in Romania.[131] The resulting code modifications would allow the release from prison of former politicians so that they didn't serve their full sentences. More importantly, the Social Democratic Party's aim was to prevent any investigations made against the current government on the basis of corruption, while they are serving in government; these Penal Code and Penal Procedure Code changes were designed to make it more difficult for the DNA prosecutors

126 European Commission, 'Report from the Commission to the European Parliament and the Council on the "EU Anti-Corruption Report"' (2014) 13–14 <https://eur-lex.europa.eu/resource.html?uri=cellar:058aecf0-d9b7-11e3-8cd4-01aa75ed71a1.0012.01/DOC_1&format=PDF> accessed 15 February 2019.

127 A Jurma, 'DNA (National Anti-Corruption Department): A Specialized Structure for Combating High Level Corruption in Romania' *Journal of Eastern European Criminal Law No 2/2014* (2015) <https://ssrn.com/abstract=2551997> accessed 15 February 2019.

128 A Adi and DG Lilleker, *#rezist—Romania's 2017 Anti-Corruption Protests: Causes, Development and Implications* (Quadriga University of Applied Sciences 2017) 29–35 <http://eprints.bournemouth.ac.uk/29647/1/romanian_protests_2017_publication_FINAL_nk.pdf> accessed 15 February 2019.

129 Mungiu-Pippidi (n 124).

130 ibid.

131 European Commission (n 125).

to investigate politicians in power. The DNA reacted to these new changes to the Codes by declaring that such modifications would make the fight against corruption less effective in Romania.[132] In January 2017, within a day of this declaration, the biggest protest since the fall of Communism took place, and more than 300,000 people demonstrated against the government's proposals in front of Victoria Palace in Bucharest.[133] In February 2017, the protests reached a record turnout of half a million people, and the pressure from the protestors forced the Government to withdraw the modification bills.[134] DNA may have won that battle, but this was the beginning of a long war, during which the Social Democratic Party gradually imposed phased changes to the Codes, while also discrediting the DNA. In particular, they accused the DNA of abuses of power that their investigative strategies were based on coercion and that the DNA illegally cooperated with the Romanian Intelligence Service in going after politicians from the Social Democratic Party.

These claims became more credible in 2018, when a parliamentary committee obtained some of the classified protocols of cooperation between DNA and the Romanian Intelligence Service. Once the committee declassified the protocols and reports, it was found that the Romanian Information Service organised wiretaps for the DNA in the cases the agency was investigating.[135] According to reports presented to the parliamentary committee by the Romanian Information Service, there were more than a quarter of a million wiretap warrants issued between 2005 and 2014.[136] This broad-sweep approach to surveillance allowed Romanian Information Service officers (members of the least accountable agency in the country) the ability to compromise politicians and judges by handpicking which of them would be handed over to the DNA and which may be held in reserve for blackmail and extortion. As a result, the Constitutional Court ruled that Romanian Information Service should no longer be allowed to organise wiretaps for the DNA.[137]

Since the fall of Communism in Romania—despite some superficial attempts—successive governments have not really tried to challenge the privilege of the top chiefs in the Romanian Information Service, the military or the police.[138] On the

132 Mungiu-Pippidi (n 124).

133 Carmen Paun, 'Romanians Protest Government Plan to Commute Sentences' (2017) <www.politico.eu/article/romanians-protest-government-plan-to-commute-sentences/> accessed 15 February 2019.

134 Elizabeth Roberts and Cosmin Stan, 'Romania Protests Continue over Plans to Revive Corruption Bill' *CNN* (2017) <https://edition.cnn.com/2017/02/06/europe/romania-protests-update/index.html> accessed 15 February 2019.

135 New Europe, 'Can Romania Move Forward When Burdened by Allegations of Deep Linkages between the Anti-corruption Agency and State Security Services?' (2018) <www.neweurope.eu/article/romanias-secret-protocols-cast-a-deep-shadow-over-its-upcoming-eu-presidency/> accessed 15 February 2019.

136 Mungiu-Pippidi (n 124).

137 Mungiu-Pippidi (n 124).

138 Daniel Dragomir, 'Romania's Anti-corruption Crackdown Echoes a Darker Past' *EUObserver* (2018) <https://euobserver.com/opinion/140824> accessed 15 February 2019.

contrary, these high-ranking officials receive preferential treatment and perks, such as high pensions. The Romanian Information Service pensioner, for example, receives on average than €1,000+ per month, compared to a national average of just over than €200.[139] This degree of untouchability and privilege for the Romanian Information Service has harmed the DNA reputation and the good work that it has done in the last eight years, to some degree. It has also escalated an open conflict between the head of the DNA, Laura Codruta Kovesi and the Social Democratic Party since they arrived back in government in 2016.[140]

On 22 February 2018, Justice Minister Toader asked the Klaus Iohannis, President of Romania, to dismiss DNA chief Kovesi by invoking 20 intolerable acts, facts relating to her activities as head of DNA.[141] These claims were based on leaked recordings, in which Kovesi was allegedly asking the prosecutors to go after the prime minister and to move faster with big corruption cases; evidence was based on media reporting, rather than proper investigation. A scandal followed, as prosecutors from the local DNA branch in Ploiesti, who had been the most active in investigating top politicians, were accused of pressuring witnesses and fabricating evidence.[142] The President Iohannis refused the government's request to remove Kovesi, and Iohannis was a vocal supporter of the DNA's efforts to fight corruption. After this refusal, Justice Minister Toader went to the Constitutional Court to invoke a constitutional conflict between power of the Presidency and government. The Romanian Government argued that the Justice Minister had the authority to make decisions related to prosecutors and that the President had no legal instruments to evaluate prosecutor behaviour.[143] The President's office argued that the president is the one who appoints the DNA chief, at the Justice Minister's proposal; therefore, as the President has the right to refuse an appointment that he views or considers unfit, thus the President also has the right to refuse the removal of the DNA chief prosecutor.[144] In late May 2018, the Constitutional Court ruled that President Iohannis did not have the right to overrule the Justice Minister Toader's request, thus instructing the President to dismiss Kovesi as head of DNA. President Iohannis put off making a decision for almost two months, and there were discussions within government to push for suspending President

139 Mungiu-Pippidi (n 124).

140 A Mungiu-Pippidi, 'Bucharest vs Brussels: Wrangling over the EU's new Chief Prosecutor' *Hertie School of Governance blog* (2019) <www.hertie-school.org/en/debate/detail/content/bucharest-vs-brussels-wrangling-over-the-eus-new-chief-prosecutor/> accessed 15 March 2019.

141 Radu-Sorin Marinas, 'Romania's President Removes Chief Anti-corruption Prosecutor' *Reuters* (2018) <https://uk.reuters.com/article/uk-romania-corruption/romanias-president-signs-decree-to-remove-chief-anti-corruption-idUKKBN1JZ0MK> accessed 15 February 2019.

142 Mungiu-Pippidi (n 124).

143 L Ilie, 'Romanian Minister Calls for Prosecutor's Sacking, Graft Crackdown Under Threat' *Reuters* (2018) <www.reuters.com/article/us-romania-government/romanian-minister-calls-for-prosecutors-sacking-graft-crackdown-under-threat-idUSKCN1G62F2> accessed 15 February 2019.

144 Marinas (n 141).

Iohannis if he did not dismiss Kovesi as head of DNA. On 9 July 2018, President Iohannis signed the decree to remove Kovesi in accordance with the decision of the Constitutional Court.[145] Kovesi's tenure was a success as the head of DNA: she successfully prosecuted a former prime minister, several ministers, members of parliament, and many powerful political leaders at the regional and local level. Currently, Kovesi is one of three candidates for the newly created position of chief prosecutor in the newly created European Public Prosecutor's Office (EPPO),[146] and after her hearing at the European Parliament on 27 February 2019, she is considered the frontrunner candidate.[147]

In February 2016, the Romanian Constitutional Court ruled that the Romanian Intelligence Service overstepped its legal authority when it became too involved in anti-corruption investigations for the DNA.[148] Furthermore, the Constitutional Court declared the use of the Romanian Intelligence Service phone-tapping evidence by the DNA to be unconstitutional, even with a warrant, and this also suggests that anti-corruption policy under Kovesi came into conflict with the rule of law.[149] The Minister of Justice suggested that during the four-year period that Kovesi was chief, DNA opened investigations against 3,420 judges and prosecutors —over half of the magistrates in Romania. These investigations remained open and were never brought to trial, but used to coerce the court system.[150] Furthermore, new evidence gathered through freedom of information requests shows that the entire executive branch, parliament and the high courts have been wiretapped since 2010 by the Romanian Intelligence Service, at the request of DNA.[151] Although, in 2016, the Constitutional Court ruled that Romanian Intelligence Service should no longer be empowered to organise wiretaps for the DNA, this leaves substantial material in the hands of the secret service that can be used to blackmail magistrates and politicians. However, none of this was raised by the Commission in the

145 Kit Gillet, 'Romanian Prosecutor Who Took on Entrenched Corruption Is Fired' *New York Times* (2018) <www.nytimes.com/2018/07/09/world/europe/romania-prosecutor-fired.html> accessed 15 February 2019.

146 Lili Bayer, 'MEPs Back Romanian Graft-Buster for EU Prosecutor' *Politico* (2019) <www.politico.eu/article/laura-codruta-kovesi-romania-anti-corruption-chief-fights-for-top-eu-prosecutor-post/> accessed 27 February 2019.

147 Editorial Board, 'The Right Woman to Be Europe's Chief Prosecutor: EU Should Resist Romanian Demands and Appoint Laura Codruta Kovesi' *Financial Times* (2019) <www.ft.com/content/f1b11402-3a85-11e9-b72b-2c7f526ca5d0> accessed 15 March 2019.

148 Irina Marica, 'Romanian Intelligence Service Wiretapping Is Unconstitutional, Court Rules' *Romanian Insider* 18 February 2016 <www.romania-insider.com/romanian-intelligence-service-wiretapping-is-unconstitutional-court-rules> accessed 15 March 2019.

149 Zselyke Csaky, 'Romania's Attack on the Rule of Law Is Personal, Not Ideological' *Freedom House* (2018) <https://freedomhouse.org/blog/romania-s-attack-rule-law-personal-not-ideological> accessed 15 February 2019.

150 T Toader, 'The "Coercion" in Romanian Anti-Corruption Campaign' *Financial Times* (2019) <https://amp.ft.com/content/5c6b14a8-4023-11e9-b896-fe36ec32aece?fbclid=IwAR0HShCR27IeeXAshXsekxlLfhp_pHtqtCpd46g3oRp_Ov0BSrB7QqZdXa8> accessed 15 March 2019.

151 Mungiu-Pippidi (n 140).

2018 CVM report,[152] which entirely ignores the Romanian Intelligence Service's role in undermining the rule of law and due judicial process, in the quest to fight corruption in Romania.

As well as the EU's straining of the rule of law in Romania through overzealous use of the CVM, according to Professor Mungiu-Pippidi,[153] another legal and ethical aspect of the EU anti-corruption campaign in Romania is that many of those who were acknowledged as anti-corruption champions seem now, in retrospect, to have been cronies and lawbreakers themselves. For example, two of the leading prosecutors, Horia Georgescu (the head of the National Integrity Agency) and Alina Bica (the head of the Anti-Organised Crime Unit) were later both convicted for corruption.[154] These examples feed into a typical post-Communist political notion of a gang of crooks targeting another such group for political power, as well as access to public funds and resources. One would think that the EU would be concerned about this possibility, and reflect this in the EU's CVM reports—yesterday's anti-corruption champions are becoming today's criminals—but there has been no consideration of these events or raised concerns in the EU anti-corruption reports for Romania.[155] Last, and most worrying, is that DNA (under Kovesi) prosecuted all three potential challengers to President Iohannis' re-election bid in Autumn 2019. They were indicted by anti-corruption prosecutors, but nobody was charged with bribery or any other related corruption offense.[156] In the latest CVM report of 2018, there was no mention of these problematic factors going forward to the Romanian 2019 Presidential elections.

The Commission, meanwhile, continues to promote to Western Balkan countries the Romanian example of convicting large numbers of high-level officials for corruption as the most effective means of corruption fighting and being the benchmark for cleaning corrupt politicians from the system—and thus, putting these states onto a clear path to becoming members of the EU. Romania's achievements in successfully establishing effective anti-corruption agencies (in particular the DNA and its record of an average of nearly six hundred convictions per year under Kovesi) are very impressive, including a prime minister, ministers, generals and members of parliament from every political party. However, the balance to these efforts is the creation of a culture of anti-corruption political populism. No new political class has emerged, clean from corruption[157]; the right accuses the left, and vice versa, leading to open conflict between members of political parties and the judiciary, thus weaponising anti-corruption campaigns for political control or power gain.

152 ibid.
153 Mungiu-Pippidi (n 124).
154 Mungiu-Pippidi (n 124).
155 Mungiu-Pippidi (n 140).
156 ibid.
157 Mungiu-Pippidi (n 124).

The following chapter will assess the next case study on Albania, and it explains the EU interaction with a Candidate States for EU. The case study on UK and Romania showed how the EU engaged with an old (former) Member States and a new Member States in perusing anti-corruption reforms and to what extent both country made use of reflexive governance in establishing its anti-corruption policy field. For the UK, it was evident that it made use of reflexive governance approach, but for Romania it was based more on hard law and top-down approach. Furthermore, Romania in 2017 backslid in the rule of law and anti-corruption reform, and the EU Anti-Corruption Report did not have much of an impact in improving the anti-corruption framework for Romania. However, the case of Romania has offered some valuable lessons for EU Candidate States such as Albania and how it can develop more sustainable anti-corruption policy. The focus of the next chapter on Albania is to evaluate the assistance of the EU to support Albania in its efforts in establishing an anti-corruption policy field and evaluate whether the interaction between the European Union and Albania reveals any forms of reflexive governance or is similar to Romania through a mix of hard law and soft law.

6 Albania

6.1 The EU anti-corruption report for Albania

This chapter analyses and explains the steps that Albania has taken in developing an anti-corruption policy field from 1990 until 2016. This chapter distinguishes three different phases during which Albania has tried to establish an anti-corruption policy, after the downfall of the Communist regime in the early 1990s. We also evaluate the EU's support for Albania in the country's anti-corruption efforts and whether the interaction between the EU and Albania reveals forms of reflexive governance.

6.2 Post-communist Albania and anti-corruption

6.2.1 1990–1997: corruption as a new political chess game

Albania was the last country in South and Eastern Europe in the 1990s to experience the fall of the Communist system.[1] The country has struggled to create stable democratic institutions and proper governmental structures to this day, as it was one of the poorest Communist countries in Europe and had arguably the most oppressive Communist regime in the region. The intense degree of oppression under Communist rule effectively eliminated all forms of opposition and dissidence in Albania, and the effects of this are still prevalent, slowing down the subsequent transition to pluralism and democracy. In 1991, Albania established itself as a parliamentary representative democratic republic.[2] The Prime Minister became the head of government, and the President became the head of state. As a result, under the new post-Communist system, the power is shared between the executive branch (the government), the legislature (parliament) and the judiciary. Since 1992, the governments have been dominated by

1 Miranda Vickers and James Pettifer, *Albania: From Anarchy to a Balkan Identity* (NYUP 2000) 55–75.

2 Miranda Vickers, *The Albanians: A Modern History* (I.B. Tauris and Co 2014) 210–35.

the Democratic Party (conservatives: centre right) and the Socialist Party (social-democrats: centre left).[3]

Corruption has been a central issue in Albanian post-Communist politics, and the 1990s were characterised by a high degree of political conflict, weak internal party democracy, electoral fraud, parliamentary boycotts and the continuously changing rules of the election game in almost every parliamentary election. However, a corruption discourse emerged between the Democratic Party (the first non-Communist party, conservative in nature) and the newly reformed Socialist Party (the old Communist party), who constantly accused one another of being corrupt. However, the notion of corruption was, at the time, a new one in the public debate in Albania; some members of parliament opposed the introduction of a legal definition of corruption, arguing that, at that point, they still did not know its relevant legal meaning.

Corruption made its first appearance in Albanian legislation in 1991, characterised as a phenomenon that could undermine the freedom and independence of the country. The National Intelligence Service was assigned to fight corruption under this provision. Furthermore, corruption as an offence appeared for the first time in February 1992 under the Albanian Criminal Code. Under the heading 'Political Corruption', this was defined as 'receiving, or accepting to receive, for oneself or for others, a financial or other reward in order to carry out actions that go against the national interests'.[4] The former Communist party that governed Albania during the first transition phase introduced this article, and it was for this reason that the peculiar decision was made to put the National Intelligence Service—the old secret police—in charge of addressing corruption,[5] on the premise that corruption undermines the freedom and independence of the country and goes against the Albanian national interest.

The 'national interest' was a term used widely in the Communist era at which time it held two particular meanings. One type of national interest is in the context of international politics, meaning the interests of Albania on the international stage.[6] These interests flex according to different combinations of group interests or international interests. The other type of national interest refers to state interests at the highest level of national politics, governmental interest or the Albanian government representing the interests of the people.

3 Andon Kume, 'Study on the Approximation of the Albanian Electoral Legislation with the Code of Good Practice on Electoral Matters of the Venice Commission (EC)' *Academic Journal of Interdisciplinary Studies* 4 (2) (2015) 77–84.

4 Law No 7553 (2005) 'Changes to the Criminal Code of the Republic of Albania' Tirana 4 February 1992.

5 Blendi Kajsiu, 'The Birth of Corruption and the Politics of Anti-Corruption in Albania, 1991–2005' *Nationalities Papers: The Journal of Nationalism and Ethnicity 41* (6) (2013) 1008–25.

6 Mirela Bogdani and John Loughlin, *Albania and the European Union: The Tumultuous Journey towards Integration and Accession* (I.B. Tauris and Co 2007) 7–14.

Therefore, it is difficult to measure and clarify what constitutes or may be classified as going against the 'national interest' in exchange for financial gain, and how corruption was viewed as a crime 'against the national interest' in Albania under the criminal code in 1992. The notion of corruption as a phenomenon, and the choice of the National Intelligence Service to address the issue suggests that Albania was still not developing proper structures to deal with the issue of corruption and was mainly borrowing phrases and terms from the Communist regime in developing new legislation. This marked the start of the Albanian political process in creating systems to deal with the hurdles of the Communist past in their fight against corruption. Public officials had to adapt to the post-Communist political ethos—Western-style good governance, wherein personal favours from governmental and private sources were no longer acceptable.[7] However, Albania still relied on the National Intelligence Service at this stage, using personnel from the secret police structure of the Communist era to deal with corruption, rather than establishing an independent anti-corruption agency to deal with corruption-related cases.

During the beginning of the post-Communist era, in particular between the years 1990–1997, corruption became a common topic in the broader political discussion—and mainly used for labelling and denigrating the old Communist elite. The Democratic Party adopted the first anti-corruption legislation, a Presidential Decree in 1992, requesting the declaration and verification of wealth for private businesses and public officials during the period 1990–1992.[8] The Democratic Party government supported the Presidential Decree and acknowledged this effort as a major anti-corruption legislation because 'the red corruption in Albania was very deep'.[9] The term 'red corruption' was used to refer to the former Communist elite that was, over a short period of time, transformed into a capitalist coterie. The negative political discourse reacting to corruption was used as an effective tactic to denigrate this previously privileged group of leaders and cast them as a corrupt clique.[10] This response marked the start of the post-Communist political strategy to use corruption to fight political opponents as well as political battles, where opponents distinguished themselves from the Communist establishment that ruled Albania for almost 50 years. A similar tactic has been seen in many CEE countries with a Communist past.

The legislation in 1992 became a key instrument when the Democratic Party (conservative political party in Albania) came into the government pushed

7 Robert C Austin and Jonathan Ellison, 'Post-Communist Transitional Justice in Albania' *East European Politics and Societies 22* (2) (2008) 373–401.

8 Presidential Decree 203, 'On the Declaration and Verification of Earned Profit (Për Deklarimin dhe Verifikimin e Fitimeve të Realizuara)' Tirana 5 June 1992 *Journal of Official Acts* (Fletorja Zyrtare) 3 164.

9 Blendi Kajsiu, *A Discourse Analysis of Corruption: Instituting Neoliberalism Against Corruption in Albania, 1998–2005* (Routledge 2015) 51.

10 Smoki Musaraj, 'Passport Troubles: Social Tactics and Places of Informal Transactions in Post-Socialist Albania' *Anthropology of East Europe Review 27* (2) (2009) 159–75.

forward in prosecuting those in the privileged political class of the former Communist rule, mainly under conditions in which Albanian was mismanaged between 1990 and 1992, and in particular, on the basis of committing financial crimes during the transition phase.[11] This tactic was used against the old Communist elite to hold them to account, at least in part—albeit not for their political atrocities during the Communist era. Instead, they could be held liable for financial crimes, and corruption was frequently used in referring to the country's management between the transition phases in 1990–1992 as betrayal of the national interest in exchange for personal financial gain. The government issued a report on the Communist elite management during 1990–1992, which became the main piece of evidence in the trial against the last Communist leader, Ramiz Alia, and the newly elected chairmen of the Socialist Party, Fatos Nano, who both were convicted and jailed under corruption charges.[12]

The report was prepared in under a month and comprised an overview of an audit of the luxurious spending of the Communist elite during the transition phase from 1990 to 1992. Berisha (the leader of the Democratic Party) felt that in a nation suffering in poverty and food shortages, the public would support actions against their former Communist leaders that focused on financial abuses.[13] This new government was interested in two things: first and foremost, to distinguish themselves and New Democracy Party as clearly as possible as non-Communist—even though many leading members were part of the former Communist politburo—and secondly, to fight their new political opponents, in particular, the then-chairman of the Socialist Party, Nano. These concerns vastly outweighed any priority to actually develop an anti-corruption policy field in Albania.

As a result, President Berisha picked financial issues related to corruption, rather than serious political crimes that could have been identified during Communist period. It is clear that, up to this time, the anti-corruption policy field had started to slowly emerge, with the introduction of legislation presenting corruption as being against the state interest. However, at this stage, it was not intended to build an anti-corruption policy field in and of itself, but rather to use corruption to fight political opponents and denigrate their political credibility by calling them corrupt, regardless of which party was leading the country after the 1992 general elections.

This narrative was demonstrated in the trial of the final Albanian Communist leader Ramiz Alia, brought to trial on the basis of corruption, rather than the wider crimes for which he was responsible during the Communist era.[14] The intention and efforts of the government were not to develop an anti-corruption

11 Fred C Abrahams, *Modern Albania: From Dictatorship to Democracy in Europe* (NYUP 2015) 55–72.

12 Ian Jeffries, *Eastern Europe at the Turn of the Twenty-First Century: A Guide to the Economic Transition* (Routledge 2012) 85–91.

13 Kajsiu (n 5).

14 Jeffries (n 12) 85–91.

policy. Although the new post-Communist government wanted to develop a track record in tackling high-profile cases related to corruption, the intention was to denigrate and destroy key former members of the previous politburo.

The government intention under the Democratic Party to push for investigating and imprisoning former members of the politburo was based on two reasons. Firstly, the last Communist leader Ramiz Alia, Nexhmije Hoxha (wife of former Communist leader Enver Hoxha), and the leader of the Socialist Party, Fatos Nano, symbolised the Communist era in the eyes of many Albanians and had to be prosecuted for their leading roles in Communist Albania.[15] Secondly, the new government wanted to clearly distinguish themselves in the estimation of the international community as emphatically non-Communist and able to lead Albania into the EU. Corruption was used as a means to prosecute and imprison key members of the previous politburo: Nexhmije Hoxha was sentenced for nine years in 1993, Nano was sentenced to 12 years in prison in 1994, and Alia was placed under house arrest in August 1992;[16] in August 1993, his detention was converted into imprisonment. However, they all went free in 1997, and Nano was compensated, as the charges were found to be politically motivated by the Democratic Party government.

These former leaders were imprisoned on the basis of their abuse of power and misappropriation of state funds during 1990–1992.[17] The parliament commission that investigated the activities of the Albania government of 1990–1992 suggested that the government at the time abused humanitarian aid given by the Italian state during the 1990–1992 economic crisis. Therefore, rather than attempting to prosecute these former leaders for their involvement in the Communist administration or crimes that they committed during Communist era, the label 'corruption' was an effective way to punish them.[18] The charges levelled at Socialist Party leader Nano for corruption were not driven by an anti-corruption agenda, but rather from a political motivation. The Vienna-based International Helsinki Federation for Human Rights argued that the jailed opposition leader was convicted under a heavily politically-motivated trial and appealed for his release.[19] This is a clear example of how the government at the time was not focusing on developing an anti-corruption policy field, but using corruption as a way to prosecute and jail political opponents. As a human rights activist observed, the Democratic Party in government did not simply want to fight corruption at this period, but win elections by intimidating their opponents.[20] This was evidenced in the 1996 Preliminary elections, where the Democratic Party won an outright majority and the election was highly

15 Abrahams (n 11) 55–72.
16 Jeffries (n 12) 85–91.
17 Vickers and Pettifer (n 1) 247–266.
18 Clarissa De Waal, *Albania Today: A Portrait of Post-Communist Turbulence* (I.B. Tauris & Co 2007) 8–12.
19 Vickers and Pettifer (n 1) 247–66.
20 Abrahams (n 11) 55–72.

contested. Human Rights Watch, the UN, the Organisation for Security and Cooperation in Europe (OSCE), the Council of Europe, the EU and the US government all called on the Albanian government to declare these elections invalid due to electoral violations and election fraud.[21]

Later on, in 1995, corruption shifted as a topic and began to relate to the public administration. In particular, bribery in the public sector became a concern in 1995, since Albania started to privatise its state entities.[22] The government introduced changes to the Albanian Criminal Code as a response to concerns about bribery of public officials, adding that a *'bribe-presenter is freed from criminal charge when he/she reports the act of bribe-giving before the start of a legal investigation'* to Article 109 of the Albanian Criminal Code.[23] The idea behind this change was to encourage the reporting of bribery in the public sector. In 1995, the High State Audit was criticised by the public and members of parliament for ignoring claims about corruption. This ranged from smuggling petrol and weapons to former Yugoslavia and the Middle East, to corruption being used as a means to pass through the border in Albania.[24] As a result, corruption at this stage started to disseminate out into the black market and get a foothold in the informal economy. The director of the high state audit in Albania at the time acknowledged that bribery was a problem in state agencies and had started to become common practice in public administration. There was a tendency towards the use of corruption, and it started to emerge in the economy, marking the start of a discourse around corruption in the financial sector. For example, government officials fixed and lowered prices in relation to the liberalised prices of the free market for financial gain.[25]

However, even in the midst of this growth of corruption throughout Albania, there was no government intention to develop an anti-corruption policy field to address these allegations. These practices were accepted by public officials and reported in the media—but no one was prosecuted for corruption at this stage. Corruption in public administration and the informal sector was not viewed as a problem at this stage, but as a means to an end. Corruption as an issue only took central stage in political discussion where it was used to fight opponents during elections. However, the emergence of corruption in the black market and in the financial sector had a huge impact on how Albania reacted after the collapse of the Ponzi scheme in March 1997, and those events shaped how corruption was treated after that time, in terms of developing an anti-corruption policy field.[26]

21 Karen Dawisha and Bruce Parrot, *Politics, Power and the Struggle for Democracy in South-East Europe* (CUP 1997) 352.

22 Kajsiu (n 5).

23 Rezarta Tahiraj, 'Law and Corruption in Albania and in the South-Eastern European Countries: A Comparative Analysis' *Mediterranean Journal of Social Sciences* 5 (7) (2014) 136–47.

24 Kajsiu (n 9) 51–7.

25 Kajsiu (n 5).

26 Theodore Kaltsounis, *The Democratization of Albania: Democracy from Within* (Palgrave Macmillan 2010) 78–80.

During this early period of post-Communist Albania, there was no unified understanding or meaning around corruption, covering bribery, smuggling, organised crime and speculation about alleged corrupt activities. Nevertheless, it is possible to draw some key examples of how corruption was used for political purposes during 1990–1997 in Albania. The phrase 'corruption' was primarily linked to the transition phase from Communism to post-Communism, and there was no proper agreement on developing an anti-corruption policy field. Despite a growing discussion about corruption during the period 1990–1997, there was no clear intention to develop an anti-corruption policy field; this only came after 1998, as a consequence of the collapse of the Ponzi schemes (known as the Pyramid schemes) and the support of international actors paying closer attention to anti-corruption policy shortcomings in Albania.

6.2.2 The collapse of the pyramid schemes and the international support to fight corruption in Albania, 1997–2009

Albania made its first attempts to develop a proper anti-corruption policy field between 1997 and 2009. There were internal and external factors that pushed Albania to shape an anti-corruption policy and make the fight against corruption more of a policy priority. The new Socialist Party came into government, elected in 1997, made fighting corruption one of their key policy priorities, and in 1998, with the assistance of the World Bank, the government introduced the first Albanian anti-corruption strategy, closely following the World Bank's programme to address corruption.[27] There were three main reasons why the Albanian government introduced the anti-corruption strategy in 1998, with the support of international actors.

Firstly, the new government under the Socialist Party wanted to distinguish themselves from the previous government under the leadership of the Democratic Party in the eyes of the Albanian electorate. Secondly, the international actors—mainly the World Bank and IMF—had a lot of leverage over the new Albanian government, and a major priority was to restructure Albania's financial sector, as a result of the collapse of the economy in 1997. Thirdly, the collapse of the country's pyramid schemes in 1997—the main factor in the collapse of the economy—and the subsequent civil unrest and political turmoil that resulted in early elections to solve the crises were all significant elements, which required the acknowledgment of corruption as a major problem that needed to be addressed through a comprehensive anti-corruption policy. Under huge pressure, the government had to respond to these internal issues, as well as the concerns of major international actors, and as a result adopted an anti-corruption strategy in 1998.

27 Albania Council of Ministers, 'Combating Corruption in Albania: A Comprehensive Reform Program' Republic of Albania: Council of Ministers (1998).

Pyramid schemes had been operating in the country since 1992, and on an increasing scale, and their sudden collapse pulled the country into chaos, widespread violence, plundering and food shortages within weeks. The common perception of this incident was unexpected from an analytical point of view, as the economic reforms after 1992 were considered as a successful model and in line with the 'Washington consensus'.[28] The IMF economic reform policymakers later observed that the unexpected collapse of the Albanian economy was as a result of the country's false understating of capitalism and market economy.[29]

The pyramid schemes were Ponzi schemes: mainly companies and firms registered as foundations or charities, banking under complicated Ponzi methods. This informal structure of the economic sector was not considered problematic by the financial authorities in Albania at the time, and corruption was not viewed as an issue. The pyramid scheme money-borrowing firms did not have to report on their sources of capital and loans, and under the regulations of the time, these were not recorded in their balance sheets. These firms were presenting themselves as 'charity foundations', and quickly gained a major foothold in the Albanian economy between 1992 and 1997. Their activities expanded into equity investment, business trading, tourism, oil, property markets, transport and food processing.[30] Investing in these pyramid schemes has become very attractive to citizens because of the high interest rates received in return. In late 1996 in Albania, the monthly profit was around 50 per cent in these banking firms. The Democratic Party of Albania when in government between 1992 and 1997 offered some credibility to these schemes, even though the IMF and World Bank had warned and recommended the government to closely supervise the so-called foundations. Albanian citizens that invested in these schemes felt that the government supported it because the executives of these schemes were closely associated with key government members—and the government did, in fact, publicly back the scheme. Even more importantly, these pyramid schemes supported and financed the Democratic Party of Albania's campaign in the 1996 general election. The schemes had become very important to the Albania economy, as they had accumulated more than US$ 1.2 billion, about 50 per cent GDP.

The pyramid schemes' collapse contributed to the social, economic and political turmoil, which saw Albania go through a massive reconstruction and, in fact, start building governmental structures again from the beginning.

The government under the Socialist Party of Albania, as well as the international actors, now saw the urgent need to push for the introduction of an anti-corruption strategy and to develop an anti-corruption policy field in order

28 Pawel Bozyk, *Globalization and the Transformation of Foreign Economic Policy* (Ashgate 2012) 211–6.

29 DJ Bezemer, 'Post-Socialist Financial Fragility: The Case of Albania' *Cambridge Journal of Economics 25* (1) (2001) 1–3.

30 Carlos Elbirt, 'Albania Under the Shadows of the Pyramid Schemes' *Transition: The Newsletter about Reforming Economics 8* (5) (1997) 8–10.

to address many fundamental issues connected to the collapse of the economy in 1997. Furthermore, key international actors pushed for reforms to reconstruct Albania's administrative structures. Thus, corruption was observed as a common problem that had allowed pyramid schemes to flourish without appropriate government supervision; furthermore, the schemes corruptly obtained support from the Democratic Party government itself.

We can easily understand the earlier delay in government action on corruption due to the influence that these schemes had in the country—especially given the fact that half of the Albanian GDP was encompassed by these schemes. By the end of 1996, the IMF had grasped the dangerous implications for the country's economy and warned the Albanian government against the pyramid schemes; the World Bank had been doing this publicly since 1996 and even earlier within government circles.[31] However, since the parliamentary elections were due in 1996, the Democratic Party in government had refused to act, fearing that any response would have a major impact on their general election results. For these reasons, the Socialist Party government wanted to clearly define themselves as clearly opposing pyramid schemes in 1998, identifying corruption as one of the major contributing factors that enabled these schemes to operate unchecked in Albania.

Now, other international actors besides the World Bank began to influence the socialist government to establish an anti-corruption policy field and make it a key political priority. World Bank research found that bribes were widespread in Albania, a finding also supported by USAID. USAID funded programmes, initiatives and outreach programmes to educate Albanians against corruption and also funded research to identify Albanians' attitudes to and understanding of corruption. The international community felt that it was now crucial to educate Albanian society in the proper meaning of corruption, through public-awareness campaigns that emphasised corruption and bribery, and in particular, corruption related to the public sector, to prevent any future Ponzi scheme becoming established on a national scale. Furthermore, international actors saw this period as an opportunity to engage civil society in shaping anti-corruption policy in Albania.

This strong movement to developing an anti-corruption field led the Albanian government to change the criminal code in 2004 regarding cases relating to corruption. Assisted by the Council of Europe, the definition of corruption was reframed, defining corruption as 'any irregular benefit or a promise for such benefit, for oneself or for other people—in order to carry out or neglect an action which pertains to his or her function'.[32] Furthermore, the title of Article 259 of the 1995 Criminal Code was changed from 'asking for a bribe' to 'passive corruption of persons who exercise public duties'.[33] In other words, the criminal code

31 ibid.

32 Law No 9275 (2004), 'On Change in the Criminal Code Approved by the Law 7895' 27 January 1995 Penal Code of the Republic of Albania.

33 ibid.

replaced 'bribery' for 'corruption'. Therefore, corruption became restricted to the public sector, but was linked with bribery.[34]

Up to this point, Albania had been monitored by the IMF, the World Bank and the Council of Europe in implementing a number of internationally recommended reforms, putting the country on a path for further integration into the global market and making it more welcoming to international capital and investors. However, for EU integration prospects, Albania had to address corruption more thoroughly and establish a comprehensive anti-corruption policy field. The European Commission found that the deficiency in tackling corruption was largely due to the lack of political will to address it as an issue. A review of the international anti-corruption effort in Albania argued that the politicians—directly or by collusion with criminals and/or business people—take from the public purse and engage in a range of corrupt schemes. Around this time, the Commission started to fund some projects against corruption in Albania, which was implemented by the Council of Europe. Through these types of projects, the EU and other international actors active in Albania found that civil society perceived that Albania's efforts in fighting corruption were superficial. The conditions were not favourable for Albania to cure corruption, as it was widespread in every aspect: institutions, politicians and the culture of engagement with public institutions. The only hope seemed to be intervention and assistance from the outside, and EU integration could become an important factor in addressing corruption. Albanian internal anti-corruption policy and efforts were insufficient: the lack of political will, the socio-economic issues, and limited administrative capacities and resources to address corruption as a problem all conspired to thwart the country finding a resolution independently.

In 2006, Albania signed the Stabilisation and Association Agreement (SAA) with the EU, and this marked the start of EU support for an anti-corruption policy field that would address key aspects of Albania's governing structures. The SAA entered into force in 2009. This was a new process between the EU and Albania and came with policy commitments for the country; the agreement consisted of new contractual relationships with trade preferences and financial assistance to support the countries' progress in meeting the requirements for EU future membership. The SAA rested on four building blocks for Albania:

1. The SAA consists of a legally binding agreement between the EU and each country in the Stabilisation and Association Process (SAP);
2. Bilateral Free Trade Agreements between all countries participating in the SAP;
3. Trade preferences, which unilaterally grant almost totally free access to EU markets for goods from the Balkans; and
4. Financial assistance planned in consultation with the partner countries, EU member states and the international community.

34 Kajsiu (n 9) 51–7.

The beginning of EU-Albania relations (formal negotiations for a bilateral SAA) began in 2003 and came into full force six years later. The SAA anticipated the establishment of an Association Agreement to be implemented progressively over a maximum transitional period. The EU-Albania SAA was extensive and, like all other SAAs, based largely on the Europe Agreements. It covered a wide range of areas, from political dialogue to regional cooperation and from freedom movement of goods, services, workers and capital to mutual co-operation in justice and home affairs.

The SAA was not specifically aimed at Albania, but was part of the EU's efforts to develop an anti-corruption policy field. The intention of the EU, as was highlighted in 2003 at the EU–Western Balkans Summit, was as a result of the Thessaloniki Declaration to integrate the Western Balkans countries into the EU in the future. The EU at this time wanted to maintain stability in the region by offering EU integration, rather than develop an anti-corruption policy field in the Western Balkans region.

The Thessaloniki Western Balkans Summit highlighted the numerous challenges faced by both the EU and the countries of the region, ranging from security concerns, the consolidation of democracy and the rule of law to economic development and regional cooperation. However, organised crime and corruption were observed by the EU (as specified in the Thessaloniki Western Balkans Summit Communication) as a real obstacle to democratic stability, the rule of law, economic development and development of civil society in the region and were also a source of concern for EU security.

Once the SAA came into force, Albania was subject to a more rigorous evaluation through the so-called 'Progress Report', issued on an annual basis, making key recommendations on specific policy fields where there are shortcomings. After 2009, the issue of corruption quickly became a key topic every year in the Progress Report and has been mentioned ever since as a problematic issue. Therefore, it marked the emergence of the EU supporting and requesting Albania to introduce tangible measures to prevent and fight corruption in more concrete terms. Since 2010, Albania has engaged more closely with the EU in establishing an anti-corruption policy field by introducing fundamental structural changes—mostly changing legislation, developing new institutional structures to address corruption and anti-corruption plans, which led to the emergence of a broader anti-corruption policy field covering many sectors that were viewed to be prone to corruption. Furthermore, fighting corruption is also a way to pass other key legislation and make necessary structural changes to government.

6.2.3 The EU conditionality and Albania's obstacles in developing an anti-corruption policy

Post-Communist Albania has proven to be one of the most challenging cases for fighting corruption and organised crime, reforming the public administration and the judiciary. Since the successful integration of the CEE states into the EU, the EU has wanted to try to replicate similar success in the Western Balkans region. However, the long-standing ethnic disputes, the widespread corruption and organised crime, lack of functional democracy, institutionally weak civil societies and the failure of the full integration of Bulgaria and Romania have all created many barriers for the EU policy's success in the Western Balkans region. The EU established an instrument called the Stabilisation Process for the Western Balkans, which was adopted at the Western Balkans Summit in 2003 for the EU's key interest in integrating the Western Balkans region into the EU.

Since the SAA came into force in Albania, the country has been subject to closer monitoring by the EU in developing meaningful and long-term sustainable reform for the purpose of the European integration process. Since 2009, Albania has paid more attention to developing an anti-corruption policy field with the assistance of the EU, as well as other international organisations. In contrast to the first post-Communist governments between 1992 and 1997 and between 1997 and 2005, the debate about the issue of corruption in Albania shifted more towards policymaking and capacity building. Furthermore, after 2009, the EU has pushed Albania to establish a policy field that would address corruption in different areas, especially in the judiciary, for the sole purpose of joining the EU.

In the latest EU Progress Report for Albania, issued in April 2018, it was clearly stated that Albania must show tangible evidence in the fight against corruption, and clear progress in addressing the five key priorities for opening the negotiation process for EU membership, potentially by the end of 2019.

The five key priorities areas are on reforms in the public administration, the judiciary, the fight against organised crime, the fight against corruption and upholding human rights. These areas are seen by the EU to be fundamentally important for reforming Albania in order to have any EU accession success. The issue concerning corruption is raised regularly in all of the Progress Reports as a leading problem in the first three areas. Before evaluating these, which the EU views to be highly problematic due to the high level of corruption involved, it is important to consider the EU-Albania relationship that led up to this point, where both the EU and Albania are working to establish an anti-corruption policy field in the country.

6.3 Albanian relations with the European Union

Albania has been an official candidate for accession to the EU since June 2014 and a member of NATO since 2009. Albanian support for membership in the EU and NATO is amongst the highest in Europe, making this the least controversial issue in the country. Almost all political parties are in agreement on EU membership, just as they were on NATO, making these two issues completely uncontroversial and non-opposing in the political debate. Opposing the EU membership would be political suicide for any Albanian party, taking into account the high support for European integration among Albanian citizens in general. The objective of full EU membership is accepted without question, as the latest 2018 Balkan Public Barometer showed that over 83 per cent of the citizens support the EU integration process. However—there are divergent opinions about how to reach it. Political parties frequently try to win votes by promising that they will be the one to lead Albania into the EU quicker than their political opponents, and this has been the case since the 2005 general elections.

Following the traditional patterns of confrontation, as was observed in the two previous periods of post-Communist Albania in this chapter, in addition to corruption, delaying any EU-related policy or reform has become a characteristic of the political debate since 2009. The 2013 election was the latest evidence demonstrating that the Democratic Party—who had governed Albania from 2005 to 2009 and then in 2009 to 2013 a coalition government of between the Democratic Party and Socialist Movement for Integration 2013—were not able to obtain the EU candidate statutes and were beset with scandals related to corruption. On 23 June 2014, under the Greek EU Presidency, the Council of the EU agreed to grant Albania candidate status, endorsed by the European Council a few days later. As a result, since then, Albania has been a candidate state for EU and has engaged with the EU in high-level dialogue to develop policies that are key to fulfilling the five main priorities. In 2018, the Commission recommended open accession talks with Albania, and the EU Council has suggested the end of 2019 as a possible starting point for opening accession talks. Let's now consider, chronologically, Albania's relations with the EU to understand how long it took to get into a dialogue for establishing an anti-corruption policy as part of the country's efforts to join the EU in the near future.

6.3.1 The chronological path to accession

The first official interaction between the EU and Albania was in 1992, when a 'Trade and Cooperation Agreement' was signed, Albania thus becoming eligible for funding under the EU Poland and Hungary Assistance for the Restructuring of the Economy (PHARE) programme.[35] The PHARE programme is a pre-accession instrument for the European Community's financial and technical cooperation with CEE countries. Its objectives revolve around two key priorities. Firstly, helping the administrations of the countries to acquire the capacity and resources to implement the Commission's acquis and to assist the national and regional administrations; the PHARE programme supported regulatory and supervisory bodies in the candidate countries to familiarise themselves with the EU objectives and procedures. Secondly, PHARE helps countries to bring their industries and basic infrastructure up to the EU standards by mobilising the investment required, particularly in areas where the EU rules are increasingly demanding—for instance with regards to the environment, transport, industry, product quality and working conditions.[36]

35 K Beshku and O Malltezi, *Albania and Europe in a Political Regard* (Cambridge Scholars Publishing 2013) 49–51.

36 Filip Keereman and Istvan Szekely, *Five Years of an Enlarged EU: A Positive Sum Game—A Positive Sun Game* (Springer 2010) 98–104.

In 1997, the EU Council of Ministers adopted a regional approach, aimed at strengthening stability in South-Eastern Europe and promoting cooperation between the states in the region. This marked an important development for Albania, Bosnia and Herzegovina, Croatia, and Macedonia, as the approach established political and economic conditionality as the basis for a transparent policy towards the development of bilateral relations in the fields of trade, financial assistance and economic cooperation, as well as a contractual basis for the development of bilateral relations between these states and the EU.[37]

In 1999, the EU proposed the new SAP for five countries in South-Eastern Europe, including Bosnia and Herzegovina, Croatia, Macedonia, Albania, Montenegro, Serbia and Kosovo.[38] Accordingly, the EU started to develop new contractual relations with these countries for stabilisation and association agreements. From 1999, Albania started to benefit from 'Autonomous Trade Preferences' with the EU, by extending generalised tariff preferences to Albania. As a result, Albania started to benefit from unilateral trade concessions under the EU's autonomous trade measures (AMTs).[39] An extension of duty-free access to the EU market was also established for products from Albania in 2000. The EU was Albania's main commercial partner by 2005, representing about 74 per cent of Albania's total imports and around 85 per cent of the total exports, making Albania one of the highest EU-trade-dependent countries.[40]

The European Council in June 2000 confirmed that all the SAP countries were potential candidates for EU membership. In November 2000 at the Zagreb Summit, the SAP was officially recognised by the EU and the Western Balkan countries, including Albania.[41] In 2001, the EU established an instrument called the Community Assistance for Reconstruction, Development and Stabilisation (CARDS) programme specifically designed for the SAP countries to support projects previously funded by the PHARE programmes.[42] The programme was the main financial instrument of the EU's SAP—a total of €5.13 billion was secured for all CARDS actions during 2000–2006, as after that day it would be replaced by the Instrument for Pre-Accession Assistance (IPA), which would cover both candidate and potential candidate countries.[43]

37 Eli Gateva, *European Union Enlargement Conditionality* (Palgrave Macmillan 2015) 124–74.

38 Robert Elsie, *Historical Dictionary of Albania* (2nd edn, Scarecrow Press Inc 2010) 130–4.

39 Johannes Stahl, *Rent from the Land: A Political Ecology of Post-Socialist Rural Transformation* (Anthem Press 2012) 125–6.

40 Aristidis Bitzenis, *The Balkans: Foreign Direct Investment and EU Accession* (Ashgate 2009) 247–50.

41 FA Tatham, *Enlargement of the European Union* (Kluwer Law International 2009) 165–70.

42 Andreas Staab, *The European Union Explained: Institutions, Actors, Global Impact* (Indiana UP 2013) 208–10.

43 Andrew Geddes, Charlie Lees and Andrew Taylor, *The European Union and South East Europe: The Dynamics of Europeanization and Multi-Level Governance* (Routledge/UACES 21 2013) 153–269.

The Commission recommended, in June 2001, for the EU to engage in the negotiations of the SAA with Albania.[44] At the European Council in 2001, the Commission was asked to present a draft negotiating directive for the negotiation of an SAA with Albania[45]; in October 2002, these directives were adopted, and on 31 January 2003 the Commission officially launched the negotiations for an SAA between the EU and Albania.[46] That June, at the Thessaloniki Western Balkans Summit, the SAP was defined as EU policy for the Western Balkans, and the EU perspective for these states was confirmed. Therefore, countries participating in the SAP started to be eligible for EU accession and would join the EU once they were ready.[47] In December 2005, the EU Council made the decision on the principles of a revised European Partnership for Albania, and on 12 June 2006, the SAA was signed at the General Affairs and External Relations Council in Luxembourg.[48]

On 9 November 2006, the Commission begun discussing visa facilitation negotiations with Albania, and by April the following year the visa facilitation agreement was reached.[49] EU Commissioner Franco Frattini cited this as the first step towards full elimination of the visa requirements and the free movement of Albanian citizens in the EU—a positive step towards future integration into the EU. The visa facilitation agreement entered into force on 1 January 2008, and two months later, Frattini opened a dialogue towards the liberalisation of the visa regime between Albania and the EU.[50] The SAA ratification process was completed by all member states on 14 January 2009, and on 1 April 2009 the SAA entered into force. Thereafter, Albania formally applied for membership in the EU on 28th April 2009.[51]

On 16 November 2009, the EU Council asked the Commission to prepare an assessment of Albania's readiness to start accession negotiations with the EU.[52] Albania responded to the Commission's questionnaire by 14 April 2010, but the EU did not immediately grant candidacy status, due to the long-lasting political disputes in the country, as well as the high levels of corruption.

44 Ridvan Peshkopia, *Conditioning Democratization: Institutional Reforms and EU Membership, Conditionality in Albania and Macedonia* (Anthem Press 2015) 7–18.

45 Sven Gänzle, Stefan Grimm and Davina Makhan, *The European Union and Global Development: An 'Enlightened Superpower' in the Making?* (Palgrave Macmillan 2012) 57–74.

46 Darjel Sina and Arjan Vasjari, 'Albania's Integration in EU' *Mediterranean Journal of Social Sciences 4* (6) (2013) 305–13.

47 Federiga Bindi and Irina Angelescu, *The Foreign Policy of the European Union: Assessing Europe's Role in the World* (Brookings Institution Press 2012) 153–65.

48 Gergana Noutcheva, *European Foreign Policy and the Challenges of Balkan Accession: Conditionality, Legitimacy and Compliance* (Routledge 2012) 55–89.

49 Michela Ceccorulli and Nicola Labanca, *The EU Migration and the Politics of Administrative Detention* (Routledge 2014) 23–42.

50 European Communication, 'Commission Launches Dialogue with Albania on Visa Liberalisation' COM (2008) 127 final.

51 Elsie (n 38) 130–4.

52 Paul Craig and Gráinne De Búrca, *The Evolution of EU Law* (OUP 2011) 188–215.

The Commission proposed visa-free travel for Albania on 27 May 2010. The adopted proposal enabled Albanians to travel to Schengen countries without needing a short-term visa.[53] The EU Council approved visa-free travel to the Schengen Area for Albanian citizens on 8 November 2010, which entered into force on 15 December 2010. On 10 October 2012 the Commission recommended that Albania be granted EU candidate status, subject to the completion of key measures in certain areas.

6.3.2 Candidate status delay—corruption and organised crime factors

In August 2012, the Albanian parliament rejected a proposal by the EU to abolish immunity for parliament members, ministers, key judges and individuals in influential public offices. The EU required that the immunity should be abolished for public officials, along with eleven other key issues. As a result, the candidate status was further delayed for Albania.[54] A constitutional amendment was unanimously passed in September 2012 that limited the immunity of parliamentarians and other key positions that had previously enjoyed immunity from prosecution in Albania.[55] The Commission saw the immunity of high public-officeholders as an obstacle in terms of prosecuting high-level officials against corruption and involvement in organised crime-related cases and pushed hard for Albania to lift this immunity.

The Commission evaluated the progress of Albania in October 2012, in complying with 12 key conditions to achieve official candidate status and start accession negotiations. Only four priorities were met, while two were well underway, and the remaining six had made moderate progress.[56] The report suggested that, if Albania managed to hold a fair and democratic parliamentary election in June 2013 and also implemented the remaining changes to comply with the eight key priorities, even though all priorities had not been fully satisfied, the EU Council would recommend granting Albania candidate status.

Albania held a general election on 23 June 2013, generally regarded as free and fair, thus satisfying the EU pre-condition.[57] On 17 July 2013, the EU delegation to Albania cited that Albania had met many of these conditions and could well become an official candidate by December 2013.

53 KB Eisele, *The External Dimension of the EU's Migration Policy: Different Legal Positions of Third-Country Nationals in the EU: A Comparative Perspective* (Brill Nijhoff 2014) 278–84.

54 Gledis Gjipali, Freedom House Annual Report on Albania (2012) <https://freedomhouse.org/sites/default/files/NIT13_Albania_3rdProof_0.pdf> accessed 30 May 2019.

55 Arat Vorpsi, Legal Adviser at the Constitutional Court of Albania (2014) <http://constitutional-change.com/is-there-a-need-of-a-deep-constitutional-reform-in-albania/> accessed 30 May 2019.

56 Henry F Carey, *European Institutions, Democratization, and Human Rights Protection in the European Periphery* (Lexington Books 2014) 338–47.

57 Peshkopia (n 44) 177–82.

On 16 October 2013, the Commission issued its annual report and concluded that the Albanian election was held in an orderly manner in which progress was made in meeting also other conditions. As a result, the Commission recommended granting to Albania the EU candidate status.[58] The EU Parliament meeting on 5 December 2013 suggested that the Council should acknowledge the progress made by Albania and grant the EU candidate status without undue delay. However, several EU member states, in particular Denmark and the Netherlands, remained opposed to granting Albania candidate status until it demonstrated that its recent progress could be sustained. Thus, at its meeting in December 2013, the EU Council decided to postpone the decision on candidate status until June 2014 to see evidence of whether recent progress could be sustained and in particular whether there was a clear effort to fight corruption and organised crime.[59] Under the Greek EU Presidency on 24 June 2014, the EU Council agreed to grant Albania the EU candidate status, which was endorsed by the European Council a few days later. This coincided with the 10th anniversary of the 'Agenda 2014', proposed by the Greek Government in 2004, as part of the EU-Western Balkans Summit in Thessaloniki, for boosting the integration of all the Western Balkan states into the European Union.[60]

At the fifth High-Level Dialogue meeting between Albania and EU in March 2015, the EU Commissioner for Enlargement informed Albania that for the EU to open accession talks, Albania was still required to meet two key conditions.[61] Firstly, the government needed to reopen political dialogue with the parliamentary opposition. Secondly, Albania must deliver quality reforms for all five earlier identified areas: i.e. reforming the public administration, rule of law, fighting corruption and organised crime, and respecting human rights.[62] This official stance was fully supported by the European Parliament through passing a Resolution Comment in April 2015, which essentially approved all conclusions drawn by the Commission's 2014 Progress Report on Albania.[63] The Government outlined the next step would be to submit a detailed progress report on the implementation of the five key reforms to the Commission in Autumn 2015, with hopes of starting the accession negotiations process in late 2016.[64]

58 David Phinnemore and Lee McGowan, *A Dictionary of the European Union* (Routledge 2015) 9–11.

59 Eva Teqja, 'Western Balkans, The Long Way of Integration: Albania's Perception about the Process' *Journal of Global Faultlines* 2 (1) (2014) 70–94.

60 Phinnemore and McGowan (n 58) 9–11.

61 European Union, Albania Joint Conclusions on the Fifth High Level Dialogue on the Key Priorities, (24 March 2015) <http://eeas.europa.eu/delegations/albania/documents/press_releases/20150324_5th_hld_operational_conclusions.pdf> accessed 30 May 2019.

62 ibid.

63 European Parliament, Resolution on the 2014 Progress Report on Albania (2015) <www.europarl.europa.eu/oeil/popups/ficheprocedure.do?lang=en&reference=2014/2951%28RSP%29> accessed 30 May 2019.

64 European Union, Albania Joint Conclusions on the Fifth High Level Dialogue on the Key Priorities (n 66).

The Progress Report issued on 10 November 2015 emphasised the importance of addressing these five key priorities and gave recommendations as to what Albania should do to cooperate with the EU accession negotiations process.[65] Corruption was evidently an obstacle to accession, especially in the public administration sector and the judicial system. In the following section, there will be an analysis and overview on how the EU identified these areas and whether Albania has developed an anti-corruption policy field with the assistance of the EU in the public administration and the judiciary.

6.4 Reforming the public administration

The Commission's Progress Reports have repeatedly indicated that Albania must reform its public administration, depoliticising it, because the Albanian public administration is not impartial to political affiliations. Furthermore, corruption is a prevailing issue in many layers of the public administration.

The EU suggested reforms to establish a professional public administration in Albania and implement preventive anti-corruption measures. The Commission recommended (in the joint EU and Albania working groups) that Albania needs to adopt a Public Administration Reform (PAR) Strategy to ensure financial sustainability first. Further efforts must be made by Albania in implementing the amendments to the Civil Service Law (CSL) and ensure transparency, objectivity and meritocracy in selection procedures for low- and middle-level managers. In other words, recruitment should be done on the basis of merit, not on political affiliation, as the current practice has led many observers to believe that corruption practices flourish because of close network groups. In addition, Albania must ensure that continuous training is provided to all human resource management units, including in local government, for a collective and clear implementation of applicable legislation. The EU is paying critical attention to the application of the legislation in Albania, ensuring it is consistent with EU standards. However, Albania lacks the proper application of the law on the organisation and functioning of the public administration, and the EU has encouraged the establishment of an efficient public administration structures, making the reduction of corrupt practices in the public administration a key priority.

The Progress Reports also repeatedly recommend that Albania takes concrete measures to enhance the independence and the monitoring capacity of the Ombudsman and the Supreme State Audit in their areas of competence and ensure proper follow-up to their findings and recommendations. The Commission has also recommended that Albania should ensure that the draft Code of Administrative Procedures is fully in line with EU/SIGMA best practices. Albania was also encouraged to take steps for full implementation of the Law on High State

65 Commission Staff Working Document, Albania 2015 Progress Report (2015) <http://ec.europa.eu/enlargement/pdf/key_documents/2015/20151110_report_albania.pdf> accessed 30 May 2019.

Control, as well as further measures for strengthening the capacity and independence of the Supreme State Audit Institution. Furthermore, the Commission encouraged Albania to address existing challenges related to independent institutions, by exploring the option of putting in place a horizontal legal framework. This procedure would enact the appointment and dismissal of directors of independent institutions, creating a merit-based, transparent selection process for their members and guaranteeing their institutional autonomy.

All of the recommendations in the latest Progress Report issued by the Commission for reforming the public administration in Albania can be understood as requiring Albania to adopt EU good governance norms. The EU, in other words, hopes to see that there is more transparency, non-politically influenced independent institutions, open government and an effective civil service in Albania, in which staff are recruited according to an open and merit-based selection policy. This approach also contributes to the broader framework of establishing an anti-corruption policy field in Albania, by tackling corruption in key areas of public administration. Albania is a challenging case in reforming the administrative structure and implementing preventing corrupt practices, as the research will show. There are some limitations insofar as the recommendations are concerned, as the EU can play a supporting role in Albania to make concrete changes in reforming the public administration, but reducing the level of corruption in the public administration is still a challenge for Albanian institutions. Nevertheless, the EU recommendations and Progress Reports have presented an opportunity to develop an anti-corruption policy field that will also lead to reforming sectors such as the public administration.

Post-Communist Albania has proven to be a challenging case for successful reform and fighting corruption within the public administrative system, because from the first election in 1992 up to the latest election in June 2017, every political party that comes to power fills the state institutions with its own people, closely affiliated with the party in power.[66] Thus, an administrative structure inherited from the Communist regime was still closely related to the legacy of the one party-state, dominating all levels of state administration by the political party in government. The EU has recommended the development of a permanent and professional administration regulated by specific laws. However, such change is still a long way off in Albania, because there is still the paradoxical reality of a persistently politicised post-Communist administration which clings onto power.[67]

The electoral victory of the Democratic Party in the first phase of post-Communist Albania brought a radical anti-Communist agenda to the very heart

66 Blendi Kajsiu, Aldo Bumci and Albert Rakip, *Albania—A Weak Democracy a Weak State: Report on the State of Democracy in Albania* (Albanian Institute for International Studies 2015).

67 Eva Dhimitri, Aida Gabeta and Majlinda Bello, 'Regional Development Theories and Modes, A Comparative Analysis of Challenges of Regional Development in Albania' *The USV Annals of Economics and Public Administration Journal 15* (2) (2015) 50–8.

of the post-Communist administration programme. Although the first Democrat government contained a group closely related to the former regime, most Communist-era employees were widely seen as upholders of that system and therefore unsuitable for any kind of partnership with the new regime created after 1992.[68] Given the lack of independent employees, the next step was to fill state structures with anti-Communist activists who lacked relevant experience and specialities. The post-Communist regime had limited options when it came to independent professionals and expertise. A new administration containing party loyalists and anti-Communist activists was possibly even more poorly equipped to handle the challenges of transition into a new liberal democracy than the prior Communist-era administration would have been.[69]

The influence of the anti-Communists in reorganising the state administration was mainly facilitated by the absence of a proper framework for guaranteeing the independence and safeguarding of public employees from any undue political influence. The notion of separating the administration from the party in government (not to mention a career-management system) was completely foreign to the Albanian political establishment in the mid-1990s, when the government approved the first-ever civil service law. Until its adoption, the working status of all public employees was regulated merely by temporary amendments to the Communist labour code.[70] The labour code allowed the supervisors of state institutions, who were by definition political appointees, to fire any employees under their responsibility whenever they thought it was necessary. However, since the same supervisors were also allowed to work on reform needs, there were practically no provisions to protect the state employees from potentially arbitrary decisions by their supervisors.[71] Therefore, during the first stage of transition between 1992 and 1997, practices established during decades of one-party rule remained in place. The next stage of reforms between 1997 and 2000 (when the Socialist Party came to power after the 1997 elections with the intervention of the international community) was focused on reforming the public administration, among other things.

In 1997, the World Bank, the EU, the European Bank for Reconstruction and Development, and the IMF designed a joint Strategy for Recovery and

68 Arolda Elbasani, 'Europeanization Travels to the Western Balkans: Enlargement Strategy, Domestic Obstacles and Diverging Reforms' in Arolda Elbasani (eds) *European Integration and Transformation in the Western Balkans: Europeanization or Business as Usual?* (Routledge 2013) 3–22.

69 Kajsiu (n 9) 93.

70 Teuta Nunaj, 'The Training of Albanian Public Administration: An Analysis of Training Policies and Their Impact in the Professional Development of Civil Servants' *Journal of Educational and Social Research* (MCSER Publishing 6 (3) 2016) 149–58.

71 Arolda Elbasani, 'EU Administrative Conditionality and Domestic Downloading: The Limits of Europeanization in Challenging Contexts' *KFG Working Paper Series No 2* (July 2009) KFG The Transformative Power of Europe Free University Berlin <http://userpage.fu-berlin.de/kfgeu/kfgwp/wpseries/WorkingPaperKFG_2.pdf> accessed 30 May 2019.

Growth, which highlighted public administration amongst the key elements for future reforms.[72] In particular, the World Bank underlined reforms in governance as one of the central pillars of its intervention and the most significant challenge facing the Albanian government.[73] The government at the end of 1997 formally approved a new 'Strategy for State Institution and Public Administration Reform' (SIPAR), entirely funded by international institutions. Also, the international institutions fully supported and drafted new legislation to regulate different aspects of state bureaucracy between 1997 and 2000, with a view to also tackling corruption more effectively.

However, once in power, the Socialists saw the administration as politically biased against them, and cleaned house, re-stocking it with their own political supporters in key public positions. Although no official data were made public, its estimated that during just the first year of Socialist government, 1500 of the total public employees (nearly 15 per cent) were released and replaced by the incoming party's loyalists.[74] Again, most employees were once again replaced with people chosen because of political connections, rather than the professional expertise needed to carry out the job. The existing legislation, effectively used by the outgoing majority, allowed for a similar restructuring of the old administration in favour of Socialist loyalists.

This practice was witnessed again after the 2005 elections. A parliamentary report prepared by the opposition in 2006 revealed that, after the elections, when the Democratic Party were in, government had approved an internal instruction prioritising candidates that had played a distinctive role in elections for employment in the public administration.[75] Several sources suggest that within the first year, around 4500 employees (almost half of the overall state administration) were dismissed.[76] This included around 1300 out of 2500 civil servants. Most places left vacant were filled with political activists. The parliamentary report, which builds on information provided by state department statistics, listed a range of cases where public employees were recruited in clear contravention of the requirements for the position.[77] This practice was further confirmed after the 2009 elections, with the inclusion of new coalition parties, which had seemingly placed their own supporters in the ministries and institutions they

72 World Bank, 'Albania Beyond the Crisis: A Strategy for Recovery and Growth' Report 18658-ALB World Bank (1998).

73 World Bank, 'Albania: Country Assistance Evaluation' Report 21390 World Bank (2000).

74 Freedom House, 'Nations in Transit. Country Report: Albania' (Freedom House 2008) <https://freedomhouse.org/report/nations-transit/2018/albania> accessed 30 May 2019.

75 Mihovil Škarica, 'Public Administration Reforms in a Fragile Institutional Framework: The Case of Albania' *Croatian and Comparative Public Administration Journal 12* (3) (2011) 210–42.

76 ibid.

77 Artan Karini, 'Aid-Supported Public Service Reform and Capacity Development in Post-Communist Albania' *International Journal of Public Administration 36* (7) (2013) 469–81.

managed[78]; similar practices were witnessed again after the 2013 and 2017 general elections when the Socialists were elected to government.

This has become a characteristic in Albania, and the party or coalition in government makes full use of legal loopholes and inventive strategies to stretch laws in order to fill state institutions with politically affiliated candidates. At present, civil servants are typically recruited through temporary contracts.[79] A council of ministers' decree approved in 2004 allows for temporary contractual appointments of civil servants. Though employed through the 2004 decree, contractual employees often keep the position for longer periods, typically until confirmed in the same role through an open recruitment process. An example is the Ministry of Interior, where all 111 winners of open competition have been in a working relationship with the institution before. Such practices, at the border of legality, have served to undermine the procedures for merit-based appointments.[80]

Many dismissed civil servants have been accused of corruption or engaging in some form of corrupt activity. However, few have been prosecuted and sentenced for engaging in bribery or corrupt activities. Accusations are dropped once the accused are replaced or a new government takes charge. The changes and replacements in key posts of the government with party loyalists make it hard to determine corrupt practices and identify at what level corruption takes place. This is because the civil servants that are appointed in key posts could engage in corruption practices (for example, giving public contracts or operating in a closed network), which makes it hard even to detect corrupt activities in the public administration, let alone fight it.

For these reasons, the EU has been keen to push Albania for administrative reforms to reduce the corrupt activities and establish an independent public administration at the same time, uninfluenced by parties in government. The EU has been involved in the international initiatives to rebuild the Albanian state. However, EU leverage was initially limited to the control of assistance and pressure of aid conditionality applied in concert with other foreign donors. The promise of enlargement policies has activated the policy of EU conditionality and a progressive range of requirements related to public administration.[81] In addition, the SAP II provided new instruments, targeting of specific areas of reform, monitoring the state of compliance, a new programme of aid and assistance, and upgrading of the institutional relations depending on the state of reforms to ensure that the target countries comply with required reforms.[82] However, the task of transforming the public administration, the lack of reformist

78 ibid.

79 Elbasani (n 68).

80 European Commission, 'Commission Opinion on Albania's Application for Membership of the European Union' COM (2010) 68.

81 Elbasani (n 68).

82 European Neighbourhood Policy and Enlargement Negotiations, 'Albania—Financial Assistance under IPA II' <http://ec.europa.eu/enlargement/instruments/funding-by-country/albania/index_en.htm>

elites and the undeveloped institutional infrastructure have inhibited a meaningful transformation of the public administration into a depoliticised and professional administration as required by the EU standards.

In terms of developing an anti-corruption policy field, there are some grounds for developing a policy that will address the level of corruption within the public administration. However, the close network group that each government brings to the public administration makes any attempt to reduce the level of corruption hard to break through. From a reflexive governance theory point of view, the EU recommendations and conditions to reform the public administration are based on some ongoing efforts from Albania to form a professional and impartial civil service administration. Nevertheless, one cannot clearly determine whether Albania has the will to establish a professional and impartial public administration that is detached from the political parties that govern the country. There is ongoing support by the EU in terms of co-finance training to establish a professional public administration and learn from other best practice in the EU. We can safely conclude that within public administration, the EU and Albania are not yet engaging in a reflexive governance approach because the EU has requested Albania to implement key legislation that will protect civil servants. Even so, in terms of developing an anti-corruption policy field, there is an element of reflexiveness because Albania acknowledges that there is an issue with corruption in the public administration. The EU is assisting Albania in reforming the public administration to prevent corruption and, as a result, contributing to establishing a broader anti-corruption policy field that also pays attention to corruption in the public administration sector.

Furthermore, in reforming the public administration and addressing the issue of corruption, the EU has identified in its 2015 Report that Albania must reform the Justice system; this recommendation was reiterated in 2016, and in the most recent Report issued in April 2018, this was cited as the most problematic sector in Albania and where corruption is broadly widespread. The judiciary has also been the key institution where corruption-related cases have not been prosecuted accordingly.

6.5 Reforming the judiciary

The judicial system in Albania is viewed to be highly problematic, and corruption is widespread throughout the judicial system. The EU has identified that the judicial system is one of the most corrupt sectors in Albania, and reforming it is the key to any future EU membership. As a result, on 22 July 2016 Albania unanimously passed new judicial reform, which required amending one-third of the Constitution. These constitutional changes pave the way to establishing a procedure for re-evaluating judges and prosecutors in Albania, known as the 'vetting process' and setting up new specialised bodies, including the Special Anti-Corruption and Organised Crime Structure (SPAK) and the National Bureau of Investigation (NBI), which will assist in the fight against corruption and organised crime. These institutions have yet to be created, and in its latest

Progress Report issued for Albania in April 2018, the Commission has reiterated the need to do so.

Bowing to pressure from the EU and other international partners (in particular the US), Albania engaged in a long process (over a year and a half, between 2014 and 2016) of reforming the judicial system and building a foundation to address and fight corruption in the justice system more effectively. These reforms are anticipated to make a contribution to the broader anti-corruption policy Albania is developing with EU and US assistance for the sole purpose of EU membership.

The judiciary is considered to be one of the most problematic sectors in the country; this is identified by several sources including Freedom in the World[83] and the Human Rights Report.[84] The law on legal aid was lately improved, but still, access to justice is very much restricted for less fortunate groups of citizens due to high judicial fees as noted in the 2014 Progress Report.[85] This perception is also supported by the Global Corruption Barometer,[86] which reports that more than three-quarters of surveyed citizens perceive the judiciary to be highly corrupt.

As a result, the EU has funded a EURALIUS IV project: Consolidation of the Justice System in Albania, under IPA 2013; funds for Albania for this project amount to almost EUR 4 million. It originally began in September 2014 and was planned to run until December 2017. Following comprehensive justice reform, the EURALIUS project has been extended for another three years, and EURALIUS V started in April 2018 with a budget of around EUR 7.5 million. The project supports the Albanian Ministry of Justice, the Office for the Administration of the Judiciary Budget, the High Council of Justice, the High Court, the General Prosecutor Office, the Courts, the National Judicial Conference, the Parliamentary Law Committee, the School of Magistrates, the National Chamber of Advocacy and the National Chamber of Notaries. The reforms cover five areas of intervention:

1) Justice reform and organisation of the ministry;
2) High Council of Justice and High Court;
3) Criminal justice and prosecution office;
4) Judicial administration and efficiency; and
5) Legal professions and the School of Magistrates.

83 Freedom House 'Report on Albania' (Freedom House 2018) <https://freedomhouse.org/report/freedom-world/2018/albania> accessed 30 May 2019.

84 Human Rights, 'Human Rights Report on Albania' (2015) <www.state.gov/documents/organization/253027.pdf> accessed 30 May 2019.

85 European Commission, Albania Progress Report, COM (2014) 700 final. <http://ec.europa.eu/enlargement/pdf/key_documents/2014/20141008-albania-progress-report_en.pdf> accessed 30 May 2019.

86 Transparency International, 'Transparency International Global Corruption Barometer' (2013) 16–17 <http://issuu.com/transparencyinternational/docs/2013_globalcorruptionbarometer_en?e=2496456/3903358#search> accessed 30 May 2019.

These projects are aimed at supporting Albania in reforming the judicial system and reducing the level of corruption that takes place within the justice system.

The former head of EURALIUS[87] Mission in Albania, Joaquin Urias, in an interview for *The Voice of America*, stated that the whole judicial system in Albania is corrupt. He indicated that the practice of knowing somebody who helps you or paying for assistance is understood as something very normal in the Albanian judicial system. Judges demand money, lawyers give money to judges; even prosecutors take money,[88] and this makes successfully reforming the judicial system extremely difficult. In turn, this makes it very difficult to develop a coherent anti-corruption policy to address the issues concerning corruption in the judicial system. In Urias's view, the first solution would be to have an independent institution, such as the High Council of Justice, to take extremely harsh measures against every form of corruption. Furthermore, the High Council of Justice should not be politically influenced, and the appointment of judges must become transparent. All measures that have been taken in recent years to discipline corrupt actions are insufficient and have mainly been just a facade to show to the EU that Albania is doing something about tackling corruption in the justice system.

In August 2015, the chairman of the Albanian Parliamentary Commission on Justice Sector Reform, Fatmir Xhafaj, also endorsed the EURALIUS and EU position on the justice system and the claims regarding dealing with high levels of corruption in the justice system. Xhafaj said that the parliamentary commission had come to acknowledge the current situation as critical and has observed that the justice system doesn't need just a makeover, but a thorough surgical intervention to push out the root of corruption.[89]

The Commission has firmly indicated that it is critical for Albania to reform and tackle the high level of corruption in the judicial system for any future EU membership success, and this stand has been supported by a few key EU member states, in particular Germany. EU member states have shown concerns that investors from EU states are cancelling projects that would create jobs because of the corruption that exists in the justice system—hence most investment companies

87 'EURALIUS IV project, "Consolidation of the Justice System in Albania", funded by EU, started in September 2014 and will last until December 2017. With its five areas of intervention, the project will support the Albanian Ministry of Justice, the Office for the Administration of the Judiciary Budget, the High Council of Justice, the High Court, the General Prosecutor Office, the Courts, the National Judicial Conference, the Parliamentary Law Committee, the School of Magistrates, the National Chamber of Advocacy and the National Chamber of Notaries as its main beneficiaries. The project comprises ten full time top experts from EU Member States and Albania, sitting in the premises of the main beneficiaries.' <www.euralius.eu/old/index.php/en/about-us/2015-08-31-09-03-55/euralius-iv> accessed 2 April 2019.

88 Joaquin Urias, 'The Whole Judicial System in Albania is Corrupt' *VOA* 29 May 2014 <www.infocip.org/en/?p=1199> accessed 30 May 2019.

89 Aleksandra Bogdani, 'Albanian Justice System Slammed as Totally Corrupt' *Balkan Insight* 5 June 2015 <www.balkaninsight.com/en/article/judges-in-albania-pays-up-to-300-000-for-their-positions-report-says> accessed 30 May 2019.

put their cases under International Arbitration because of the lack trust in the Albanian justice system. The UK ambassador in Albania has noted that legislation against corruption and bribery in the country makes it almost impossible to invest in the current, corrupt environment.[90]

The Commission suggested, in the joint EU and Albania working groups, that Albania needs to show progress on the judicial reform in relation to the main components of the reform process of 2016–2018. This is particularly true in implementing constitutional changes, criminal justice, legal education, efficiency of justice, legal professions and the fight against corruption in the judiciary.[91] The ad hoc Parliamentary Committee on Judicial Reform is required to submit a written report to the Commission upon completion of each of the stages of progress on these main components, including the degree of inclusiveness, the participation of key judicial bodies and institutions.[92] This can be observed as a process where Albania, with the assistance of the EU, is developing an anti-corruption policy field that will cover the justice system sector.

In terms of a reflexive governance approach, the EU here is supporting the ongoing efforts that Albania is making in fighting corruption in the judiciary. This is even though, as pointed out above, the changes so far have been merely a façade, rather than concrete efforts to fight corruption in the justice system. The Commission has asked Albania to provide information on the state of preparation of the justice reform strategy (2014–2020) and on efforts made to prepare for sector budget support.[93] Albania is also required to report on the outcome of the working groups on the justice reform strategy, including the review of the code of criminal procedure. The EU is checking to see whether Albania can prepare a strategy for reforming completely the justice system by 2020. From a reflexive governance perspective, the EU is not directly engaging with Albania in a reflexive approach—but there are elements where the EU will support co-financing in the preparation of the justice reform strategy.

Currently, the Albania's judicial reforms are at the stage of re-evaluating judiciary officials, 800 judges and prosecutors, as well as a number of other members of the judiciary. This process only started in November 2017 and will take about five years to complete. This process is delivering its first tangible results, as some members of the judiciary, judges and prosecutors were unable to justify their financial assets and have been recommended for further investigation on charges of engaging in corrupt practices. However, one can only make a comprehensive analysis of the success of the re-evaluation process (known as

90 British Embassy Albania, 'Analysis of the Justice System in Albania—2015' 13 July 2015 <www.gov.uk/government/world-location-news/analysis-of-the-justice-system-in-albania-2015> accessed 30 May 2019.

91 European Union (n 64).

92 ibid.

93 European Commission, 'IPA (II) Indicative Strategy Paper for Albania (2014–2020)' 16–19. <http://ec.europa.eu/enlargement/instruments/funding-by-country/albania/index_en.htm> accessed 30 May 2019.

the vetting process in Albania) after it has been completed, and the number of judiciary officials charged on corruption and unethical practices so far is very low. However, the re-evaluation process looks promising to date, and the judiciary reform passed in 2016 has put Albania in an encouraging position to close Chapters 23 and 24 on the judiciary and fundamental right acquis, once the EU opens accession talks with Albania in late 2019.

The process of re-evaluating the judiciary officials is fundamental for the success of implementing the judiciary reform. According to a report presented in July 2015 by the Parliamentary Commission, some alarming concerns about the level of corruption in the justice system were raised; likewise, in the EU 2015 Progress Report. Among the most concerning findings reported is the allegation that judges pay between €100,000 and €300,000 to the High Council of Justice in order to get better posts, such as those judges within rural areas, where they are able to collect higher amounts of money in bribes.[94] The 336-page dossier suggests that the corruption cycle begins with police officers who accept cash to destroy evidence, ranging to prosecutors who accept between €1,000 and €2,000 to resist pressing charges. Furthermore, the report finds that paying a judge to change a sentence allegedly costs between €60,000 and €80,000. The report, which analyses the operations of the Albanian justice system since it was established in its present form in 1998, also claims that there is compelling evidence that some judges take bribes from both sides in court cases.[95] Among the publication's recommendations is the removal of the country's president as the head of the High Council of Justice in order to guarantee the independence and impartiality of the courts and to de-politicise the selection process used to appoint High Court judges.[96] Therefore, the process of re-evaluating judiciary officials is crucial for the success of implementing the judiciary reform and fighting corruption at its core in Albania. To sum up, based on the evidence provided in this chapter, the judicial system is highly problematic in Albania, and corruption is widespread thought the justice system. The country has made some efforts to tackle this, and the judicial reform passed in 2016 is promising. However, to date, fighting corruption is modest and insufficient.

6.6 The future for Albania and the anti-corruption policy field

Therefore, there are some efforts to develop an anti-corruption policy in Albania, with support from the EU, to address key outstanding issues related to corruption. The EU has engaged, in some respects, in a reflexive governance approach with Albania, developing the grounds for an anti-corruption policy to tackle the issue of corruption by giving assistance for further training, supporting legislation,

94 Blendi Kajsiu, 'Nations in Transit 2018: Albania' Freedom House (2018) <https://freedomhouse.org/report/nations-transit/2018/albania> accessed 30 May 2019.

95 ibid.

96 ibid.

facilitating peer review to learn from best practice and co-financing with the Albanian government strategies for the next five years. These efforts and ongoing activities are a sign that Albania, together with the EU, is developing grounds to establish an anti-corruption policy field that will address corruption in the justice system. However, the efforts that Albania has made so far have been insufficient in fighting corruption and developing a coherent anti-corruption policy field that addresses corruption in the judicial system, public administration and other key sectors. The latest Council of Europe's Group of States against Corruption Report on Albania, issued on July 2018, found that Albania has so far fully complied with just four of the ten recommendations it issued in its evaluation report in 2014.[97] The other six recommendations have only been partially implemented—and this is an indication that Albania has yet to take anti-corruption reform seriously.

The following section offers the overall conclusion for the three case studies and gives some insights to cross-cutting themes between the countries. Furthermore, it summaries how the countries made use of reflexive governance approach and whether the EU Anti-Corruption Report was a positive instrument in enhancing the anti-corruption policy for the UK and Romania. Last, it concludes with Albania's main obstacles in establishing a coherent anti-corruption policy, increasing more political will to make corruption a high priority and developing an effective judicial system that can fight corruption and organised crime at the highest level—thus putting the country in a favourable position for future membership to the European Union.

6.6.1 Concluding remarks on the country studies

The EU Anti-Corruption Report and the EU policy overall had a positive impact in supporting the national anti-corruption discourse in the countries case study, addressing the issue of corruption in terms of developing national anti-corruption policy. The UK and Romania have responded somewhat positively to the Report recommendations, but they differ when it comes to applying them into concrete policy actions. Albania has responded to a lesser degree to the European Commission's influence in developing anti-corruption policy. Rather than embracing reflexive-governance and taking full ownership of its anti-corruption measures by implementing the Commission's recommendations in the annual EU country reports and GRECO recommendations, Albania has instead required more of a 'hard law' approach, responding to the European Council threats of withholding accession talks to the Union in the last few years.

In the UK, the Report's recommendations were incorporated into the national anti-corruption policy. In December 2014, the UK published its first national Anti-Corruption Plan and, in its progress update in May 2016, emphasised that

97 Council of Europe's Group of States against Corruption (GRECO) 'Report on Albania (2018)' <https://rm.coe.int/greco-rc4-2018-4-fourth-evaluation-round-corruption-prevention-in-resp/16808c3a35> accessed 30 May 2019.

of the 66 actions proposed in the Plan, 62 actions were delivered. The Report played a role in this process, and we can therefore say that overall it had a positive impact. Furthermore, the UK engaged in reflexive governance in developing its national plan.

After the Brexit vote took place in June 2016, there were some initial concerns that the country—due to the reorientation of its policy priorities and resource allocations—would diminish its anti-corruption policies. However, in 2017, the UK introduced the Criminal Finances Act 2017, the Money Laundering, Terrorist Financing and Transfer of Funds Regulations 2017, and there are future plans to launch a public beneficial ownership register. These measures suggest that even after leaving the EU, the UK will continue aligning its regulations to the same standards as those adopted by the EU and international standards. For the UK to realise its vision of a 'Global Britain'—the country's new foreign policy initiative post-Brexit—it must preserve its role in the international fight against corruption and should not neglect anti-corruption committees, as well as continuing to advocate for transparency. It remains to be seen in the years to come—after the country's exit from the EU in 2019—whether the UK's fight against corruption will be set back or maintained. What is encouraging is that the UK has a strong and vibrant civil society, including robust NGOs like TI-UK and Global Witness, who have played a critical part in the UK governments' past anti-corruption initiatives. The engagement with civil society shows that the UK has all the potential to continue to engage in reflexive governance in developing future anti-corruption laws and policies.

In contrast, in the case of Romania, the Report had rather limited results in implementing the Report's recommendations into robust and tangible policy actions. Romania's efforts since the Report was published were focused mainly on strengthening the National Anti-corruption Directorate and producing results in terms of convictions of high level officials. Furthermore, the political turmoil in November 2015, with the collapse of Victor Ponta's government due to corruption allegations, and the formation of a technocratic government led by Dacian Ciolos have contributed to difficulties in implementing the Report's recommendations. In terms of a reflexive governance approach, the Report did have a positive impact—the country has engaged with local actors, and local issues concerning corruption addressed in the Report were tackled, including the informality and corruption in the public health care system. Using reflexive governance, the Report was able to reflect broader EU policy concerns for the country through examining more local issues (such as corruption in the healthcare system, in which citizens indicated they had to engage frequently, in order to access medicines and treatment). However, overall, the reflexive governance approach has not been as successful in Romania, and additional hard law adopted by the EU seems to have worked more successfully when developing an anti-corruption policy. In short, Romania has mainly responded in developing anti-corruption policy only when the Commission has threatened with freezing subsidies and to withhold development funds to Romania. The Commission has put forward a proposal to cut funds to member states that do not uphold the rule of law and aimed to exert pressure on countries such as Hungary, Poland and Romania, and this received the backing of European Parliament in January 2019.[98]

The chapter on Romania offers evidence for us to confidently conclude that the EU has played an important role in instigating and maintaining the fight against corruption in the country. The most important measurement tool that the EU has for this is the CVM, allowing enhanced verification and monitoring of progress in judicial and anti-corruption reforms after Romania's accession to the EU in 2007. However, simply demonstrating that the EU has significant leverage in this area does not automatically mean that anti-corruption activities have been successful overall, as the chapter showed—nor that they will necessarily have a long-lasting effect on the country in sustaining anti-corruption reforms.

The Commission continues to monitor and supervise Romania's anti-corruption activity though the CVM, even though on 1 January 2019, Romania took the rotating presidency of the Union. The CVM's 2018 report argued that 'the CVM has an important role in Romania as driver for reform, as well as a tool to track progress'.[99] Although it is an important mechanism to maintain anti-corruption reform momentum, in its pursuit of the 'big fish' (i.e. high-level officials and CEOs of large corporations) at all costs, coupled with EU demands to produce more conviction results, the CVM has in fact strained the rule of law in Romania, according to Mungiu-Pippidi.[100] The Commission's main target in advancing and maintaining specific anti-corruption champions in key positions, such as DNA chief Laura Kovesi, has also been counterproductive in terms of sustaining the anti-corruption momentum. There is a risk that the EU appears to have a biased view against Romania and that the pursuit of anti-corruption within government has gone too far, in comparison with other member states joining in 2004 and 2007. This all-consuming zeal for pursuing corruption has generated governmental instability, creating open conflicts between the parliament and the judiciary.

The lesson, perhaps, that Western Balkan countries can learn from Romania is that, once effective anti-corruption agencies are in place, staffed by dedicated prosecutors such as Kovesi, there should be also in place an adequate supervision to monitor these agencies, so that there is no risk for abuse of power and that they respect the rule of law—i.e. ensuring checks and balances on anti-corruption

98 European Parliament, 'Member States Jeopardising the Rule of Law Will Risk Losing EU Funds' (2019) <www.europarl.europa.eu/news/en/press-room/20190109IPR23011/member-states-jeopardising-the-rule-of-law-will-risk-losing-eu-funds> accessed 30 May 2019.

99 European Commission, 'Report from the Commission to the European Parliament and the Council on Progress in "Romania under the Cooperation and Verification Mechanism"' Strasbourg 13.11.2018 COM (2018) 851 final <https://ec.europa.eu/info/sites/info/files/progress-report-romania-2018-com-2018-com-2018-851_en.pdf> accessed 10 February 2019.

100 Alina Mungiu-Pippidi, 'Bucharest vs Brussels: Wrangling over the EU's new Chief Prosecutor' Hertie School of Governance (2019) <www.hertie-school.org/en/debate/detail/content/bucharest-vs-brussels-wrangling-over-the-eus-new-chief-prosecutor/> accessed 15 March 2019.

institutions. The EU should not turn a blind eye to due process, simply because the techniques are producing high indictment and conviction rates. Such checks and balances would resist practices becoming commonplace such as those of the Ploiesti DNA branch, faking evidence to indict a politician, or the Romanian Intelligence Service avoiding due process regarding mass wiretaps.

Finally on Romania—and most importantly, for lessons for states with authoritarian tendencies or a Communist past—a new political class must emerge and be supported. So far, those removed from the political and civil service systems on corruption charges have been replaced by family members or proxies of those corrupt politicians or inner circles of senior civil servants. Therefore, the absence of an alternative political class fundamentally undermines the good work of anti-corruption in the country because the same corrupt groups are recycled back into the system, effectively replaced by surrogates with identical issues and challenges. Furthermore, after Romania's backsliding on anti-corruption laws in 2017, whilst the CVM has been operational since 2007, it is time to review the EU's anti-corruption approach in Romania and invest more in sustainability of anti-corruption reforms, rather than just working on increasing the number of people being prosecuted for corruption and adopting legislation issued as a checklist in the annual CVM reports.

In the case of Albania, the institutional anti-corruption framework introduced with the assistance of the international community and the EU appears to be promising. However, we can conclude that the framework remains largely ineffective due to a lack of proper implementation due to lack of political will, over-politicising anti-corruption policy, and insufficient resources allocated to anti-corruption efforts. The Albanian governments, since the collapse of Communism, have not properly addressed the root causes of corruption. So far, the country has adopted laws and institutions in line with international and EU standards as required, but paid little attention as to whether and how legislation is actually going to work on the ground. These adopted laws and policies may merely be a façade to please international institutions.

Furthermore, consecutive Albanian governments have ticked off EU requirements, without making serious efforts on substantive changes to social norms against corruption in terms of developing a comprehensive anti-corruption policy field in the country. These concerns, noted by the Report, were also found in the GRECO report on Albania issued in 2018. In the European Council's June 2018 meeting, concerns were raised about Albania's efforts to fight grand and political corruption, and the Council remained unimpressed the zero-conviction rate for high-ranking public officials. These issues factored as reasons against opening accession talks with Albania in 2018. The European Council has postponed its decision for the possibility of opening accession talks with Albania for EU membership for late 2019, with a view that in the meantime, Albania must be able to demonstrate a genuine track record on fighting corruption and organised crime.

It should be noted that Albania went through major judicial reform in June 2016, and the Parliament amended nearly one-third of the Constitution (45 articles). On paper, these constitutional amendments are aimed at re-establishing the justice system and setting up new institutions to fight organised crime and corruption, with a view to reducing politicians' long-standing influence. Some of these institutions include the Independent Qualification Commission (EU and US magistrates are overseeing this process as part of the International Monitoring Operation team which is re-evaluating the judicial system), the Special Anti-Corruption and Organised Crime Structure (SPAK), and the National Bureau of Investigation (NBI), which will assist in the fight against corruption and organised crime. So far, SPAK and NBI have not been established, as the staff, including special anti-corruption prosecutors and investigators, are being vetted. All these structural changes are key conditions set out by the EU in order to open accession talks for EU membership.

The Independent Qualification Commission only began its work in November 2017; its mandate is to re-evaluate 800 judges and prosecutors, as well as a number of other members of the judiciary. By January 2019, only 100 members of the current judicial system had been re-evaluated and are undergoing an investigation based on three criteria: assets, background and a proficiency assessment—almost half resulted in dismissal or voluntary resignation. The process so far is encouraging, but can only properly be analysed when fully completed—which, at the current pace, looks like five years at the minimum. At this point, it is also difficult to estimate whether the new justice system will fight corruption more effectively although, on paper, it seems to be going in the right direction so far. The vetting process and implementation of the judicial reform is proving challenging, having left Albania without a Constitutional Court or a Supreme Court. This leaves the government and its main decision-making institutions free from checks and balances and from scrutiny by the main courts for abuses of power or unconstitutional decisions taken by the government. Re-evaluation of the judicial system is also having an impact on access to justice for Albanian citizens with pending cases in the courts. The vetting process has given priority to the Constitutional Court, after only seven out of nine sitting judges proved adequate as part of the judiciary. The Supreme Court has four out of 19 judges sitting, and it is therefore impossible to deliberate hearings, as judges cannot be quorate to hear a case with such low numbers—by January 2019, there are about 23,900 pending cases. These issues (lack of access to justice, the lack of a high court which can hold government decisions to account, lack of checks and balances in the separation of power in the country) were discussed by the Venice Commission.[101] The opinion given was that the re-evaluation process is a necessary measure for fighting corruption in the judiciary, but that vetting bodies should accelerate the re-evaluation process and allow other reforms to take effect.

101 Council of Europe, 'European Commission for Democracy through Law (Venice Commission) Albania opinion on draft constitutional amendments enabling the vetting of politicians' Opinion No 942/2018 Strasbourg 17 December 2018 <www.venice.coe.int/webforms/documents/default.aspx?pdffile=CDL-AD(2018)034-e> accessed 30 May 2019.

In closing, Albania has demonstrated overall that it has made little use of reflexive governance, only involving civil society and the business community in consulting on anti-corruption reforms in a very limited capacity, and findings and recommendations of such stakeholders have not been incorporated into plans or policy. There has been minimal country ownership of anti-corruption policy, and the EU interplay with Albania has been based mainly on conditionality set by the European Commission and supported strongly by the European Council (for example, in postponing accession talks with the EU until tangible reforms are passed and a track record in fighting grand and political corruption at high level is developed). In other words—the hard law approach associated with accession for EU membership, rather than a reflexive governance approach, characterises the development of the anti-corruption policy field in Albania.

In conclusion, the three countries we have considered closely all took a different approach in developing their anti-corruption laws and policies, in how they engaged with reflexive governance, in how they included different stakeholders into the process of developing their anti-corruption strategies, and in how they approached their relations with the EU when it came to anti-corruption related reforms. The UK engaged well with different stakeholders and taking a reflexive governance approach: non-state actors played an important role in initiating anti-corruption policies and laws, and the recommendations issued by the Commission under the EU Anti-Corruption Report were mostly reflected into the UK anti-corruption strategy. Whereas, in the case of Romania, the EU played a key role, in particular through the CVM to initiating anti-corruption reforms, which were mainly achieved through a combination of soft and hard law approaches. The reflexive governance approach was mostly seen in issues of corruption concerning the healthcare sector, which the Report took it up in its recommendations. In Albania, the reflexive governance approach was missing, and only a hard law approach—when the EU and international put pressure on the country by threatening to withhold accession talks for EU membership—saw Albania respond by initiating anti-corruption reforms and policy.

Section 3

7 The future of EU anti-corruption policy

7.1 Introduction

This chapter is an overview of our analysis of the EU Anti-Corruption Report and considers in some detail the areas of relevance for future EU anti-corruption policy, in particular, the European Semester process. The chapter is divided into two parts, the first being a brief summary evaluation of the Report's achievements. We then discuss the latest phase of the EU anti-corruption policy—post-2017—under the European Semester, suggesting deficiencies, gaps and areas that could be given closer attention in future EU anti-corruption policy objectives. Both sections offer an assessment from the perspective of the theory of reflexive governance. In this analysis there are examples given where reflexive governance occurred as a result of the Report's impact, how future EU anti-corruption policy could be strengthened by making further use of reflexive governance mechanisms, and how reflexive governance can be helpful to member states in developing their own anti-corruption policies.

7.2 The impact of the EU anti-corruption report

The Report attempted to improve the overall EU anti-corruption policy in five key areas, with some success. First, the Report officially recognised that more sectors were vulnerable and prone to corruption practice in the EU and the member states, in particular, in the area of public procurement and political party funding, thereby raising awareness of the policy field of corruption in the EU. Second, the Report has offered some new insights on the level of corruption and the damaging effects that it has in the EU and the member states. Third, the Report contributed towards thinking about the negative effect of corruption in economic terms, by officially estimating the cost of corruption at the EU level—which it identified to be at least €120 billion (£99 billion) annually. Fourth, the Report has allowed the EU Commission to engage in a dialogue with member states and civil society to rethink anti-corruption policy and establish conditions for mutual learning. As a result, both the EU and member states can learn from best practice in designing more effective anti-corruption policies and future legislation, and include civil society to play a role in shaping anti-corruption policy at EU and national levels. Finally—and most significantly—the Report made the inclusion of civil society an integral part in the process of writing the Report and justifying its findings. This approach allowed NGOs, journalists, academics and anti-corruption experts with key knowledge for each individual member state to play a role in how the Report was crafted. Thus, the Commission enabled external actors to have a direct impact on influencing anti-corruption policy at EU and national levels.

The Report raised the profile of addressing corruption from a policy and law perceptive, pushing it up the agenda for fighting corruption in the EU and member states. It was a key part of the development of an anti-corruption policy field in the EU and can be characterised as the flagship anti-corruption monitoring instrument of the Commission to date. The Report embodies the Commission's efforts and commitments to support member states in acknowledging their anti-corruption policy shortcomings. Analysing the Report from a reflexive governance perspective, we can clearly see an innovative problem-solving component. The Commission, through the Report, is supporting member states to acknowledge their anti-corruption policy shortcomings and engage in an innovative problem-solving exercise to enhance their anti-corruption policies and tools.

Another area in which the Report had an impact was identifying public procurement as a sector highly vulnerable to corrupt practices. As a result, the Report dedicated a thematic chapter to public procurement and recognised the policy shortcomings to address the high level of corruption at EU and member state level in relation to it.[1] As outlined in Chapter 2, public procurement was selected as a case study by the Commission to assess the costs of corruption for a sub-sector of the EU economy. Under the thematic chapter in the Report, the Commission can be understood to be trying to trigger a process and a dialogue by which governments at different levels—national, regional, local and other public bodies, as well as NGOs, academia, and the media—engage in developing wider anti-corruption strategies to prevent corruption in public procurement. Furthermore, the Report had an impact by further recognising the level of corruption in public procurement and the importance of addressing corruption in this key sector of the economy, thus protecting economic growth. Public procurement has a strong economic significance in the EU, with around 20 per cent of the EU's GDP annually spent by government.[2] In a global context, public procurement represents around a third of public spending in developed countries. Therefore, corruption in the domain of governmental contracting can have significant economic costs, and the Report encourages member states to strongly acknowledge their policy shortcomings in addressing corruption in this area.[3] This

1 HB Christopher, 'Highlight of the EU Procurement Reforms: The New Directive on Concessions' *European Procurement and Public Private Partnership Law Review 9* (1) (2014) 1–2.

2 'Identifying and Reducing Corruption in Public Procurement in the EU: Development of a Methodology to Estimate the Direct Costs of Corruption and Other Elements for an EU-Evaluation Mechanism in the Area of Anti-Corruption' (PwC and Ecorys 2013).

3 OECD, *Government at a Glance 2013* (OECD 2013).

is an example of the reflexive governance component of active participation: the Report has led to wider participation of different levels of government and non-government bodies engaging in shaping anti-corruption measures to prevent corruption in public procurement.

The Report also highlighted the association of corruption in different areas, undermining policy success. For instance, corruption allows organised crime and criminal organisations to thrive; corruption undermines the functioning of the rule of law; a high perception of corruption reduces voter turnout in national parliamentary elections and lowers trust in EU institutions.[4] Member states have accepted that the association of corruption affects other sectors as stipulated in these examples. This is another example of the reflexive governance component of proceduralism: the Report suggests that corruption is associated with other areas, and member states have reflected and acknowledged the effect that corruption has on other sectors, as well as their policy shortcomings in this regard. However, the Report has not succeeded in influencing member states to take prompt action in addressing these sectors.

The Report made the EU member states aware of the risks corruption poses to EU funds. Mihály Fazekas argues that EU funds can deteriorate the quality of government, and as a result, they increase the risk of corrupt practices.[5] Research suggests that this has been the case in many countries that joined the EU in 2004 and 2007. According to Fazekas, there are three reasons this might occur. Firstly, EU funds are often disbursed on investment projects where public discretion is fairly high, and it is acknowledged that discretionary spending is more associated with corruption compared to non-discretionary spending. Secondly, EU funds offer a large pool of public resources for rent extraction of public means. Thirdly, EU funds contribute to weakening the relationship between domestic civil society, taxation and policy implementation.[6] As a result, EU member states must make part of their anti-corruption agenda addressing corruption related to EU funds. From a reflexive governance theory perspective, this is an example of the proceduralism component: the Report suggests that EU funds are exposed to corruption. Therefore, when designing policy and preventive measures in the future, member states could also consider including EU fund protection and relevant preventative measures. In other words, after the Report, member states are reflecting on their own anti-corruption policy shortcomings in addressing EU funds.

The economic costs incurred by corruption at EU level were formally recognised in the Report, with an estimate that corruption possibly amounts to €120 billion

4 R Holland, 'EU Anti-Corruption Report Shows Long Road Ahead' *Compliance Week 11* (122) (March 2014) 10–12.

5 M Fazekas and others, 'Are EU Funds a Corruption Risk? The Impact of EU Funds on Grand Corruption in Central and Eastern Europe' in A Mungiu-Pippidi (ed), *The Anticorruption Frontline: The ANTICORRP Project Vol 2* (Barbara Budrich Publishers 2014) 68–89.

6 ibid.

per year in the EU. The EU Commissioner for Home Affairs at the time, Cecilia Malmstrom, considered the high level of corruption in Europe as 'breath-taking', and the €120 billion figure triggered a debate as to what might be the actual cost of corruption.[7] The resulting analysis of the €120 billion figure opened a new discussion about the real cost of corruption in the EU. Research by Parliamentary Research Services in the 'Cost of Non-Europe Report' on Organised Crime and Corruption suggests that corruption actually costs the EU between €179 billion and €990 billion in GDP terms on an annual basis.[8] (The Report does not take into account other areas, indirectly affected by corruption, whereas this 'Cost of Non-Europe Report' considers costs in terms of lost tax revenues and foreign investment, as a result of the environment created by corruption in the EU and the member states.)

A study conducted by Mungiu-Pippidi applied a different approach in calculating the costs of corruption in the EU and concluded that the estimate of €120 billion in the Report miscalculates the actual costs of corruption. Mungiu-Pippidi argues that the costs are probably more in the range of €323 billion, about three times more than the Report's estimation.[9] These estimates have led other researchers to pay much closer attention to the cost of corruption, not only in economic terms but also in the social and political costs that corruption has in the EU, which the Report fails to address. This is another clear example of the reflexive governance component of active participation. The Report's official estimate of corruption costs has led to various pieces of research and ongoing discussions for evaluating the actual cost of corruption in the EU, to thinking about how the Commission came up with the €120 billion figure, and considering what areas it covered to estimate that cost. This process has actively involved different participants from civil society to contribute to the debate by providing research—such as by the Parliamentary Research Services in their report and the work of Mungiu-Pippidi in challenging the Commission's figure—active participation going far beyond the Commission and member states' findings.

Furthermore, the Report has had an impact in supporting a dialogue between the Commission, member states and civil society to further prioritise anti-corruption policy, and through preventative anti-corruption measures in other policy areas that can contribute to tackling corruption. From a reflexive governance theory perspective, this is an example of regulation of self-regulation: the EU

7 James Fontanella-Khan, 'Corruption in the EU Costs Business €120bn a Year,' Study Finds *Financial Times* (3 February 2014) <www.ft.com/cms/s/0/28f11862-8cf9-11e3-ad57-00144feab7de.html#axzz46ZcUiQmi> accessed 30 May 2019.

8 Wouter van Ballegooij and Thomas Zandstra, 'Organised Crime and Corruption: Cost of Non-Europe Report' Annex II—Corruption European Parliament, EPRS PE 579.319 (March 2016) 26–48. <www.europarl.europa.eu/RegData/etudes/STUD/2016/579319/EPRS_STU(2016)579319_EN.pdf> accessed 30 May 2019.

9 A Mungiu Pippidi, 'The Good, the Bad and the Ugly: Controlling Corruption in the European Union' *Hertie School of Governance Work Package: WP3 Corruption and Governance Improvement in Global and Continental Perspectives* (2016) 11–30.

Anti-Corruption policy is encouraging the creation of a dialogue between stakeholders to further prioritise their anti-corruption policy.

A highly significant impact of the Report was in establishing an anti-corruption experience-sharing programme. This would serve well as a platform for interested parties and stakeholders to engage in a dialogue on how to best address challenges identified in the Report, as well as to improve laws and policies by learning from each other's experiences in tackling the issue of corruption more effectively.[10] Since the publication of the Report in 2014, there have been four similar events in the form of a workshop organised in the framework of the programme of peer learning under the Report initiatives, covering areas such as asset declaration, whistle-blowing and healthcare corruption.[11] This would demonstrate reflexive governance in the form of collective learning. Through the Report, the Commission is supporting member states to engage in collective and mutual learning exercises; the Report provides a platform for learning between member states to learn from each other's best practice and enhance their anti-corruption policy. The Report itself is a form of reflexive governance where participants are actively engaging in enhancing their anti-corruption policy shortcomings and engaging in local experimentations as well. This is a clear example of the impact the Report had in engaging in a process of learning, which is a key component of the theory of reflexive governance, as stipulated in more detail in Chapter 3.

However, the impacts of the Report thus far have not embodied all of the seven key components of the theory of reflexive governance—in contrast to our findings in Chapter 3 (analysing the Report from a reflexive governance perspective), in which all of the seven key components of the theory of reflexive governance are apparent. In fully evaluating the impact of the Report, it would be ideal to compare it with the second edition of the Report, which was anticipated to come out at the end of 2016. The second Report was expected to be more indicator-driven and would have provided the opportunity to reflect on the progress made. Such a comparison would have offered somewhat more concrete assessment on the impact that the first Report had on the member states, in addition to what we offer here. However, since there has been no follow-up assessment of the extent to which member states have taken action on the recommendations made by the first Report, and since the Commission has discontinued future editions, it can only be said that the Report's major impact was in laying the foundation for developing an anti-corruption policy framework in the EU and raising corruption as an issue in the broader policy discussion in the EU.

10 Susan Rose-Ackerman and Paul D Carrington, *Anti-Corruption Policy: Can International Actors Play a Constructive Role?* (Carolina Academic Press 2013) 3–35.

11 European Commission, 'The Experience Sharing Programme to Support Member States, Local NGOs and Other Stakeholders in Addressing Specific Challenges Identified in the EU Anti-Corruption Report' (2016) <http://ec.europa.eu/dgs/home-affairs/what-we-do/policies/organized-crime-and-human-trafficking/corruption/experience-sharing-programme/index_en.htm> accessed 30 May 2019.

For the Report to have had a more significant and concrete impact, it would have required some time to gain sufficient visibility, due to it being a relatively new instrument and a new development at supranational level.[12] From an overall reflexive governance perspective, the Report was designed as a form of self-regulation and embodies key characteristics of reflexive governance theory.

The Report's general purpose was to engage member states in regulation of self-regulation processes in order to further improve their anti-corruption measures and anti-corruption legislation—identified as often poorly enforced. Thus, in analysing the general purpose of Report, its central impacts are characteristically self-regulatory and have been achieved.

We now consider why the Report was terminated after its first edition and also look in more detail at the development of anti-corruption policy in the EU post-2017.

7.3 The EU anti-corruption policy—the end of the report in 2017

The second EU Anti-Corruption Report was expected to be published in February 2016, two years after the first; an ongoing biannual assessment. The Commission then suggested postponing this until the Autumn of 2016; then, in January 2017, the Commission decided to drop the Report altogether as an anti-corruption monitoring instrument, having decided instead that corruption would be monitored under the European Semester process.

The first Report—initiated by member states and with the support of the European Parliament—published in 2014 was in one sense designed to provide the Commission with information to monitor the progress of the fight against corruption in individual member states. It made each individual member state aware of their own shortcomings in their laws and institutional settings to combat corruption more effectively. The Report provided important information on corruption cases, in particular, offering a description of the level of corruption throughout the EU—broad corruption trends—and an outline about the developments of anti-corruption laws and policies in all member states. Finally, the Report identified cross-cutting corruption risks with cross-border dimensions and offered non-legally binding recommendations to each individual member state in areas identified as most vulnerable to corruption practices. Therefore, as an instrument, the Report was an important point of reference in the fight against corruption across the member states and included many sectors—not just the economic process which the European Semester monitors.

On 25 January 2017, the Commission Vice President Frans Timmermans announced to the European Parliament the termination of the EU Anti-Corruption Report as an anti-corruption monitoring instrument, despite the fact

12 M Krambia-Kapardis, 'Perception of Political Corruption as a Function of Legislation' *Journal of Financial Crime 21* (1) (2014) 44–55.

that the research and work for the second Report by experts were largely completed and ready for publication.[13] TI-EU and other transparency campaigners have requested materials prepared for the second Report to be released via freedom of information legislation, but the Commission has so far refused to do so—it seems that the second Report research will never be published.[14]

Timmermans' letter to the European Parliament suggests that the 2014 Report served well as the basis for dialogue with member states and was a useful instrument for background information to evaluate areas affected by corruption. Furthermore, Timmerman acknowledges that it opened a wider debate on corruption both at the EU level and within individual member states. However, in the Commission's view, during the period between when the Report was published and 2017, the wider policy framework at EU level has evolved in a number of ways. The Commission's perspective is that fighting corruption should be addressed through economic policy, and therefore combating corruption is now part of the European Semester process of economic governance—where a number of the country reports now also include specific analysis of corruption risks and related challenges associated with corruption practices.

Furthermore, Timmermans suggested that the Commission wanted to continue the dialogue with member states in anti-corruption reforms through the European Semester process and issue country-specific recommendations under the European Semester scope. This approach suggests that the Commission will take up anti-corruption-related policy matters in the context of economic policy dialogue between member states and EU institutions. Timmermans' letter suggests that corruption remains a key issue in several member states, and its economic impact makes it essential that it is addressed through the European Semester framework. The Commission now believes that the annual dialogue with member states on economic policies through the European Semester process is the best forum to address issues related to corruption. In Timmermans's letter, the Commission admits reservations about the suitability of the format adopted by the 2014 Report—acknowledging the complex nature of corruption—but is convinced that the European semester is the more efficient approach to developing the anti-corruption field within the EU.

The Commission's decision to terminate the Report and instead address corruption-related policy issues through the European Semester process has not been welcomed by European scholars and EU civil society organisations working within the field. Local research correspondents and experts, who worked on the 2014 Report, wrote a joint letter to the Commission, calling for the Report's continuation,[15] and the decision was likewise criticised by 56 civil society organisations, who called for the EU to live up to its commitments in the fight against

13 Transparency.eu, Timmermans' Letter (2018) <http://transparency.eu/wp-content/uploads/2017/02/20170130-Letter-FVP-LIBE-Chair.pdf> accessed 30 May 2019.

14 ibid.

15 ibid.

corruption. According to academics in the field, the Report was far from a perfect tool and had several limitations (as we discussed in Chapter 2)—nevertheless, it was a first attempt to take the issue of corruption seriously from a policy perspective to outline common standards to all member states and treat corruption not just as a problem that prevents economic growth, but also one with an impact on the development of a society.

Furthermore, the Commission's decision to terminate the Report as mechanism is a major blow to the fulfilment of Articles 67 (3) and 83 of the Treaty on the Functioning of the European Union (TFEU), whereby the Union is expected to take measures to prevent and combat crime, including by setting minimum penal standards and the objectives on fighting economic crime and corruption, as set by the Stockholm Programme.[16]

In the view of TI-EU, the discontinuation of the Report is a clear message that the Commission no longer considers fighting corruption a political priority.[17] Corruption is once again considered a serious problem in just a few individual member states, as was the view before the adoption of the Report. This is quite a contradiction when evaluating the scale of the problem in many member states—as we saw in detail in Chapter 2—which remains formidable, with ongoing challenges to good governance, the rule of law and anti-corruption reforms across the EU.

The real reasons behind why the Report was scrapped are unclear, but it's highly likely that it was a political decision taken by the Commission, with pressure from some important member states scrutinised in the Report. There is no clear evidence to support this claim, but inquiries from TI-EU are highly suggestive.[18] Furthermore, before deciding to discontinue the Report, the Commission held no consultation with the European Parliament, not even with the Commission's own expert group who prepared the Report. Therefore, it seems that there were political factors at play—perhaps the Commission decided to not expose all member states—and it is hard not to infer that fighting corruption is considered by the EU to be a bureaucratic exercise, which should be conducted largely behind closed doors. This retreat to the bureaucratic comfort zone by the Commission is a decision that reflects the lack of will and commitment to fighting corruption under the Juncker's purview, even though some of the biggest corruption scandals have occurred during this period. For example, the Volkswagen emissions scandal of 2015 (known as the 'Dieselgate Scandal') wherein member states including Germany, the UK, Spain and Luxembourg failed to clamp down on emissions cheating; Volkswagen had used illegal software to mask emission of

16 Marco Hafner and others, 'The Cost of Non-Europe in the Area of Organised Crime and Corruption' Annex II—Corruption European Union EPRS PE 579.319 (March 2016) <www.europarl.europa.eu/RegData/etudes/STUD/2016/579319/EPRS_STU%282016%29579319_EN.pdf> accessed 30 May 2019.

17 Transparency.eu (n 14).

18 Transparency.eu, 'EU Anti-Corruption Report—No Answers Please, We're the Commission' (2017) <https://transparency.eu/no-answers/> accessed 30 May 2019.

dangerous nitrogen oxides (NOx) on tests.[19] Furthermore, it was revealed in 2017 that Volkswagen fraudulently secured €400 million in loans from the European Investment Bank (EIB) to develop the engine at the heart of Dieselgate, through an investigation by the European Anti-Fraud Office (OLAF) into loans provided by the EIB in 2009 to help the world's biggest carmaker develop an engine that would comply with increasing emission rules in the EU and the U.S.A.[20] OLAF itself cannot take judicial action, but it has sent recommendations to public prosecutors in Braunschweig, who are leading criminal inquiries into Volkswagen.[21]

We will now consider in some detail the European Semester process and how the anti-corruption field fits into the Commission's new approach in the post-Report era.

7.4 The European semester process

Since the financial and sovereign debt crises in 2009–2010, the EU has introduced a series of changes and policies in its institutional design for economic governance. According to Amy Verduna and Jonathan Zeitlin, at the centre of these institutional changes is the European Semester Process.[22] The European Semester brings together within a single policy co-ordination cycle a variety of EU governance instruments with different legal bases, from the Stability and Growth Pact, Macroeconomic Imbalance Procedure and Fiscal Compact, to the Europe 2020 Strategy and the Integrated Economic and Employment Policy Guidelines.[23] In this cycle, the Commission and the European Council set priorities for the EU, review national performance, budgets and reform programmes, and issue country-specific recommendations, backed up in some cases by financial sanctions. Each member state receives a single integrated set of country-specific recommendations, except for those under a bailout programme. These recommendations cover a wide range of policy fields, including issues such as wage determination, education and health care, which fall under the primary competence of member states and where the EU's legislative powers are severely limited. In 2018, the country-specific recommendations also included corruption as an issue and recommended actions to some member states to improve their anti-corruption framework, which will be discussed further in the section below.

19 Marco Frigessi di Rattalma, *The Dieselgate: A Legal Perspective* (Springer Switzerland 2017).

20 ibid.

21 Patrick McGee, 'Volkswagen fined €1bn by German state prosecutors', *Financial Times* (13 June 2018) <www.ft.com/content/240cd18a-6f24-11e8-852d-d8b934ff5ffa> accessed 30 May 2019.

22 Amy Verdun, and Jonathan Zeitlin, 'Introduction: the European Semester as a New Architecture of EU Socioeconomic Governance in Theory and Practice' *Journal of European Public Policy* 25 (2) (2018) 137–48.

23 Amy Verdun and Alfred Tovias, *Mapping European Economic Integration* (Palgrave Macmillan UK 2013).

The European Semester was also designed to reinforce the EU economic governance. The legal basis for the process is the so-called 'Six-Pack'—six legislative acts that reformed the Stability and Growth Pact.[24] These measures included stronger sanctions for the Stability and Growth Pact's Excessive Deficit Procedure, a new Macroeconomic Imbalance Procedure for detecting and correcting non-fiscal imbalances that could have negative effect on other member states (based on a scoreboard of economic indicators, in-depth country reviews and country-specific recommendations, and backed by a financial sanctions for persistent non-compliance), an Commission ex ante review of Euro-area national budgets (not limited to Eurozone countries), and Reverse Qualified Majority Voting for overturning Commission proposals under the excessive deficit and imbalance procedures.[25]

Since 2010, the design of the European Semester was mainly about extending and strengthening the powers and capacities of European institutions to monitor, coordinate and sanction the economic and budgetary policies of member states, especially but not exclusively within the Eurozone. It has changed since its inception, most significantly by the Juncker Commission in 2015, to also include a social dimension, with specific guidelines and targets on poverty and social inclusion.[26]

The first European Semester cycle took place in 2011 and was dominated by the pursuit of fiscal consolidation and macroeconomic austerity. As the sovereign debt crisis within the Eurozone morphed into a broader economic and employment crisis, a significant rebalancing between social, economic and employment objectives was also included in the policy orientation of successive European Semesters. In its current form, the European Semester begins each November with the Commission's Annual Growth Survey, which identifies the key reform priorities for the EU, and offers general policy guidance to the member states for the coming year.[27] Figure 7.1 illustrates how the European Semester Cycle works in practice.

In February each year, the Commission publishes a country report laying out its analysis of the key challenges and reform progress of each member states, which are preceded and followed by a dialogue with national governments. Based on the Commission's annual growth survey and the European Council conclusions in its March meeting, socio-economic priorities and policy orientations are adopted for

24 Antonio Estella, *Legal Foundations of EU Economic Governance* (CUP 2018).

25 Mark Dawson, 'New Governance and the Displacement of Social Europe: The Case of the European Semester' *European Constitutional Law Review 14* (1) (2018) 191–209.

26 Aleksandra Maatsch, 'Effectiveness of the European Semester: Explaining Domestic Consent and Contestation' *Max Planck Institute for the Study of Societies Cologne MPIfG Discussion Paper 17/6* (2017).

27 Jonathan Zeitlin and Bart Vanhercke, 'Socializing the European Semester: EU Social and Economic Policy Co-Ordination in Crisis and Beyond' *Journal of European Public Policy 25* (2) (2018) 149–74.

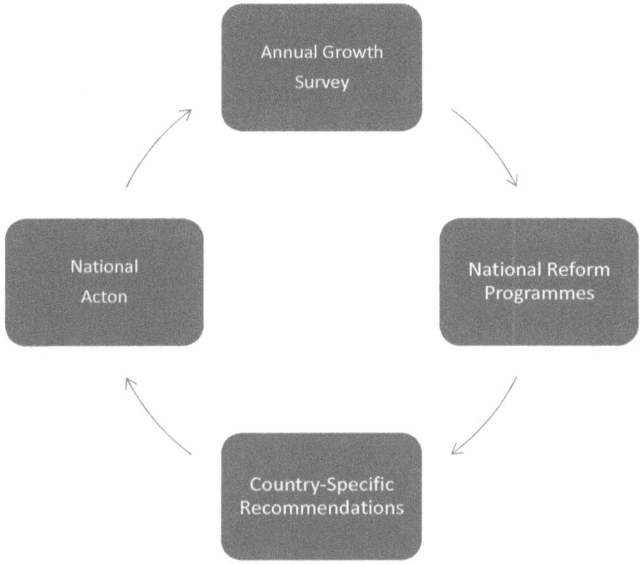

Figure 7.1 The European semester policy coordination cycle

the EU.[28] By early April, the member states submit their National Reform Programmes, and fiscal stability or Convergence Programmes. In May, the Commission evaluates these programmes and proposes country-specific recommendations, which in turn are reviewed and sometimes amended by committees of member state officials preparing the work of the European Council. The revised country-specific recommendations are then endorsed by the Council and later adopted in June or July. The European Parliament then adopts resolutions and reports on the Commission's Annual Growth Survey and the country-specific recommendations each year, and it may invite the Presidents of the Commission, European Council and Eurogroup to discuss the European Semester.[29]

In 2018, in its country-specific recommendations, the European Semester also included corruption as a topic after the Commission decided in 2017 to drop the EU Anti-Corruption Report and incorporate it into the European Semester. The next section explains in detail the recommendations issued in the European Semester for each of the member states.

28 Verdun and Zeitlin (n 23).

29 James D Savage and David Howarth, 'Enforcing the European Semester: the Politics of Asymmetric Information in the Excessive Deficit and Macroeconomic Imbalance Procedures' *Journal of European Public Policy* 25 (2) (2018) 212–230.

7.4.1 European Semester 2018 anti-corruption recommendations

The Commission stated that their efforts to address corruption in the member states would continue within the European Semester process framework post-2017. However, the recommendations issued to member states in 2018 speak a different language and do not show any additional ambition to improve the anti-corruption policy or any new efforts for a more comprehensive approach in seriously fighting corruption in the EU. In the latest European Semester country-specific recommendation reports, issued on May 2018, the Commission not only mentions corruption as an issue for 13 out of 28 member states, but only proposes anti-corruption recommendations for seven of them (namely, the Czech Republic, Hungary, Italy, Latvia, Malta, Romania and Slovakia).

The recent European Semester country-specific recommendations for 2018 shows that the scope of anti-corruption recommendations is very narrow under the European Semester framework, and it recommends anti-corruption action to only to few member states, rather than all (as was the case under the Report). Thus, overall the European Semester process remains a somewhat inadequate replacement for the Report. An overview of each European Semester country-specific recommendations 2018 is provided in Appendix A.

The European Semester country-specific recommendations issued in May 2018 mention corruption as an issue for only 13 out of 28 member states (Bulgaria, Croatia, Cyprus, Czech Republic, Hungary, Italy, Latvia, Lithuania, Malta, Portugal, Romania, Slovakia and Slovenia). We'll now briefly consider the corruption-related issues identified here and the Commission's recommendations for improving anti-corruption policy in these countries.

Bulgaria[30]

Corruption was mentioned as an issue in the following areas: public procurement, the business environment and the judiciary.

Public procurement: The European Semester country-specific for Bulgaria found that many of the measures included in the National Public Procurement Strategy have been put in place—however, the Bulgarian authorities needed to put more effort into ensuring their effective implementation. According to the business community and NGOs, the overall public-procurement landscape has already shown signs of improvement, but these encouraging signs are yet to fully be established, and transparency and corruption, in particular, are still a matter of high concern. The increased use of direct awards and the high number of single bids continue to significantly hamper the system's transparency

30 European Commission, 'European Semester: Country Specific Recommendation on the 2018 National Reform Programme of Bulgaria and Delivering a Council Opinion on the 2018 Convergence Programme of Bulgaria' COM (2018) 402 final <https://ec.europa.eu/info/sites/info/files/file_import/2018-european-semester-country-specific-recommendation-commission-recommendation-bulgaria-en.pdf> accessed 30 May 2019.

and its effectiveness. The first independent evaluation of the new control functions of the Public Procurement Agency is still ongoing, and it's difficult to make an assessment of its success at this point. Regular updates are necessary to ensure further optimisation of the Agency's control functions and maintain the reforms. There are still problems with administrative capacity, including at the municipal level, and further efforts at professionalising this area are required to improve effectiveness and the economy overall.

Business environment: This requires further improvement. Though a number of reforms have been adopted, their practical implementation is lagging behind; businesses are still concerned about corruption, institutional shortcomings and insufficient labour supply. Progress in public administration reform and e-government is also slow. Improving good governance practices in the public sector could benefit from more transparency, clearer rules and a long-term perspective.

The judiciary: The new elections to the Supreme Judicial Council has had a positive impact on constitutional and legislative reform in 2015/2016, addressing shortcomings in the fight against corruption and organised crime. Legislation was adopted in early 2018 establishing a new unified anti-corruption authority to strengthen prevention and deterrence of high-level corruption, and this will help to improve the system of prosecution in high-level corruption cases.

Recommendations: NONE

The European Semester country-specific report for Bulgaria has not issued any recommendations for specific actions; this was also true of the EU Anti-Corruption Report in 2014, because the Commission monitors the judicial reform and the fight against corruption and organised crime in Bulgaria under the CVM.

Czech republic[31]

Corruption was mentioned as an issue in the following areas: public procurement and the business environment.

Public procurement: The Czech Republic continues to face challenges in improving the transparency and efficiency of public procurement and preventing corruption. Steps have been taken to improve the public-procurement framework, such as using electronic procedures, but the level of competition remains a concern, as nearly half of all public tenders result in a single-bid procedure. The Czech authorities have invested in the National Electronic Tool to boost transparency and efficiency, but the process must still become more accessible and there is scope for removing administrative barriers for public procurement. Although both central and local authorities have started undertaking targeted initiatives to train staff involved in procurement procedures, setting up joint

31 European Commission, 'European Semester: Country Specific Recommendation on the 2018 National Reform Programme of Czech Republic and Delivering a Council Opinion on the 2018 Convergence Programme of Czech Republic' COM (2018) 402 final <https://ec.europa.eu/info/sites/info/files/file_import/2018-european-semester-country-specific-recommendation-commission-recommendation-czechrepublic-en.pdf> accessed 30 May 2019.

procurement measures and acquiring specialist expertise in certain areas remain major challenges. Whilst several major reforms of the anti-corruption strategy have been adopted, some areas remain unaddressed, and corruption and bribery are still ongoing concerns for businesses and the public.

Business environment: While several major reforms of the anti-corruption strategy have been adopted, there is still a considerable scope for improving this area if corruption and bribery are addressed appropriately.

Recommendations: YES

- Improve the long-term fiscal sustainability, in particular, of the pension system.
- Address the shortcomings and weaknesses in public-procurement practices, notably by enabling more quality-based competition and implementing anti-corruption measures.

Spain[32]

Corruption was mentioned as an issue in the following areas: public procurement and general comments.

Public procurement: Spain continues to have challenges in improving transparency in public procurement. Whilst there has been progress with the adoption of a new law on public sector contracts in November 2017, the new legislation can only be effective in improving the transparency of public procurement if it is implemented properly and if governance structures are improved, in particular the mechanisms of procurement procedures at all levels of government.

General comments: Corruption was also discussed more generally as an issue to be addressed in order to boost trust in the Spanish economy and its governmental institutions to increase productivity growth. Some progress has been made in the transparency of party financing and disclosure of assets and conflicts of interest, as well as the independence of the justice system. However, public and business perception of transparency and trustworthiness is still low.

Recommendations: NO

Croatia[33]

Corruption was mentioned as a general issue.

32 European Commission, 'European Semester: Country Specific Recommendation on the 2018 National Reform Programme of Spain and Delivering a Council Opinion on the 2018 Convergence Programme of Spain' COM (2018) 402 final <https://ec.europa.eu/info/sites/info/files/2018-european-semester-country-specific-recommendation-commission-recommendation-spain-en.pdf> accessed 30 May 2019.

33 European Commission, 'European Semester: Country Specific Recommendation on the 2018 National Reform Programme of Croatia and Delivering a Council Opinion on the 2018 Convergence Programme of Croatia' COM (2018) 402 final <https://ec.europa.eu/info/sites/info/files/file_import/2018-european-semester-country-specific-recommendation-commission-recommendation-croatia-en.pdf> accessed 30 May 2019.

General comments: Croatia's Anti-Corruption Action Plan 2017–2018 needs to be fully implemented in order to deliver on the objectives of the anti-corruption strategy 2015–2020. Several key elements still require improvement, in particular, regarding the asset and conflict-of-interest disclosures, as well as raising awareness of whistle-blowing reporting channels. An effective control of risks in public procurement is required, as currently it is vulnerable to corruption practices due to a large share of in-house contracting by state-owned entities.

Recommendations: NO

Italy[34]

Corruption was mentioned as an issue in the following areas: public procurement and the business environment.

Italy has improved its anti-corruption framework by revising its statute of limitations, as well extending the protection of whistle-blowers to private sector workers and aligned the offence of corruption among private parties with international standards, but it is still not adequate. In 2014, Italy had the largest number of incoming and pending criminal cases in the EU at the second and third instances—making it in one of the longest trial lengths. The European Semester indicates that the National Anti-Corruption Authority has a key role in the implementation of the new anti-corruption framework and repression of corruption could be improved by increasing the efficiency of criminal justice.

Recommendations: Yes

- Reducing the length of civil trials in all instances by enforcing and streamlining procedural rules, including those under consideration by the legislator.
- More effective anti-corruption prevention measures and repression of corruption by reducing the length of criminal trials, as well as implementing the new anti-corruption framework.
- Italy should ensure proper enforcement of the new framework for publicly owned enterprises and increase its efficiency through a new annual competition law, especially its implementation in the local authority level.

Cyprus[35]

Corruption was mentioned as a general issue.

34 European Commission, 'European Semester: Country Specific Recommendation on the 2018 National Reform Programme of Italy and Delivering a Council Opinion on the 2018 Convergence Programme of Italy' COM (2018) 402 final <https://ec.europa.eu/info/sites/info/files/2018-european-semester-country-specific-recommendation-commission-recommendation-italy-en.pdf> accessed 30 May 2019.

35 European Commission, 'European Semester: Country Specific Recommendation on the 2018 National Reform Programme of Cyprus and Delivering a Council Opinion on the 2018 Convergence Programme of Cyprus' COM (2018) 402 final <https://ec.europa.eu/info/sites/info/files/file_import/2018-european-semester-country-specific-recommendation-commission-recommendation-cyprus-en.pdf> accessed 30 May 2019.

Corruption remains a challenge in Cyrus, even though a national anti-corruption strategy and action plan were adopted in December 2017. The existing anti-corruption body remains inadequately resourced, although the government is considering the establishment of a new independent agency in Cyprus, which might receive more funded/allocated resources. Various legislative initiatives, such as draft laws on whistle-blower protection, lobbying and asset declarations, are currently under parliamentary scrutiny. If adopted, these would help to strengthen Cyprus anti-corruption framework.

Recommendations: NO

Latvia[36]

Corruption was mentioned as an issue in the following areas: the business environment and money laundering.

Business environment: Corruption continues to hamper Latvia's business environment, and the prevention of conflicts of interest remains rigid and formalistic. The delay in legislating on whistle-blower protection is detrimental to the accountability and efficiency of public administration. Regulation of the insolvency process has been notably strengthened over the years, thus limiting the opportunities for abuses, however. The Council for the Judiciary needs to support the specialisations of judges' expertise dealing with cases related to the abuses of the insolvency system.

Money laundering: Latvian banks serving non-resident clients are exposed to a high risk of involvement in money laundering, creating challenges to the integrity of the financial system in Latvia with potential to damage its reputation, and have a negative effect in investment and economic growth. The anti-money laundering framework has recently been strengthened, and Latvia has recently adopted a law aimed at significantly limiting the exposure of the financial sector to money-laundering risks, enhancing the exchange of information between financial institutions and law enforcement agencies and curbing transactions with shell companies. Continuous efforts would be needed to achieve sustainable improvement, and the consequences of the adopted law and its effectiveness will need to be monitored in the future.

Recommendations: Yes

- Continue to strengthen the efficiency of the public sector, in particular, with regard to local authorities and state-owned enterprises.
- Strengthen the accountability of public administration by protecting whistle-blowers, preventing conflicts of interest and following up on the results of the ongoing assessment of past insolvency proceedings.

36 European Commission, 'European Semester: Country Specific Recommendation on the 2018 National Reform Programme of Latvia and Delivering a Council Opinion on the 2018 Convergence Programme of Latvia' COM (2018) 402 final <https://ec.europa.eu/info/sites/info/files/file_import/2018-european-semester-country-specific-recommendation-commission-recommendation-latvia-en.pdf> accessed 30 May 2019.

Lithuania[37]

Corruption was mentioned as a general issue.

Corruption remains an issue in Lithuania, although the country has made progress in strengthening its corruption-prevention framework by adopting legislation on lobbying and whistle-blower protection for both public- and private-sector workers. However, implementing legislation remains a challenge in Lithuania. Corruption in the health sector still raises concerns, despite the commendable results of the government's 'clean hands' programme.

Recommendations: NO

Hungary[38]

Corruption was mentioned as an issue in the following areas: public procurement and the judiciary.

The European Semester country report stated that according to several indicators, Hungary's exposure to corruption appears to have increased over the past years, and the risks of corruption could negatively affect the country's growth potential. The functioning of the prosecution service is of crucial importance to fight corruption and money laundering, and while measures to fight low-level corruption appear to have been applied with some success, there is not enough focus on starting investigations into high-level cases. Although steps have been taken regarding public procurement, there is still limited transparency and restrictions on access to information on competition in tendering processes and public-procurement contracts.

Recommendations: Yes

- Continue simplifying the tax system, in particular, by reducing sector-specific taxes.
- Improve the quality and transparency of the decision-making process through effective social dialogue and engagement with other stakeholders and by regular, adequate impact assessments.
- Reinforce the anti-corruption framework, strengthen prosecutorial efforts and improve transparency and competition in public procurement inter alia through making data gained from the e-procurement system accessible to the public.

37 European Commission, 'European Semester: Country Specific Recommendation on the 2018 National Reform Programme of Lithuania and Delivering a Council Opinion on the 2018 Convergence Programme of Lithuania' COM (2018) 402 final <https://ec.europa.eu/info/sites/info/files/file_import/2018-european-semester-country-specific-recommendation-commission-recommendation-lithuania-en.pdf> accessed 30 May 2019.

38 European Commission, 'European Semester: Country Specific Recommendation on the 2018 National Reform Programme of Hungary and Delivering a Council Opinion on the 2018 Convergence Programme of Hungary' COM (2018) 402 final <https://ec.europa.eu/info/sites/info/files/2018-european-semester-country-specific-recommendation-commission-recommenda tion-hungary-en.pdf> accessed 30 May 2019.

- Strengthen competition, regulatory stability and transparency in the services sector, notably in retail.

Malta[39]

Corruption was mentioned as an issue in the following areas: the justice system and money laundering.

Justice system: Corruption remains a challenging issue in Malta, and the justice system continues to face many problems with regards to its efficiency. Strengthening the legal and institutional framework to fight corruption remains weak, and strengthening its anti-corruption framework is required to ensure a healthier business environment. Governance shortcomings in the anti-corruption framework may adversely affect the business climate and weigh negatively on investment. The effectiveness of the country's efforts to fight corruption needs to be improved, especially with regards to the investigation and prosecution of corruption-related cases. Therefore, improving the governance framework is vital to also preserving Malta's reputation and attractiveness as an international investment destination in Europe.

Money laundering: Some progress has been made in improving cross-border cooperation in Malta, but money laundering is a problematic issue. The Malta Financial Services Authority still appears understaffed, and concerns remain regarding its capacity to supervise a large cross-border financial system, in particular its non-bank segment. In the services sector in particular, the online gaming industry has significantly contributed to the country's sustained economic growth, and this may create challenges to the financial system's integrity, and therefore a strong anti-money laundering framework is essential. Malta has recently transposed the Fourth Anti Money Laundering Directive into national law, and authorities have recently presented an integrated strategy to fight money laundering and terrorist financing. However, challenges remain in ensuring proper implementation and effective enforcement of the recently adopted regulatory framework.

Recommendations: Yes

- Strengthen overall governance framework, in particular, by enhancing the national supervision of internationally oriented financial businesses licensed in Malta.
- Ensure the enforcement of the Anti-Money Laundering framework, and step up the fight against corruption more effectively.

39 European Commission, 'European Semester: Country Specific Recommendation on the 2018 National Reform Programme of Malta and Delivering a Council Opinion on the 2018 Convergence Programme of Malta' COM (2018) 402 final <https://ec.europa.eu/info/sites/info/files/file_import/2018-european-semester-country-specific-recommendation-commission-recommendation-malta-en.pdf> accessed 30 May 2019.

Portugal[40]

Corruption was mentioned as a general issue.

Portugal has revised its public-procurement code in order to promote transparency, competition and better management of public contracts. The implementation of the new rules should be monitored, including the impact of the stricter rules on the use of direct awards. The Portuguese justice system continues to improve its efficiency, although the length of proceedings in administrative courts remains a challenge, in corruption-related cases that are dealt with in court. Corruption and lack of transparency are still perceived by businesses as areas of concern. While progress has continued as regards prosecuting corruption, efforts to improve a culture of integrity in public institutions have not so far shown sufficient results.

Recommendations: NO

Romania[41]

Corruption was mentioned as an issue in the following areas: public procurement and the judiciary.

Public procurement: The efficiency and transparency of the public-procurement process remains pivotal to addressing key policy challenges to Romania, including efficiency in public spending, the fight against corruption, and promoting innovation and sustainable and inclusive growth. Romania has made some progress in implementing the public-procurement strategy, but the plan is not yet fully implemented. The institutional framework for effective audit and fraud control still remains a challenge, and lack of transparency and corruption continue to be associated with public procurement in the healthcare infrastructure investments and regional hospitals.

Justice system: Corruption remains a major issue in the justice system in Romania, and developments throughout the past year have largely brought into question the irreversibility and sustainability of Romania's substantial progress on reforming its judiciary, as well as tackling corruption at a high level. Judicial independence is being challenged, and pressure is being put on judicial institutions and the legal framework for fighting corruption—thus progress on

40 European Commission, 'European Semester: Country Specific Recommendation on the 2018 National Reform Programme of Portugal and Delivering a Council Opinion on the 2018 Convergence Programme of Portugal' COM (2018) 402 final <https://ec.europa.eu/info/sites/info/files/file_import/2018-european-semester-country-specific-recommendation-commission-recommendation-portugal-en.pdf> accessed 30 May 2019.

41 European Commission, 'European Semester: Country Specific Recommendation on the 2018 National Reform Programme of Romania and Delivering a Council Opinion on the 2018 Convergence Programme of Romania' COM (2018) 402 final <https://ec.europa.eu/info/sites/info/files/2018-european-semester-country-specific-recommendation-commission-recommendation-romania-en.pdf> accessed 30 May 2019.

remaining challenges is being further held back. The implementation of the 2016–2020 national anti-corruption strategy developing further measures to prevent and fight corruption is progressing at technical level, but more tangible political support is required, as corruption and governance issues in the public sector persist at all levels and are among the top challenges for the business environment.

The Commission continues to monitor the judicial reform and the fight against corruption in Romania under the CVM, and therefore the European Semester country-specific report did not cover this in the country-specific recommendations for Romania, but made reference to it because of its relevance for the development of a positive socio-economic environment in Romania.

Recommendations: Yes

- Increase the predictability of decision-making by enforcing the systematic and effective use of regulatory impact assessment, and stakeholder consultation and involvement in the design and implementation of reforms.
- Improve the transparency and efficiency of public procurement; in particular, prioritise large infrastructure public-procurement projects in major sectors such as transport, healthcare, waste and waste water.
- Strengthen corporate governance of state-owned enterprises.

Slovenia[42]

Corruption was mentioned as an issue in the following areas: public procurement, the business environment; general comments.

Slovenia struggles with inefficiency and lack of transparency in public procurement; competition between bidders is comparatively low, as indicated by the low number of bids received per tender and by the high ratio of negotiated procedures without prior call. The professionalisation of those involved in procurement is also low, and there are few safeguards against corruption and collusion among bidders. In particular, the independence of the National Review Commission is limited in Slovenia, due to the procedure for appointing members. Economic crime and corruption are estimated by the authorities to have caused significant damage in the past years; some anti-corruption reforms are still pending in the country.

Recommendations: NO

42 European Commission, 'European Semester: Country Specific Recommendation on the 2018 National Reform Programme of Slovenia and Delivering a Council Opinion on the 2018 Convergence Programme of Slovenia' COM (2018) 402 final <https://ec.europa.eu/info/sites/info/files/2018-european-semester-country-specific-recommendation-commission-recommendation-slovenia-en.pdf> accessed 30 May 2019.

Slovakia[43]

Corruption was mentioned as an issue in the following areas: public procurement, business environment and the judiciary.

Public procurement: Slovakia has taken important steps towards achieving a well-functioning system of public procurement, and efforts have been made to introduce quality award criteria; mandatory electronic tools for conducting public-procurement procedures should be in place by October 2018. Satisfactory performance has not yet been achieved in the areas of internal controls, transparency, digitisation, professionalisation and strategic public procurement—nevertheless, even though not optimally efficient, comprehensive prior verifications have been carried out on all projects funded through the European Social and Investment Funds. This is also reflected in Slovakia's scores related to anti-competitive practices, which remain somewhat above the EU average, despite some improvement. More than half of businesses perceive corruption as widespread in public procurement managed by national authorities, and there are still only limited signs of commitment to fighting corruption.

Business environment: Complex administrative procedures, excessive and fast-changing business regulations, and poor quality of regulatory bodies heavily affect Slovakia's business environment. While the country lost ground in some international comparisons, it has identified a number of measures to improve the quality of the business environment and boost investment. Slovakia has also strengthened its framework for regulatory impact assessment, extending its use in recent years. However, high regulatory barriers remain in the business services sector, with levels of restrictiveness higher than the EU average for architects, engineers, tax advisers, lawyers, patent agents, real estate agents and tourist guides.

Justice system: Slovakia has made no progress in stepping up the fight against corruption within the judiciary. Corruption perceptions remain high, and prosecutions for such offences have fallen further. The perception of corruption has further deteriorated in the wake of the murder of an investigative journalist, who had made findings on a wide range of high-level corruption cases. The proportion of high-level cases prosecuted is extremely low, and the lack of accountability for police and public prosecutors has not been resolved, hindering the fight against corruption and investigations of sensitive corruption cases.

Recommendations: Yes

- Increase the use of quality-related and lifecycle cost criteria in public-procurement operations.

43 European Commission, 'European Semester: Country Specific Recommendation on the 2018 National Reform Programme of Slovakia and Delivering a Council Opinion on the 2018 Convergence Programme of Slovakia' COM (2018) 402 final <https://ec.europa.eu/info/sites/info/files/file_import/2018-european-semester-country-specific-recommendation-commission-recommendation-slovakia-en.pdf> accessed 30 May 2019.

- Reducing the fragmentation of the public research system and stimulating business innovation, including for small- and medium-sized businesses.
- Fighting corruption, including by ensuring enforcement of existing legislation and by increasing accountability at the level of police and prosecution.
- Improving the effectiveness of the justice system, in particular, by safeguarding independence in judicial appointment procedures is necessary for Slovakia.

7.4.2 Country-specific recommendation summary

The European Semester country-specific recommendations issued in May 2018 mention corruption as an issue for almost half of the member states in areas mainly related to economic growth. Recommendations were only made anti-corruption measures for seven member states and mainly focused on improving transparency in public procurement and the business environment in order to boost foreign investments and thus improve economic performance.

We'll now move on to consider the future of anti-corruption policy in the EU and examine the limitations of the European Semester in addressing corruption.

7.5 EU anti-corruption policy under the European semester process

The highlight of the EU's ambitions for a comprehensive anti-corruption policy was in 2011, after the European Council had asked the Commission to develop a comprehensive anti-corruption policy to continue the work of the so-called Stockholm programme in the area of justice and home affairs. As a result, the Commission issued a communication on 'Fighting Corruption in the EU' in June 2011 under former Home Affairs Commissioner Cecilia Malmström. As discussed in Chapter 1, the communication promised a number of steps and measures with regard to developing an EU anti-corruption policy and was by far the most ambitious anti-corruption policy proposal at the EU level.

The Commission's Communication on 'Fighting Corruption in the EU' in June 2011 promised a number of policy actions, including:

1) A special EU monitoring and assessment mechanism, known as the EU Anti-Corruption Report;
2) Establishing an expert group to oversee the EU Anti-Corruption Report;
3) Publishing the Eurobarometer survey every two years;
4) An experience-sharing programme between member states and the EU;
5) Accelerating negotiations on EU participation in the Council of Europe's Group of states Against Corruption (GRECO); and
6) Ensuring the fulfilment of the EU's obligation, following the ratification of the UN Convention Against Convention (UNCAC) in 2008, to carry out a self-assessment of its anti-corruption capacities.

In January 2019, nearly eight years after the Communication, the ambition for a wider EU anti-corruption policy is still to be achieved. Let's review what happened to those ambitious objectives:

1) The EU Anti-Corruption Report in 2014 was abolished after a single publication.
2) The expert group has not met for over two years since the Report was terminated.
3) The Commission is still negotiating participation with GRECO.
4) The Commission is still conducting the legal analysis that would allow it to complete the self-assessment mandated by UNCAC, and to date it has failed to complete this assessment.

All that remains in 2019 are the Eurobarometer surveys—the EU's efforts to fight corruption and develop a wider EU anti-corruption policy in 2019 are very far from its 2011 ambitions. It is fair to say that the Juncker Commission, from the point of view of the anti-corruption field, is doing nothing new, but in fact is backtracking away from the Barroso Commission anti-corruption objectives of eight years ago.

Commission policy is now pursuing the objectives of the Report through the European Semester; however, this is far from a comprehensive approach. By contrast, the Report issued recommendations to all member states on addressing corruption, and not just those areas related to public procurement and improving the business environment, as the European Semester 2018 has issued. The European Semester is not an adequate alternative to replace the Report, but a poor substitute.

7.5.1 European semester process: narrow scope and opaque reasoning

When it comes to monitoring corruption, the European Semester is not comprehensive—corruption is viewed only as an element contributing towards poor economic governance and the shadow economy. No social dimension is considered and no recommendations made encompassing the political sphere. The country-specific recommendations are for just a quarter of the member states, and there is no consideration of how wider anti-corruption policy can be improved across the member states—unlike the output from the 2014 Report. The reasoning and rational behind why the Commission issued recommendations for addressing corruption to some member states and not others is neither clear and reasonable nor justified. The 2014 Report, by contrast, described its data collection methodology and the process by which it decided upon recommendations for each of the 28 member states.

7.5.2 Failures to promote good governance and the rule of law

The European Semester framework primarily addresses corruption on the basis of its potential impact on growth and competitiveness in the EU. The country-specific recommendations in the European Semester 2018, as shown above, have paid little attention to the impact that corruption has on good governance or rule of law, illegal political party financing, police and the judicial system. This is concerning, because a member state like Hungary, in the TI Corruption Perceptions Index of 2018,[44] ranks even lower than Montenegro, a candidate state for the EU. In the EU and Western Balkans strategy, issued by the Commission in February 2018, the Western Balkans countries—in particular Montenegro—are described as showing elements of state capture[45] and corruption at all levels of government and administration—one of the main obstacles to their EU membership aspirations. Similar elements of state capture can also be observed in Hungary under the ruling Fidesz party, led by Viktor Orbán.[46] Its officials have been misusing public funds, much of which come from EU-funded projects, and made efforts to shut down the activities of independent voices in civil society and academia when these voices have spoken against the government's corrupt practices.

A similar pattern of action to that observable in Hungary is also seen by the Law and Justice party currently governing Poland.[47] Other member states are taking hostile action against investigating journalism looking into corruption probes. In Romania, for example, the government is using the EU's new data protection rules to stifle a probe by a group of investigative reporters (the RISE Project), an award-winning investigative journalism outlet in Romania looking into the abuse of EU funds in the country.[48] On 9 November 2018, the Romanian Data Protection Authority ordered the RISE Project to reveal its sources, under the threat of a fine of up to €20 million based on the EU's General Data Protection Regulation (GDPR) directive 679/2016.[49] Furthermore, between 2017 and 2018 in three member states (Malta, Slovakia and Bulgaria), three journalists, Jan Kuciak in Slovakia,[50] Daphne Caruana Galizia

44 transparency.org, 'The 2018 Corruption Perceptions Index' (2018) <www.transparency.org/whatwedo/publication/corruption_perceptions_index_2018> accessed 30 May 2019.

45 European Commission, 'A credible enlargement perspective for and enhanced EU engagement with the Western Balkans' COM (2018) 65 final <https://ec.europa.eu/commission/sites/beta-political/files/communication-credible-enlargement-perspective-western-balkans_en.pdf> accessed 30 May 2019.

46 M Fazekas and IJ Tóth, 'From Corruption to State Capture: A New Analytical Framework with Empirical Applications from Hungary' *Comparative Political Studies 41* (4–5) (2016) 638–73.

47 Konrad Niklewicz, 'Safeguarding the Rule of Law within the EU: Lessons from the Polish Experience' *European View 16* (2) (2017) 281–91.

48 Organised crime and corruption reporting project 'Romania Orders Journalists Investigating Corruption to Give Up Sources'. <www.occrp.org/en/daily/8878-romania-orders-journalists-investigating-corruption-to-give-up-sources> accessed 30 May 2019.

49 Nikolaj Nielsen, 'EU Data Verdict Imminent On Romania's €20m Reporters' Fine' *EUObserver* (25 January 2019) <https://euobserver.com/justice/144008> accessed 15 February 2019.

50 Chris Harris, 'Jan Kuciak Murder: How Has Journalist's Slaying Changed Slovakia?' *Euro News* (21 February 2019) <www.euronews.com/2019/02/21/jan-kuciak-murder-how-has-journalist-s-slaying-changed-slovakia> accessed 25 February 2019.

in Malta[51] and Viktoria Marinov in Bulgaria,[52] were killed whilst investigating corruption and connections between top government officials and organised crime networks.[53] These concerns are not mentioned in the European Semester, and, unlike the 2014 Report, it does not mention the protection of whistle-blowers, nor what steps each of the member states should take to improve the environment for investigative journalism working on corruption cases.

7.5.3 No room for a broader dialogue: civil society exclusion

The Commission's current policy in addressing corruption through the European Semester framework gives the impression that the fight against corruption is merely a bureaucratic and a box-ticking exercise, which should be conducted behind closed doors between Commission officials and a few member states. In the current format, under the European Semester process, there is no room or opportunity for an open discussion that could include the Commission, all member states and civil society in considering how to address corruption more effectively. On the other hand, under the 2014 Report, the Commission engaged with these stakeholders in a dialogue about addressing corruption concerning each of the member states and came up with wider recommendations then those being produced now.

The Report added value towards establishing a comprehensive anti-corruption strategy, encouraging member states in developing their own anti-corruption strategies and supporting their efforts, and bringing civil society concerns into the anti-corruption agenda. Since the Report was published, countries such as Estonia, Finland and the UK have developed anti-corruption strategies which have included actions based on addressing some of the Report's recommendations. The European Semester engages in no such strategic dialogue with member states, and there is no indication of the prospect of formalising a separate anti-corruption policy with the member states.

The Report's objective of formalising an anti-corruption strategy for member states meant that respective government officials agreed on objectives and recommendations, their rationale and priorities, and thus integrated transnational, European, national, regional and local government priorities in anti-corruption strategies and action plans. The Report encouraged each member state to establish anti-corruption strategy, and if all member states adopted one, it would have

51 Margaret Atwood, 'A Year After Her Murder, Where Is The Justice For Daphne Caruana Galizia?' *The Guardian* (16 October 2018) <www.theguardian.com/commentisfree/2018/oct/16/murder-justice-daphne-caruana-galizia-malta> accessed 15 February 2019.

52 Theodor Troev and Kerin Hope, 'Bulgarian Reporter Investigating Misuse Of EU Funds Murdered' *Financial Times* (2018) <www.ft.com/content/43c3de8a-caf3-11e8-9fe5-24ad351828ab> accessed 15 February 2019.

53 Theodor Troev and Kerin Hope, 'The Journalists Killed In EU Member States In The Past Year' *Financial Times* (2018) <www.ft.com/content/e806a7c4-cae5-11e8-9fe5-24ad351828ab> accessed 15 February 2019.

clearly shown the scope of ambition in fighting corruption. Furthermore, a clear anti-corruption strategy with policy objectives and commitments would make it easier for the EU, civil society and researchers to hold governments to account on their commitments in fighting corruption on a more regular basis. It is hard to say to what extent the Report was successful in supporting member states to develop their own anti-corruption strategy, as the second Report would have highlighted more clearly their efforts in the past years, but intention was there—the absence of continuing reports is a missed opportunity in developing better accountability tools for member states in assessing their anti-corruption commitments.

Therefore, the European Semester process, in its current form, is not an adequate alternative as a substitute for the EU Anti-Corruption Report. However, the European Semester process can be improved, and it has the potential to produce some positive progress on anti-corruption reforms in the member states in the future if the Commission improves some aspects of its current format. The next chapter—the overall conclusion of the book—offers some recommendations and analyses how the European Semester process can be improved and build on the work laid out by the EU Anti-Corruption Report. Furthermore, the conclusion gives some suggestions on how the European Semester can make more use of the reflexive governance approach and include the civil society and non-state stakeholders in the anti-corruption policymaking at the EU level.

7.6 Improving the European semester process in analysing corruption

The topic of corruption has been part of the purview of the European Semester since it was established in 2010, as part of efforts to improve the business environment and public administration in the EU. However, there have been concerns about the low rate of implementation of country-specific recommendations issued as part of the European Semester framework, with a take-up of approximately 30 per cent overall, according to a monitoring study by TI-EU.[54] Therefore, the European Semester process has a long way to go to become a credible and effective instrument for delivering reforms in the member states. Nevertheless, two elements of the European Semester framework might be improved as a starter towards this process: its implementation method and its corruption risk assessment analysis of member states.

7.6.1 Implementation

The implementation of the country-specific recommendations proposed by the Commission as part of the European Semester process has been inadequate. An analysis by the European Parliamentary Research Service (EPRS), the Bruegel

54 Transparency International EU, 'European Semester Policy Position' (2017) <https://transparency.eu/resource/european-semester-policy-position/> accessed 30 May 2019.

think tank, and the Institute of International and European Affairs show that there is a low rate of implementation of the country-specific recommendations under the European Semester framework in the past five years.[55] Part of the issue, and a core element, is that the European Semester framework is not widely known or understood by the member states. Since it does not include the contributions of civil society like the EU Anti-Corruption Report, there is little input from non-state actors—leaving no room for scrutinising its findings. It is, therefore, perceived merely as a bureaucratic exercise. In the field of anti-corruption, as discussed in the previous chapters, non-state actors like NGOs, think tanks, academics, as well as business and trade unions play an important role in shaping and scrutinising governments' commitments in fighting corruption.

Therefore, the Commission's policy in moving forward should consider engaging with as many relevant groups as possible, as it did with the Report, and embrace the reflexive governance approach—thereby increasing pressure for reform at the national level and addressing some of the recommendations about corruption cited in the European Semester process. This significant improvement would have the potential to communicate Commission recommendations to a wider audience, and through consultations with non-state actors, it could make more comprehensive findings about the state of corruption in each of the member states. Furthermore, the consultation and involvement of non-state actors has the potential to develop more targeted policy recommendations against corruption in future European Semester country reports. As a result, the Commission would be able to improve the process of writing and issuing the recommendations related to corruption in the European Semester process for member states with greater credibility and transparency—and thereby reaching beyond member states' governments and building upon the reflexive governance approach that was started under the EU Anti-Corruption Report.

The current wording of European Semester recommendations is vague, and it is difficult to evaluate how member states should implement anti-corruption policy actions. For example, the country-specific recommendations in 2018 for the Czech Republic noted challenges in preventing corruption in public procurement and recommended the country to develop 'more quality-based competition' by implementing anti-corruption measures.[56] This language is not very helpful in terms of formulating and developing a coherent anti-corruption policy, to say the least. When comparing it with the 2014 Report, in the Report there was an acknowledgment of the problem of corruption in public procurement and

55 Konstantinos Efstathiou and Guntram B Wolf, 'Is the European Semester Effective and Useful?' *Bruegel Think Tank, Policy Contribution Issue 9 June 2018* <http://bruegel.org/wp-content/uploads/2018/06/PC-09_2018_3.pdf> accessed 30 May 2019.

56 European Commission, 'Recommendation for a Council Recommendation on the 2018 National Reform Programme of the Czech Republic and delivering a Council opinion on the 2018 Convergence Programme of the Czech Republic' COM (2018) 403 final <https://ec.europa.eu/info/publications/2018-european-semester-country-specific-recommendations-czech-republic_en> accessed 30 May 2019.

a range of best-practice examples in improving the situations, as well as information on how other member states had successfully implemented anti-corruption reforms. These elements of sharing of best practice in member states, one of the core elements of the reflexive governess approach, is notably absent in the European Semester framework, as far as developing anti-corruption incentives and measures.

However, the European Semester can be improved in this respect. For example, once the country reports are published under the European Semester framework, the Commission could consult with civil society groups and stakeholders, openly and transparently, on how corruption-related issues identified in the relevant county-specific report should be translated into concrete policy recommendations, and what actions must be taken, developing indicators to track the progress achieved. As a result, stakeholders and non-state actors can be invited to comment and contribute on the annual growth survey and country reports under the European Semester process. The consultation could be in the form of workshop or two-day roundtable, as was conducted in preparation of the 2014 Report. These consultations meetings or workshops would support the work of the Commission in coming up with more inclusive findings and producing more comprehensive recommendations, which would translate well in supporting member states to fight corruption more effectively.

The Commission might also consider developing a new a system to track progress in the implementation of anti-corruption measures under the European Semester framework. The Commission approach with the 2014 Report was to use biannual Reports to track the progress in the member states—unfortunately there never was a second Report to measure the progress made in between, and the EU policy approach never materialised in this respect—partially due to lack of political will. However, for the European Semester process to be more successful in implementing anti-corruption recommendations, it can set out implementation deadlines (as is the case currently for Greece, in the context of the macroeconomic adjustment programme). Such an approach would entail the development of more effective anti-corruption measures for each of the member states and keep the anti-corruption reform momentum going. Following the publication of the annual growth survey in the early Autumn, the Commission might consider holding an open consultation with non-state actors and stakeholders on the implementation and impact of previous anti-corruption recommendations under the European Semester framework.

The outcome of the discussions and engagement with non-state stakeholders and civil society organisations should be published online, ahead of the European Semester teams' formal country visits in the Autumn, thus making the European Semester process more transparent and inclusive for all stakeholders. When the country reports are published in the Spring, they might also include a clear assessment of the implementation of the previous year's recommendations, based on consultations with non-state stakeholders and civil society organisations. Furthermore, by way of greater transparency, the country reports under the European Semester framework should disclose details of the consultation process with state and non-state actors, as well as what actions have been agreed to address corruption more effectively. For example, as described in Chapter 2, the Commission issued conclusions of the discussion with non-state actors and their inputs in the 2014 Report. If such an approach is designed into the current format of the European Semester, the EU will also be able to build on the reflexive governance approach that it began under the 2014 Report, where it reached out beyond the government and its institutions. At this point, the European Semester has reverted to a system where only the Commission and the government engage in anti-corruption policy formulation—a regression to a top-down approach.

7.6.2 Risk assessment analysis

Another key improvement that the European Semester could make is to improve its risk assessment and justify why corruption is mentioned as an issue only to some member states and not others. As we have seen, in 2018, corruption was only mentioned as an issue for 13 out of 28 member states, and only 7 out of 28 member states received policy recommendations on addressing corruption as an issue. An obvious example of obscure and questionable analysis is in the case of Croatia, ranked 57 in TI's 2017 Corruption Perceptions Index (CPI), indicating serious problems with corruption in the public sector. The 2014 Report identified several issues relating to corruption in state-owned enterprises, public procurement, the healthcare system, lack of whistle-blowing, and favouritism within and politicising of public administration. Furthermore, in recent years, the government in Croatia has been clamping down on independent media and civil society. However, the 2018 European Semester country report noted only the business climate as a concern; nothing was mentioned regarding these other highly significant areas. In this instance, at least, the European Semester risk assessment is inadequate and very limited in scope. The reflexive governance approach in this respect would also help to enhance the European Semester if it adopts this approach, as it will mirror the issues concerned with corruption in these member states at the EU level and thus engage in multi-level approach. This would be far more likely to deliver a coherent anti-corruption policy.

Another example of the inadequacies of the European Semester risk assessment is in the UK. In 2017, the UK's National Crime Agency made a strategic threat assessment and found that corruption is becoming a key vulnerability in the logistics sector, i.e. corrupt workers at ports, and airports facilitating breaches of border control.[57] There are also corrupt individuals working in the financial and legal sectors, instrumental in facilitating money laundering and fraud in the UK. Neither corruption, in general, nor money laundering, specifically, was cited as issues for concern in the UK.

57 National Crime Agency. 'National Crime Agency Annual Report and Accounts 2016–17' (2017) <https://nationalcrimeagency.gov.uk/who-we-are/publications/25-nca-annual-report-2016-17/file> accessed 30 May 2019.

Despite the lack of clarity on how the European Semester process justifies the mention of corruption (or lack thereof), there is scope for improvement. One positive change might be if the Commission were to conduct comprehensive risk assessments and publish its analyses of the main corruption risks in each member states every two to three years, feeding this information into the European Semester process to make it more comprehensive when evaluating corruption risks in the EU. This risk assessment could be drawn from independent studies and surveys, similar to the corruption risk assessment carried out by the 2014 Report. Furthermore, the Commission could encourage and support the member states to commission independent experts to conduct their own independent risk assessments and include those findings in the European Semester country report annexes. Thus, the European Semester would be drawing information from a wider pool about the risk of corruption to various sectors; these findings would help to determine the main corruption risks in each member states.

Furthermore, the Commission could develop standard indicators for tracking anti-corruption progress or regress in all member states, possibly every one or two years—something that had been planned for the Report to do biennially. The development of these indicators was planned in the 2014 Report as concepts, as mentioned in Chapter 2, but due to the Report's cancellation, they never fully materialised. It is difficult to determine how useful or successful they would have been without seeing the second Report. Indicators are necessary to track progress in member states and are significant in spotting regress or failure to implement anti-corruption policy and keep corruption-fighting on the political agenda. Furthermore, the Commission could consider consulting with member states and other non-state actors on the methodology for the corruption risk assessment and developing indicators (both of these were undertaken for the 2014 Report). Findings can be included in factsheets published as part of the European Semester process, and, in such a way, future European Semester country reports may be able to build on these developments; using the reflexive governance approach in this way will better reflect the reality of the state of corruption in the member states and inform more coherent policy. Currently, with interaction between just the Commission and the member states government, it is easy to dismiss risks that corruption poses to different public sectors.[58] For the sake of economic growth or increasing employment, for example, in defence contracts or foreign investment (shown in the country cases studies in Section II of this book), member states are prone to tolerate undue behaviour. Pressed by these more immediate concerns, member states may hide

58 Oliver Bullough, 'How Britain Let Russia Hide Its Dirty Money' *The Guardian* (25 May 2018) <www.theguardian.com/news/2018/may/25/how-britain-let-russia-hide-its-dirty-money> accessed 30 May 2019.

corruption under the carpet, only to feel the effects later, such as through moneylending in the property and housing market in the UK.[59]

The mounting evidence of serious back-sliding by many member states on anti-corruption commitments, respecting the rule of law and protecting the freedom of press[60] (in particular, safeguarding investigative journalists working on corruption probes), provides a strong impetus for this analysis on the adequacy of the European Semester as a replacement for the Report. Since the Commission's grand ambition for developing a comprehensive anti-corruption policy in 2011, about eight member states have fallen more than ten points, and a quarter of member states have scored 50 or lower in the TI Index, according to TI in 2018.[61] This is an indication of a serious—and increasing—problem with corruption and the need for a comprehensive anti-corruption policy in the EU.

7.7 The future for the European semester process and EU anti-corruption policy

In the letter that Commissioner Timmermans wrote to the EU Parliament concerning the discontinuation of the Report, he argued that the first and only Report, published in 2014, had provided data and the basis for a broader EU anti-corruption framework. Thus, subsequent Reports were not necessary. It is clear that the Commission is trying to strengthen the European Semester and its economic governance; such an approach is seen in other policy areas, such as justice. The EU Justice Scoreboard (the Commission's latest initiative to monitor member states' justice systems, introduced in late 2013) is now also part of the European Semester process. The EU Justice Scoreboard allows the Commission to obtain information on the performance of national judicial systems and provides comparable data on the independence, quality and efficiency of national justice systems.[62] Member States may receive specific recommendations as part of the European Semester process about their judicial systems, mainly focusing on civil, commercial and administrative cases to pave the way for a more investment, business-friendly environment. However, in the European Semester process, there is no reflection on how to address systematic abuses of

59 Transparency International UK, 'London Property: A Top Destination for Money Launderers' (2016) <www.transparency.org.uk/publications/london-property-tr-ti-uk/> accessed on 30 May 2019.

60 Coralie Pring and Jon Vrushi, 'Tackling the Crises of Democracy, Promoting Rule of Law and Fighting Corruption' *Transparency International* (29 January 2019) <www.transparency.org/news/feature/tackling_crisis_of_democracy_promoting_rule_of_law_and_fighting_corruption> accessed 15 February 2019.

61 Transparency International 'Corruption Perceptions Index 2018' (2018) <www.transparency.org/cpi2018> accessed 15 February 2019.

62 Alexander Strelkov, 'EU Justice Scoreboard: A New Policy Tool For "Deepening" European Integration?' *Journal of Contemporary European Studies 27* (1) (2018) 15–27.

democratic and rule of law principles across EU member states. Similarly, with corruption, the European Semester does not offer new insights on the social impact that corruption has, as well as its damaging effects on the EU and the member states.

Since the European Semester process is the Commission's new central monitoring instrument and is integrating different policy areas, including corruption, it is important that the Commission either integrates the social dimension of corruption into the European Semester process or establishes it in other policy areas which go beyond the economic scope of considering corruption (i.e. protection of European funds, public-procurement tenders and improving the business environment for foreign investors). The 2014 Report closely examined the social dimension of corruption in individual member states and issued wide-ranging recommendations, such as:

- strengthening accountability and integrity standards;
- strengthening internal control mechanisms within public authorities;
- strengthening asset disclosure systems;
- improving effectiveness of policies for addressing conflicts of interest;
- implementing more effective policies to address corruption risks at local level;
- improving effectiveness of courts, prosecution services and law enforcement bodies against corruption;
- safeguarding the independence and capacity of anti-corruption agencies;
- ensuring freedom from obstruction for criminal proceedings on corruption charges concerning elected politicians;
- implementing effective protection mechanisms for whistle-blowers;
- limiting risks of foreign bribery;
- taking more determined measures to ensure transparency of lobbying;
- developing mechanisms and policies to effectively address corruption risks related to state-owned and state-controlled companies; and
- developing e-tools to enhance transparency of public spending and decision-making in public administration.

These areas are barely mentioned as issues for the member states in the European Semester process in 2018. Furthermore, European Semester country-specific recommendations only extend to one area (public procurement) where corruption poses a serious threat. Given the importance of the areas listed above, and the negative impact that corruption presents in the member states, the Commission should not overlook them and must explore other avenues to continue to address corruption in policy areas not yet covered in the European Semester process, including the social dimension of corruption in its policy approach. Post-2019, it would be in the Commission's best interests to include corruption as an element in policies aimed at cracking down on organised crime, protection of whistle-blowers and empowering of specialised anti-corruption agencies at the member state level, given its importance and negative impacts.

7.7.1 Including organised crime in EU anti-corruption policy objectives

The Commission's future anti-corruption policy agenda on addressing the policy and legal gaps in fighting organised crime would be more effective if it were to include corruption as a component that facilitates undue behaviour. Corruption and organised crime often go together. Organised-crime groups feed corruption and often actively try to corrupt customs officials, immigration authorities, law enforcement, the judiciary, and procurement processes to gain access to sensitive information, as well as to bypass law enforcement boundaries. Three criminal phenomena—organised crime, corruption, and money laundering—are often closely related. In order to design effective anti-corruption policy, it is imperative to include organised-crime networks at the same time.

Susan Rose-Ackerman finds that organised crime requires corruption as an enabling tool for some organised criminal activities.[63] If it were not for corruption, some of the illicit activities by organised crime groups would not flourish. In its last comprehensive assessment in 2013, Europol has identified about 3,600 organised-crime groups operating in the EU,[64] and in its European Union Serious and Organised Crime Threat Assessment 2017[65] and the Internet Organised Crime Threat Assessment 2018, it suggested that more than 5000 organised-crime groups operating on an international level are currently under investigation in the EU.[66] The figure in 2018 suggests that there is a substantial increase of organised-crime groups operating in the past five years in the EU. This increase is because organised-crime groups are integrating new technologies into their modi operandi and building new criminal-business models around technology. Therefore, the integration of new technologies by organised-crime groups has an impact on criminal activities across the spectrum of serious and organised crime in the EU. This includes the expansion of online trade and widespread availability of encrypted communication channels. A Commission study suggested that crimes such as fraud range in worth from €500 million to €5 billion in the EU.[67] However, similarly to corruption, the

63 Susan Rose-Ackerman and Bonnie J Palifka, *Corruption and Government: Causes, Consequences, and Reform* (CUP 2016) 294–316.

64 Europol, 'Report on EU Serious and Organised Crime Threat Assessment' (2013) 6. <www.europol.europa.eu/content/eu-serious-and-organised-crime-threat-assessment-socta> accessed 10 February 2019.

65 Europol, 'The European Union (EU) Serious and Organised Crime Threat Assessment (SOCTA) 2017' (2017) 14 <www.europol.europa.eu/activities-services/main-reports/european-union-serious-and-organised-crime-threat-assessment-2017> accessed 10 February 2019.

66 Europol, 'Internet Organised Crime Threat Assessment 2018' (2018) 14 <www.europol.europa.eu/internet-organised-crime-threat-assessment-2018> accessed 10 February 2019.

67 Marco Hafner and others, 'The Cost of Non-Europe in the Area of Organised Crime and Corruption' Annex II—Corruption European Union EPRS PE 579.319 (March 2016) <www.europarl.europa.eu/RegData/etudes/STUD/2016/579319/EPRS_STU%282016%29579319_EN.pdf> accessed 30 May 2019.

cost of organised crime at EU level is in fact very difficult to assess due to the difficulty in collecting independent data from organised-crime offenders.

Many post-Communist countries have had issues with organised crime, corruption, and money laundering (for more, see Chapter 2 and the 2014 Report's findings). However, the European Semester process has made no reference to organised crime in the 2018 country-specific recommendations. Research on post-Communist countries has identified that the collapse of the Communist system benefitted both legitimate investors and organised-crime groups, as the entire wealth of the state in post-Communist countries was up for grabs at low or no cost. Both legitimate businesses and criminal groups sought to share in the wealth of these countries. In some post-Communist countries, organised-crime groups managed to create an atmosphere of insecurity and the threat of violence, driving competitors away, especially recognised international firms.[68] This left the criminal groups with an open field to become state entities and access the wealth of the state. Foreign investment from legitimate business was reduced in post-Communist countries; this was also witnessed in the Western Balkan countries, aiming to join the EU in the future.[69] Kukhianidze noted that this behaviour is caused by the weakness of state institutions, which created an environment for the growth of organised-crime groups, and thus allowed them to use corruption to infiltrate governments and businesses.[70]

The objective here is not for us to try to resolve the problem of organised crime—nor should the European Semester process attempt to solve it, single-handed, in the future. Rather, it is to make the case that in addressing organised crime in future policy areas, the EU should also involve corruption as a key component. Corruption is a symptom of deeper problems than the EU is currently addressing under the European Semester, and when organised crime has a strong foothold, many of the anti-corruption reform proposals will only have a superficial impact.

A study conducted by the EPRS identifies that there are barriers in the fight against organised crime, and the main obstacles are that there is a lack of ratification, transposition, implementation and enforcement in the EU.[71] The research finds that there is a lack of horizontal and vertical integration in terms of the consistency with monitoring instruments regarding organised crime. The main examples are in relation to the rule of law more generally, and criminal law, as well as between international, EU, national, regional and local governance levels. A possible explanation of the lack of implementation of adequate standards may be a reflection of many factors, mainly concerning institutional

68 Rose-Ackerman and Palifka (n 64).

69 Valbona Zeneli, 'Corruption, Foreign Direct Investment, and International Marketing in the Western Balkans' *Thunderbird International Business Review 58* (3) (2015) 277–91.

70 Alexandre Kukhianidze, 'Corruption and Organized Crime in Georgia Before and After the "Rose Revolution"' *Central Asian Survey 28* (2) (2009) 215–34.

71 Hafner and others (n 14).

capacity and the political will to push higher the agenda of tackling organised crime. In some member states, the recommendations of the 2014 Report suggested that anti-corruption agencies, police, and judicial authorities face difficulties and challenges in their effectiveness due to insufficient resources, and, in some cases, politicisation. It must be noted that, in this area, this remains a shared competence between the EU and its member states, but member states remain in charge of law enforcement and judicial procedures to fight organised crime.

By including corruption in policies against organised crime, the EU would also strengthen the procedural component of reflexive governance. Proceduralism (as discussed in Chapter 3) allows for multi-level actors and areas to be part of a process in policymaking and enable member states to ensure that, when a future anti-corruption action plan is designed, organised crime is included—thus contributing to developing a far-reaching policy against organised crime in the EU.

7.7.2 Including the protection of whistle-blowers to EU anti-corruption policy objectives

Throughout this book, we have seen a pattern on how corruption affects people differently and how different sectors are seriously threatened by corrupt practices. We have considered different examples of how corruption weakens the very fabric of democracy, economy, society, the political system and the judiciary[72]—as a result, the legal and political forms of corruption have become part of the larger debate in Europe. We have shown some of the key gaps in the systems across the EU and exposed the inadequate regulation and policies to address corruption promptly—as a result, the Commission estimates the total financial cost of corruption to be as high as €120 billion per year, having an adverse impact on all of the member states' public resources.[73] No country is immune to corruption, and all face challenges on policy success in addressing the high cost incurred by corruption.

As we have seen, corruption typically happens behind closed doors, away from the public eye. Whistle-blowers find it far from easy or straightforward to report on corruption cases. As recently as 2018, three journalists were murdered in the EU because they exposed corruption at the highest level, as well as the abuse of EU funds.[74] According to a survey conducted by TI, in the EU, nearly 74 per cent of those who have witnessed or experienced corruption did not report it.[75] Although

72 A Mungiu-Pippidi, *The Quest for Good Governance: How Societies Develop Control of Corruption* (CUP 2015) 1–26.

73 JB Auby and E Breen, *Corruption and Conflicts of Interest: A Comparative Law Approach* (Edward Elgar 2014) 3–15.

74 Theodor Troev and Kerin Hope, 'The Journalists Killed In EU Member States In The Past Year' *Financial Times* (2018). <www.ft.com/content/e806a7c4-cae5-11e8-9fe5-24ad351828ab> accessed 15 February 2019.

75 David Schultz and Khachik Harutyunyan, 'Combating Corruption: The Development of Whistleblowing Laws in the United States, Europe, and Armenia' *International Comparative Jurisprudence 1* (2) (2015) 87–97.

progress has been made in preventing corruption in the EU, in laws and regulation, it is still far from sufficient, due to the gaps in whistle-blower protection legislation, where people can be unsafe in questioning practices that have some form of corruption involved.

Whistle-blowers are crucial in exposing corrupt practices. However, despite being widely acknowledged as a key source in disclosing corruption and other misconduct associated with corrupt practices, whistle-blowers regularly pay the price for their candour due to the lack of legal protection. The research in the EU finds that there are inadequate laws in place when it comes to whistle-blower-protection legislation; a study conducted by TI in 2014 found that only 4 out of 28 EU member states have comprehensive legal frameworks for whistle-blower protection. A recent study, conducted by Vigjilenca Abazi at the Maastricht Centre for European Law,[76] found that only 9 out of 28 EU member states have adequate laws in place for whistle-blower protection. The other member states have partial, poor or no legal framework at all in place as shown in Table 7.1.

In future, the European Semester country chapters could pay particular attention in evaluating the level of legal whistle-blower protection in all of the member states and make sound recommendations on implementing adequate legal protections for whistle-blowers in the short and medium term. In April 2018, the Commission published a proposal for an EU-wide Whistle-blower Directive to strengthen

Table 7.1 Whistle-blower protection in EU member states

Comprehensive legalisations	*Partial legalisations*	*Limited/no legalisations*
France	Austria	Bulgaria
Ireland	Belgium	Croatia
Luxembourg	Cyprus	Finland
Netherlands	Czech Republic	Lithuania
Romania	Denmark	Portugal
Slovakia	Estonia	Spain
Slovenia	Germany	
Sweden	Greece	
UK	Hungary	
	Latvia	
	Malta	
	Poland	

Source: Vigjilenca Abazi, 'Legal Analysis on the Competences of the European Union for Legislation on Whistleblower Protection' Greens/EFA Group,' European Parliament (22 May 2017)

76 Vigjilenca Abazi, 'Legal Analysis on the Competences of the European Union for Legislation on Whistleblower Protection' Greens/EFA Group, European Parliament (22 May 2017) <http://extranet.greens-efa-service.eu/public/media/file/1/5179> accessed 10 February 2019.

whistle-blower protection across the EU.[77] In its proposal, the Commission defines a whistle-blower as someone reporting or disclosing information on violations of EU law which they observe in their work-related activities. The proposal for the directive comes as a result of recent scandals, such as Dieselgate, Luxleaks, the Panama Papers, the Fipronil case and Cambridge Analytica, all of which have shown major wrongdoing happening inside organisations and which have a negative impact across the EU.[78] In many cases, these scandals cause damage to the environment, public health and safety, and to national or EU public finances. The proposed legislation will give much greater protection for individuals who wish to come forward when they encounter corruption or illegality in their workplace. This proposal will have to be negotiated between the European Parliament and European Council before being adopted. However, in the meantime, future European Semester process could engage in providing a thorough evaluation of the current legal frameworks for whistle-blower protection in all member states and support them to develop more adequate legal protection for whistle-blowers. The reflexive governance approach can be useful for the Commission in engaging with member states and non-state actors to mirror the actual legal protection and in particular its applications for whistle-blowers and investigative journalists, therefore enhancing a wider legal protection at the EU level.

7.7.3 Empowering specialised anti-corruption institutions at the member state level

The EU Anti-Corruption Report suggested that all member states should strongly consider examining their own anti-corruption policy shortcomings and come up with their own national anti-corruption action plans. Research throughout the different chapters in this book indicates the importance of having an institutional infrastructure in place to fight corruption and implementing national anti-corruption action plans. In the 2014 Report, especially in the country chapter recommendations in Chapter 2, there is an extensive list of reasons supporting the idea that establishing an anti-corruption agency is vitally important to implement key anti-corruption policy objectives. Furthermore, the Report's country chapter recommendations make a strong case for member states to strengthen their anti-corruption agencies and institutions, especially in many post-Communist countries, and highlight the Romania National Anticorruption Directorate as the model that member states can follow. The Report also indicates that it is crucial for member states to make their anti-corruption agencies more independent from political influence and increase their capacity

77 European Commission, 'Proposal for a Directive of the European Parliament and the Council on the Protection of Persons Reporting on Breaches of Union Law' COM (2018) 218 final.

78 European Commission, Press Release: 'Whistleblower Protection: Commission Sets New, EU-wide Rules' (2018) <http://europa.eu/rapid/press-release_IP-18-3441_en.htm> accessed 10 February 2019.

to implement national anti-corruption policies and strategies. In the European Semester process, there is no mention of member states establishing an anti-corruption agency or a special department to deal with corruption.

When analysing the recommendations for each of the member states in both reports (the 2014 Report and European Semester 2018), there is a clear indication that many member states lack any proper institutional infrastructure to fight corruption and implement national anti-corruption strategies effectively. Thus, in the future European Semester process it would be highly encouraging for the Commission to include an analysis of the anti-corruption agencies in member states and offer an assessment of their effectiveness, and the resources that each member state allocates to its anti-corruption agency. Furthermore, the Commission could engage member states to further improve their anti-corruption agencies, by showing them best practice examples from other successful anti-corruption agencies and pointing out that all member states should have their anti-corruption agencies in line with international anti-corruption standards. The Commission could make more use of reflexive governance approach to this end, in particular, engaging in mutual learning of best practices.

At the end of 2012, anti-corruption practitioners, experts, international practitioners, representatives of anti-corruption bodies across the world, high representatives of the UNDP, UNODC, WB, OECD, and TI came up with 16 principles to ensure the independence and effectiveness of anti-corruption agencies. These common principles are mainly intended to improve the operations of anti-corruption agencies. Known as the Jakarta Statement on Principles for Anti-Corruption Agencies, they were approved by the International Association of Anti-Corruption Authorities and by UNCAC country parties to promote and strengthen the effectiveness of anti-corruption agencies. Future European Semester country-specific reports should recommend that all member states should adopt common principles and standards for anti-corruption agencies based on the Jakarta Statement.[79]

The Jakarta Statement is not legally binding: it is a political statement to make countries reflect on their own anti-corruption agencies and be more committed in improving their anti-corruption standards. Furthermore, the Jakarta Statement supports anti-corruption agencies to have a stronger mandate and better resources available to anti-corruption agencies in order to perform their duties and fight corruption more effectively. Future European Semester reports could review whether anti-corruption agencies fully meet these international criteria and support member states to make their anti-corruption agencies come into line with international standards. Some elements are crucial for anti-corruption agencies to be in place, in order to be effective, and the European Semester could, at least, flag those main points. Patrick Meagher and Caryn

79 UNODC, 'The Jakarta statement on Principles of Anti-Corruption Agencies' (2012) <www.unodc.org/documents/corruption/WG-Prevention/Art_6_Preventive_anti-corruption_bodies/JAKARTA_STATEMENT_en.pdf> accessed 10 February 2019.

Voland have identified ten key factors for an effective anti-corruption agency: political mandate, legal status cross-agency coordination, prevention and monitoring government implementation of anti-corruption policy, accountability, independence, transparency, powers, professional staff and sufficient resources.[80]

Future EU anti-corruption policy could focus on key factors that might have an influence on anti-corruption agencies' performance, such as their independence and legal status, their financial and human resources, their investigation history, their prevention track record, their accountability, cooperation with other member states and international organisations, as well as their education, outreach projects and the national public perception of their performance.

First and foremost, it is vital that anti-corruption agencies are independent and, as Article 6 of UNCAC indicates that anti-corruption agencies are provided with the necessary independence to undertake their roles effectively and free from any undue influence.[81] Meagher and Voland indicate that, in many cases, the incumbent government uses anti-corruption agencies as a weapon against their political opponents.[82] Meagher suggests that anti-corruption agencies are often controlled by incumbent governments, using them to attack members of the opposition, as well as punishing members of their own party who are perceived to have stepped out of line.[83] Along the same lines, Robert Klitgaard observed that anti-corruption agencies and anti-corruption campaigns are, at times, used to fight political opponents rather than to fight corruption.[84] Thus, future EU anti-corruption policy could address, in the country-specific reports, the level of independence of anti-corruption agencies in the member states and, at the same time, monitor whether anti-corruption agencies are used as a weapon to fight political opponents, rather than fight corruption. Therefore, the benchmark of an independent anti-corruption agency is the most important element, because it should have public respect and credibility that it is actually fighting corruption. The European Semester process could serve as a platform to encourage member states to establish independence from political interference for their national anti-corruption agencies, so that they cannot be controlled or used for political purposes.

80 Patrick Meagher, 'Anticorruption Agencies: Rhetoric versus Reality' *The Journal of Policy Reform 8* (1) (2005) 69–103.

81 UNODC, 'United Nations Convention against Corruption Article 6 Preventive Anti-corruption Body or Bodies' (2004) 10 <www.unodc.org/documents/brussels/UN_Convention_Against_Corruption.pdf> accessed 10 February 2019.

82 Patrick Meagher and Caryn Voland 'Anti-corruption Agencies (ACAS): Office of Democracy and Governance Anti-corruption Program Brief' *IRIS Discussion Papers on Institutions and Development* University of Maryland, (2006) 8–10.

83 Meagher (n 81).

84 Robert Klitgaard, 'Addressing Corruption Together' OCDE (2015) 41–66, <www.oecd.org/dac/conflict-fragility-resilience/publications/FINAL%20Addressing%20corruption%20together.pdf> accessed 10 February 2019.

The 2014 Report, in its member states' recommendations chapters, points out in numerous cases that member states should allocate more resources to their anti-corruption agencies and institutions dealing with corruption-related cases. It is vital that anti-corruption agencies have an adequate budget and human resources in place to perform their functions effectively. In future, the European Semester could encourage the member states' governments to allocate sufficient funds to their anti-corruption agencies in order to increase their resources and capacity. An adequate budget allocated to anti-corruption agencies is also an important indicator of the government's political will to fight corruption. Research finds that many anti-corruption agencies in the EU have complained of their limited resources and of the uncertainties of their budget allocation regarding sufficient financial support to run their investigations. While all governments in the EU face budget constraints, Francesca Recanatini notes that the allocation of limited resources for anti-corruption agencies might be an indication of the lack of a genuine commitment to member states' anti-corruption agencies' mission by their governments and their political will to fight corruption.[85] Therefore, future EU anti-corruption policy should also focus its objectives to support anti-corruption agencies in securing adequate financial means in order to have sufficient resources in place to assist fighting corruption more effectively.

In the 2014 Report it was noted that there is a lack of cooperation between anti-corruption institutions and other stakeholders to address corruption-related cases. However, the success of anti-corruption agencies depends on cooperation with other organisations, because it drives anti-corruption agencies to achieve their targets and to commit to concrete forms of cooperation to address corruption more effectively.[86] It is therefore crucial that anti-corruption agencies cooperate with other cross-border anti-corruption agencies in sharing information and provide assistance in cross-border arrests of corruption suspects. Such cooperation would also help to tackle issues that are related to cross-border crime, which falls within the border EU anti-corruption policy long-term objectives. There are some encouraging developments at the EU level, with the decision to create a European Public Prosecutor's Office (EPPO) in June 2017.

In 2013, the Commission proposed a regulation on the establishment of an EPPO, based on Article 86 TFEU, and 20 EU member states reached an agreement on the establishment of a new EPPO under enhanced cooperation. The EPPO will be an independent EU body based in Luxembourg and will have the authority to investigate and prosecute fraud, corruption and other crimes involving EU funds and crimes against the EU budget. The Netherlands and Malta also joined this initiative in August 2018, and there are now 22 member states in enhanced cooperation on the establishment of the EPPO. So far, Denmark,

85 Susan Rose-Ackerman, *International Handbook on the Economics of Corruption Volume 2* (Edward Elgar Publishing 2013) 528–71.

86 Meagher (n 81).

Hungary, Ireland, Poland, Sweden, and the UK have not signed up to this initiative and oppose the idea of EPPO. The EPPO is envisaged to take up its functions by the end of 2020/2021 and will complement the work of the European Anti-Fraud Office (OLAF). This is an important step forward because, as we have seen throughout our discussion in this book, corruption and crime have a cross-border dimension. Until all member states sign up to the EPPO, EU funds will still be vulnerable to corruption in countries such as Hungary and Poland. According to a recent report, nearly one-fifth of OLAF's investigations and recommendations for financial irregularities in Structural and Agricultural Funds were issued to Hungary and Poland.[87]

The country-specific reports of the future European Semester process have the potential to become a good platform to call out more strongly those countries which are misusing EU funds and encourage member states to become part of the EPPO in order to be more successful in cracking down on grand corruption cases and fighting corruption in public procurement more effectively—the stated focus for the Commission's focus since its 2018 strategy statement.[88]

7.8 Conclusion

In closing, we have demonstrated throughout this chapter and in the book that under the EU Anti-Corruption Report, the EU attempted to develop a comprehensive policy against corruption across the member states at the EU level and thus develop a separate anti-corruption policy field. Furthermore, the Report showed that the EU has the tools to prompt member states to develop common anti-corruption standards and that these initiatives were enhanced through using a reflexive governance approach (in particular, through mutual learning about anti-corruption best practices). In this area, it is vital that there is a way for mutual learning and exchange of best practices to take place across countries. Under the Report, member states could do that, working jointly with the EU towards achieving higher common anti-corruption standards—this component is missing under the European Semester.

Nevertheless, for any future progress in this regard, more political will is required from the EU and, in particular, from the member states. In the current political climate, it is difficult to build a common political will to make anti-corruption a top policy priority—taking into consideration that EU focus now is on countering the rise of populism and extremism in political parties, as well as reaching an agreement with the UK after Brexit. The current format of the

87 European Anti-Fraud Office, 'OLAF Report 2017: Eighteenth Report of the European Anti-Fraud Office, 1 January to 31 December 2017' (2017) <https://ec.europa.eu/anti-fraud/sites/antifraud/files/olaf_report_2017_en.pdf> accessed 10 February 2019.

88 Anne Weyembergh and Chloé Brière, 'The Future Cooperation between OLAF and the European Public Prosecutor's Office' *New Journal of European Criminal Law 9* (1) (2018) 62–82.

European Semester is limited with regard to fostering mutual learning of anti-corruption best practices—an area which could provide a good basis for building political will and support in pursuing a more comprehensive policy against corruption. Lack of political will is often invoked as a reason for failure of anti-corruption policy reforms; in states with poor governance, where transparency, accountability, participation and the rule of law are limited (such as in CEE and South East Europe), generating political will can be very challenging to achieve.

Furthermore, the EU current anti-corruption policy, both as it is advanced under the European Semester and more generally, the EU has not addressed corruption as a general threat to the rule of law, human rights and democracy across the member states. Instead, corruption has been targeted by EU prior to the 2014 Report and now under the European Semester, merely as a negative side effect of the proper function of the internal market. Therefore, it can be said that the EU initiatives that started under the Report were paused halfway through and must not be abandoned as the EU progresses its anti-corruption policy, as well as its reflexive governance approach to the EU anti-corruption policy. The EU must be willing to build sufficient political will to establish a more ambitious anti-corruption policy at the EU level, post-EU Anti-Corruption Report.

One important lesson from the Report—from the enlargement of the EU in the 2000s and now in the negotiation phase with candidate states from the Western Balkans—is that in order to increase the effectiveness of evaluation of best anti-corruption practices, the assessment process must be openly transparent and offer an opportunity for the participation of members of civil society and independent experts. This is another element missing in the current anti-corruption policy under the European Semester. A process whereby governments are evaluating governments behind closed doors is not suitable in the policy area of anti-corruption, and the EU is going backwards under the European Semester in this regard. Participation by civil society makes an important contribution in understanding the corruption trends in the member states and in the EU. What was well begun in the Report should not now be abandoned.

Finally, Report critics have questions about whether the EU should be addressing corruption within the member states or whether member states should be fighting corruption on their own. However, as we have shown through many different examples in this book, member states cannot fight corruption in isolation—as with climate change, no member states can tackle these challenges alone. This consideration should be part of a more fundamental question about the objectives and the role of the EU in the next decade in how it will face corruption as a policy issue. Should the EU's prime focus be economic integration, treating factors such as corruption only in terms of their effects on this process, or should the EU's aim be to create a union of values, where the focus on negative impacts from corruption are on those affecting society, the rule of law, democracy, human rights, climate change and income inequality?

The EU has moved beyond the single market agenda in the last ten years, evidenced in the enlargement process that took place in the 2000s. The current strategy, published in 2018, is to expand the Union in the Western Balkans in the next decade and to focus on the promotion of the rule of law, democracy, human rights and fighting corruption. However, this leaves open to question whether the EU should adopt the same policy approach towards all member states, creating specific tailor-made policy targets for each, in the way it began in the 2014 Report. Based on the findings of this book, the answer would be yes—in particular taking into account the backsliding of the rule of law in Poland, Hungary and Romania.

The EU has the tools and capacity to develop common anti-corruption standards, the scope for which was laid out in the EU Anti-Corruption Report. However, it remains to be seen whether there is the political will to take positive action in the fight against corruption—the main challenge for the EU in the next decade.

Conclusion

The EU Anti-Corruption Report identified serious shortcomings in the EU member states' domestic laws and policies to prevent and fight corruption. In particular, the Report—as shown in Chapter 2—identified systematic failures of member states to address conflicts of interest between politicians and business. Political party financing, public tenders and contracts were highlighted as particular areas of concern. Furthermore, the Report showed there were lack of policies and laws preventing revolving doors between government officials and corporations, which has become one of the contributing factors for the public to lose confidence in public officials and trust in the public institutions. In short, the Report findings concluded that all the member states need to do more to prevent corruption and restore public trust in government, as well in the European Union.

The Report also indicated that the trust in member states' leaders has fallen dramatically because of the interactions between business and the public sector taking place behind closed doors—leaving EU taxpayer and citizens with serious doubts about whose interests are being looked after and addressed. Furthermore, like crime, corruption has a cross-border dimension, which impacts all member states and is therefore a major threat to the integrity and function of the single market. In assessing the member states, the Report offered a sobering warning against complacency about corruption in the EU; and as we showed in Chapters 1 and 2, there is a lack of legal instruments to combat corruption more rigorously. The Report was designed to be published every two years, with its first publication in February 2014, but was instead quietly dropped by the Commission in 2017, in favour of evaluating corruption through the EU Semester Process. Although the Report was only issued once, it did have some impact on the overall anticorruption policy debate and the development of the border anticorruption policy in the EU.

The 2014 Report improved EU anti-corruption policy in five areas—a significant achievement, and strong foundation on which the EU could have built a more coherent anti-corruption policy.

Firstly, the Report officially recognised that beyond the internal market, other sectors were vulnerable and prone to corruption in the EU (public procurement and political party funding in particular), thereby raising awareness of corruption as a policy field. The Commission went so far as to put forward a proposal, in May 2018, for the Council to put sanctions in place with regard to EU funding and impose regulation on the protection of the Union's budget in the event of generalised deficiencies in the rule of law within member states. Secondly, the Report offered the public new insight into corruption levels and its damaging effects on the Union. In particular, the Report included a study on member states' legislative shortcomings on fighting and preventing corruption. Thirdly, the Report contributed to a broader anti-corruption policy discussion, thinking about the negative effect of corruption in economic terms by offering an estimation of the cost of corruption in the EU of at least €120 billion (£99 billion) per year. Fourthly, the Report facilitated the Commission in engaging in an open dialogue with member states, including civil society in the Report's preparation. This approach facilitated mutual learning for member states in rethinking their anti-corruption policy approach. As a result, both the EU and member states learned from the best as well as the worst practices in fighting and preventing corruption and, therefore, designing more comprehensive anti-corruption policies and laws. The final major impact—and the Report's biggest achievement—was to include civil society in the process of establishing the Report and allowing NGOs, journalists, academics and anti-corruption experts with key knowledge on each member state to play a role in shaping the Report. In this way, these external actors could have a direct impact on influencing anti-corruption policy at EU and national levels.

The Report identified public procurement as a sector highly vulnerable to corrupt practices. Public procurement has a strong economic significance in the EU, with around 20 per cent of the EU's GDP annually spent by government. In the thematic chapter in the Report, the Commission achievement was to trigger a dialogue by which governments at different levels—national, regional, local and other public bodies, as well as NGOs, academia, and the media—engage in developing wider anti-corruption strategies to prevent corruption in public procurement.

Analysing some of these examples from a reflexive governance perspective, the Report contained a key component of the theory of reflexive governance as shown in Chapter 3: active participation and innovative problem-solving. Through the Report, the Commission supported member states to acknowledge the shortcomings of their anti-corruption policy, and engage in an innovative problem-solving exercise with non-state actors and the EU to enhance their anti-corruption policies and corruption-prevention tools. Furthermore, the Report offered an opportunity to engage in wider participation: different levels of government and non-governmental bodies shaping anti-corruption measures, such as corruption prevention in public procurement. In this way, the Report engaged with the reflexive governance component of active participation—an approach which is now missing under the European Semester, which has reverted back to a restricted practice, where just the Commission and member states engage in policy discussion.

Another example of where the Report engaged in reflexive governance was through making use of proceduralism—acknowledging the impact corruption has on other policy areas. For instance, corruption allows organised crime and criminal organisations to thrive; thus, corruption undermines the functioning of the rule of law. A high perception of corruption reduces voter turnout in national parliamentary elections and lowers trust in EU institutions. The Report did not succeed in influencing member states to view corruption as an enabler for organised crime, but it did (using the reflexive governance component of proceduralism) suggest that the broader definition of corruption should seek to include the association of corruption in other policy sectors, as stipulated in these examples above and shown in Chapter 3. The Report engaged with the reflexive governance approach again (in this case, active participation) when the Commission officially offered an estimation of the economic costs incurred by corruption at the EU level; according to the Report, corruption may amount to €120 billion per year in the EU. Sparked by this estimation, different studies were launched, as we discussed in Chapter 7, and the resulting analysis opened new discussions about the real cost of corruption in the EU. Some suggested that corruption in fact costs the EU between €179billion and €990 billion in GDP terms on an annual basis (this increased figure takes into account other areas not covered by the Report, which are indirectly affected by corruption, such as the costs in terms of lost tax revenues and foreign investment, as a result of the environment created by corruption in the EU and the member states). The process of analysing the €120 billion figure has actively involved different participants from civil society and non-state actors to contribute to the debate by providing research—thus embracing the reflexive governance component of active participation by going far beyond the Commission and member states' findings. We observe the regulation of self-regulation component of reflexive governance in the open dialogue—supported by the Report—between the Commission, member states and civil society to further prioritise anti-corruption policy. This is a clear example of regulation of self-regulation, as explained in Chapters 2 and 3, where through the Report the EU encouraged a dialogue between different stakeholders to prioritise their anti-corruption policy and reflect on their shortcomings. In a final example of reflexive governance, in this case collective and mutual learning, the Report itself served as a platform where different stakeholders engaged in improving anti-corruption laws and policies by learning from each other's experiences and best practices. Since the publication of the Report in 2014, a workshop was held in which mutual learning took place, with member states and non-state actors sharing best practice in, for example, asset declaration, protecting whistle-blowers, or preventing corruption in the healthcare system. This was a clear example of how the Report engaged in a process of collective learning, a key component of the theory of reflexive governance, as explained in more detail in Chapter 3.

However, the Report had also shortcoming and some failures in areas where it did not live up to the expectations set when it was first announced in 2011. For example, the Report included little new data and mainly relied on studies conducted by the UN, GRECO, OECD, TI and other organisations with expertise in anti-corruption issues. The Report did amass some original data collection—in particular from the two surveys it performed on citizen and business perceptions of corruption in the EU (the Eurobarometer surveys). However, none of the surveys demonstrated sufficient added-value or usefulness to the public and policymakers. In general, they reconfirmed what had been provided previously by other organisations with a longer history of studying and monitoring corruption.

Another failure of the Report was the lack of formal assessment procedure within its framework with regard to following up on country recommendations (although some follow-up on country-specific recommendations was envisaged for the second Report). Furthermore, the areas and sectors covered were limited, and no detailed recommendations were issued. TI assessments of the overall Report suggest that there was a lack in specific recommendations, and those that were issued were very broad—in particular, the recommendations for the protection of whistle-blowers, access to information and lobbying were very vague. In 2011, when the Commission communicated its plans for establishing the Report, it stated that 'whistle-blowers, access to information, and lobbying/ regulating revolving doors for EU and member states public officials' would be evaluated in depth at the Report's publication in February 2014.

Furthermore, the Commission made other promises when establishing the Report which were dropped three years later, once the Report came out in 2014 (for example, the evaluation of law enforcement, judicial and police cooperation within the EU), and by so doing, limited the Report's potential impact and reach. The Report was also supposed to cover asset recovery, accounting standards, statutory audit for EU companies, and enhancing integrity in sport and match fixing, as well as an evaluation of the EU's external policies in regard to EU candidate states, potential candidates and neighbouring countries (essentially, the Western Balkans), making recommendations on policy reforms in addressing their anti-corruption policy shortcomings. However, when Report came out in 2014 it did not include any of these areas and thus fell short of its original intent to be a comprehensive anti-corruption reporting mechanism.

The main limitation of the Report was that it did not include the European institutions. The Commission initially suggested it would evaluate the level of corruption within EU institutions and offer suggestions for policy reforms to prevent and fight corruption. However, the published Report did not cover this area, as the DG Home Affairs in charge of the Report, under former Commissioner Cecilia Malmström, thought that it would come across as biased if it was evaluating its own institutions. This decision negatively impacted how the Report was viewed, and it received criticism on this basis; outside experts could have been commissioned to audit EU institutions with complete probity, and in the future perhaps the Commission may do so. This is unlikely to occur anytime soon, however, taking into consideration the rise of populism and Euroscepticism within the EU, as such a report on corruption levels within EU institutions would play into the populist and Eurosceptic narrative. Having said that, should the EU and its institutions accede to GRECO, they would face significant scrutiny and a thorough evaluation on corruption. Whether or not this happens, any future comprehensive anti-corruption policy initiative or monitoring mechanism must include an assessment on corruption within EU institutions.

The greatest contribution the Report made was in raising awareness of local or national corruption issues within the wider EU public policy debate by issuing separate country chapters for each member states, as detailed in second part in Chapter 2. The Report attempted to show, country by country, the anti-corruption policy and strategy shortcomings for each member state, pushing the anti-corruption policy higher on the agenda and creating opportunities for exchanging ideas in order to improve laws and policies. Even though it is right to criticise the Commission for collecting existing evidence, rather than conducting new analysis about corruption, the Report itself acted as an important reference point in understanding the lack of policy in the country report issued to each member state and thus supported member states in developing new instruments to prevent corruption.

When assessing the Report and more broadly the EU anti-corruption policy overall, as analysed in Part 2 of this book, and in particular, in the case study on the UK and Romania, the Report had a positive impact in supporting national anti-corruption efforts and reflected some of the outstanding policy concerning corruption. The UK and Romania (as shown in Chapters 4 and 5) have responded somewhat positively to the Report's recommendations, but they differ when it comes to transferring these recommendations into concrete policy actions, and as well as in their interaction with the EU in developing anti-corruption prevention measures. In the case of the UK, the Report's recommendations were incorporated into the national anti-corruption policy—in particular under first national anti-corruption plan. The UK engaged in reflexive governance in developing its national plan, and NGOs like TI-UK and Global Witness have played a critical part in pushing the UK government anti-corruption initiatives, the most prominent examples being the Bribery Act of 2010, the London Anti-Corruption Summit of 2016 and the UK Anti-Corruption Strategy. This engagement with civil society shows that the UK has all the potential to continue to engage in a reflexive governance approach in developing future anti-corruption laws and policies. Even after Brexit and leaving the Union, the UK would appear to have the will to engage with the EU in the fighting corruption and ensure its laws and policies remain in line with common international and EU standards, as explained in Chapter 4.

In the case of Romania, however, the Report had a limited result in translating recommendations into robust and tangible policy actions. Romania's efforts have been focused mainly on strengthening the National Anti-corruption Directorate. Furthermore, the Commission continues to monitor and supervise Romania's anti-corruption activity through the Cooperation and Verification Mechanism (CVM). The Report and CVM recommendations were both the same, and the Report simply duplicated the CVM. However, since the Report was published, Romania has been through a political turmoil, with the collapse of Victor Ponta's government due to corruption allegations. Thus, the Commission and the Romanian government's priority after the Report was to support the National

Anti-corruption Directorate activities in producing results in terms of convictions of high-level officials and maintaining specific anti-corruption champions in key positions, such as DNA chief Laura Kovesi. As explained in Chapter 5, this approach has been counterproductive in terms of sustaining the anti-corruption momentum, after Kovesi was dismissed by the justice minister Tudorel Toader in 2018. In terms of a reflexive governance approach, the Report did, however, have a positive impact on Romania—the country has engaged with local actors and local issues concerning corruption addressed in the Report, including the informality and corruption in the public healthcare system. Through reflexive governance, the Report was able to reflect broader EU policy concerns for the country by examining local issues not touched by the CVM. However, overall, the reflexive governance approach has not been as successful in Romania in developing anti-corruption laws and policies, whilst additional hard law adopted by the EU seems to have worked more successfully when developing an anti-corruption policy (as explained in more detail in Chapter 6). Romania has largely responded in developing anti-corruption policy only when the Commission has threatened freezing subsidies and withholding development funds. In other words, Romania has required a blend of hard and soft law approach for anti-corruption policy reform. The situation has further deteriorated in 2018/2019, as Romania is undergoing a judicial reform which is weakening the independence and capacity of the judiciary and has put forward plans to pass a decree that would provide legal instruments to overturn corruption convictions for politicians—in other words an corrupt-officials amnesty. The Commission has warned the country against such a course of action and has proposed cutting funds to member states that do not uphold the rule of law—aimed at exerting pressure on Romania—which received the backing of European Parliament in 2019.

In the original outline for this book, the idea of using Albania as a case study was to compare the EU's approach to a member state with a candidate state. In fact, the Commission dropped its initial plan to include candidate states in the Report, because it didn't want to treat member and candidate states in the same way when monitoring their anti-corruption shortcomings. In Chapter 6, we considered the institutional anti-corruption framework introduced by the international community and the EU and how it appeared to be receiving a promising welcome in Albania. However, this framework remains largely ineffective in practice due to a lack of proper implementation and lack of political will—as over-politicised anti-corruption policy and insufficient resources are allocated to anti-corruption efforts. So far, for the sake of EU membership, Albania has adopted laws and policies and is introducing anti-corruption institutions which are in line with international and EU standards as required by the Commission. However, the country has paid little attention to whether and how these institutions and legislation are going to work in practice. The adopted laws and policies may merely be a façade to please international institutions and the Commission. Needless to say, Albania went through major judicial reform in June 2016, and parliament amended nearly one-third of the Constitution, with a view to reforming the judicial system and fighting corruption at the highest level. On paper, these constitutional amendments will create the institutional infrastructure to fight organised crime and corruption and reduce politicians' long-standing influence. As we saw in Chapter 6, overall, Albania has made little use of the reflexive governance approach, and it has mainly been the Commission and the Albanian government who engaged in anti-corruption policy discussion. Involving the civil society and the business community in consulting on anti-corruption reforms has been very limited. Furthermore, the findings and recommendations of non-state actors or stakeholders have not been incorporated in concrete anti-corruption plans or long-term policy. In Albania there has been minimal country ownership of anti-corruption policy, and the EU interplay with the country has been based mainly on conditionality set by the Commission in its country progress report, with strong support from the European Council and powerful member states (for instance, postponing accession talks with the EU until tangible reforms are passed, and Albania has established a track record of fighting grand and political corruption at high level). As we concluded in Part 2, the hard-law approach associated with accession for EU membership, rather than a reflexive governance approach, characterises the development of the anti-corruption policy field in Albania.

The initial plan for this book was to make a comparison between the first EU Anti-Corruption Report and the second edition of the Report, tracking the progress in-between and comparing the recommendations issued for each member states in the first and the second Report. However, as discussed in Chapter 7, in January 2017, the Commission announced to the European Parliament its decision to scrap the Report, despite the fact that the expert research and work for the second Report were largely completed and ready for publication. In the Commission's letter to the European Parliament, informing it about the termination of the Report—the EU's anti-corruption flagship initiative by far—stated that the 2014 Report had been a policy exercise that facilitated a constructive dialogue with member states and was a useful instrument to collect background information about the impact of corruption. The Commission later announced that the work of the Report would be taken over by the European Semester process; the Commission's perspective was that fighting corruption should be addressed through economic policy. Therefore, combating corruption has now become part of the European Semester process of economic governance—where a number of the country reports now also include specific analysis of corruption risks and related challenges associated with corruption practices. The decision to terminate the Report and replace its work with the European Semester process means that the Commission's new approach will take up anti-corruption-related policy matters in the context of economic policy dialogue between member states and EU institutions, leaving no room for participation by non-state actors. Corruption will be evaluated only in terms of having a negative impact on economy growth and the function of the internal market.

This decision has not been welcomed by European scholars and EU civil society organisations working within the field, and, as we see in the in-depth analysis of the European Semester in Chapter 7, it is clear that the 'semester-isation' of the anti-corruption policy in the EU has resulted in damage, and the EU has backtracked in its efforts to address the social and political dynamics of corruption. Local research correspondents and experts who worked on the 2014 Report have also united in their disappointment regarding the Commission's decision to scrap the Report and substitute its work with the European Semester. The 2018 European Semester mentions corruption as an issue for 13 out of 28 member states, but only proposes anti-corruption recommendations for 7 out of these—clearly demonstrating that the scope of anti-corruption recommendations is very narrow under the European Semester framework. Furthermore, it recommended anti-corruption action to only to few member states, rather than all, as was the case under the Report. Overall, the European Semester process remains an inadequate replacement for the Report. This view is shared by the majority of non-state actors working on the anti-corruption field within the EU; in a joint letter to the Commission, 56 civil society organisations have called for the Report's continuation and for the EU to live up to its commitments in the fight against corruption.

In closing, the Report's critics questioned whether the EU should be addressing corruption within the member states or whether member states should be fighting corruption on their own. As this book has shown, member states cannot fight corruption through domestic efforts—as with climate change, no country can tackle these challenges alone. Therefore, such considerations should be part of a more fundamental question about the objectives and the role of the EU in the next decade in how it will address corruption as a policy issue. Should the EU's prime focus be economic integration, treating factors such as corruption only in terms of their negative impact on the function of the internal market, or should the EU's objective be to create a union of values, where the focus on negative impacts from corruption is on those affecting society, the rule of law, democracy, human rights, climate change and income inequality?

In 2019, the EU has moved beyond the single market agenda, evidenced in the enlargement process that took place in the 2000s and as well as its plan for future enlargement in the Western Balkans. The current strategy, published in 2018, is to expand the Union in the Western Balkans in the next decade and focus on the promotion of the rule of law, democracy, human rights and fighting corruption. However, this leaves open to question whether the EU should adopt the same policy approach towards all member states, creating specific tailor-made policy targets for each, in the way it began in the 2014 Report, or continue under the European Semester Process—an inadequate instrument to address corruption? Based on the findings of this book, the answer would be that a bespoke, case-by-case approach is needed—in particular, taking into account the backsliding of the rule of law in Poland, Hungary and Romania.

As we have demonstrated in Chapter 1 and throughout the book, the EU has the tools and capacity to develop common anti-corruption standards, the scope for which was laid out in the EU Anti-Corruption Report. Furthermore, through a reflexive governance approach, the Report managed to integrate non-state actors in shaping anti-corruption policy and help the Commission as well as member states to try and tackle the root of corruption problems, including local issues into a wider EU policy approach—something missing under the European Semester process.

In moving forward, it remains to be seen whether there is sufficient political will to take positive action in the fight against corruption and develop a comprehensive anti-corruption policy, which began with such promise under the Report. And this, surely, is the main challenge for the EU in the next decade.

Appendix A

Table 1 European Semester Country-Specific Recommendations in 2018 Corruption in the European Semester Process for 2018 is only mentioned as an issue for concern to thirteen member states and it issued recommendations to only seven states.

Country	*Corruption*	*Recommendations 1*
Austria	X	X
Belgium	X	X
Bulgaria	✓	X
Croatia	✓	X
Cyprus	✓	X
Czech Republic	✓	✓
Denmark	X	X
Estonia	X	X
Finland	X	X
France	X	X
Germany	X	X
Hungary	✓	✓
Ireland	X	X
Italy	✓	✓
Latvia	✓	✓
Lithuania	✓	X
Luxembourg	X	X
Malta	✓	✓
The Netherlands	X	X
Poland	X	X

(*Continued*)

Table 1 (Cont.)

Country	*Corruption*	*Recommendations 1*
Portugal	✓	X
Romania	✓	✓
Slovakia	✓	✓
Slovenia	✓	X
Spain	X	X
Sweden	X	X
United Kingdom	X	X

Bibliography

Books

Abrahams FC, *Modern Albania: From Dictatorship to Democracy in Europe* (NYUP 2015).

Ackerman J, and Ballesteros IS, 'The Global Explosion of Freedom of Information Laws' *Administrative Law Review 58* (*1*) (2006) 85–130.

Adi A, and Lilleker DG, *#rezist—Romania's 2017 Anti-Corruption Protests: Causes, Development and Implications* (Quadriga University of Applied Sciences 2017) 29–35 <http://eprints.bournemouth.ac.uk/29647/1/romanian_protests_2017_publication_FINAL_nk.pdf>.

Aggarwal A, Ginsburg O, and Fojo T, 'Cancer Economics, Policy and Politics: What Informs the Debate? Perspectives from the EU, Canada and US' *Journal of Cancer Policy 2* (*1*) (2014) 1–11.

Andersson J, and Rindzevičiūtė E, *The Struggle for the Long-Term in Transnational Science and Politics* (Routledge 2015).

Argyris C, and Schön D, *Organizational Learning II: Theory, Method and Practice* (Addison Wesley 1996) 39–43.

Armour J, Awrey D, Davies P, Enriques L, Gordon JN, Mayer C, and Payne J, *Principles of Financial Regulation* (OUP 2016).

Armstrong KA, 'The Lisbon Strategy and Europe 2020: From the Governance of Co-ordination to the Co-ordination of Governance', in Copeland P, and Papadimitriou D (eds), *The EU's Lisbon Strategy: Evaluating Success, Understanding Failure* (Palgrave Macmillan 2012) 208–28.

Barcevičius E, Weishaupt JT, and Zeitlin J, 'Tracing the Social OMC from Its Origins to Europe 2020', in Barcevičius E, Weishaupt JT, and Zeitlin J (eds), *Assessing the Open Method of Coordination: Institutional Design and National Influence of EU Social Policy Coordination* (Palgrave Macmillan 2014) 16–39.

Beshku K, 'Albania and the Western Balkans in the European Context at the Beginning of the 1990s: How Did the Normative Power of the European Community/Union Affect Them?' in Beshku K, and Malltezi O (eds), *Albania and Europe in a Political Regard* (Cambridge Scholars Publishing 2013) 49–60.

Bew P, 'The Committee on Standards in Public Life: Twenty Years of the Nolan Principles 1995–2015' *Political Quarterly Journal 86 (3)* (2015) 411–18.

Bezemer D, 'Post-Socialist Financial Fragility: The Case of Albania' *Cambridge Journal of Economics 25 (1)* (2001) 1–23.

Bilbao-Ubillos J, *The Economic Crisis and Governance in the European Union: A Critical Assessment* (Routledge 2014) 32–51.

Bitzenis A, *The Balkans: Foreign Direct Investment and EU Accession* (Ashgate 2009).

Bogdan I, 'Post-Accession Constitutionalism with a Human Face: Judicial Reform and Lustration in Romania' *European Constitutional Law Review 6 (1)* (2011) 28–58.

Bogdani M, and Loughlin J, *Albania and the European Union: The Tumultuous Journey Towards Integration and Accession* (IB Tauris 2007).

Börzel T, 'Coming Together or Drifting Apart? Political Change in New Member States, Accession Candidates, and Eastern Neighbourhood Countries' *MAXCAP Working Paper Series No 03* Freie Universität Berlin (2014).

Börzel T and Cichowski RA, 'Law, Politics, and Society in Europe', in Börzel T, and Cichowski RA (eds), *The State of the European Union 6: Law, Politics, and Society* (OUP 2003) 2–29.

Börzel T, Pamuk Y, and Stahn A, 'Good Governance in the European Union' *Berlin Working Paper on European Integration No 7* Berlin (2008).

Börzel T, and Stapel S, 'Mapping Governance Transfer by 12 Regional Organizations: A Global Script in Regional Colors', in Börzel T, and Hüllen VV (eds), *Governance Transfer by Regional Organizations: Patching Together a Global Script* (Macmillan 2015) 22–48.

Bovis CH, 'Highlight of the EU Procurement Reforms: The New Directive on Concessions' *European Procurement and Public Private Partnership Law Review 9 (1)* (2014) 1–2.

Bozyk P, *Globalization and the Transformation of Foreign Economic Policy* (Ashgate 2012).

Brown AJ, Lewis D, Moberly R, and Vandekerckhove W (eds) *International Handbook on Whistleblowing Research* (Edward Elgar 2014).

Bryane M, 'Issues in Anti-Corruption Law: How Can Code of Conduct Laws Be Drafted in order to Reduce Corruption in a Public Sector like Romania' *European Law Journal 18 (2)* (2012) 289–322.

Buscaglia E, 'An Analysis of Judicial Corruption and Its Causes: An Objective Governing-Based Approach' *International Review of Law and Economics 21 (2)* (2001) 233–49.

Calleja A, *Unleashing Social Justice Through EU Public Procurement* (Routledge 2016).

Capussela AL, *State-Building in Kosovo: Democracy, Corruption and the EU in the Balkans* (IB Tauris 2015).

Carp R,'The Struggle for the Rule of Law in Romania as an EU Member State: The Role of the Cooperation and Verification Mechanism' *Utrecht Law Review 10 (1)* (2016) 1–16.

Carr I, (2013), 'Development, Business Integrity and the UK Bribery Act 2010' in Horder J, and Alldridge P (eds), *Modern Bribery Law: Comparative Perspectives* (CUP 2013) 128–59.

Castells M, 'The Network Society: From Knowledge to Policy', in Castells M, and Cardoso G (eds), *The Network Society: From Knowledge to Policy* (Johns Hopkins Center for Transatlantic Relations 2005) 3–23.

Clayton N, 'An Overview on the Inconsistencies of Approach in Regulating the Capital Position of Banks: Will the United Kingdom Step Out of Line with Europe?' *Journal of Banking Regulation 14 (2)* (2013) 107–33.

Cohen N, 'Informal Payments for Health Care—The Phenomenon and Its Context' *Health Economics, Policy and Law 7 (3)* (2012) 285–308.
Collins H, *Regulating Contracts* (OUP 1999).
Connolly R, *The Economic Sources of Social Order Development in Post-Socialist Eastern Europe* (Routledge 2013).
Cawley R, 'The Influence of European Union Policies and Regulation' in Lemstra W, and Melody WH (eds), *The Dynamics of Broadband Markets in Europe Realizing the 2020 Digital Agenda* (CUP 2014) 25–52.
Crona BI, and Parker JN, 'Learning in Support of Governance: Theories, Methods, and a Framework to Assess How Bridging Organizations Contribute to Adaptive Resource Governance' *Ecology and Society 17 (1)* (2012) 32–39.
Darling A, *Back from the Brink: 1000 Days at Number 11* (Atlantic Books 2012).
Dawson M, *New Governance and the Transformation of European Law: Coordinating EU Social Law and Policy* (CUP 2011).
Dawson M, 'New Governance and the Displacement of Social Europe: The Case of the European Semester' *European Constitutional Law Review 14 (1)* (2018) 191–209.
De Schutter O, and Lenoble J, *Reflexive Governance: Redefining the Public Interest in a Pluralistic World* (Hart 2010).
De Waal C, *Albania Today: A Portrait of Post-Communist Turbulence* (IB Tauris 2007).
Deakin S, and Rogowski R, 'Reflexive Labour Law, Capabilities and the Future of Social Europe' in Rogowski R, Salais R, and Whiteside N (eds), *Transforming European Employment Policy—Labour Market Transitions and the Promotion of Capability* (Edward Elgar 2011) 229–54.
Deming HS, *Anti-Bribery Laws in Common Law Jurisdictions* (OUP 2012).
Denca SS, 'Romania The Black Sea Atlanticist' in Baun M, and Mare D, *The New Member States and the European Union: Foreign Policy and Europeanization* (Routledge 2013) 175–89.
Dewing I, and Russell P, 'Whistleblowing, Governance and Regulation before the Financial Crisis: The Case of HBOS' *Journal of Business Ethics 134 (1)* (2016) 155–69.
Dhimitri E, Gabeta A, and Bello M, 'Regional Development Theories and Modes, A Comparative Analyse: Challenges of Regional Development in Albania' *USV Annals of Economics and Public Administration Journal 15 (2)* (2015) 50–58.
Dimitrova A, 'The Effectiveness and Limitations of Political Integration in Central and Eastern European Member States: Lessons from Bulgaria and Romania' *MAXCAP Working Paper Series No 10* Freie Universität Berlin (2015)
Dimitrova A, and Buzogany A, 'Post-Accession Policy-Making in Bulgaria and Romania: Can Non-State Actors Use EU Rules to Promote Better Governance?' *Journal of Common Market Studies 52 (1)* (2014) 139–56.
Dimitriu R, 'Romania: First Steps to Whistleblowers' Protection' in Thüsing G, and Forst G (eds), *Whistleblowing—A Comparative Study Ius Comparatum—Global Studies in Comparative Law* (Springer 2016) 243–62.
Ducu A, 'Could the Present Economic-Financial Crisis Give a New Impetus to the Fight against Corruption and the Underground Economy?' *Internal Auditing and Risk Management 8 (2)* (2013) 35–46.
Dussuyer I, Mumford S, and Sullivan G, 'Reporting Corrupt Practices in the Public Interest: Innovative Approaches to Whistleblowing' in Graycar A, and Smith RG (eds), *Handbook of Global Research and Practice in Corruption* (Edward Elgar 2011) 429–62.

Eisele K, *The External Dimension of the EU's Migration Policy: Different Legal Positions of Third-Country Nationals in the EU: A Comparative Perspective* (Brill Nijhoff 2014).

Elbasani A, 'EU Administrative Conditionality and Domestic Downloading: The Limits of Europeanization in Challenging Contexts' *KFG Working Paper Series No 2* Freie Universität Berlin (2009).

Elbasani A, 'Europeanization Travels to the Western Balkans: Enlargement Strategy Domestic Obstacles and Diverging Reforms' in Elbasani A (eds), *European Integration and Transformation in the Western Balkans: Europeanization or Business as Usual?* (Routledge 2013) 3–22.

Elbirt C, 'Albania under the Shadows of the Pyramid Schemes' *Transition: the Newsletter about Reforming Economics 8 (5)* 8–10 (1997).

Elsie R, *Historical Dictionary of Albania* (2nd edn, Scarecrow Press 2010).

Enache M, 'The Evolution of the Justice Reform in Romania' *US-China Law Review 9 (3)* (2012) 175–83.

Estella A, *Legal Foundations of EU Economic Governance* (CUP 2018).

Etienne J, 'Different Ways of Blowing the Whistle: Explaining Variations in Decentralized Enforcement in the UK and France' *Regulation and Governance 9 (4)* (2015) 309–24.

Ewing K, Rowbottom J, and Tham JC, *The Funding of Political Parties: Where Now?* (Routledge 2012) 256–57.

Fabri D, 'The Whistleblowing Dilemma in Malta Continues: A Personal View and Analysis' in Thüsing G, and Forst G (eds), *Whistleblowing—A Comparative Study* (Springer 2016) 187–202.

Fazekas M, Chvalkovska M, Skuhrovec I, Tóth J, and King PL, 'Are EU Funds a Corruption Risk? the Impact of EU Funds on Grand Corruption in Central and Eastern Europe' in Mungiu-Pippidi A (ed), *The Anticorruption Frontline the ANTICORRP Project Vol 2* (Budrich Publishers 2014) 68–89.

Fazekas M, and Tóth IJ, 'From Corruption to State Capture: A New Analytical Framework with Empirical Applications from Hungary' *Comparative Political Studies 41 (4–5)* (2016) 638–73.

Fisher J, (2015) 'Risk Recklessness and Policing the Financial Markets' in Ryder N, Turksen U, and Hassler S (eds), *Fighting Financial Crime in the Global Economic Crisis* (Routledge 2015) 7–28.

Fisher J, Denver D, and Benyon J, *Central Debates in British Politics* (Routledge 2015).

Fletcher C, and Herrmann D, *The Internationalisation of Corruption: Scale Impact and Countermeasures* (Routledge 2012).

Frigessi Di Rattalma M, *The Dieselgate: A Legal Perspective* (Springer Switzerland 2017).

Gallagher T, *Romania and the European Union: How the Weak Vanquished the Strong* (Manchester UP 2009).

Ganev VI, 'Post-Accession Hooliganism: Democratic Governance in Bulgaria and Romania after 2007' *East European Politics and Societies 27 (1)* (2013) 26–44.

Gateva E, 'Post-Accession Conditionality—Translating Benchmarks into Political Pressure?' *East European Politics 29 (4)* (2013) 420–42.

Gateva E, *European Union Enlargement Conditionality* (Palgrave Macmillan 2015).

Geddes A, Lees C, and Taylor A, *The European Union and South East Europe: The Dynamics of Europeanization and Multi-Level Governance* (Routledge 2013).

Gray J, 'Financial Regulation before and after Northern Rock' in Gray J, and Akseli O (eds), *Financial Regulation in Crisis? the Role of Law and the Failure of Northern* (Edward Elgar 2011) 72–87.

Grødeland A, 'Public and Elite Perceptions of Supranational Courts: The European Perspective' *Review of Central and East European Law 39 (1)* (2014) 41–94.

Habermas J, *Between Facts and Norms Contributions to a Discourse Theory of Law and Democracy* (Polity 1996).

Hafner M, Taylor J, Disley E, Thebes S, Barberi M, Stepanek M, and Levi M, 'The Cost of Non-Europe in the Area of Organised Crime and Corruption: Annex II—Corruption' EPRS PE 579319 (March 2016) <www.europarl.europa.eu/RegData/etudes/STUD/2016/579319/EPRS_STU%282016%29579319_EN.pdf>.

Hall MJB, 'The Sub-Prime Crisis the Credit Crunch and Bank "Failure": An Assessment of the UK Authorities' Response' in Kaufman G, and Bliss R (eds), *Financial Institutions and Markets: The Financial Crisis: An Early Retrospective* (Palgrave Macmillan 2012) 93–125.

Hammergren LA, *Justice Reform and Development: Rethinking Donor Assistance to Developing* (Routledge 2014).

Harrison K, and Ryder N, *The Law Relating to Financial Crime in the United Kingdom* (Routledge 2016).

Hart HLA, *The Concept of Law* (2nd edn, Clarendon Press 1997).

Harvey J, 'The Limitation of the Law in Relation to Financial Crime: Back to Basics' *Journal of Criminal Law 82 (3)* (2018) 193.

Hein M, 'The Fight against Government Corruption in Romania: Irreversible Results or Sisyphean Challenge?' *Europe-Asia Studies 67 (5)* (2015) 747–76.

Hendry J, 'Governance Proceduralisation and Justice: Some Challenges to the Legal Paradigm' *Law and Critique: Special Issue on Governance Civil Society & Social Movements 19 (3)* (2008) 345–61.

Heywood PM, 'Integrity Management and The Public Service Ethos in The UK: Patchwork Quilt rr Threadbare Blanket?' *International Review of Administrative Sciences 78 (3)* (2012) 474–93.

Heywood PM (ed), *Routledge Handbook of Political Corruption* (Routledge 2015)

Heywood PM, and Rose J, 'Curbing Corruption or Promoting Integrity? Probing the Hidden Conceptual Challenge' in Hardi P, Heywood PM, and Torsello D (eds), *Debates on Corruption and Integrity: Perspectives from Europe and the US* (Palgrave Macmillan 2015) 102–19.

Hillion C, 'EU Enlargement' in Craig PC, and De Búrca G (eds), *The Evolution of EU Law* (OUP 2011) 188–215.

Hipper AM, *Beyond the Rhetorics of Compliance: Judicial Reform in Romania* (Springer 2015).

Holland R, 'EU Anti-Corruption Report Shows Long Road Ahead' *Compliance Week 11 (122)* (2014) 10–12.

Horký O, 'The Impact of the Shallow Europeanisation of the 'New' Member States on the EU's Actorness: What Coherence between Foreign and Development Policy?' in Gänzle S, Grimm S, and Makhan D (eds), *The European Union and Global Development: An 'Enlightened Superpower' in the Making?* (Palgrave Macmillan 2012) 57–74.

Huberts LWJC, Pijl D, and Steen A, 'Integrity and Corruption' in Fijnaut CJCF, Muller E, and Rosenthal U (eds) *Police: Studies on Its Operation and Organization* (Samsom 1999) 57–79.

Ivanov K, 'The 2007 Accession of Bulgaria and Romania: Ritual and Reality' in Schmidt-Pfister D, and Moroff H (eds), *Fighting Corruption in Eastern Europe: A Multilevel Perspective* (Routledge 2013) 103–13.

Jeffries I, *Eastern Europe at the Turn of the Twenty-First Century: A Guide to the Economic Transition* (Routledge 2012).

Johnston R, and Pattie C, 'Funding Local Political Parties in England and Wales: Donations and Constituency Campaigns' *British Journal of Politics and International Relation 9 (3)* (2007) 365–95.

Jones P, and Tickner P, *Fraud and Corruption in Public Services* (Routledge 2016).

Jurma A, 'DNA (national Anti-Corruption Department): A Specialized Structure for Combating High Level Corruption in Romania' *Journal of Eastern European Criminal Law No 2/2014* (2015) <https://ssrn.com/abstract=2551997>.

Kajsiu B, 'The Birth of Corruption and the Politics of Anti-Corruption in Albania 1991–2005' *Nationalities Papers: The Journal of Nationalism and Ethnicity 41 (6)* (2013) 1008–25.

Kajsiu B, *A Discourse Analysis of Corruption Instituting Neoliberalism against Corruption in Albania 1998-2005* (Routledge 2015).

Kajsiu B, Bumci A, and Rakip A, '*Albania—A Weak Democracy a Weak State: Report on the State of Democracy in Albania*' Albanian Institute for International Studies (2015).

Kaltsounis T, *The Democratization of Albania: Democracy from Within* (Palgrave Macmillan 2010).

Karini A, 'Aid-Supported Public Service Reform and Capacity Development in Post-Communist Albania' *International Journal of Public Administration 36 (7)* (2013) 469–81.

Karklins R, *The System Made Me Do It: Corruption in Post-Communist Societies* (Routledge 2005).

Keereman F, and Szekely I, *Five Years of an Enlarged EU: A Positive Sum Game—A Positive Sun Game* (Springer 2010) 98–104.

Kelsen H, *Pure Theory of Law* (2nd edn, University of California Press 1967).

Kett P, 'The Role of the G20 and B20 in the Fight against Corruption' in Manacorda S, Centonze F, and Forti G (eds), *Preventing Corporate Corruption: The Anti-Bribery Compliance Model* (Springer 2014) 287–93.

Khorana S, and Ferguson KB, and William KA, 'Governance Issues in the EU's e-Procurement Framework' *Journal of Common Market Studies 53 (2)* (2015) 292–310.

Kjaer PF, *Between Governing and Governance on the Emergence Function and Form of Europe's Post-National Condition* (Hart 2010).

Klitgaard R, 'Addressing Corruption Together' OECD (2015) 41–66, <www.oecd.org/dac/conflict-fragility-resilience/publications/FINAL%20Addressing%20corruption%20together.pdf>.

Knyrim R, and Trieb G, 'Whistleblowing Hotlines in Austria' *International Data Privacy Law 1 (1)* (2011) 70–75.

Kokkinis A, 'The Financial Services Act 2012: The Recent Overhaul of the United Kingdom's Financial Regulatory Structure' *International Company and Commercial Law Review 24 (9)* (2013) 325–28.

Kolb AY, and Kolb DA, 'Experiential Learning Theory: A Dynamic Holistic Approach to Management Learning Education and Development' in Armstrong S, and Fukami CV (eds), *The SAGE Handbook of Management Learning Education and Development* (Sage 2011) 42–68.

Kostadinova P, and Giurcanu M, 'Political Blackmail Institutional Infighting and Electoral Politics: The Fate of Governing Parties during the Great Recession (2008–12) in Romania and Bulgaria' *Politics and Policy 43 (6)* (2015) 789–821.

Krambia-Kapardis M, 'Perception of Political Corruption as a Function of Legislation' *Journal of Financial Crime 21 (1)* (2014) 44–55.

Kukhianidze A, 'Corruption and Organized Crime in Georgia before and after the 'rose Revolution' *Central Asian Survey 28 (2)* (2009) 215–34.

Kume A, 'Study on the Approximation of the Albanian Electoral Legislation with the Code of Good Practice on Electoral Matters of the Venice Commission (EC)' *Academic Journal of Interdisciplinary Studies 4 (2)* (2015) 77–84.

Kurtoglu MG, and Komsuoglu A, 'A Critical Assessment of the Transformative Power of EU Reforms on Reducing Corruption in the Balkans' *Southeast European and Black Sea Studies 15 (3)* (2015) 301–26.

Lazowski A, 'And Then They Were Twenty-Seven ... A Legal Appraisal of the Sixth Accession Treaty' *Common Market Law Review 44 (2)* (2007) 401–30.

Lenoble J, and Maesschalck M, *Reflexive Governance: Redefining the Public Interest in a Pluralistic World* (Hart 2010).

Lessig L, 'Institutional Corruptions' *Edmond J Safra Working Papers No 1* Cambridge, MA: Harvard University Press (2013).

Levine SS, and Prietula M, 'How Knowledge Transfer Impacts Performance: A Multi-Level Model of Benefits and Liabilities' *Organization Science 23 (6)* (2012) 1748–66.

Levitz P, and Pop-Eleches G, 'Monitoring Money and Migrants: Countering Post-Accession Backsliding in Bulgaria and Romania' *Europe-Asia Studies 62 (3)* (2010) 461–79.

Lewis D, 'Ten Years of Public Interest Disclosure Legislation in the UK: Are Whistleblowers Adequately Protected?' *Journal of Business Ethics 82 (2)* (2008) 497–507.

Lewis D, 'Is a Public Interest Test for Workplace Whistleblowing in Society's Interest?' *International Journal of Law and Management 57 (2)* (2015) 141–58.

Lewis M, 'Informal Payments and the Financing of Health Care in Developing and Transition Countries' *Health Affairs 26 (4)* (2007) 984–97.

Little G, and Stopforth D, 'The Legislative Origins of the MPs' Expenses Scandal' *The Modern Law Review 76 (1)* (2013) 83–108.

Loorbach D, 'Transition Management for Sustainable Development: A Prescriptive Complexity-Based Governance Framework' *Governance 23 (1)* (2010) 161–83.

Lord N, *Regulating Corporate Bribery in International Business: Anti-corruption in the UK and Germany* (Routledge 2014).

Luhmann N, 'The Self-Reproduction of Law and Its Limits' in Luhmann N, *Essays on Self-Reference* (Columbia University Press 1990) 227–45.

Luhmann N, *Theory of Society Vol 1* (Stanford University Press 2012).

Luhmann N, *A Sociological Theory of Law* (2nd edn, Routledge 2014).

Luhmann N, 'Some Problems with Reflexive Law' in Teubner G, and Febbrajo A (eds), *State Law and Economy as Autopoietic Systems Regulation and Autonomy in a New Perspective European Yearbook in the Sociology of Law* (Giuffrè 1992) 389–415.

Maatsch A, 'Effectiveness of the European Semester: Explaining Domestic Consent and Contestation' *Max Planck Institute for the Study of Societies Cologne MPIfG Discussion Paper 17/6* (2017).

Magone JM, 'Introduction: The 'great Transformation' of European Politics: A Holistic View' in Magone JM (ed), *Routledge Handbook of European Politics* (Routledge 2015) 1–37.

Manea T, 'Medical Bribery and the Ethics of Trust: The Romanian Case' *Journal of Medicine and Philosophy 40 (1)* (2015) 26–43.

Maton J, 'UK Bribery Act 2010' *Employee Relations Law Journal 36 (3)* (2010) 37–45.

McCourquodale R, and Simons P, (2007) 'Responsibility beyond Borders: Responsibility for Extraterritorial Violations by Corporations of International Human Rights Law' *Modern Law Review 70 (4)* 598–625.

McGowan L, and Phinnemore D, *A Dictionary of the European Union* (Routledge 2015).

McPhilemy S, 'Formal Rules versus Informal Relationships: Prudential Banking Supervision at the FSA before the Crash' *New Political Economy 18 (5)* (2013) 748–67.

Meagher P, 'Anticorruption Agencies: Rhetoric versus Reality' *The Journal of Policy Reform 8 (1)* (2005) 69–103.

Meagher P, and Voland C, 'Anti-corruption Agencies (acas): Office of Democracy and Governance Anti-corruption Program Brief' *IRIS Discussion Papers on Institutions and Development* (University of Maryland 2006).

Mendelski M, 'EU-Driven Judicial Reforms in Romania: A Success Story?' *East European Politics 28 (1)* (2012) 23–42.

Mendelsohn MF, 'United States' in Mendelsohn MF (ed), *The Anti-Bribery and Anti-Corruption Review 4th Edn Law Business Research* (Gideon Roberton2016) 255–89.

Mocanu MC, 'Is the Appeal against Delay in Court Proceedings a Means of Appeal for Withdrawal?' *Contemporary Readings in Law and Social Justice 5 (2)* (2013) 609–12.

Moldovan A, and Van de Walle S, 'Gifts or Bribes? Attitudes on Informal Payments in Romanian Health Care' *Public Integrity 15 (4)* (2013) 383–99.

Morgan KO, *The Oxford History of Britain* (OUP 2010).

Mungiu Pippidi A, 'How Media and Politics Shape Each Other in the New Europe' *Romanian Journal of Political Science 8 (1)* (2008) 69–78.

Mungiu Pippidi A, *A Quest for Good Governance: How Societies Develop Control of Corruption* (CUP 2015).

Mungiu Pippidi A, 'The Good the Bad and the Ugly: Controlling Corruption in the European Union' *European Research Center for Anti-Corruption and State-building* (2013) Working Paper No. 35, 1–66.

Mungiu Pippidi A, 'Romania's Italian-Style Anticorruption Populism' *Journal of Democracy Issue 29 (3)* (2018) 104–16.

Mugarura N, 'The Implications of Brexit for UK Anti-Money Laundering Regulations' *Journal of Money Laundering Control 21 (1)* (2018) 5.

Musaraj S, 'Passport Troubles: Social Tactics and Places of Informal Transactions in Post-Socialist Albania' *Anthropology of East Europe Review 27 (2)* (2009) 159–75.

Neamtu B, and Dragos DC, 'Fighting Corruption in Public Procurement: The Case of Romania' in Racca GM, and Yukins CR (eds), *Integrity and Efficiency in Sustainable Public Contracts Balancing Corruption Concerns in Public Procurement Internationally* (Bruylant 2015) 1–22.

Niklewicz K, 'Safeguarding the Rule of Law within the EU: Lessons from the Polish Experience' *European View 16 (2)* (2017) 281–91.

Noutcheva G, 'Bulgaria and Romania's Accession to the EU: Postponement Safeguards and the Rule of Law' *CEPS Policy Briefs No 102* (2006).

Noutcheva G, *European Foreign Policy and the Challenges of Balkan Accession: Conditionality Legitimacy and Compliance* (Routledge 2012).

Noutcheva G, and Dimitar B, 'The Successful Laggards: Bulgaria and Romania's Accession to the EU' *East European Politics and Societies 22 (1)* (2008) 114–44.

Nunaj T, 'The Training of Albanian Public Administration: An Analysis of Training Policies and Their Impact in the Professional Development of Civil Servants' *Journal of Educational and Social Research 6 (3)* (2016) 149–58.

Nurmandi A, and Sunhyuk K, 'Making e-Procurement Work in a Decentralized Procurement System' *International Journal of Public Sector Management 28 (3)* (2015) 198–220.

Ogarcă R, 'Whistleblowing in Romania' *Young Economists Journal Special Issue 7* (2009) 105–14.

Olsen BE, and Sørensen KE, *Regulation in the EU* (Thomson 2006).

Pasculli L, 'Corruptio Legis: Law as a Cause of Systemic Corruption: Comparative Perspectives and Remedies Also for the Post-Brexit Commonwealth' in Proceedings of 6th Annual International Conference on Law *Regulations and Public Policy (LRPP 2017) 5–6 June 2017 Singapore (2017)* 189–97.

Peshkopia R, 'The Ontology of Human Rights Socialization the Case of Albania' in Carey HF (ed), *European Institutions Democratization and Human Rights Protection in the European Periphery* (Lexington Books 2014) 338–47.

Peshkopia R, *Conditioning Democratization: Institutional Reforms and EU Membership Conditionality in Albania and Macedonia* (Anthem Press 2015).

Peters S, 'Soft Law as a New Mode of Governance' in Diedrichs U, Reiners W, and Wessels W (eds), *The Dynamics of Change in EU Governance* (Edward Elgar 2011) 21–51.

Piana D, *Judicial Accountabilities in New Europe: From Rule of Law to Quality of Justice* (Routledge 2016).

Piga G, and Tatrai T, *Public Procurement Policy* (Routledge 2016).

Prado M, 'The Paradox of Rule of Law Reforms: How Early Reforms Can Create Obstacles to Future Ones' *University of Toronto Law Journal 60 (2)* (2010) 555–78.

Pülzl H, and Lazdinis M, 'May the Open Method of Coordination Be a New Instrument for Forest Policy Deliberations in the European Union?' *Forest Policy and Economics 13 (6)* (2011) 411–18.

Recanatini F, 'Anti-Corruption Authorities: An Effective Tool to Curb Corruption?' in S Rose-Ackerman and T Søreide (eds), *International Handbook on the Economics of Corruption Volume 2* (Edward Elgar 2011) 528–70.

Rhodes R, 'Recovering the Craft of Public Administration' *Public Administration Review 76 (2)* (2015) 638–47.

Riste MG, 'EU Enlargement and Anticorruption: Lessons Learned from Romania' *Journal of European Integration 34 (5)* (2012) 429–46.

Ristei M, 'The Politics of Corruption: Political Will and the Rule of Law in Post-Communist Romania' *Journal of Communist Studies and Transition Politics 26 (3)* (2010) 341–62.

Rodin S, 'The European Union and the Western Balkans: Does the Lisbon Treaty Matter?' in Bindi F, and Angelescu I (eds), *The Foreign Policy of the European Union: Assessing Europe's Role in the World* (Brookings Institution Press 2012) 153–65.

Rogowski R, 'The European Social Model and Law and Policy of Transitional Labour Markets in the European Union' in Rogowski R (ed), *The European Social Model and Transitional Labour Markets—Law and Policy* (Ashgate 2008) 9–27.

Rogowski R, 'ALACs and the Concept of Citizen Participation in the Light of European Law' (October 25 2010) *Warwick School of Law Research Paper No 2010/25.*

Rogowski R, *Reflexive Labour Law In The World Society* (Edward Elgar 2013).

Rogowski R, *'luhmann Niklas 1927–98' Wiley Blackwell Encyclopedia of Sociology* (2nd edn, Wiley Blackwell 2015) 1–6.

Rose-Ackerman S, 'Corruption and Conflicts of Interest' in Auby BJ, and Breen E (eds), *Corruption and Conflicts of Interest: A Comparative Law Approach* (Edward Elgar 2014) 3–15.

Rose-Ackerman S, and Carrington P (eds), *Anti-Corruption Policy: Can International Actors Play a Constructive Role?* (Carolina Academic Press 2013).

Rose-Ackerman S, *International Handbook on the Economics of Corruption Volume 2* (Edward Elgar 2013) 528–71.

Rose-Ackerman S, and Palifka BJ, *Corruption and Government: Causes Consequences and Reform* (CUP 2016).

Rousso A, and Steves F, 'The Effectiveness of Anti-Corruption Programs: Preliminary Evidence from the Post-Communist Transition Countries' in Rose-Ackerman S (ed), *International Handbook on the Economics of Corruption* (Edward Elgar 2006) 278–82.

Ryder N, Turksen U, and Hassler S (eds), *Fighting Financial Crime in the Global Economic Crisis* (Routledge 2015).

Sabel CF, and Zeitlin J, 'Learning from Difference: The New Architecture of Experimentalist Governance in the EU' *European Law Journal 14 (3)* (2008) 271–27, 278–80.

Sadurski W, *Rights before Courts: A Study of Constitutional Courts in Postcommunist States of Central and Eastern European* (2nd edn, Springer 2014).

Savage A, *Leaks Whistleblowing and the Public Interest: The Law of Unauthorised Disclosures* (Edward Elgar 2016).

Savage JD, and Howarth D, 'Enforcing the European Semester: The Politics of Asymmetric Information in the Excessive Deficit and Macroeconomic Imbalance Procedures' *Journal of European Public Policy 25 (2)* (2018) 212–30.

Scott C, 'Reflexive Governance Meta-Regulation and Corporate Social Responsibility: The 'heineken Effect'' in Boeger N, Murray R, and Villiers C (eds), *Perspectives on Corporate Social Responsibility* (Edward Elgar 2008) 170–85.

Scott J, and Trubek DM, 'Mind the Gap Law and New Approaches to Governance in the European Union' *European Law Journal 8 (1)* (2002) 1–18.

Schnell S, 'Mimicry Persuasion or Learning? the Case of Two Transparency and Anti-Corruption Policies in Romania' *Public Administration and Development 35 (4)* 2015) 277–87.

Schultz D, and Harutyunyan K, 'Combating Corruption: The Development of Whistleblowing Laws in the United States Europe and Armenia' *International Comparative Jurisprudence 1 (2)* (2015) 87–97.

Schwindt-Bayer LA, and Tavits M, *Clarity of Responsibility Accountability and Corruption* (CUP 2016).

Scîntee SG, and Vlădescu C, 'Primary Health Care in Romania after 20 Years of Reforms' in Bartlett W, Božikov J, and Rechel B (eds), *Health Reforms in South East Europe* (Palgrave Macmillan 2012) 130–47.

Sedelmeier U, 'Anchoring Democracy from Above? the European Union and Democratic Backsliding in Hungary and Romania after Accession' *Journal of Common Market Studies 52 (1)* (2014) 105–21.

Semenova E, Edinger M, and Best H, 'Patterns of Parliamentary Elite Recruitment in Post-Communist Europe: A Comparative Analysis' in Semenova E, and Edinger M (eds) *Parliamentary Elites in Central and Eastern Europe: Recruitment and Representation* (Routledge 2014) 284–308.

Senden L, *Soft Law in European Community Law* (Bloomsbury 2004)

Senden L, 'Self-Regulation and Co-Regulation in European Law: Where Do They Meet?' *Electronic Journal of Comparative Law 9 (1)* (2005) 1–26.

Sjafjell B, and Wiesbrock A (eds) *Sustainable Public Procurement under EU Law: New Perspectives on the State as Stakeholder* (CUP 2016).

Škarica M, 'Public Administration Reforms in a Fragile Institutional Framework: The Case of Albania' *Croatian and Comparative Public Administration Journal 12 (3)* (2011) 210–42.

Staab A, *The European Union Explained: Institutions Actors Global Impact* (Indiana University Press 2013).

Stahl J, *Rent from the Land: A Political Ecology of Postsocialist Rural Transformation* (Anthem Press 2012).

Stepurko T, Pavlova M, Gryga I, and Groot W, 'Informal Payments for Health Care Services—Corruption or Gratitude? A Study on Public Attitudes, Perceptions and Opinions in Six Central and Eastern European Countries' *Communist Post-Communist Stud 46 (4)* (2013) 419–31.

Stepurko T, Pavlova M, Gryga I, and Groot W, 'To Pay or Not to Pay? A Multicountry Study on Informal Payments for Health-Care Services and Consumers' Perceptions' *Health Expectations 18 (6)* (2014) 2978–93.

Strelkov A, 'EU Justice Scoreboard: A New Policy Tool For 'Deepening' European Integration?' *Journal of Contemporary European Studies 27 (1)* (2018) 15–27.

Sukhdev J, Moran M, and Williams K, 'Power Politics and the City of London after the Great Financial Crisis' *Journal of Government and Opposition 49 (3)* (2015) 400–425.

Szarek-Mason P, *The European Union's Fight against Corruption: The Evolving Policy Towards Member States and Candidate Countries* (CUP 2010).

Tahiraj R, 'Law and Corruption in Albania and in the South-Eastern European Countries: A Comparative Analysis' *Mediterranean Journal of Social Sciences 5 (7)* (2014) 136–47.

Tambora M, Pavlova M, Golinowskaa S, Sowada C, and Groot W, 'The Formal-Informal Patient Payment Mix in European Countries: Governance, Economics, Culture, or All of These?' *Health Policy 113 (3)* (2013) 284–95.

Tänzler D, Maras K, and Giannakopoulos A (eds) *The Social Construction of Corruption in Europe* (Ashgate 2012).

Tatham AF, *Enlargement of the European Union* (Kluwer Law International 2009).

Teqja E, 'Western Balkans, the Long Way of Integration: Albania's Perception about the Process' *Journal of Global Faultlines 2 (1)* (2014) 70–94.

Teubner G, 'Substantive and Reflexive Elements in Modern Law' *Law and Society Review 17 (2)* (1983) 239–85.

Teubner G, *Law as an Autopoietic System* (Blackwell 1993).

Tiryakioğlu M, 'Learning-Based Technology Transfer Policies and Late Development: The South Korea Experience' in Yülek M, and Taylor TK (eds), *Designing Public Procurement Policy in Developing Countries: How to Foster Technology Transfer and Industrialization in the Global Economy* (Springer 2012) 141–56.

Tismaneanu V, 'Romanian Exceptionalism? Democracy Ethnocracy and Uncertain Pluralism in Post-Ceauşescu Romania' in Dawisha K, and Parrot B (eds) *Politics Power and the Struggle for Democracy in South-East Europe* (CUP 1997) 403–52.

Toma R, 'Perceptions of Ethics and Corruption in Romania: The Need for Civic Engagement' in Belasen AT, and Toma R (eds) *Confronting Corruption in Business: Trusted Leadership Civic Engagement* (Routledge 2016) 127–66.

Topan A, 'The Resignation of the Santer-Commission: The Impact of 'Trust' and 'Reputation'' *European Integration Online Papers (EIoP) 6* (2002) 1–14.

Trauner F, 'Bilateral Patterns of Cooperation on Readmission: Premises and Impact on Human Rights Observance' in Ceccorulli M, and Labanca N (eds), *The EU Migration and the Politics of Administrative Detention* (Routledge 2014) 23–42.

Trubek DM, and Trubek LM, 'The Open Method of Co-ordination and the Debate over 'Hard' and 'Soft' Law' in Zeitlin J, and Pochet P, with L Magnusson (eds) *The Open Method of Co-ordination in Action: The European Employment and Social Inclusion Strategies* (Peter Lang 2005) 83–103.

Trubek DM, and Trubek LM, 'The World Turned Upside Down: Reflections on New Governance and the Transformation of Law' *Wisconsin Law Review (2)* (2010) 719–26.

Turner S, *Understanding the Tacit* (Routledge 2014).

Văduva S, *From Corruption to Modernity: The Evolution of Romania's Entrepreneurship* (Springer 2016).

Van der Meer M, Visser J, and Wilthagen T, 'Adaptive and Reflexive Governance: The Limits of Organized Decentralization' *European Journal of Industrial Relations 11 (3)* (2005) 347–65.

Van Erp J, Huisman W, and Vande Walle G (eds), *The Routledge Handbook of White-Collar and Corporate Crime in Europe* (Routledge 2015).

Van Heerde-Hudson J, and Fisher J, (2013) 'Parties Heed (with Caution): Public Knowledge of and Attitudes Towards Party Finance in Britain' *Sage Journals Party Politics 19 (1)* 41–60.

Vandekerckhove W, 'European Whistleblower Protection: Tiers or Tears?' in Lewis D (ed), *A Global Approach to Public Interest Disclosure: What Can We Learn from Existing Whistleblowing Legislation and Research?* (Edward Elgar 2013) 15–33.

Van Vooren B, *EU External Relations Law and the European Neighbourhood Policy: A Paradigm for Coherence* (Routledge 2012).

Verdun A, and Tovias A, *Mapping European Economic Integration* (Palgrave Macmillan 2013).

Verdun A, and Zeitlin J, 'Introduction: The European Semester as a New Architecture of EU Socioeconomic Governance in Theory and Practice' *Journal of European Public Policy 25 (2)* (2018) 137–48.

Vasjari A, 'Albania's Integration in EU' *Mediterranean Journal of Social Sciences 4 (6)* (2013) 305–13.

Vergragt PJ, and Brown HS, 'Sustainable Mobility: From Technological Innovation to Societal Learning' *Journal of Cleaner Production 15 (11–12)* (2007) 1104–15.

Vickers M, *The Albanians: A Modern History* (IB Tauris 2014).

Vickers M and J Pettifer *Albania: From Anarchy to a Balkan Identity* (New York University Press 2000).

Weyembergh A, and Brière C, 'The Future Cooperation between OLAF and the European Public Prosecutor's Office' *New Journal of European Criminal Law 9 (1)* (2018) 62–82.

Wiesbrock A, and Sjåfjell B, 'Public Procurement's Potential for Sustainability' in Sjåfjell B, and Wiesbrock A (eds), *Sustainable Public Procurement under EU Law: New Perspectives on the State as Stakeholder* (CUP 2015) 230–42.

Yanga LM, 'UK Bribery Act 2010: Implications for Business in Africa' *International Journal of Law and Management 56 (1)* (2014) 3–28.

Zeitlin J, 'The Open Method of Coordination in Action Theoretical Promise Empirical Realities Reform Strategy' in Zeitlin J, and Pochet P, with L Magnusson (eds) *The Open Method of Co-ordination in Action: The European Employment and Social Inclusion Strategies* (Peter Lang 2005) 447–503.

Zeitlin J, and Vanhercke B, 'Socializing the European Semester: EU Social and Economic Policy Co-Ordination in Crisis and Beyond' *Journal of European Public Policy 25 (2)* (2018) 149–74.

Zeneli V, 'Corruption Foreign Direct Investment and International Marketing in the Western Balkans' *Thunderbird International Business Review 58 (3)* (2015) 277–91.

European Commission Reports and Papers

European Commission, 'White Paper on European Governance' COM (2001) 428 final 7–11.

European Commission, 'Commission Decision of 13 December' 2006 C (2006) 6569.

European Commission, 'Commission Decision of 13/XII/2006' C (2006) 6570 final.

European Commission, 'Commission Opinion on Albania's Application for Membership of the European Union' COM (2010) 68.

European Commission 'Communication on Europe 2020: A Strategy for Smart Sustainable and Inclusive Growth' COM (2010) 2020 final.

European Commission, 'Communication Fighting Corruption in the EU' COM (2011) 308 final.

European Commission, 'Interim Report from the Commission to the European Parliament and the Council on Progress in Romania/Bulgaria under the Cooperation and Verification Mechanism' COM (2012) 56/57 final.

European Commission, 'On Progress in Romania under the Cooperation and Verification Mechanism' COM (2012) 410 final.

European Commission, 'Annual Report on Financial Assistance for Enlargement (IPA PHARE CARDS Turkey Pre-accession Instrument Transition Facility' (2013).

European Commission, Flash Eurobarometer 398 on Internal Market Report (2013) <http://ec.europa.eu/public_opinion/archives/ebs/ebs_398_en.pdf>.

European Commission, Special Eurobarometer 397 on Corruption (2013) <http://ec.europa.eu/public_opinion/archives/ebs/ebs_397_en.pdf>.

European Commission, 'Identifying and Reducing Corruption in Public Procurement in the EU Development of a Methodology to Estimate the Direct Costs of Corruption and Other Elements for an EU-Evaluation Mechanism in the Area of Anti-corruption' PwC Ecorys (2013) <https://ec.europa.eu/anti-fraud/sites/antifraud/files/docs/body/identifying_reducing_corruption_in_public_procurement_en.pdf>.

European Commission, 'EU Anti-Corruption Report' COM (2014) 38 final.

European Commission, 'Albania Progress Report' COM (2014) 700 final of 8102014 <https://ec.europa.eu/neighbourhood-enlargement/sites/near/files/pdf/key_documents/2014/20141008-albania-progress-report_en.pdf>.

European Commission, 'Annex 1: Belgium to the EU Anti-Corruption Report' COM (2014) 38 final <http://ec.europa.eu/dgs/home-affairs/what-we-do/policies/organized-crime-and-human-trafficking/corruption/anti-corruption-report/docs/2014_acr_belgium_chapter_en.pdf>.

European Commission, 'Annex 10: France to the EU Anti-Corruption Report' COM (2014) 38 final <http://ec.europa.eu/dgs/home-affairs/what-we-do/policies/organized-crime-and-human-trafficking/corruption/anti-corruption-report/docs/2014_acr_france_chapter_en.pdf>.

European Commission, 'Annex 11: Croatia to the EU Anti-Corruption Report' COM (2014) 38 final <http://ec.europa.eu/dgs/home-affairs/what-we-do/policies/organized-crime-and-human-trafficking/corruption/anti-corruption-report/docs/2014_acr_croatia_chapter_en.pdf>.

European Commission 'Annex 12: Italy to the EU Anti-Corruption Report' COM (2014) 38 final <http://ec.europa.eu/dgs/home-affairs/what-we-do/policies/organized-crime-and-human-trafficking/corruption/anti-corruption-report/docs/2014_acr_italy_chapter_en.pdf>.

European Commission 'Annex 13: Cyprus to the EU Anti-Corruption Report' COM (2014) 38 final <http://ec.europa.eu/dgs/home-affairs/what-we-do/policies/organized-crime-and-human-trafficking/corruption/anti-corruption-report/docs/2014_acr_cyprus_chapter_en.pdf>.

European Commission 'Annex 14: Latvia to the EU Anti-Corruption Report' COM (2014) 38 final <http://ec.europa.eu/dgs/home-affairs/what-we-do/policies/organized-crime-and-human-trafficking/corruption/anti-corruption-report/docs/2014_acr_latvia_chapter_en.pdf>.

European Commission, 'Annex 15: Lithuania to the EU Anti-Corruption Report' COM (2014) 38 final <http://ec.europa.eu/dgs/home-affairs/what-we-do/policies/organized-crime-and-human-trafficking/corruption/anti-corruption-report/docs/2014_acr_lithuania_chapter_en.pdf>.

European Commission, 'Annex 16: Luxembourg to the EU Anti-Corruption Report' COM (2014) 38 final <http://ec.europa.eu/dgs/home-affairs/what-we-do/policies/organized-crime-and-human-trafficking/corruption/anti-corruption-report/docs/2014_acr_luxembourg_chapter_en.pdf>.

European Commission, 'Annex 17: Hungary to the EU Anti-Corruption Report' COM (2014) 38 final <http://ec.europa.eu/dgs/home-affairs/what-we-do/policies/organized-crime-and-human-trafficking/corruption/anti-corruption-report/docs/2014_acr_hungary_chapter_en.pdf>.

European Commission, 'Annex 18: Malta to the EU Anti-Corruption Report' COM (2014) 38 final <http://ec.europa.eu/dgs/home-affairs/what-we-do/policies/organized-crime-and-human-trafficking/corruption/anti-corruption-report/docs/2014_acr_malta_chapter_en.pdf>.

European Commission, 'Annex 19: The Netherlands to the EU Anti-Corruption Report' COM (2014) 38 final <http://ec.europa.eu/dgs/home-affairs/what-we-do/policies/organized-crime-and-human-trafficking/corruption/anti-corruption-report/docs/2014_acr_netherlands_chapter_en.pdf>.

European Commission, 'Annex 2: Bulgaria to the EU Anti-Corruption Report' COM (2014) 38 final <http://ec.europa.eu/dgs/home-affairs/what-we-do/policies/

organized-crime-and-human-trafficking/corruption/anti-corruption-report/docs/2014_acr_bulgaria_chapter_en.pdf>.

European Commission, 'Annex 20: Austria to the EU Anti-Corruption Report' COM (2014) 38 final <http://ec.europa.eu/dgs/home-affairs/what-we-do/policies/organized-crime-and-human-trafficking/corruption/anti-corruption-report/docs/2014_acr_austria_chapter_en.pdf>.

European Commission, 'Annex 21: Poland to the EU Anti-Corruption Report' COM (2014) 38 final <http://ec.europa.eu/dgs/home-affairs/what-we-do/policies/organized-crime-and-human-trafficking/corruption/anti-corruption-report/docs/2014_acr_poland_chapter_en.pdf>.

European Commission, 'Annex 22: Portugal to the EU Anti-Corruption Report' COM (2014) 38 final <http://ec.europa.eu/dgs/home-affairs/what-we-do/policies/organized-crime-and-human-trafficking/corruption/anti-corruption-report/docs/2014_acr_portugal_chapter_en.pdf>.

European Commission, 'Annex 23: Romania to the EU Anti-Corruption Report' COM (2014) 38 final <http://ec.europa.eu/dgs/home-affairs/what-we-do/policies/organized-crime-and-human-trafficking/corruption/anti-corruption-report/docs/2014_acr_romania_chapter_en.pdf>.

European Commission, 'Annex 24: Slovenia to the EU Anti-Corruption Report' COM (2014) 38 final <http://ec.europa.eu/dgs/home-affairs/what-we-do/policies/organized-crime-and-human-trafficking/corruption/anti-corruption-report/docs/2014_acr_slovenia_chapter_en.pdf>.

European Commission, 'Annex 25: Slovakia to the EU Anti-Corruption Report' COM (2014) 38 final <http://ec.europa.eu/dgs/home-affairs/what-we-do/policies/organized-crime-and-human-trafficking/corruption/anti-corruption-report/docs/2014_acr_slovakia_chapter_en.pdf>.

European Commission, 'Annex 26: Finland to the EU Anti-Corruption Report' COM (2014) 38 final <http://ec.europa.eu/dgs/home-affairs/what-we-do/policies/organized-crime-and-human-trafficking/corruption/anti-corruption-report/docs/2014_acr_finland_chapter_en.pdf>.

European Commission, 'Annex 27: Sweden to the EU Anti-Corruption Report' COM (2014) 38 final <http://ec.europa.eu/dgs/home-affairs/what-we-do/policies/organized-crime-and-human-trafficking/corruption/anti-corruption-report/docs/2014_acr_sweden_chapter_en.pdf>.

European Commission, 'Annex 28: United Kingdom to the EU Anti-Corruption Report' COM (2014) 38 final <http://ec.europa.eu/dgs/home-affairs/what-we-do/policies/organized-crime-and-human-trafficking/corruption/anti-corruption-report/docs/2014_acr_united_kingdom_chapter_en.pdf>.

European Commission, 'Annex 3: Czech Republic to the EU Anti-Corruption Report' COM (2014) 38 final <http://ec.europa.eu/dgs/home-affairs/what-we-do/policies/organized-crime-and-human-trafficking/corruption/anti-corruption-report/docs/2014_acr_czech_republic_chapter_en.pdf>.

European Commission, 'Annex 4: Denmark to the EU Anti-Corruption Report' COM (2014) 38 final <http://ec.europa.eu/dgs/home-affairs/what-we-do/policies/organized-crime-and-human-trafficking/corruption/anti-corruption-report/docs/2014_acr_denmark_chapter_en.pdf>.

European Commission, 'Annex 5: Germany to the EU Anti-Corruption Report' COM (2014) 38 final <http://ec.europa.eu/dgs/home-affairs/what-we-do/pol

icies/organized-crime-and-human-trafficking/corruption/anti-corruption-report/docs/2014_acr_germany_chapter_en.pdf>.

European Commission, 'Annex 6: Estonia to the EU Anti-Corruption Report' COM (2014) 38 final <http://ec.europa.eu/dgs/home-affairs/what-we-do/policies/organized-crime-and-human-trafficking/corruption/anti-corruption-report/docs/2014_acr_estonia_chapter_en.pdf>.

European Commission, 'Annex 7: Ireland to the EU Anti-Corruption Report' COM (2014) 38 final <http://ec.europa.eu/dgs/home-affairs/what-we-do/policies/organized-crime-and-human-trafficking/corruption/anti-corruption-report/docs/2014_acr_ireland_chapter_en.pdf>.

European Commission, 'Annex 8: Greece to the EU Anti-Corruption Report' COM (2014) 38 final <http://ec.europa.eu/dgs/home-affairs/what-we-do/policies/organized-crime-and-human-trafficking/corruption/anti-corruption-report/docs/2014_acr_greece_chapter_en.pdf>.

European Commission, 'Annex 9: Spain to the EU Anti-Corruption Report' COM (2014) 38 final <http://ec.europa.eu/dgs/home-affairs/what-we-do/policies/organized-crime-and-human-trafficking/corruption/anti-corruption-report/docs/2014_acr_spain_chapter_en.pdf>.

European Commission, Democracy though law—Venice Commission CDL-REF (2014) 015 2-15 <www.venice.coe.int/webforms/documents/defaultaspx?pdf>file=CDL-REF(2014)015-e>.

European Commission, 'Report from the Commission to the European Parliament and the Council on the 'EU Anti-Corruption Report'' (2014) 13–14 <https://eur-lex.europa.eu/resourcehtml?uri=cellar:058aecf0-d9b7-11e3-8cd4-01aa75ed71a100 1201/DOC_1&format=PDF>.

European Commission, 'Flash Eurobarometer 374 on Business' Attitudes Towards Corruption in the EU' (2014) <http://ec.europa.eu/public_opinion/flash/fl_374_en.pdf>.

European Commission, (2016) 'On Progress in Romania under the Cooperation and Verification Mechanism Report from the Commission to the European Parliament and the Council' COM (2016) 41 final.

European Commission, 'Report from the Commission to the European Parliament and the Council on Progress in Romania under the 'co-operation and Verification Mechanism'' (2016) 10 <https://ec.europa.eu/transparency/regdoc/rep/1/2016/EN/1-2016-41-EN-F1-1.PDF>.

European Commission, 'Country Report Romania on Including an In-Depth Review on the Prevention and Correction of Macroeconomic Imbalances' SWD (2016) 91 final.

European Commission, 'On Progress in Romania under the Co-operation and Verification Mechanism' COM (2016) 41 final.

European Commission, 'The Experience Sharing Programme to Support Member States Local NGOs and Other Stakeholders in Addressing Specific Challenges Identified in the EU Anti-Corruption Report' (2016) <https://ec.europa.eu/home-affairs/what-we-do/policies/organized-crime-and-human-trafficking/corruption/experience-sharing-programme_en>.

European Commission, 'Albania—Financial Assistance under IPA II' (2018) <https://ec.europa.eu/neighbourhood-enlargement/instruments/funding-by-country/albania_en>.

European Commission, 'European Semester: Country Specific Recommendation on the 2018 National Reform Programme of Bulgaria and Delivering a Council Opinion on the 2018 Convergence Programme of Bulgaria' COM (2018) 402 final <https://ec.europa.eu/info/sites/info/files/file_import/2018-european-semester-country-specific-recommendation-commission-recommendation-bulgaria-en.pdf>.

European Commission, 'European Semester: Country Specific Recommendation on the 2018 National Reform Programme of Czech Republic and Delivering a Council Opinion on the 2018 Convergence Programme of Czech Republic' COM (2018) 402 final <https://ec.europa.eu/info/sites/info/files/file_import/2018-european-semester-country-specific-recommendation-commission-recommendation-czechrepublic-en.pdf>.

European Commission, 'European Semester: Country Specific Recommendation on the 2018 National Reform Programme of Spain and Delivering a Council Opinion on the 2018 Convergence Programme of Spain' COM (2018) 402 final <https://ec.europa.eu/info/sites/info/files/2018-european-semester-country-specific-recommendation-commission-recommendation-spain-en.pdf>.

European Commission, 'European Semester: Country Specific Recommendation on the 2018 National Reform Programme of Croatia and Delivering a Council Opinion on the 2018 Convergence Programme of Croatia' COM (2018) 402 final <https://ec.europa.eu/info/sites/info/files/file_import/2018-european-semester-country-specific-recommendation-commission-recommendation-croatia-en.pdf>.

European Commission, 'European Semester: Country Specific Recommendation on the 2018 National Reform Programme of Italy and Delivering a Council Opinion on the 2018 Convergence Programme of Italy' COM (2018) 402 final <https://ec.europa.eu/info/sites/info/files/2018-european-semester-country-specific-recommendation-commission-recommendation-italy-en.pdf>.

European Commission, 'European Semester: Country Specific Recommendation on the 2018 National Reform Programme of Cyprus and Delivering a Council Opinion on the 2018 Convergence Programme of Cyprus' COM (2018) 402 final <https://ec.europa.eu/info/sites/info/files/file_import/2018-european-semester-country-specific-recommendation-commission-recommendation-cyprus-en.pdf>.

European Commission, 'European Semester: Country Specific Recommendation on the 2018 National Reform Programme of Latvia and Delivering a Council Opinion on the 2018 Convergence Programme of Latvia' COM (2018) 402 final <https://ec.europa.eu/info/sites/info/files/file_import/2018-european-semester-country-specific-recommendation-commission-recommendation-latvia-en.pdf>.

European Commission, 'European Semester: Country Specific Recommendation on the 2018 National Reform Programme of Lithuania and Delivering a Council Opinion on the 2018 Convergence Programme of Lithuania' COM (2018) 402 final <https://ec.europa.eu/info/sites/info/files/file_import/2018-european-semester-country-specific-recommendation-commission-recommendation-lithuania-en.pdf>.

European Commission, 'European Semester: Country Specific Recommendation on the 2018 National Reform Programme of Hungary and Delivering a Council Opinion on the 2018 Convergence Programme of Hungary' COM (2018) 402 final <https://ec.europa.eu/info/sites/info/files/2018-european-semester-country-specific-recommendation-commission-recommendation-hungary-en.pdf>.

European Commission, 'European Semester: Country Specific Recommendation on the 2018 National Reform Programme of Malta and Delivering a Council Opinion on the 2018 Convergence Programme of Malta' COM (2018) 402 final <https://ec.europa.eu/info/sites/info/files/file_import/2018-european-semester-country-specific-recommendation-commission-recommendation-malta-en.pdf>.

European Commission, 'European Semester: Country Specific Recommendation on the 2018 National Reform Programme of Portugal and Delivering a Council Opinion on the 2018 Convergence Programme of Portugal' COM (2018) 402 final <https://ec.europa.eu/info/sites/info/files/file_import/2018-european-semester-country-specific-recommendation-commission-recommendation-portugal-en.pdf>.

European Commission, 'European Semester: Country Specific Recommendation on the 2018 National Reform Programme of Romania and Delivering a Council Opinion on the 2018 Convergence Programme of Romania' COM (2018) 402 final <https://ec.europa.eu/info/sites/info/files/2018-european-semester-country-specific-recommendation-commission-recommendation-romania-en.pdf>.

European Commission, 'European Semester: Country Specific Recommendation on the 2018 National Reform Programme of Slovenia and Delivering a Council Opinion on the 2018 Convergence Programme of Slovenia' COM (2018) 402 final <https://ec.europa.eu/info/sites/info/files/2018-european-semester-country-specific-recommendation-commission-recommendation-slovenia-en.pdf>.

European Commission, 'European Semester: Country Specific Recommendation on the 2018 National Reform Programme of Slovakia and Delivering a Council Opinion on the 2018 Convergence Programme of Slovakia' COM (2018) 402 final <https://ec.europa.eu/info/sites/info/files/file_import/2018-european-semester-country-specific-recommendation-commission-recommendation-slovakia-en.pdf>.

European Commission, 'Recommendation for a Council Recommendation on the 2018 National Reform Programme of the Czech Republic and Delivering a Council Opinion on the 2018 Convergence Programme of the Czech Republic' COM (2018) 403 final <https://ec.europa.eu/info/publications/2018-european-semester-country-specific-recommendations-czech-republic_en>.

European Commission, 'Proposal for a Directive of the European Parliament and the Council on the Protection of Persons Reporting on Breaches of Union Law' COM (2018) 218 final.

European Commission, 'A Credible Enlargement Perspective for and Enhanced EU Engagement with the Western Balkans' COM (2018) 65 final <https://ec.europa.eu/commission/sites/beta-political/files/communication-credible-enlargement-perspective-western-balkans_en.pdf>.

European Commission, 'IPA (II) Indicative Strategy Paper for Albania (2014–2020)' 16–19 <http://ec.europa.eu/enlargement/instruments/funding-by-country/albania/index_en.htm>.

European Commission Instrument for Pre-Accession Assistance (IPA II) 2014–2020: Supporting Rule of Law Enforcement Agencies in Bosnia and Herzegovina (2011).

European Communications, Studies and Reports

Abazi V, 'Legal Analysis on the Competences of the European Union for Legislation on Whistleblower Protection' Greens/EFA Group, European Parliament (22 May 2017) <http://extranet.greens-efa-service.eu/public/media/file/1/5179>.

Albania Council of Ministers, *Combating Corruption in Albania: A Comprehensive Reform Program* Republic of Albania: Council of Ministers (1998).

Council of Europe's Group of States against Corruption (GRECO) 'Report on Albania (2018)' <https://rm.coe.int/greco-rc4-2018-4-fourth-evaluation-round-corruption-prevention-in-resp/16808c3a35>.

European Anti-Fraud Office, 'OLAF Report 2017: Eighteenth Report of the European Anti-Fraud Office, 1 January to 31 December 2017' (2017) <https://ec.europa.eu/anti-fraud/sites/antifraud/files/olaf_report_2017_en.pdf>.

European Communication, Commission Launches Dialogue With Albania On Visa Liberalization COM (2008) 127 final.

European Council, Presidency Conclusions 21–22 June 11177/1/07 (2007).

European Court of Auditors, 'Special Report EU Pre-accession Assistance for Strengthening Administrative Capacity in the Western Balkans: A Meta-Audit No 21' (2016) <www.eca.europa.eu/Lists/News/NEWS1609_13/SR_WESTERN-BALKANS _EN.pdf>.

European Parliament, 'How Can European Industry Contribute To Growth And Foster European Competitiveness' *Study for the ITRE Committee* (August 2014).

European Parliament, 'eGovernment: Using Technology to Improve Public Services and Democratic Participation' EPRS—PE 565890 (2015).

European Parliament, 'Resolution on the 2014 Progress Report on Albania' (2015) <www.europarl.europa.eu/oeil/popups/ficheproceduredo?lang=en&reference=2014/2951%28RSP%29>.

European Parliament, 'Briefing on the Western Balkans Frontline of the Migrant Crisis' (2016) <www.europarl.europa.eu/RegData/etudes/BRIE/2016/573949/EPRS_BRI(2016)573949_EN.pdf>.

European Parliament, 'Resolution on the 2015 Report on Montenegro' (2015/2894 (RSP)) (2016).

European Parliament Think Tank, 'Briefing: The Western Balkans' Berlin Process: A New Impulse for Regional Cooperation' (2016) <www.europarl.europa.eu/RegData/etudes/BRIE/2016/586602/EPRS_BRI(2016)586602_EN.pdf>.

Eurobarometer, 'Flash Eurobarometer for Romania' (2015) <http://ec.europa.eu/COMMFrontOffice/PublicOpinion/indexcfm/Survey/getSurveyDetail/yearFrom/1973/yearTo/2016/surveyKy/2084>.

European Union, 'Albania Joint Conclusions on the Fifth High Level Dialogue on the Key Priorities' (24 March 2015) <http://eeas.europa.eu/delegations/albania/documents/press_releases/20150324_5th_hld_operational_conclusions.pdf>.

Europol, 'Report on EU Serious and Organised Crime Threat Assessment' (2013) 6 <www.europol.europa.eu/content/eu-serious-and-organised-crime-threat-assessment-socta>.

Europol, 'The European Union (EU) Serious and Organised Crime Threat Assessment (SOCTA) 2017' (2017) 14 <www.europol.europa.eu/activities-services/main-reports/european-union-serious-and-organised-crime-threat-assessment-2017>.

Europol, 'Internet Organised Crime Threat Assessment 2018' (2018) 14 <www.europol.europa.eu/internet-organised-crime-threat-assessment-2018>.

Van Ballegooij W, and Zandstra T, 'Organised Crime and Corruption: Cost of Non-Europe Report Annex II—Corruption' EPRS Service PE 579319 (2016) 72–88 <www.europarl.europa.eu/thinktank/en/document.html?reference=EPRS_IDA(2016)558779>.

Other International Reports and Papers

Bar Association Joint Report by IBA OECD and UNODC.

British Embassy Albania, 'Analysis of the Justice System in Albania—2015' 13 July 2015 <www.gov.uk/government/world-location-news/analysis-of-the-justice-system-in-albania-2015>.

Electoral Commission, 'Donations and Loans: Guidance for Regulated Donees in Great Britain' (2010) <www.electoralcommission.org.uk/__data/assets/electoral_commission_pdf>_file/0019/13708/026-regulated-donees-guidance-final.pdf>.

Gjipali G, 'Freedom House Annual Report on Albania' (2012) <https://freedomhouse.org/sites/default/files/NIT13_Albania_3rdProof_0.pdf>.

Freedom House, *Nations in Transit Country Report: Albania* (Freedom House 2008).

Freedom House, 'Public Procurement: An Operational Approach' 20 March 2013 <http://freedomhouse.ro/en/indexphp/stiri/events/item/134-press-release-conference-public-procurement-an-operational-approach>.

Freedom House, 'Report on Albania' (Freedom House 2015) <https://freedomhouse.org/report/freedom-world/2015/albania>.

Freedom House 'Report on Albania' (Freedom House 2018) <https://freedomhouse.org/report/freedom-world/2018/albania>.

Human Rights, 'Human Rights Report on Albania' (2015) <www.state.gov/documents/organization/253027.pdf>.

House of Commons Foreign Affairs Committee 'The Use of UK-Manufactured Arms in Yemen' House of Commons Fourth Report of Session 2016–17 (2018) 33 <https://publications.parliament.uk/pa/cm201617/cmselect/cmfaff/688/688.pdf>.

House of Commons Committee on Members' Expenses, the Operation of the Parliamentary Standards Act 2009: First Report of Session 2010–12 Vol 2 (2012).

HM Government, 'Guidance on Proceeds of Crime Act 2002' Money Laundering Provisions 7–8 (2013) <www.gov.uk/government/uploads/system/uploads/attachment_data/file/257962/30-poca.pdf>.

HM Government, 'The UK Anti-Corruption Plan' (2014) 10–56 <www.gov.uk/government/uploads/system/uploads/attachment_data/file/388894/UKantiCorruptionPlan.pdf>.

HM Government, Progress Update on the UK Anti-Corruption Plan (2016) 2–7 <https://assets.publishing.service.gov.uk/government/uploads/system/uploads/attachment_data/file/522802/6.1689_Progress_Update_on_the_UK_Anti-Corruption_Plan_v11_WEB.PDF>.

HM Government, 'UK Anti-Corruption Strategy 2017–2022' (2017) <www.gov.uk/government/publications/uk-anti-corruption-strategy-2017-to-2022>.

HM Treasury, 'A New Approach To Financial Regulation: Building A Stronger System' (2011) <www.gov.uk/government/uploads/system/uploads/attachment_data/file/81411/consult_newfinancial_regulation170211.pdf>.

Home Office, 'Annual Report and Accounts 2014–15' (2015) 9 <www.gov.uk/government/uploads/system/uploads/attachment_data/file/441284/HO_AR_14-15_print.pdf>.

House of Commons Committee on Members' Expenses, 'The Operation of the Parliamentary Standards Act 2009: First Report of Session 2010–12 Volume 2' (2012).

House of Commons, 'The Code of Conduct and the Guide to the Rules Relating to the Conduct of Members' Chapter 1 and 2 (2015) <www.publications.parliament.uk/pa/cm201516/cmcode/1076/107601.htm>.

IBA, 'Report of the Task Force on Extraterritorial Jurisdiction IBA Legal Practice Division London' (2009) <http://tinyurl.com/taskforce-etj-pdf>.

IBA, 'Response of the Working Group of the International Bar Association Anti-Corruption Committee to the Ministry of Justice Consultation on Guidance about Commercial Organisations Preventing Bribery' (2010).

IBA, 'Risks and Threats of Corruption and the Legal Profession' (2010) <www.oecd.org/investment/anti-bribery/46137847.pdf>.

Kajsiu B, 'Nations in Transit 2018: Albania' (Freedom House 2018) <https://freedomhouse.org/report/nations-transit/2018/albania>.

Ministry of Justice, 'Guidance about Commercial Organisations Preventing Bribery (section 9 of the Bribery Act 2010) Response to Consultation CP11/10 (CP(R) 7/11) (2011) <www.justice.gov.uk/downloads/legislation/bribery-act-2010-guidance.pdf>.

Ministry of Justice, 'National Anticorruption Strategy for the Period 2012–2015' op 11 <http://rai-see.org/wp-content/uploads/2015/08/Romania-National_Anti_Corruption_Strategy-2012_2015-Annex_1.pdf>.

National Crime Agency 'National Crime Agency Annual Report and Accounts 2016–17' (2017) <https://nationalcrimeagency.gov.uk/who-we-are/publications/25-nca-annual-report-2016-17/file>.

OECD, *Integrity in Public Procurement—Good Practice from A to Z* (OECD 2007) <www.oecd.org/development/effectiveness/38588964.pdf>.

OECD, *Government at a Glance 2013* (OECD 2013).

OECD, 'Addressing Corruption Together by Robert Klitgaard' (OCDE 2014) 41–66 <www.oecd.org/dac/governance-peace/publications/FINAL%20Addressing%20corruption%20together.pdf>.

Open Government Partnership '09 Implementation of the Law 'On Protection of Whistleblowers' Capacity Building, Amendments and its Bylaws: Albania' (2016) <www.opengovpartnership.org/commitment/09-implementation-of-law-on-protection-of-whistleblowers-capacity-building-amendments-and>.

Presidential Decree 203, 'On the Declaration and Verification of Earned Profit (për Deklarimin Dhe Verifikimin E Fitimeve Të Realizuara)' 5 June 1992 *Journal of Official Acts (fletorja Zyrtare) 3* (1992) 164.

Republic of Romania Assembly, 'Strategy on Justice System Reform Strategy Project Ad Hoc Parliamentary Committee on Justice System Reform Group of High Level Experts' Euralius (2015) 2–4 <www.euralius.eu/images/Justice-Reform/Strategy-on-Justice-System-Reform_24-07-2015.pdf>.

Romanian Academic Society, 'Beyond Perception: Has Romania's Governance Improved after 2004?' (2011) <www.sar.org.ro/polsci/?p=573>.

Transparency International, 'National Integrity Systems TI Country Study Report United Kingdom' (TI-UK 2009).

Transparency International UK, 'Corruption in the UK: Overview and Policy Recommendations 4-volume Report' (TI-UK 2011) 16–26 <www.transparency.org.uk/publications/corruption-in-the-uk-overview-policy-recommendations/>.

Transparency International, 'Business Principles for Countering Bribery' (TI-UK 2013) <www.transparency.org/whatwedo/publication/business_principles_for_countering_bribery>.

Transparency International, 'Transparency International Global Corruption Barometer' (TI 2013) 16–17 <http://issuu.com/transparencyinternational/docs/2013_globalcorruptionbarometer_en?e=2496456/3903358#search>.

Transparency International, 'Corruption Perception Index' (TI 2014) <www.transparency.org/cpi2014/infographic/regional/european-union-and-westerneurope>.

Transparency International, "Report on the EU Integrity System' (TI 2014) <https://transparency.eu/wp-content/uploads/2016/10/EU_Integrity_System_Report.pdf>.

Transparency International, 'Report on Whistleblowing in Europe Legal Protections for Whistleblowing in the EU' (TI 2014) <www.transparency.org/whatwedo/publication/whistleblowing%5Fin%5Feurope%5Flegal%5Fprotections%5Ffor%5Fwhistleblowers%5Fin%5Fthe%5Feu>.

Transparency International, 'Corruption Perceptions Index 2015' (TI 2015) <www.transparency.org/cpi2015#results-table>.

Transparency International UK, 'London Property: A Top Destination for Money Launderers' (2016) <www.transparency.org.uk/publications/london-property-tr-ti-uk/>.

Transparency International EU, 'European Semester Policy Position' (2017) <https://transparency.eu/resource/european-semester-policy-position/>.

Transparency International 'Corruption Perceptions Index 2018' (2018) <www.transparency.org/cpi2018>.

transparencyorg, 'The 2018 Corruption Perceptions Index' (2018) <www.transparency.org/whatwedo/publication/corruption_perceptions_index_2018>.

UNODC, 'United Nations Convention against Corruption Article 6 Preventive Anti-corruption Body or Bodies' (2004) 10 <www.unodc.org/documents/brussels/UN_Convention_Against_Corruption.pdf>.

UNODC, 'United Nations Convention against Corruption Article 6 Preventive Anti-corruption Body or Bodies' (2003) 10 <www.unodc.org/documents/brussels/UN_Convention_Against_Corruption.pdf>.

UNODC, 'Report Corruption in the Western Balkans: Bribery as Experienced by the Population' (2011) <www.unodc.org/documents/data-and-analysis/statistics/corruption/Western_balkans_corruption_report_2011_web.pdf>.

UNODC, 'The Jakarta Statement on Principles of Anti-Corruption Agencies' (2012) <www.unodc.org/documents/corruption/WG-Prevention/Art_6_Preventive_anti-corruption_bodies/JAKARTA_STATEMENT_en.pdf>.

UNODC, 'Report on Drug Money: The Illicit Proceeds of Opiates Trafficked on the Balkan Route' (2015) <www.unodc.org/documents/data-and-analysis/Studies/IFF_report_2015_final_web.pdf>.

US Dept of State, 'Human Rights Report on Albania' (2015) <www.state.gov/documents/organization/253027.pdf>.

World Bank, 'Albania beyond the Crisis: A Strategy for Recovery and Growth' Report 18658-ALB World Bank (1998) <http://documents.worldbank.org/curated/en/952321468768673016/pdf/multi-page.pdf>.

World Bank, 'Albania: Country Assistance Evaluation' Report 21390 World Bank (2000) <http://documents.worldbank.org/curated/en/746131468768319009/Albania-Country-assistance-evaluation>.

World Bank, 'Korea's Move to e-Procurement' (2004) <http://documents.worldbank.org/curated/en/913231468272393912/Koreas-move-to-e- procurement>.

World Bank, 'Governance & Anti-Corruption' (2016) <http://web.worldbank.org/WBSITE/EXTERNAL/WBI/EXTWBIGOVANTCOR/0menuPK:1740542~pagePK:64168427~piPK:64168435~theSitePK:174053000.html>.

Press Releases and Journalism

Atwood M, 'A Year After Her Murder, Where Is The Justice For Daphne Caruana Galizia?' *The Guardian* (16 October 2018) <www.theguardian.com/commentisfree/2018/oct/16/murder-justice-daphne-caruana-galizia-malta>.

Barrington R, 'Reflections on a Decade in the Fight against Corruption and the Coming' *Transparency International UK* (2019) <www.transparency.org.uk/reflections-on-the-fight-against-corruption/>.

Barrington R, 'What Does Brexit Mean for the UK's Fight against Corruption?' (2016) <www.transparency.org.uk/what-does-brexit-mean-for-the-uks-fight-against-corruption/>.

Bayer L, 'MEPs Back Romanian Graft-Buster for EU Prosecutor' *Politico* (2019) <www.politico.eu/article/laura-codruta-kovesi-romania-anti-corruption-chief-fights-for-top-eu-prosecutor-post/>.

Bogdani A, 'Albanian Justice System Slammed as Totally Corrupt' *Balkan Insight* 5 June 2015 <www.balkaninsight.com/en/article/judges-in-albania-pays-up-to-300-000-for-their-positions-report-says>.

'Brexit: What Next for the Anti-Corruption Movement in the UK?' *Corruption Watch* (2016) <www.cw-uk.org/single-post/2016/07/05/Brexit-What-Next-for-the-Anti-Corruption-Movement-in-the-UK>.

British Embassy Albania, 'Analysis of the Justice System in Albania 2015' 13 July 2015 <www.gov.uk/government/world-location-news/analysis-of-the-justice-system-in-albania-2015>.

Buckley N, 'Former Romanian Prime Minister Jailed For Taking Bribes' *Financial Times* 6 January 2014 <www.ft.com/cms/s/0/a43e56b8-7707-11e3-a253-00144feabdc0 html#axzz41gLEJh9z>.

Bullough O, 'How Britain Let Russia Hide Its Dirty Money' *The Guardian* (25 May 2018) <www.theguardian.com/news/2018/may/25/how-britain-let-russia-hide-its-dirty-money>.

Campbell D, Siddique H, Kirk A, and Meikle J, 'NHS Hires up to 3000 Foreign-Trained Doctors in a Year to Plug Staff Shortage' *Guardian* 28 January 2015 <www.theguardian.com/society/2015/jan/28/-sp-nhs-hires-3000-foreign-doctors-staff-shortage>.

Csaky Z, 'Romania's Attack on the Rule of Law Is Personal, Not Ideological' *Freedom House* (2018) <https://freedomhouse.org/blog/romania-s-attack-rule-law-personal-not-ideological>.

Chiriac M, 'Romania Names Ex-Commissioner as New PM' *Balkan Insight* 11 November 2015 <https://balkaninsight.com/2015/11/11/ex-commissioner-is-romania-s-new-prime-minister-11-10-2015/>.

Dolan C, We Have an Anti-corruption Report: So Now What?' *Politico* 2 May 2014 <www.politico.eu/article/we-have-an-eu-anti-corruption-report-now-what/>.

Dragomir D, 'Romania's Anti-Corruption Crackdown Echoes a Darker Past' *EUObserver* (2018) <https://euobserver.com/opinion/140824>.

Efstathiou K, and Wolf GB, 'Is the European Semester Effective and Useful?' *Bruegel Think Tank, Policy Contribution Issue 09 June 2018* <http://bruegel.org/wp-content/uploads/2018/06/PC-09_2018_3.pdf>.

European Commission, 'Daily News: Western Balkans Conference in Berlin on 28 August 2014 – President Barroso, Vice President Oettinger and Commissioner

Füle to Attend' *European Commission Press Release Database* <http://europa.eu/rapid/midday-express-26-08-2014.htm>.

European Commission, Press Release: 'Whistleblower Protection: Commission Sets New, EU-wide Rules' (2018) <http://europa.eu/rapid/press-release_IP-18-3441_en.htm>.

'Fighting Corruption: A Manifesto for a More Secure, Prosperous and Resilient UK' *Transparency Internation`al* (2017) <www.transparency.org.uk/publications/ge-2017-manifesto/>.

'Finmeccanica: The Italian Judge Accepts the Requests Made by Agustawestland to Bring to an End the Indian Case' (*Leonardo* 28 August 2014) <www.leonardocompany.com/en/-/finmeccanica-accolte-gip-richieste-agustawestland>.

Fontanella K 'Corruption in the EU Costs Business €120bn A Year Study Finds' *Financial Times* (3 February 2014) <www.ft.com/cms/s/0/28f11862-8cf9-11e3-ad57-00144feab7dehtml#axzz46ZcUiQmi>.

Gillet K, 'Romanian Prosecutor Who Took on Entrenched Corruption Is Fired' *New York Times* (2018) <www.nytimes.com/2018/07/09/world/europe/romania-prosecutor-fired.html>.

'Global Arms Industry: First Rise in Arms Sales since 2010, Says SIPRI' (*SIPRI* 2017) <www.sipri.org/media/press-release/2017/global-arms-industry-first-rise-arms-sales-2010-says-sipri>.

Harris C, 'Jan Kuciak Murder: How Has Journalist's Slaying Changed Slovakia?' *Euro News* (21 February 2019) <www.euronews.com/2019/02/21/jan-kuciak-murder-how-has-journalist-s-slaying-changed-slovakia>.

HM Government, 'Home Secretary Announces New National Economic Crime Centre to Tackle High Level Fraud and Money Laundering' (2017) <www.gov.uk/government/news/home-secretary-announces-new-national-economic-crime-centre-to-tackle-high-level-fraud-and-money-laundering>.

Hough D, 'Will Brexit Britain Lose Its Lead in the Fight against Corruption?' *The Conversation* (2018) <https://theconversation.com/will-brexit-britain-lose-its-lead-in-the-fight-against-corruption-72128>.

Ilie L, 'Romanian Minister Calls for Prosecutor's Sacking, Graft Crackdown under Threat' *Reuters* (2018) <www.reuters.com/article/us-romania-government/romanian-minister-calls-for-prosecutors-sacking-graft-crackdown-under-threat-idUSKCN1G62F2>.

Jovanovic I, 'Whistleblowers Get Better Protection in Serbia' *Balkan Insight* 5 June 2015 <www.balkaninsight.com/en/article/whistleblowers-get-better-protection-in-serbia>.

'In Denial—The European Union Conceals Romania's Backsliding on Corruption' *The Economist* 3 July 2008 <www.economist.com/node/11670671>.

Marica I, 'Romanian Intelligence Service Wiretapping Is Unconstitutional, Court Rules' *Romanian Insider* 18 February 2016 <www.romania-insider.com/romanian-intelligence-service-wiretapping-is-unconstitutional-court-rules>.

Marinas RS, 'Romania's President Removes Chief Anti-Corruption Prosecutor' *Reuters* (2018) <https://uk.reuters.com/article/uk-romania-corruption/romanias-president-signs-decree-to-remove-chief-anti-corruption-idUKKBN1JZ0MK>.

Marini A, 'Problems in Bulgaria Are Systemic, in Romania—Political' *EU Inside* (2016) <www.euinside.eu/en/news/problems-in-bulgaria-are-systemic-in-romania-political>.

McGee P, 'Volkswagen Fined €1bn by German State Prosecutors' *Financial Times* (13 June 2018) <www.ft.com/content/240cd18a-6f24-11e8-852d-d8b934ff5ffa>.

'MPF Firma Acordo De Leniência Com Rolls-Royce' *Ministério Público Federal* (17 January 2017) <www.mpf.mp.br/pr/sala-de-imprensa/noticias-pr/mpf-firma-acordo-de-lenienciacom-rolls-royce>.

Mungiu-Pippidi A, 'Bucharest vs Brussels: Wrangling over the EU's New Chief Prosecutor' *Hertie School of Governance blog* (2019) <www.hertie-school.org/en/debate/detail/content/bucharest-vs-brussels-wrangling-over-the-eus-new-chief-prosecutor/>.

New Europe, 'Can Romania Move Forward When Burdened by Allegations of Deep Linkages between the Anti-Corruption Agency and State Security Services?' (2018) <www.neweurope.eu/article/romanias-secret-protocols-cast-a-deep-shadow-over-its-upcoming-eu-presidency/>.

Nielsen N, 'EU Data Verdict Imminent on Romania's €20m Reporters' Fine' *EUObserver* (25 January 2019) <https://euobserver.com/justice/144008>.

'Patients Bearing Gifts: In Central and Eastern Europe Patients Offer Bribes and Low-Paid Doctors Accept Them' *The Economist* 24 March 2015 <www.economist.com/news/europe/21647087-central-and-eastern-europe-low-paid-doctors-accept-bribes-and-patients-offer-them-patients-bearing>.

Paun C, 'Romanians Protest Government Plan to Commute Sentences' (2017) <www.politico.eu/article/romanians-protest-government-plan-to-commute-sentences/>.

Pegg D, and Evans R, 'Airbus Braces for a Difficult Landing after Corruption Allegations' *The Guardian* (5 November 2017) <www.theguardian.com/business/2017/nov/04/airbus-year-corporate-confessions-difficult-landing>.

'Press Release: BAE Systems PLC Pleads Guilty and Ordered to Pay US $400 Million Criminal Fine' *Department of Justice* (1 March 2010) <http://fcpa.stanford.edu/fcpac/documents/3000/002249.pdf>.

Pring C, and Vrushi J, 'Tackling the Crises of Democracy, Promoting Rule of Law and Fighting Corruption' *Transparency International* (29 January 2019) <www.transparency.org/news/feature/tackling_crisis_of_democracy_promoting_rule_of_law_and_fighting_corruption>.

Roberts E, and Stan C, 'Romania Protests Continue over Plans to Revive Corruption Bill' *CNN*, (2017) <https://edition.cnn.com/2017/02/06/europe/romania-protests-update/index.html>.

'Romania Orders Journalists Investigating Corruption to Give up Sources' *Organised Crime and Corruption Reporting Project* (2018) <www.occrp.org/en/daily/8878-romania-orders-journalists-investigating-corruption-to-give-up-sources>.

'Rolls-Royce Settles Bribery Probes in UK, US and Brazil' (*Reuters* 16 January 2017) <www.reuters.com/article/us-rolls-royce-hldg-fraud-settlement-idUSKBN15025C>.

Russell J, 'BAE Pays Fine to Settle Tanzania Corruption Probe' *The Telegraph* (21 December 2010) <www.telegraph.co.uk/finance/newsbysector/industry/defence/8216551/BAE-pays-fine-tosettle-Tanzania-corruption-probe.html>.

'The Companies We Keep: What the UK's Open Data Register Actually Tells Us about Company Ownership' *Global Witness* (2018) <www.globalwitness.org/en/campaigns/corruption-and-money-laundering/anonymous-company-owners/companies-we-keep/#chapter-0/section-1>.

'The Right Woman to Be Europe's Chief Prosecutor: EU Should Resist Romanian Demands and Appoint Laura Codruta Kovesi' *Financial Times* (2019) <www.ft.com/content/f1b11402-3a85-11e9-b72b-2c7f526ca5d0>.

Toader T, 'The 'coercion' in Romanian Anti-Corruption Campaign' *Financial Times* (2019) <https://ft.com/content/5c6b14a8-4023-11e9-b896-fe36ec32aecefbclid=IwAR0HShCR27IeeXAshXsekxlLfhp_pHtqtCpd46g3oRp_Ov0BSrB7 QqZdXa8>.

Transparencyeu, Timmermans' Letter (2018) <http://transparency.eu/wp-content/uploads/2017/02/20170130-Letter-FVP-LIBE-Chairpdf>.

Transparencyeu, 'EU Anti-Corruption Report—No Answers Please, We're the Commission' (2017) <https://transparency.eu/no-answers/>.

Troev T, and Hope K, 'Bulgarian Reporter Investigating Misuse of EU Funds Murdered' *Financial Times* (2018) <www.ft.com/content/43c3de8a-caf3-11e8-9fe5-24ad351828ab>

Troev T, and Hope K, 'The Journalists Killed in EU Member States in the Past Year' *Financial Times* (2018) <www.ft.com/content/e806a7c4-cae5-11e8-9fe5-24ad351828ab>.

'UK Overseas Territories to Open Up Ownership Registers' *Financial Times* (2018) <www.ft.com/content/5a924560-4d45-11e8-8a8e-22951a2d8493>.

'UK's Serious Fraud Office Drops Investigations of Rolls Royce Individuals, GSK' *Reuters* (2019) <www.reuters.com/article/britain-sfo/uks-serious-fraud-office-drops-investigations-of-rolls-royce-individuals-gsk-idUSL5N20H3D1>.

'Unexplained Wealth Orders: How to Catch the Corrupt and Corrupt Money in the UK' *Transparency International* (2017) <www.transparency.org/news/feature/unexplained_wealth_orders_how_to_catch_zthe_corrupt_and_corrupt_money_in_the>.

Urias J, 'The Whole Judicial System in Albania Is Corrupt' *VOA* 29 May 2014 <www.infocip.org/en/?p=1199>.

Vorpsi A, 'Is There a Need of a Deep Constitutional Reform in Albania? (2014) <http://constitutional-change.com/is-there-a-need-of-a-deep-constitutional-reform-in-albania/>.

World Law Group, 'Global Guide to Whistleblowing Programs' (2012) 11–16 <http://medialockelord.com/files/upload/WLG_Global_Guide_to_Whistleblowing_Programs-2012. pdf>.

Watt H, 'The Tory Leader's Group Donor Club: 'A Chance for Like-Minded People to Talk'' *Guardian* (2015) <www.theguardian.com/politics/2015/may/04/tories-leaders-group-donor-club-david-cameron-conservatives-dinners>.

Law

Anti-Terrorism, Crime and Security Act 2001 108-110 <www.legislation.gov.uk/ukpga/2001/24/pdf>s/ukpga_20010024_en.pdf>.

'Deferred Prosecution Agreement' SFO v Rolls Royce PLC (17 January 2017) <www.judiciary.uk/wp-content/uploads/2017/01/sfo-v-rolls-royce.pdf>.

FSA, 'Financial Services Authority (FSA) Anti-Bribery and Corruption Systems and Controls in Investment Banks' FSA/PN/035/2012 (2012) <www.fsa.gov.uk/static/pubs/other/anti-bribery-investment-banks.pdf>.

FSA, Financial Services and Markets Act 2000 'Memorandum of Understanding between the Financial Conduct Authority and the Bank of England Including the Prudential Regulation Authority' (2015) <www.bankofengland.co.uk/-/media/boe/files/memoranda-of-understanding/bank-fca-psr-and-pra-supervision-of-payment-systems.pdf>.

Plea Agreement United States V BAE Systems PLC (4 February 2010) <http://fcpa.stanford.edu/fcpac/documents/4000/002716.pdf>.

'Rolls Royce PLC' (*SFO* 17 January 2017) <www.sfo.gov.uk/cases/rolls-royce-plc/>.

'Sentencing Remarks' Regina v BAE Systems PLC, Southwark Crown Court (21 December 2010) <www.bailiiorg/ew/cases/Misc/2010/16.pdf>.

Index

Note: Page numbers followed by "n" refer to endnotes.

FSC
www.fsc.org
MIX
Papier | Fördert gute Waldnutzung
FSC® C083411

Kolibri 360 GmbH
Ferdinand-Jühlke-Straße 7
99095 Erfurt, Deutschland
produktsicherheit@kolibri360.de